Health in Diversity – Diversity in Health

Katharina Crepaz · Ulrich Becker ·
Elisabeth Wacker
Editors

Health in Diversity –
Diversity in Health

(Forced) Migration, Social
Diversification, and Health in a
Changing World

 Springer VS

Editors
Katharina Crepaz
Munich, Germany

Ulrich Becker
Munich, Germany

Elisabeth Wacker
Munich, Germany

ISBN 978-3-658-29176-1   ISBN 978-3-658-29177-8   (eBook)
https://doi.org/10.1007/978-3-658-29177-8

This Springer VS imprint is published by the registered company Springer Fachmedien Wiesbaden
GmbH part of Springer Nature.
The registered company address is: Abraham-Lincoln-Str. 46, 65189 Wiesbaden, Germany

Preface

Migration is an international topic, of interest to policy makers and scholars around the globe, and with a strong impact on the shape of modern societies. However, despite its inherent character as a transnational issue, decision-making and research on migration often remain confined to nation-state borders, and thus offer only a limited perspective on the many different aspects of the topic. The conference series "South-East African and European Conferences on Refugees and Forced Migrants" is our attempt to counteract Eurocentric views, and to foster mutual learning processes. The idea was to design a conference with our colleagues from Pwani University in Kenya, with whom both the Max Planck Institute for Social Law and Social Policy and the Technical University of Munich have a long history of collaboration in research, teaching, and scholarly exchange. For decades, Kenya has been engaged in large-scale migration within its own borders, supporting refugees from neighboring countries and providing health care for people living in shelter camps for generations; it thus provided a highly productive setting for scholarly debate about migratory movements. The conference was to be both interdisciplinary (open to scholars from legal studies, political science, sociology, anthropology, among others) and transcontinental, bringing together researchers from African and European countries in order to compare, evaluate, and possibly learn from each other's findings on migration-related topics.

The first conference, titled "Social Rights – Care – Mutual Benefits?" took place in Kilifi, Kenya, in 2016, and focused on the inclusion of (forced) migrants into host societies, on re-designing asylum procedures and systems, as well as on adopting a more benefit-based perspective on migration instead of the prominent deficit-oriented view. The event was very successful, and especially lauded for its truly international and bridge-building character; this confirmed our view that we were offering a unique scholarly gathering, and prompted the decision to make the conference a recurring event, accompanied by an edited volume to allow for public access to the topics discussed at the conference.

In March 2019, the second edition, titled "Health in Diversity, Diversity in Health?" was held in Kilifi. While the first conference was relatively open-topic, the second edition had a clear focus on the connection between (forced) migration and health. How can health care systems respond to increased diversity?

Which challenges do professionals face when dealing with diverse patient groups? What is the impact of forced migratory movements on individual health? Which preventive measures and/or new technologies might be helpful when dealing with diversity and health? These were only some of the questions raised in the presented papers as well as in the lively discussions that ensued. We are very happy that we have, once again, managed to compile an edited volume that preserves the research presented as well as the connections established at the conference by making the papers available to the interested public. We hope that scholars, practitioners and public decision-makers will find the contents of this book interesting and useful for their personal work, and would be delighted to open up a broad international dialogue on the issues raised in the present edited volume.

Elisabeth Wacker

Contents

1. Perspectives on the Nexus between (Forced) Migration and Health
in Increasingly Heterogeneous Societies 1

Katharina Crepaz

2. Historical Perspectives: Health and Migration in a Globalized Society

Mental Health in Times of Increasing Flight and Migration – A German
Perspective 13

Ulrike Kluge

Civil Strife, Migration and Health in the East African Region: Some
Historical Reflections 25

Gordon Onyango Omenya

3. Legal Perspectives: Health as a Human Right

Dimensions of Health Care and Social Services Accessibility for Disabled
Asylum Seekers in Germany 51

Cornelius Lätzsch

Protecting the Health Care Rights of Refugees: Some Legal Perspectives
from the Republic of South Africa 77

Letlhokwa George Mpedi

4. Political Perspectives: Health Care Policy, Social Policy, and Diversity

What Happens to the Healthy Immigrant Later in Life? – The Health of
(Forced) Migrants Through the Life Course 103

Andrea Goettler

Refugee-Environment Nexus: Socio-Cultural Acceptability of Eco-Friendly
Options for Household Cooking in Kenyan Refugee Camps 121

Godffrey Nyongesa Nato

Social Integration and Racist Discrimination of Young African Refugees in
Germany 135

Albert Scherr

5. Quality of Life, Diversity and Health

Health for All? Disability, Diversity and Global Health 151

Isabella Bertmann-Merz

Quality of Life: Coping Strategies and Innovations among Forced Migrants
in Encampment in the Tana Delta in Kenya 171

Sellah Lusweti, Obeka Bonventure and Halimu Shauri

6. Diversity in Refugee Camps

Violence Against Women in Camps? Exploring Links between Refugee
Camp Conditions and the Prevalence of Violence 187

Ulrike Krause

Resolving Trauma Associated with Sexual and Gender-Based Violence in
Transcultural Refugee Contexts in Kenya 209

Fathima Azmiya Badurdeen

7. Economic Perspectives on Diversity and Health

The e-ICI Framework: How to Support the Development of Digital Services
for Forced Migrants Dealing with Health Issues 233

Annalies Beck, Ayca Nina Zuch

Costs and Benefits of Forced Migration in Kenya: The Case of Kakuma
Refugee Camp 281

Samuel Mwakubo

Index of Authors **299**

1. Perspectives on the Nexus between (Forced) Migration and Health in Increasingly Heterogeneous Societies

Katharina Crepaz[1]

Keywords: Refugees, (Forced) Migration, Health, Africa, Europe

Abstract

This contribution introduces some general ideas on the nexus between (forced) migration and health in heterogeneous modern societies. It does so by first providing UNHCR data to set out a framework for the continued and even increased relevance of refugee issues in both Africa and Europe, by giving a definition of health as a human right, and by then focusing on the connection and reciprocal effects of health and (forced) migratory processes. Finally, and most importantly, an outlook on the papers featured in the edited volume and their contents is given.

Contents

Abstract..1

1   Forced Migration and Health: International Comparative Perspectives.......3

1   Katharina Crepaz | Max Planck Institute for Social Law and Social Policy and Technical University of Munich | crepaz@mpisoc.mpg.de

© Springer Fachmedien Wiesbaden GmbH, part of Springer Nature 2020
K. Crepaz et al. (eds.), *Health in Diversity – Diversity in Health*,
https://doi.org/10.1007/978-3-658-29177-8_1

2 Contents of the Edited Volume..5

Bibliography 10

1 Forced Migration and Health: International Comparative Perspectives

According to the UNHCR (2019), there are currently 70.8 million forcibly displaced people worldwide; 37,000 people a day are forced to flee their homes because of conflict and persecution (UNHCR 2019) – we are thus witnessing the highest levels of displacement ever recorded. At the time of compiling our last edited volume, in 2018, numbers were already alarming, with 65.6 million forced migrants (UNHCR 2018, quoted in Crepaz & Wacker 2019), but the situation has again worsened dramatically. Additionally, about 80% of refugees live in countries neighboring their countries of origin, which puts an uneven amount of pressure on the Global South when dealing with refugee issues; it is therefore those countries, often poverty-ridden and politically instable, who are most directly involved in hosting forced migrants. How European and African approaches to refugees and forced migrants differ and where possibilities for mutual learning and the exchange of best practices might be found was the topic of our last edited volume (entitled "Refugees and Forced Migrants in Africa and the EU: Comparative and Multidisciplinary Perspectives on Challenges and Solutions", published with Springer VS in early 2019). In the present second edition, we focus on how the current record number of (forced) migratory processes affects health and well-being on a variety of levels, and again explore a comparative outlook given by authors from both African and European countries.

In 1948, the Universal Declaration of Human Rights was established, followed in 1951 by the UN Refugee Convention as the most important international legal document on refugees and their rights and the UNHCR as its 'guardian'. Article 14 of the Universal Declaration of Human rights states that "everyone has the right to seek and enjoy in other countries asylum from persecution" (UN 2015: 30), while the Refugee Convention establishes who can be defined as a refugee: "[any person who] as a result of events occurring before 1 January 1951 and owing to well-founded fear of being persecuted for reasons of race, religion, nationality, membership of a particular social group or political opinion, is outside the country of his nationality and is unable, or, owing to such fear, is unwilling to avail himself of the protection of that country; or who, not having a nationality and being outside the country of his former habitual residence as a result of such events, is unable or, owing to such fear, is unwilling to return to it" (UNHCR 2010: 14). The Refugee Convention also introduces the principle of 'non-refoulement' in Article 33: "No Contracting State shall expel or return ('*refouler*') a refugee in any manner whatsoever to the frontiers of territories where his life or freedom would be threatened on account of his race, religion, nationality, membership of a particular social group or political opinion" (UNHCR 2010: 30) 'Non-refoulement' thus prohibits to expel refugees; however, there can be exceptions from this principle if a refugee has been convicted by a final judgement of a particularly serious crime, or if they are considered to be a danger to public security.

Although the UN Refugee Convention remains the most important international legal document on forced migration, it falls short of reflecting some of the more recent international political developments. The Convention had been established as a response to refugee and displaced persons movements in Europe after World War II, when the powers forcing them to leave their homelands were almost exclusively nation state governments. Nowadays, the actors responsible for forced migratory movements are often terrorist groups (e.g. the so-called 'Islamic State'), and refugees frequently come from what is referred to in political science as 'failed states' (e.g. countries in which the state government is not capable of establishing sovereignty and control over the whole territory, often then ruled by clans or warlords). With climate change as one of the biggest current global threats, people may also leave their homes because of natural disasters (flooding, draughts), which no nation state can be held accountable for. The Convention is also not equipped to deal with large-scale international forced migratory movements, such as the one brought about by the civil war in Syria. Despite these shortcomings, the Refugee Convention establishes an important framework of rights, and also mentions provisions on health. However, health is not mentioned in a distinct article, but is tackled in Article 24, which deals with "labor legislation and social security". It outlines that refugees shall be accorded the same treatment as nationals in respect to "[s]ocial security (legal provisions in respect of employment injury, occupational diseases, maternity, sickness, disability, old age, death, unemployment, family responsibilities and any other contingency which, according to national laws or regulations, is covered by a social security scheme)" (UNHCR 2010: 25). This social security provision contains a number of factors that could also influence a person's health status, as well as their ability to participate in work and society, and their general well-being.

Even though the article is not health-specific, it is still in line with the WHO's definition of health, which is outlined in the preamble to its Constitution of 1946: "Health is a state of complete physical, mental and social well-being and not merely the absence of disease or infirmity" (WHO 2019). Like the provisions outlined in Article 24 of the Refugee Convention, the WHO definition is broad, and encompasses many aspects of a person's possible health status. As can be imagined, a state of "complete physical, mental and social well-being" is an ideal type, and something usually quite removed from those forced to flee their homelands. Flight conditions do not normally allow for a person to reach such a state; however, the WHO Constitution also refers to "the highest attainable standard of health" (WHO 2019), thus making clear that certain environmental and personal framework conditions may keep a person from reaching the ideal state of complete well-being. The WHO explicitly states that "[t]he enjoyment of the highest attainable standard of health is one of the fundamental rights of every human being without distinction of race, religion, political belief, economic or social condition"; this highest attainable state is thus a human right, which cannot be denied on the grounds of e.g. lack of citizenship or legal status in a host country. The definition of health as a human right is vital for refugees, as it means that access to at least basic healthcare has to be provided regardless of their present status, and regardless of the country they are currently in. However, implementing this right in practice is not always easy and there are pitfalls and restrictions, as some of the contributions in this volume also highlight. Difficulties in providing health care for refugees may arise from unresponsive authorities, from the lack of provisions for mental health or – from a public health perspective – from difficulties in convincing the resident population that refugees themselves are not a threat to the host country's health or health care system. Such threat-based views could then in turn be used by anti-migration political actors to deny health care services to refugees, especially to those without official status. Lack of access to health care can thus also be viewed as a sign of social exclusion (Bivins 2013: 145). Besides political willingness to provide health care services, limited resources also constitute one of the main barriers. Some of the African countries receiving large numbers of refugees already struggle with providing health care, and especially mental health treatment, to their own populations. Similar developments are visible in Europe, where mental health is often not included in the basic healthcare provisions available for refugees, and even if it is, lack of cultural mediators or professionals trained in foreign languages and customs makes receiving appropriate care very difficult. Researchers therefore argue for the implementation of community-based approaches, rooted in the involvement of staff with a migratory or refugee background as outreach screeners and counsellors (Hecker & Neuner 2019: 68). Through these approaches, societal diversity could step beyond being viewed solely as a problem for health care systems, and in itself represent the first step towards reaching a better health care status for refugees and (forced) migrants, pursuing the goal of "health in diversity".

2   Contents of the Edited Volume

How societal diversity and improved health chances for all groups present in heterogeneous societies may be reconciled is also the topic of the present edited volume. After the first South-East African and European Conference on Refugees and Forced Migrants was held in 2016, it became clear that we wanted the common international and interdisciplinary forum for discussion to continue, as it constituted one of the rare chances to interact with scholars coming from different geographical areas and also different disciplines. While the first conference was relatively open-topic, the second edition – held in March 2019 in Kilifi, Kenya, as a joint project of the Max Planck Institute for Social Law and Social Policy, the Chair of Sociology of Diversity at the Technical University of Munich and Pwani University – had a strong focus on the relationship between (forced) migration and health. Through presentations and in-depth discussion, the scholars aimed to shed further light on how migratory movements may influence the health status of both refugees and the general populations, and how societies can be designed to be more receptive for diversity also in their health care systems. Mental health and migration, vulnerable groups (e.g. persons with disabilities, women) and health in refugee camps were also among the topics discussed. We are delighted to be able to make the papers presented in Kenya available to scholars, practitioners and public decision-makers in the form of this edited volume, tackling health and diversity from the points of view of different academic disciplines as well as different geographical contexts.

First, Ulrike Kluge and Gordon Omenya will provide some historical and current perspectives on migration and health. Ulrike Kluge focuses on the mental health care situation of refugees in Germany. She presents approaches from the Center for Intercultural Psychiatry and Psychotherapy at Charité Berlin (ZIPP), and gives an overview of the barriers that refugees may face when aiming to get mental health care in Germany. Kluge argues that multi-dimensional and multi-professional approaches are necessary to provide good mental health service for refugees.

Gordon Omenya presents some historical reflections on health and migration in the East African region. Omenya argues that the region has been conflict-ridden due to the colonial powers' division of land without paying attention to the inhabitants. He then traces how colonial governments installed health care systems in the area, and how these systems dealt with refugees leaving their homelands due to a continued stream of armed conflicts. In conclusion, Omenya provides some suggestions as to how health care systems could become more inclusive and move away from exploitative to mutually beneficial relations. Moving from historical to legal perspectives and from Africa to Germany, Cornelius Lätzsch's contribution explores the accessibility of health care and social services for asylum seekers with disabilities in Germany. The UN Convention on the Rights of Persons with Disabilities (CRPD), the EU Reception Conditions Directive (Directive 2013/33/EU) and the German Asylum Seekers Benefits Act (AsylbLG) follow different and sometimes conflicting approaches: While the UN CRPD and the Reception Conditions Directive open doors to specific support, the Asylum Seekers Benefits Act limits accessibility. Refugees with disabilities thus have to deal with inaccessible housing and restricted access to health care. Lätzsch argues for a closer collaboration between academia, social work, and politics, in order to overcome the marginalization of asylum seekers with disabilities.

Providing additional legal reflections, Letlhokwa George Mpedi's contribution focuses on the health care rights of refugees in South Africa. The article posits "health" and "refugee" as key terms, and does so by looking at important documents such as the Constitution of South Africa of 1996, which also contains the right to health. Mpedi then evaluates the current situation in South Africa by describing some of the challenges refugees face when trying to access health care services, including an imperfect public and expensive private service, limited ability to enforce the right to health care, language barriers, lack of access to information, as well as ignorance and xenophobia.

In the first paper on political perspectives, Andrea Göttler looks at the health of (forced) migrants through the life course. She reviews the role of social determinants of health associated with labor and forced migration, and discusses how studies on older labor migrants in Germany show the long-term effects of health risks in the receiving country. Göttler argues that improvements for the recognition of long-term socioeconomic barriers to health are still needed, and provides an outlook on possible future health risks of current (forced) migrants in Europe.

Geoffrey Nato's contribution then deals with micro-level possibilities for health improvement, through an analysis of more eco-friendly and sustainable energy provision options for refugee camps. He argues that creating sustainable energy options has been neglected so far, putting pressure on the environment and possibly also on the relationship with the host community that has to provide energy for the camps. Nato looks at three potential eco-friendly solutions (sustainable firewood, energy-efficient cooking stoves, alternative sources of fuel) and concludes that cultural preconceptions and ideas of hygiene must also be kept in mind when designing new and more sustainable energy sources.

Returning to Europe, Albert Scherr's article focuses on the social integration and instances of racist discrimination against young African refugees in Germany. Through biographical interviews, Scherr analyzes the problems refugees face after their arrival, and identifies a non-transparent constellation of legal and institutional conditions as well as uncertain future perspectives as some of the most pressing issues. He argues that in order to allow for inclusion, both informal and institutional support and considerable personal contributions on the part of the refugee are necessary.

Following the legal and political framework conditions, the prerequisites for ensuring a good quality of life when dealing with diversity and health are discussed. Isabella Bertmann-Merz's paper focuses on the question of access to health (care) for vulnerable groups, and on how diversity aspects are reflected to the extent that health care is available to all people without barriers and/or discrimination. The text draws on governance issues, and distinguishes between globalization and health governance, global governance and health, and governance for global health as key concepts. Bertmann-Merz focuses on the diversity dimensions migration and disability, and argues that inclusive approaches need to be intensified, while already established initiatives should be re-thought from a diversity perspective.

Sellah Lusweti, Obeka Bonventure and Halimu Shauri look at coping strategies and innovations among forced migrants in encampment in the Tana Delta (Kenya). They argue that forced migration is characterized by difficult living conditions and few job opportunities, and that forced migrants thus have to be innovative to create new support mechanisms for their life in camp surroundings. The interview data collected by Lusweti, Bonventure and Shauri in three refugee camps suggests that forced migrants in the Tana Delta have shown resilience by coming up with new solutions and/or new applications of existing products, technologies, services and organizational models to keep up with the realities of life in encampment.

The next section of the edited volume looks at refugee camps, living conditions and health possibilities/problems there in more detail. Ulrike Krause discusses violence against women in camps, and explores the links between refugee camp conditions and the prevalence of violence. Based on empirical research conducted in Uganda, Krause argues that sexual violence, domestic violence and structural discrimination constitute the main risks female refugees face in encampment, and that these forms of violence exist despite humanitarian efforts to protect and assist refugees, and especially women. She concludes that these special efforts may even sometimes contribute directly or indirectly to frustration and violence, along with the limits imposed by the camp and hierarchical procedures.

Fathima Azmiya Badurdeen's paper focuses on how trauma associated with sexual and gender-based violence (SGBV) may be resolved; it does so through looking at transcultural refugee contexts in Kenya. Based on qualitative data collected in in-depth interviews with women and girl refugees in Dadaab and Kakuma refugee camps, the article presents the context of trauma faced by women and refugees of SGBV, and the ways in which they resolve trauma and health issues using social networks and professional health care services. Azmiya Badurdeen emphasizes the need for an exploration of cultural interpretations of trauma as well as for flexible and adaptive approaches by professionals for interpreting and treating mental trauma.

Finally, the present edited volume also offers technological and economic perspectives on diversity and health, and looks at how information technology may improve access to health care. Annalies Beck and Ayca Nina Zuch investigate how new technologies may help forced migrants dealing with health issues, and provide suggestions on how the development of digital services for this target group may be improved. Beck and Zuch analyze the problems that refugees in Germany face when in need of health support, and then propose the e-ICI (e-Inclusion and Cohesion Based Innovation) approach as a possible solution. E-ICI is user-centered, and focuses on dealing with health issues in a culture sensitive way by choosing the appropriate technology (e.g. mobile apps, social media, blockchain or AI). To render such innovation possible, Beck and Zuch argue for a collaboration of doctors, scientists, developers, designers and experts in information technologies, but also the potential users themselves.

Samuel Mwakubo's paper focuses on the costs and benefits of forced migration in Kenya, arguing that forced migration may not only be a burden but also a possible asset for the host communities. The results of a Cost-Benefit Analysis (CBA) conducted for Kakuma Refugee Camp show that supply chains for goods and services demanded by refugees were formed, and that the benefits are substantial for Turkana County, but marginal for the overall country. In order to minimize the associated costs (e.g. damage to the environment), Mwakubo argues for close collaboration between governments, NGOs and UNHCR, especially in ecologically fragile areas. He thus also highlights that human health also depends on a healthy environment, following a "one health" approach.

The present volume offers a collection of African and European perspectives on (forced) migration and health, ranging from accounts of the historical development of the issue, the challenges in finding fitting approaches in law and politics, the problems and solutions in ensuring quality of life and health for diverse populations, and dealing with health risks and violence in refugee camps to the potential for health inclusion offered via new technologies and to replacing a pure burden-sharing perspective with one also focused on (forced) migrants as a possible asset. The comparative framework reveals that while there may be some differences in the challenges faced (e.g. refugee camps as a primarily African issue), the similarities prevail: both African and European countries have to find new ways of dealing with the diversification of societies, while also implementing the WHO's principle of health as a human right. Migration and health care both constitute topics to be addressed at a global scale; it is therefore important to establish research on these issues from a comparative international perspective which also allows for mutual learning processes.

Bibliography

Bivins, Roberta (2013): Immigration, Ethnicity and 'Public' Health Policy in Postcolonial Britain. In: Cox, Catherine; Marland, Hilary (eds.) *Migration, Health and Ethnicity in the Modern World.* Bastingstoke: Palgrave Macmillan, pp. 126-150.

Crepaz, Katharina; Wacker, Elisabeth (2019): Introduction: Working Together to See Further: European and African Perspectives on Refugees and Forced Migrants Compared. In: Wacker, Elisabeth; Becker, Ulrich; Crepaz, Katharina (eds.) *Refugees and Forced Migrants in Africa and the EU: Comparative and Multidisciplinary Perspectives on Challenges and Solutions.* Wiesbaden: Springer VS, pp. 1-9.

Hecker, Tobias; Neuner, Frank (2019): Mental Health Enables Integration: Re-Thinking Treatment Approaches for Refugees. In: Krämer, Alexander; Fischer, Florian (eds.) *Refugee Migration and Health: Challenges for Germany and Europe.* Cham: Springer Nature Switzerland, pp. 63-72.

UN (2015): The Universal Declaration of Human Rights. http://www.un.org/en/udhrbook/pdf/ udhr_booklet_en_web.pdf (last accessed 19/07/2019).

UNHCR (2010): Convention and Protocol Relating to the Status of Refugees. http://www.unhcr.org/3b66c2aa10 (last accessed 19/07/2019)

UNHCR (2019): Figures at a Glance. https://www.unhcr.org/figures-at-a-glance.html (last accessed 19/07/2019).

Wacker, Elisabeth; Becker, Ulrich; Crepaz, Katharina (2019) (eds.): *Refugees and Forced Migrants in Africa and the EU: Comparative and Multidisciplinary Perspectives on Challenges and Solutions.* Wiesbaden: Springer VS.

WHO (2019): WHO Remains Firmly Committed to the Principles set out in the Preamble to the Constitution. https://www.who.int/about/who-we-are/constitution (last accessed 19/07/2019)

2. Historical Perspectives: Health and Migration in a Globalized Society

Mental Health in Times of Increasing Flight and Migration - A German Perspective

Ulrike Kluge[1]

Keywords: Refugees, Mental Health, Trauma, Mental Health Care Professionals, Global Mental Health

Abstract

The chapter gives a brief introduction to the mental health care situation of refugees in Germany, presenting recent developments and discourses exemplary of one research and care delivery facility in Berlin. The impact of living conditions and access barriers on the mental health situation are presented and the main challenges regarding treatment and service structures are discussed.

Contents

Abstract..13

1 Introduction..15

2 Refugee Situation in Germany in the Context of Mental Health..............17

[1] Ulrike Kluge | Center for Cross-Cultural Psychiatry and Psychotherapy (ZIPP), Charité University Medicine Berlin & Berlin Institute for Integration and Migration Research (BIM) at Humboldt University Berlin | ulrike.kluge@charite.de

© Springer Fachmedien Wiesbaden GmbH, part of Springer Nature 2020
K. Crepaz et al. (eds.), *Health in Diversity – Diversity in Health*,
https://doi.org/10.1007/978-3-658-29177-8_2

2.1 Living Conditions in Germany...18
2.2 Language and Culture-Related Barriers..20
2.3 Administrative Barriers..20
2.4 Mental Health Conditions...20
3   Conclusion...21
Bibliography...22

1 Introduction

Impacted by political, social and ecological crises, migration and flight have become central topics in European societies in the last few years. This is challenging the mental health care system, its supply structures of psychosocial, psychiatric and psychotherapeutic care services. As a response to this, there is a growing demand for specialized treatment as well as short-term interventions (Adorjani et al. 2017). At the same time, there has been an increasing demand for training in the field of cross-cultural competences and on trauma-related issues for professionals as well as voluntary care givers in shelters and psychosocial support structures (Mehran et al 2019).

At the Center for Intercultural Psychiatry and Psychotherapy (ZIPP)[1] at Charité Berlin we have been working in this field for over 16 years. As part of a university medicine structure, the ZIPP comprises three areas: healing, research and teaching/training. The (1) care delivery facility is the ethnopsychiatric outpatient ward that is integrated into the psychiatric outpatient ward at Charité, Campus Mitte (besides five other specialized outpatient wards). The treatment comprises psychodynamic single and group therapy, psychopharmacological treatment, social work and reports during the asylum-seeking process. The team includes psychotherapists, psychiatrists, social workers, nurses and language and cultural interpreters from various cultural backgrounds (Kluge et al. 2017). The interdisciplinarity and diversity of the cultural backgrounds and migration histories of the team creates a many-voiced transcultural space. Transcultural encounters between patients and therapists from diverse cultural contexts facilitate reflection on the common grounds as well as differences. To overcome the higher degree of strangeness in trans- and intercultural understanding (Kimmerle 2000), it is necessary "to allow certain aspects to remain temporarily or permanently without being understood, to respect and acknowledge incomprehensible aspects of foreign cultural backgrounds" (Kimmerle 2002).

In 2017, we established an additional service: TransVer[2]- a psychosocial network structure with the goal of enhancing intercultural opening of the community psychiatry service system for migrants and refugees. TransVer is based on three pillars: training for mental health care workers (including supervision and case support), transfer into appropriate care delivery facilities for users and professionals, as well as a database on services. The transfer is a main part, because there is a large, fragmented community mental health system. Even mental health professionals are not familiar with the variety of services and

---

1   https://psychiatrie-psychotherapie.charite.de/en/patients/outpatient_department/center_for_inte rcultural_psychiatry_psychotherapy_zipp/

2   http://transver-berlin.de/

specialized treatment facilities. Obviously, this is even more challenging for immigrants and refugees who do not speak the language and lack information and knowledge about the German (mental) health care system. In summary, the overarching goal of those mental health services is the intercultural opening, including the reduction of language and administrative access barriers, increasing the quality of mental health care delivery for those groups and providing information to all actors and stakeholders in the field.

The (2) research at ZIPP takes place at two facilities, namely within the Research Group on Transcultural Psychiatry (TP) and the Research Group on Global Mental Health (GMH). Both groups combine the natural sciences and humanistic approaches and quantitative and qualitative research methods, ranging from epidemiological methods to ethnological fieldwork. Whereas the research group on Transcultural Psychiatry comprises Medical Humanities, Diversity Studies, Intercultural Psychotherapy, Transcultural Psychiatry, Medical Anthropology and Ethnopsychiatry, the research group on Global Mental Health integrates theory and methods from Global Mental Health, Public Mental Health and Epidemiology. Critical reflection of concepts, terms, categories and definitions used in this research area, such as culture, race, ethnicity, migrants, people with a migrant background, intercultural opening, cross-cultural competence, acculturation/integration etc. is a base of our research. TP focusses on (a) the development of new treatment approaches, tailored to refugees and immigrants, including treatment approaches via language and cultural interpreters, (b) the extent to which transcultural and migration processes have an impact on the migrating subjects and how do these processes effect identity building. Further fields of interest are (c) ways in which diverse healing systems/cultures deal with mental disorders. The research group on GMH addresses mental health disparities and mental health service delivery especially in low- and middle-income countries. The group supports the goals of the Movement for Global Mental Health (http://www.globalmentalhealth.org.).

The two research groups are closely connected to the Berlin Institute for Integration and Migration Research (BIM). BIM is an interdisciplinary research-based institute at Humboldt University that integrates 6 disciplines (Political Sciences, Sociology, Ethnology, Educational Science, Economics, Psychology, Medicine, and parts of 6 other institutes).

In this interinstitutional network, the recent research projects focus on (a) mental health and flight, (b) inclusion, exclusion und social cohesion in close cooperation with local networks, neighborhood initiatives and cultural institutions, (c) transgenerational transmission of losses and trauma narratives, (d) neurourbanistics, (e) psychosocial and labour market integration of refugees in the countries of origin, transit countries and receiving countries in relation to host community solidarity.

2   Refugee Situation in Germany in the Context of Mental Health

Worldwide, there are 68.5 million forcibly displaced people as a result of persecution, conflict, violence, or human rights violations (UNHCR: The UN Refugee Agency 2018). In Europe, Germany is the country that takes in the most refugees: approx. 1.1 million (UNO Flüchtlingshilfe 2018). As shown in figure 1, there are refugees from a variety of countries in Germany. For example, 24.7% refugees are from Syria. In 2015, about 477 000 asylum seekers filed an asylum application in Germany – 442 000 were initial applications. These numbers show an increase of 135% over the previous year (see Mediendienst Integration: https://mediendienst-integration.de). However, the Federal Office for Migration and Refugees (BAMF) only decided on 283 000 asylum applications during this period. Of relevance for mental health care is the fact that asylum seekers and refugees still receive limited medical benefits under the Asylum Seekers Benefits Act (AsylbLG § 4 and § 6).

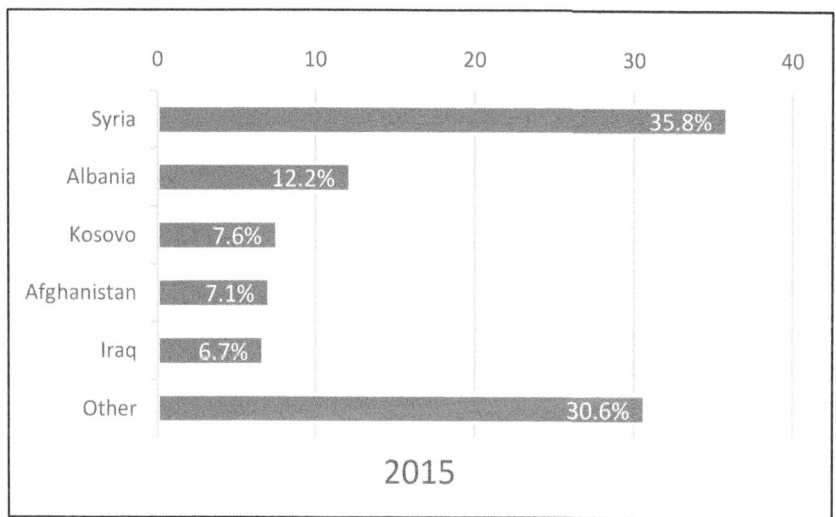

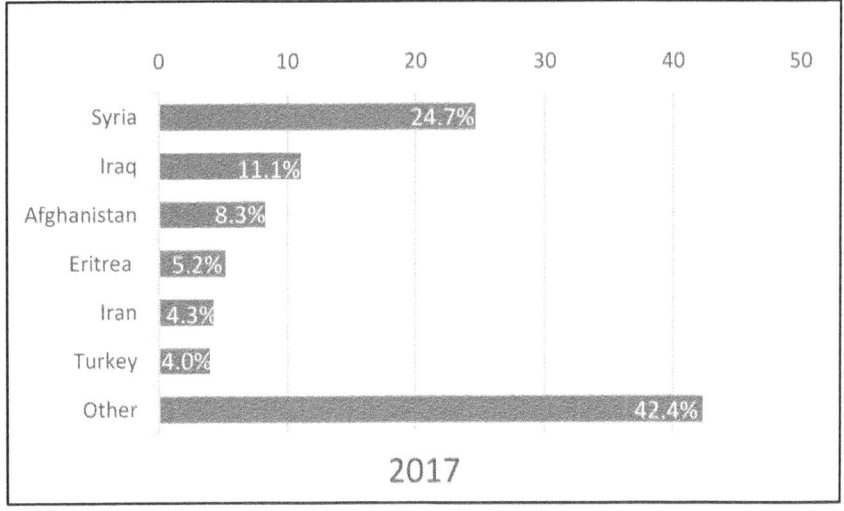

Figure 1: Countries of origin by refugees in Germany in 2015 and 2017 (after BAMF 2015, BAMF 2017).

2.1 Living Conditions in Germany

But what are the specific challenges in mental health care for asylum seekers and refugees in Germany? The biographies of refugees are often marked by uncertain living conditions in the countries of origin, potential traumatizing experiences (like war, torture, expulsion) in the countries of origin, during the flight and after arriving in the destination countries, including the risk of separation from the family and close relatives due to life-threatening events (Kluge 2016).

Most basically, existential uncertainties, e.g. concerning residential status, shape the reality of life. Moreover, refugees/asylum seekers in Germany have fewer rights compared to the German host community and the majority of society, especially as regards health care. Isolation and exclusion from the majority society shape the refugees' living conditions, particularly with regard to the housing situation (e.g. living in shelters), language barriers, discrimination experiences and other factors. Due to the existential uncertainties and limited rights, the lives of asylum seekers and refugees are characterized by passivity. Limited access to working permissions is another obstacle to integration and creates difficult financial situations. All this said, in treatment and therapy one additional factor usually burdens asylum seekers and refugees intensely: the expectations of those left at home in the country of origin, resulting in feelings of guilt, shame and often helplessness. Separation from family and close relatives due to life threatening events and the flight itself are also main factors that have an impact on mental health conditions of refugees, as well as difficulties to find a place to stay in the receiving country after the flight. After arrival, difficult living conditions in the receiving countries and, in a lot of cases, the impossibility to return influence the mental health of refugees. (Thöle et al. 2017). See figure 2 for an overview of living conditions of those groups in Germany.

The emotional burden resulting from those experiences and life histories is obvious. There are no epidemiological data on how many refugees of those who arrived since 2015 do have a mental disorder. From clinical evidence we do know that about a quarter of those asylum seekers and refugees who seek help show signs of PTSD, about 40% evidence unipolar depression, etc. The mental health burden is very high, but it is not in all cases that those challenging living conditions in the countries of origin, transit and arrival do result in a mental health disorder.

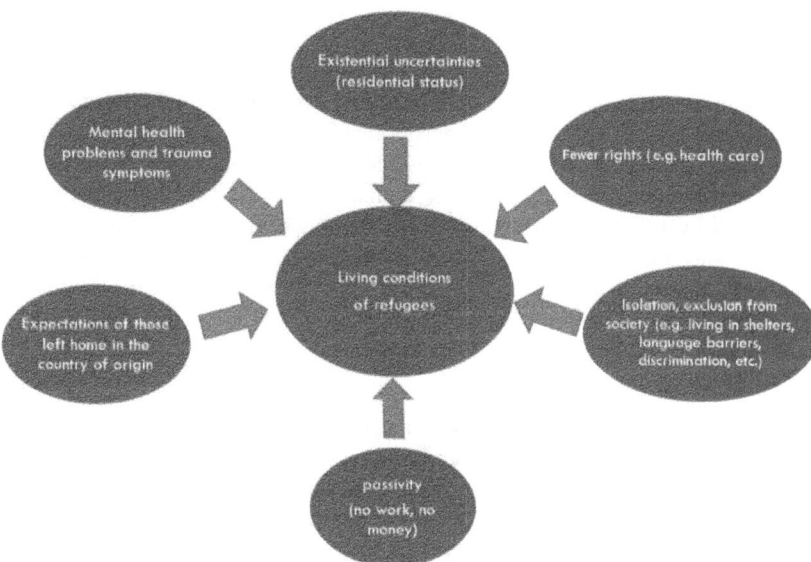

Figure 2:   Living conditions of asylum seekers and refugees in Germany.

2.2   Language- and Culture-Related Barriers

As mentioned before, isolation and exclusion from society as well as from the health care system results partly from language- and culture-related barriers. In the health care system in Germany there is still only a limited availability of professionals who speak the mother tongue of foreign patients, depending on regions and facilities in Germany. Additionally, there are no standardized training manuals for interpreters for (mental) health care: Therefore, competences are very heterogenous.

Moreover, professionals are often reluctant to involve interpreters due to concerns about reduced therapy quality. To increase the quality of interpreter-accompanied therapy we need standardized training for professionals as well as interpreters in this field, easily accessible interpreting services structures (including face-to-face, video and telephone interpretation), and the respective financial and administrative structures for those services (Kluge et al 2012).

In addition to problems revolving around mother tongue therapists and interpreters, cultural biases are another main barrier, too: They result in misunderstandings, prejudice and, in clinical practice, in uncertainties in diagnostics and treatment.

2.3   Administrative Barriers

In addition to language and culture-related barriers, asylum seekers face administrative barriers in their efforts to access mental health care in Germany. They do have fewer rights, especially in the context of health care, as mentioned above: entitlements to health care are defined by the Asylum Seekers Benefits Act (AsylbLG), § 4 and § 6, with limited coverage for the first 15 months of a person's stay in Germany (apart from some communities: Hamburg, Bremen). Moreover, mental health care for asylum seekers and refugees is still fragmented and dependent on local provisions.

2.4   Mental Health Conditions

There are single reports on the prevalence and frequency of mental health problems occurring in asylum seekers and refugees: For example, the PTSD rate is ten times higher in refugees than compared to the general population (Crumlish and O'Rourke 2010; Fazel et al. 2005), and symptoms of anxiety and depression are documented in 84.6% and 63.1% of this population group in Switzerland (Heeren et al. 2014). For Germany, no prevalence rates have been established so far.

Regarding psychiatric diagnoses, there is a resurgence of interest in the construct of complicated grief in mental health, given the importance of this reaction for refugees (Silove et al. 2017). The majority of refugees do have experienced multiple losses and separations in the context of gross human rights violations (Momartin et al. 2004). In addition, the long-debated category of complex PTSD, comprising elements of disrupted self-organization, will be included for the first time in the forthcoming ICD-11 (First et al. 2015). Early evidence suggests that the diagnosis can already be identified among refugees. There is a growing body of studies documenting cases in which PTSD is associated with psychotic-like symptoms or a genuine psychosis among refugees and post-conflict populations (Tay et al. 2015, Nygaard et al. 2017). There is now compelling evidence that schizophrenia and other psychotic disorders are more prevalent among refugees resettled in high-income countries as compared to other immigrants and host populations (Hollander et al. 2016).

Needless to say, the above-described living conditions of asylum seekers and refugees in Germany or other countries of destination and the resulting large number of social burdens require additional social and psychosocial support besides specialized treatment, such as trauma-focused treatment and therapy.

The discourse on trauma in the psycho-social field is not a new one. But it underwent a challenging renaissance in Germany and other European countries starting in 2015. There had been two main images in the media and in society: that of refugees as traumatized victims - or that of threatening perpetrators. Sverre Varvin, a Norwegian psychoanalyst argues: "Professionals, and to a large degree the public, identify the refugee's psychological suffering as problems that are "trauma-related" (Lesley & Varvin, 2016). "(…) the refugee experience is complex and comprises much more than "trauma". "Trauma", in these contexts, tends to become less of a theoretical concept and more of an object containing the deepest of human fears and images of the most terrifying violence" (Varvin, 2018).

3 Conclusion

The field of refugee mental health overlaps considerably with the larger movement of Global Mental Health: Both focus on the mental health needs of deprived populations from low-income countries.

But how can sufficient, good quality mental health services for asylum seekers and refugees in Germany be guaranteed in the future? There is a necessity for integrated care, consisting of social, political, cultural, medical and psychosocial stakeholders. There is especially a need for integrated mental health care systems, addressing psychological and social stressors in an appropriate manner, differentiating between needs ranging from psychosocial support to specialized treatment such as trauma therapy. Moreover, language and cultural barriers, as well as legal and political circumstances, need to be considered.

And what could be done? Multidimensional and -professional approaches are necessary to offer good quality mental health services for refugees. More specifically, low-threshold approaches, on a professional level as well as volunteer approaches, are needed. Psychosocial services need to be strengthened and professionals, including interpreters, have to be trained to offer adequate services for those groups.

The mental health situation of refugees in Europe is a global issue and should be understood as such in research and in the development of support structures including the expertise of professionals and researchers in the exit, transit and arrival countries.

Bibliography

Adorjan, K., Kluge, U., Heinz, A., Stamm, T., Odenwald, M., Dohrmann, K., Mokhtari-Nejad, R., Hasan, A., Schulze, TG., Falkai, P., Pogarell, O. (2017). Versorgungsmodelle für traumatisierte Flüchtlinge in Deutschland. *Nervenarzt*. doi:10.1007/s00115-017-0364-5

Crumlish, N., & O'Rourke, K. (2010). A Systematic Review of Treatments for Post-Traumatic Stress Disorder among Refugees and Asylum-Seekers. *The Journal of Nervous and Mental Disease, 198, (4, 237–251). doi:10.1097/NMD.0b013e3181d61258

Bundesamt für Migration und Flüchtlinge (2015) Migrationsbericht des Bundesamtes für Migration und Flüchtlinge im Auftrag der Bundesregierung. https://www.bamf.de/SharedDocs/ Anlagen/DE/Publikationen/Migrationsberichte/migrationsbericht-2015.pdf;jsessionid=38AA4E19 FB25B6193889987CACC2385E.1_cid286?__blob=publicationFile (last access: 20.10.2019)

Bundesamt für Migration und Flüchtlinge (2017) Migrationsbericht der Bundesregierung Migrationsbericht 2016/2017. http://www.bamf.de/SharedDocs/Anlagen/DE/Publikationen/ Migrationsberichte/migrationsbericht-2016-2017.pdf?__blob=publicationFile (last access: 20.10.2019)

Fazel, M., Wheeler, J., & Danesh, J. (2005). Prevalence of Serious Mental Disorder in 7000 Refugees Resettled in Western Countries: A Systematic Review. *The Lancet, 365, (9467, 1309–1314). doi:10.1016/S0140-6736(05)61027-6

First, M. B., Reed, G. M., Hyman, S. E., & Saxena, S. (2015). The Development of the ICD-11 Clinical Descriptions and Diagnostic Guidelines for Mental and Behavioural Disorders. *World Psychiatry : Official Journal of the World Psychiatric Association (WPA), 14, (1, 82–90). doi:10.1002/wps.20189

Heeren, M., Wittmann, L., Ehlert, U., Schnyder, U., Maier, T., & Müller, J. (2014). Psychopathology and Resident Status - Comparing Asylum Seekers, Refugees, Illegal Migrants, Labor Migrants, and Residents. *Comprehensive Psychiatry, 55, (4, 818–825). doi:10.1016/j.comppsych.2014.02.003

Hollander, A.-C., Dal, H., Lewis, G., Magnusson, C., Kirkbride, J. B., & Dalman, C. (2016). Refugee Migration and Risk of Schizophrenia and Other Non-Affective Psychoses: Cohort Study of 1.3 Million People in Sweden. *BMJ (Clinical research ed.), 352, (i1030). doi:10.1136/bmj.i1030

Kluge, U., Bogic, M., Devillé, W., Greacen, T., Dauvrin, M., Dias, S., Gaddini, A., Jensen, N K., Ioannidi- Kapolou, E., Mertaniemi, R., Puipcinós i Riera, R., Sandhu, S., Sarvary, A., Soares, J J F., Stankunas, M., Straßmayr, C., Welbel, M., Heinz, A., Priebe, S. (2012). Health Services and the Treatment of Immigrants: Data on Service Use, Interpreting Services and Immigrant Staff Members in Services Across Europe. European Psychiatry 27:S56-S62.

Kluge, U. (2016). Behandlung psychisch belasteter und traumatisierter Asylsuchender und Flüchtlinge - Das Spannungsverhältnis zwischen therapeutischem und politischem Alltag. *Nervenheilkunde* 35 (6):385-390.

Kluge, U., Romero, B., Hodzic, S. (2017). Psychotherapeutische und psychiatrische Versorgung geflüchteter Menschen mit Sprach- und Kulturmittlern. S*wiss Archives of Neurology, Psychiatry and Psychotherapy,* 168(5):133–139.

Kimmerle, H. (2002). Interkulturelle Philosophie zur Einführung. Hamburg , Junius- Verlag

Lesley, J., & Varvin, S. (2016). 'Janet vs Freud' on traumatization: A critique of the theory of structural dissociation from an object relations perspective. *British Journal of Psychotherapy*, 32(4), 436–455.

Mehran, N., Abi Jumaa, J., Valensise, L., von Bach, E., Hertner, L., Strasser, J., Kluge, U. (2019). Zur Beziehungsgestaltung zwischen geflüchteten Frauen und weiblichen Freiwilligen / Exploring the Relationship between Refugee Women and Female Volunteers. *Fortschritte Neurologie-Psychiatrie.* (accepted)

Momartin, S., Silove, D., Manicavasagar, V., & Steel, Z. (2004). Comorbidity of PTSD and Depression: Associations with Trauma Exposure, Symptom Severity and Functional Impairment in Bosnian Refugees Resettled in Australia. *Journal of Affective Disorders, 80, (2-3,* 231–238). doi:10.1016/S0165-0327(03)00131-9

Nygaard, M., Sonne, C., & Carlsson, J. (2017). Secondary Psychotic Features in Refugees Diagnosed with Post-Traumatic Stress Disorder: A Retrospective Cohort Study. *BMC psychiatry, 17, (1,* 5). doi:10.1186/s12888-016-1166-1

Silove, D., Ventevogel, P., & Rees, S. (2017). The Contemporary Refugee Crisis: An Overview of Mental Health Challenges. *World Psychiatry: Official Journal of the World Psychiatric Association (WPA), 16, (2,* 130–139). doi:10.1002/wps.20438

Tay, A. K., Rees, S., Chen, J., Kareth, M., & Silove, D. (2015). The Structure of Post-Traumatic Stress Disorder and Complex Post-Traumatic Stress Disorder amongst West Papuan Refugees. *BMC psychiatry, 15,* (111). doi:10.1186/s12888-015-0480-3

Thöle, AM., Penka, S., Aichberger, MC., Heinz, A., Kluge, U. (2017). Die (Flüchtlings-) Krise im psychotherapeutischen Behandlungszimmer. Psychother Psych Med 2018; 68(01): 30-37

UNHCR: The UN Refugee Agency (UN, Ed.). (2018). Global Trends. Forced Displacement in 2017. https://www.unhcr.org/globaltrends2017/. Accessed: 13 October 2019.

UNO Flüchtlingshilfe. (2018). Zahlen & Fakten zu Menschen auf der Flucht. https://www.uno-fluechtlingshilfe.de/fluechtlinge/zahlen-fakten/. Accessed: 13 October 2019.

Varvin, S. (2018). "Flucht und Exil: die Aufgabe der Psychoanalyse in einem entmenschlichenden Kontext". Lecture at the conference „Psychoanalytische und gruppenanalytische Behandlungsaspekte in der Arbeit mit Menschen mit Flucht- und Migrationserfahrung". October 2018 in Berlin. http://wp.belongingandcontaining.de/wp-content/uploads/2018/10/Sverre-Varvin-Flucht-und-Exil-Übersetzung.pdf. (last access: 20.10.2019).

Civil Strife, Migration and Health in the East African Region: Some Historical Reflections

Gordon Onyango Omenya[1]

Key Words: Health, Migration, Civil War, Refugees, East Africa, Postcolonial

Abstract

Issues of migration, health, civil strife and refugees are very common within the East African region. The fact that the creation of the East African states was a result of conflict in Europe cannot be underestimated. And therefore, the reorganization of boundaries among Africans and African states by the colonial masters was bound to generate conflict in the postcolonial period. True to this, the postcolonial states in East Africa were engulfed in civil strife leading to forced migration, displacements and the rise of refugee crises within the region. States such as Rwanda, Burundi, Sudan, South Sudan and Somalia symbolized the refugee crisis in this region. The colonial governments had laid the foundation of modern health systems in Africa and East Africa in particular, and the postcolonial governments inherited this system, which informed the whole idea of preventive and curative measures as far as health matters were concerned. The medical needs of the refugees would, therefore, be partially met by this system in collaboration with the United Nations High Commissioner for Refugees (UNCHR) and other non-governmental organisations (NGOs) especially for refugees living in camps. The diversity of diseases affects the refugees due to their diverse backgrounds, and health services provided by the governments of host nations, the United Nations High Commissioner for Refugees, and non-

---

1   Gordon Onyango Omenya | Kenyatta University, Nairobi-Kenya | gomenya30@yahoo.com

© Springer Fachmedien Wiesbaden GmbH, part of Springer Nature 2020
K. Crepaz et al. (eds.), *Health in Diversity – Diversity in Health*,
https://doi.org/10.1007/978-3-658-29177-8_3

governmental organisations such as the International Rescue Committee, the National Church Council of Kenya and volunteer medical practitioners represent the global, diverse and plural nature of the East African postcolonial era where modernity thrives. It also brings to the fore the north-south relations at another social level which is not necessarily capitalist or exploitative, but one which is mutually beneficial. This paper, therefore, provides a historical perspective on civil war, migration, health and the refugee crisis since the first major cases of civil strife within the East African region.

Contents

Abstract 25

1   Introduction: Background of Civil Strife 27

2   Colonialism, Refugees and Health in the East African Region 29

3   Civil Strife, Migration and the Refugee Question in East Africa 33

4   Refugee Problem and Health in Post-Independence East Africa 37

5   Conclusion 44

Bibliography 45

1 Introduction: Background of Civil Strife

Certain regions of the world experienced and continue to experience more conflict than others. Regions such as Central America, the Great Lakes region of Africa, and South-East Asia have witnessed numerous civil wars within several states, whereas other areas such as Europe and the Southern Cone of Latin America have had a relatively low frequency of internal conflict. Statistical analyses, moreover, have demonstrated that there is a regional clustering of civil war and that states bordering countries at war are significantly more likely to experience conflict themselves (see Gleditsch 2003b, Gurr and Marshall 2003). The regularity and strength of this geographical clustering casts doubt upon the conventional assumption that civil wars are independent, domestic phenomena, driven exclusively by processes and attributes within the state where the conflict occurs. Rather, international factors and relationships with other states may be very important in shaping the risk of internal conflict (Idean, 2006:1).

Although not so much connected to civil strife, the paradigm of the balance of power in Europe informed by the Peace of Utrecht of 1713 sheds more light on how European society was also conflictual before their democracies matured into what they are today. This 'school of perpetual peace' found its way into application, at the time of the next re-organisation of the European order: in the early nineteenth century, in the years immediately following the fall of Napoleon, with the Treaty of the Holy Alliance (1815) and the 'Congress System' (Ghervace, 2017). The war of the Spanish Succession exemplifies serious strife within Europe. Other dynastic concerns had to be settled, such as the Stuart claim to the succession of the English, Scottish, and Irish thrones, which had been a card used by the French to foment instability across the Channel (Ghervace, 2017). Theoretically, there is, however, ample reason to assume that autocratic successions increase the risk of both civil and interstate war from a rationalist perspective (Andrej &Anders, 2017). However, the fundamental question in rationalistic explanations of war is why the involved actors fail to reach a settlement that avoids war, given that war is always a costly option ex post (Fearon 1995). One answer is that the actors have private information about their resolve (i.e., their subjective assessment of the costs of war) and capability to wage war that they have strong incentives to misrepresent in bargaining situations, in order to arrive at a better settlement (Fearon 1995; Walter 2009). While European states have always managed to solve conflict amongst themselves, a proposition which can be explained from a theoretical point of view, a number of African states have continuously been involved in civil conflict many years after their independence.

Africa has a high prevalence of civil wars and this is commonly attributed to the ethnic diversity of its countries (Elbadawi and Sambanis, 2000:3). This inference seems self-evident to many, given that African rebel movements almost always are ethnically defined. Ethnic identities and hatred are thus seen as the cause of violent conflict. However, a more systematic analysis of the causes of civil war suggests that Africa's civil wars conform to a global pattern that is better explained by political and economic factors as well as by the extent of ethnic, cultural and religious diversity in the society (Elbadawi, 2000:3). Over the last 40 years, nearly 20 African countries (or about 40 percent of Africa south of the Sahara (SSA)) have experienced at least one period of civil war. It is estimated that 20% of SSA's population now lives in countries which are formally at war, and low-intensity conflict has become endemic to many other African states. This state of affairs has created stereotypes of Africa as a doomed continent with inescapable ethnic cleavages and violent tribal conflict. The more incidents of political violence we observe in Africa, the more support there is for this simplistic and negative perception (Elbadawi and Sambanis, 2000:1).

Statistical analyses of refugee flows that have appeared in print (notably Azam and Hoeffler 2002, Davenport et al. 2003,) have confirmed that civil wars, political repression, and regime change, are important predictors of flight. Some authors (such as Weiner 1992, Lischer 2005 and Loescher, 1993), however, have noted that international migration in general and refugee migration in particular can have important security consequences, which suggests that refugee flows and population movements due to civil wars can spur the spread of conflict both between and within states. Civil wars may also invite the international spread of infectious diseases and other public health concerns, which similarly lead to a decline in living standards and general discontent (see Ghobarah, Huth and Russett 2003).

Idean (2006) argues that the vast majority of the world's refugees never directly engage in political violence, but are rather the unfortunate victims of it. Refugees are usually thought of as victims of political violence. Periods of ethnic strife, armed conflict between rival factions, and government purges of political opposition groups, clearly place great burdens on civilian populations. People in these contexts face difficult choices: stay and risk harm, or flee to safety leaving behind one's property, homeland, and friends and family. Moreover, refugees often live in difficult conditions in their countries of destination, and are frequently dependent on humanitarian assistance. The risk of conflict is highest in anocracies that combine lack of political openness with ineffective repression, and lower in both democracies that allow for non-violent political opposition and autocracies that deter dissent (see, for example, Muller and Weede 1990). This characteristic seems to have featured a lot amongst a number of East African states.

The causes – whether political, economic or social – of civil conflict have been well addressed by numerous quantitative and qualitative studies. Two particularly influential explanations for the onset of civil conflict have been offered by Fearon and Laitin (2003), and Collier (2003). Collier (2003) has pointed to the high incidence of civil conflict in "countries with poor and declining economies" that rely on "natural resources for a large proportion of national income", and has inferred that "[...] every year that their dismal economic conditions persist increases the odds that their societies will fall into armed conflict." Fearon & Laitin (2003) on the other hand, have argued that the incidence of civil conflict is explained best by conditions that favour insurgency, including financially and bureaucratically weak states, rough terrain and large populations. Other studies have focused on the significance of other factors such as religious cleavages, ethnic fractionalisation and political repression in predicting the onset of civil conflict (Elbadawi, Sambanis, 2000). It is against this background that this paper examines and historicizes civil war and how it has impacted on the health of the refugees in East Africa in terms of accessibility and acquisition of health services.

2 Colonialism, Refugees and Health in the East African Region

Politicians from several European countries oversaw the conquest of sub-Saharan Africa at the end of the nineteenth century, dividing the bulk of the continent between the governments of Britain, France, Germany, Belgium, Portugal, and Spain (Tilley, 2016:744). The participants in the Berlin Congress of 1884–1885 that partitioned Africa agreed that possession required effective occupation, and effective occupation meant introducing soldiers, traders, missionaries, and settlers in order to validate claims to territory. This triggered a burst of international rivalry between the colonial powers. The Portuguese occupied Angola and Mozambique for fear of losing them to Britain, as they had other parts of Africa they had once claimed but never really administered. France took over equatorial Africa north of the Congo River to preempt the Belgians, and Germany seized Southwest Africa (now Namibia) and German East Africa to preempt the British (Headrick, 2014:2). With all these arrangements and claims over spheres of influence, most of the East African states (Kenya, Uganda, Tanzania, Rwanda and Burundi) fell under the British, German and Belgian protectorates.

While the motives of the European states during the partition of East Africa varied, they tended to be optimistic about the potential wealth of the new territories in terms of both natural resources and labor pools. They also embraced a vague mandate to "civilize," "improve," and "develop" the populations they ruled, setting up governance structures that invested officials, usually unfamiliar with the regions, with far more political and cultural power than most Africans possessed (Wesseling, 1996). Health activities took on an exalted role given this ethos of improvement since they were a visible and seemingly uncontroversial way to address the needs of the continent's people. Unsurprisingly, medical projects often received a significant portion of development funds earmarked for social welfare, and medical personnel made up the majority of employees in the technical services of each colonial state (Tilley, 2011:336).

The issue of health and migration can best be understood from a colonial point of view. As western forms of knowledge, health and medicine became important values that Europeans through colonialism would bequeath to Africans and the postcolonial African states. Odinga (2012:vi) argues that the socio-economic changes that accompanied the colonial governmental 'migration' and settlement in East Africa created favorable environmental conditions for the propagation and spread of different diseases earlier unknown in the region. The political machinery, on the other hand, influenced the provision and distribution of health services. Before 1914, for example, the colonial government health services were limited to the colonial officials, the railway employees and only those Africans who were in government employment. Health services were only extended to the Africans and Asians outside the colonial government employment as emergency measures to check on the spread of epidemics from the African zones to the European zones. Emphasis was put on curative as opposed to preventive medicine; on protecting the health of the male as opposed to the female (Odinga, 2012:vii). In other words, the health system in the colonial period was racialized and gendered.

As a result of the changes that emanated during World War I, the colonial government realized the necessity of extending the health services to the population that earlier had no access to the services. After the War as a matter of policy, therefore, the colonial government revised its health care provision policy. The post-World War I health policy emphasized the provision of health services to everybody and both preventive and curative medicine were given due recognition. This led to the rise of dispensaries, child welfare centres and the creation of the sanitation division in the medical department. It is, however, argued that, though this was a positive move, the African population hitherto denied the services had become unmanageable in light of the available health resources (Odinga, 2012:viii). It is also shown that the move to extend the services to the population had economic motives and was therefore not aimed at improving the health status of the population. Due to the imbalance in the provision and distribution of health services, the intensified Africans' and Asians' demand for an equitable distribution of the services, and the changing global distribution of the services, as well as the changing global outlook towards the health of the population in general, the colonial government devised new health policies in the post-World War II era. This led to the rise of the "health centre" system, and for the first time Africans were required to pay a fee for the health resources at their disposal. This further deteriorated the health of the population. Thus, instead of serving the intended purpose, the services were used as a political weapon to increase the dependence of Africans for exploitation (Odinga, 2012:viiii).

The efforts of Europeans to ameliorate the health of imperial subjects were typically beset with contradictions both because disease burdens increased and because health conditions were more difficult to control than officials expected. Conquest was violent and disruptive, radically altering landscapes and lives, and producing what medical specialist Patrick Manson aptly referred to in 1902 as a "pathological revolution" in tropical Africa (Tilley, 2016:744). Manson was referring to certain epizootics, such as rinderpest, which had swept through Eastern and Southern Africa in the 1890s, decimating cattle populations and leading to massive social and economic upheavals. He was also concerned about an ongoing pandemic of sleeping sickness (*African trypanosomiasis*)—a disease transmitted by tsetse flies and fatal to humans unless treated—that had broken out in the territories surrounding Lake Victoria, including the Congo, Uganda, the Sudan, and Tanzania . The flies' habitats had been transformed in the previous decades, bringing tsetses into closer proximity to humans and distancing them from some of the animals, especially cattle, on which they normally fed. Thus, in at least some regions, people became a convenient meal for the flies, increasing transmission rates and spreading the epidemic to new areas (Tilley, 2016:744). The challenges of controlling and preventing the spread of diseases were similar to the challenges that refugees would pose later on with their myriad forms of diseases and sicknesses especially within the postcolonial host nations in East Africa.

In Kenya for instance, the first colonial medical services were geared towards the Europeans and were only concerned with the indigenous Kenyans when epidemics struck. Ann Beck wrote in her book:

> After the Europeans had been taken care of, the administration could concern itself with the health of the Indians who were needed for the building of the railroad and for the promotion of trade. The African contingent of the population, used to tropical climates, need not be a concern of the medical administration except in emergencies. Beside, government officials knew that the various missions could take care of them; or even if they could not do so, the administration accepted this kind of wishful thinking (Beck, 1970:14).

The observation above could resonate well with the plight of refugees in East Africa where the postcolonial governments do not have any budget line for health services for refugees unless there is an outbreak of communicable diseases such as polio or cholera, which must be stopped from spreading at all cost. This scenario in itself dichotomizes refugees and gives them the identity of the Other, which in itself is a concept of 'belonging' and 'not belonging'. These binaries can always work against refugees who are very vulnerable considering that they cannot access medical services on their own within a host country.

Headrick (2014:2) observes that sleeping sickness was probably endemic in the East African region and flared into epidemics as the expansion of colonial rule increased trade and migrations throughout Africa. This dramatic social change triggered outbreaks of sleeping sickness in several areas of East and Central Africa. In response to the sleeping sickness epidemic, imperial governments sent specialists in tropical diseases to Africa to study the new scourge. Between 1901 and 1913, fifteen medical research missions (8 of them British) came to Africa to study sleeping sickness. In 1902 the Royal Society asked the London School of Tropical Medicine to dispatch a mission to Uganda. The leaders of the mission, parasitologist George C. Low and epidemiologist Cuthbert Christy, did little to advance knowledge of the disease. However, a third member of the mission, Aldo Castellani, a bacteriologist and student of Manson at the London School, established a small laboratory at Entebbe on Lake Victoria, where he identified several pathogens in the cerebrospinal fluid of sleeping sickness victims (Headrick, 2014:2). For a while, it was not clear whether the pathogen that caused sleeping sickness was a bacteria, perhaps a variety of streptococcus called "hypnococcus," or a protozoan, such as a trypanosome he called *T. ugandense*. Nevertheless, these early findings were the basis upon which western medicine flourished and which informed the postcolonial health services which refugees stood to gain from (Fevre, 2004: 568).

While rinderpest and sleeping sickness posed a major health challenge both to Africans and Europeans who migrated and settled in the East African region, this challenge was further enhanced by malaria, a deadly tropical disease that claimed so many lives of the European population due to their particular vulnerability. With the idea of malaria in mind, the Europeans took an extra effort to protect themselves from malaria, including the establishment of separate residential neighborhoods in coastal towns. Similarly, there were early European projects in mosquito control, and other European efforts were directed towards improving the health of Africans who worked directly for Europeans in mining enclaves or who lived in urban environments (Webb, 2014:xii). The discovery of African adult acquired immunity and African childhood vulnerability raised fundamental questions for European colonial medical officers about how to address the "African" malaria problem.

The 1950s and early 1960s marked the era of global malaria eradication projects and campaigns that were overseen by the World Health Organization (Webb, 2014:xiii). The projects, based on the use of synthetic insecticides for indoor residual house-spraying, dramatically reduced malaria in endemic zones but could not sustain the interruption of transmission because mosquito resistance to the insecticides emerged and the projects did not have the full support of African populations in the project zones. These conditions of vulnerability, perhaps described as 'refugee vulnerability', would also apply to refugees coming from different geographical regions and settling in the host states with unique diseases and so on in the post-independence period. The argument here is that although colonialism was brutal, violent and capitalistic in nature, there were certain attempts by the colonial governments in East Africa to put in place functional structures in the health sector that would later on take care of the various diseases that emerged within the colonial and postcolonial states. However, independent African governments did not embrace the WHO's vision of malaria pre-eradication programs, preferring to allocate scarce resources to other medical problems, yet deaths from malaria declined. This was in good measure owing to the widespread availability of the inexpensive antimalarial drug chloroquine and to the rapid urbanization of tropical Africa. In stable post-independence states, health structures such as dispensaries, health units and district hospitals have continued to exist amid various financial and structural challenges. Nevertheless, in many other African countries, civil war led to the destruction of all these structures giving rise to the refugee question and the need to access better health care in the neighboring host nations (Webb, 2014:xiii).

Based on the fact that Africans were subjected to poor quality health services during colonialism, it would suffice to deduce that although colonial healthcare was racial in nature, African health services were taken care of by the missionaries through colonial government. African district hospitals were thus put in place to address the health needs of Africans. This was the characteristic of post-colonial Africa under colonial rule. During colonialism, very few civil wars took place since most Africans were united against colonialism and would occasionally raid colonial camps and attack colonial administrators. Displacement would thus have been based on forced migration, forced labour and land alienation. Cases of refugees crossing over from other states were therefore minimal. Most Africans whose land was alienated therefore ended up living as squatters while others were confined to the African reserves. Within these reserves, the health needs of Africans were taken care of at the African District Hospitals and health centres across the East African region.

3   Civil Strife, Migration and the Refugee Question in East Africa

The United Nations (UN) Convention Relating to the Status of Refugees defines a refugee as a person who, 'owing to well-founded fear of being persecuted for reasons of race, religion, nationality, membership of a particular social group or political opinion, is outside the country of his nationality and is unable, or owing to such fear, is unwilling to avail himself of the protection of that country' (Leon, 1987:47). While this international legal definition emphasizes government persecution targeted at individuals, it is widely accepted among academics and policy-makers that those escaping general conditions of violence such as civil war and state failure also qualify as refugees. Therefore, it is customary for countries of asylum to grant some form of protection to people leaving areas broadly deemed as insecure, even if it is difficult to prove individual cases of persecution. However, in addition to persons who have fled across national borders, many people also flee to areas within the state. These are referred to as internally displaced persons (IDPs), and they lack the international legal protections afforded to international refugees (Leon, 1987:47).

Among the most dramatic events in the world today is the massive migration of people across political borders. In part, this migration represents people's search for a better livelihood; in part it is in response to political pressures (Nindi, 1987:387). State repression, insurgencies, and civil wars often have devastating consequences for societies marred by violence. Such periods of social upheaval often create massive population dislocations as individuals are forced to flee their homes in search of physical security elsewhere. Quite often, the number of forced migrants far exceeds the number of killed and injured persons during armed conflicts. Somalia, Rwanda, and Darfur are but a few recent cases of mass refugee outflows that have captured international attention thereby heralding the refugee question in East Africa, a question and problem that has not been resolved up to date. Such displacement often has lasting effects on the economy, public health, and social relations, not only for the refugees themselves, but also their host and origin communities. Moreover, as several conflicts have eluded a lasting resolution, many of these refugee crises drag on for decades, leaving people without a permanent home (Sahleyan, 2007:127). In either case, the plight of these refugees constitutes one of the greatest challenges to the international community. In East Africa, refugee camps such as Kakuma, Dadaab, (Kenya) and Nyarugusu in Tanzania have been in place for more than a decade symbolizing the epitome of the refugee crisis in East Africa.

The Rwandan genocide of 1994, the Somalia crisis, the Burundian Civil War and the two Sudanese Civil Wars, between 1955-1972 and 1983-2005, among others have caused massive displacement in East Africa. By 2014, Sudan had 665,908 refugees worldwide, and as of 2016 the number of Sudanese refugees registered with UNHCR was 650,588. Sudanese refugees are distributed mostly between Chad (48%), South Sudan (37%) and Ethiopia (6%), while most South Sudanese refugees are hosted in Kenya (MGSoG, 2017:8). There are also Sudanese refugees in Egypt; however, they are not required to register as refugees there, as the two countries have a free movement agreement, which makes it challenging to estimate the number of Sudanese in Egypt. Estimates therefore vary extremely, from 2,000 to millions (Di Bartolomeo, Jaulin & Perrin, 2012:4). Nevertheless, Kakuma Refugee Camp in Kenya is a habitat for a mixture of refugees from all the states affected by war within the region.

One of the negative consequences of armed conflict is the dislocation of large numbers of non-combatants, both within states and across national borders. This has been the case within the postcolonial political and social spaces in Sudan, Somalia, Ethiopia, Rwanda and Burundi in the East African region. Civil wars are particularly associated with large-scale forced migration, for a host of reasons. For example, Posen (1996:74-77) identifies five chief reasons for forced displacement: genocide or ethnic cleansing to achieve cultural homogeneity, politicide against proponents of certain political ideas, fear of territorial occupation by the opposing side, and the need to escape dangerous environments created by combat. All these determinants of forced migration are highly positively influenced by the occurrence of civil wars. Most are fought inside the borders of a state, often causing greater destruction than interstate wars fought on borders or focused on strategic targets. Such domestic conflict may drive people out of their homes incidentally – that is, to escape the ravages of war – or due to deliberate efforts at dislocation by the opposing sides. Civilian groups are especially vulnerable to forced migration during ethnic conflicts, which are often associated with ethnic cleansings and seizures of territory; the wave of civil and ethnic conflicts following the end of the Cold War often resulted in high-intensity violence and consequent mass movements of persecuted or endangered groups. Such large-scale movements of people have significant economic, social, and political consequences, both for individual states and entire regions. The implications of refugee flows for human security and political stability, therefore, necessitate systematic evaluations of forced migration (Iqbal and Zorn 2007:200).

Migration and settlement of displaced persons is not a new phenomenon in East Africa, and migratory movements in and out of the East and Horn of Africa are diverse and significant in volume. The flows of people in, between and from countries in the region can best be characterized as mixed migration flows. Forced migrants, including asylum seekers and refugees, and voluntary economic migrants move within the region as well as beyond for a variety of different factors, including conflicts as well as socio-economic conditions in their respective countries of origin (Marchand & Reinold, 2017:1). Forced migration occurs when people are compelled to leave their homes due to fear of persecution, for instance in the case of Eritrea (see also Gibney, 1988, Moore 2004,).

In addition, civil war, violent conflicts, political oppression and persecution are main migration drivers in some of the relevant countries. Environmental factors are also increasingly affecting countries in the region and impact people's food security, livelihoods and migration decisions (Marchand and Reinold,

2017). Somalia has been a major country of origin for mixed migration in the East and Horn of Africa especially in the past 25 years. Factors pushing people to leave the country were and are conflict, chronic insecurity, extreme poverty, famine, and until 2012, the lack of an effective central government. Migration from South Sudan is largely driven by conflicts, the latest of which is displacing millions within the country as well as across borders, which is exacerbated by an increase in food insecurity. Migration from Sudan is also driven by conflict in addition to factors such as a lack of sustainable livelihoods and employment opportunities as well as a lack of basic infrastructure and social services, and food insecurity (International Organization for Migration, 2011b). Similarly, Marchand et al. (2017:7) have observed that prolonged national service obligations, political oppression as well as poor economic conditions are considered to be the main drivers for migration particularly of young Eritreans, including unaccompanied minors. More so, drivers for migration from Ethiopia are varied, but can be summarized as being socio-economic factors along with ethnic tensions and environmental disasters that impact peoples' livelihoods. Although, some of these migration drivers are environmental in nature, most importantly, civil war and political persecutions have been the major push for the rise of refugees in the East African region.

Kenya, on the other hand, shows significantly different characteristics compared to the other countries in the East and the Horn of Africa. Kenyans are rarely found among the flows of irregular migrants in or out of the region. Instead, Kenyan migrants are largely (highly) skilled workers traveling with documents and visas, which some then fail to renew or overstay and these people become irregular as a consequence. Perhaps, this is the reason why many elite class members affected by conflict have always sought for better health care in Kenyan hospitals such as Nairobi Hospital and Kenyatta National Hospital (Marchand et al, 2016:7). Overall, due to limited options for regular migration (apart from refugees) or the administrative challenges associated with it, many migrants choose irregular channels of migration, many being well aware of the risks and vulnerabilities associated with this type of migration. These vulnerabilities have had serious consequences on accessibility to health services especially by refugees in the host countries (Marchand et al., 2016).

It is important to point out that the majority of displaced persons and refugees in the context of East Africa are women and children, including many female-headed households (UNHCR, 1991:1, UNHCR, 2010:1). Many of the displacement situations are protracted and have lasted for more than 20 years at this stage. On the other hand, new refugees continue to arrive at camps across the region. As a consequence, forced displacement is a serious concern to be addressed in the region and presents a significant challenge for achieving peace and security as well as reducing poverty, the spread of communicable diseases and supporting sustainable development in the East African region (World Bank and UNHCR, 2015). The issue of many women within refugee camps opens up the gender dimension of the question of refugees and their vulnerability to diseases and health care within the camps. It could be argued, therefore, that with their high numbers within refugee camps, the rate of sickness and infant mortality has been higher amongst women and children compared to men (UNCHCR, 2010:2, Laurie and Petchesky, 2008:1).

In East Africa, Uganda, Tanzania and Kenya are home to more than two million refugees from Somalia, South Sudan, Democratic Republic of Congo, Ethiopia, Burundi and Eritrea. The bulk of this population — about 1.47 million people — is in Uganda, despite its economy and land size being smaller than those of Kenya and Tanzania (The East African, 16/11/2018). According to a 2018 report by the African Centre for Migration and Society titled *Free and Safe Migration in East Africa*, Congolese and South Sudanese nationals running away from instability in their countries are housed in settlements and urban areas in the country, alongside local communities. One of Uganda's hallmark acts is its longstanding, free-of-charge distribution of viable agricultural land to refugees (East African Standard, 16/11/2018). With a current refugee population of about 415,000, mainly from Somalia and South Sudan, Kenya has for many years been home to hundreds of thousands of refugees from the Horn of Africa and the Great Lakes, but is now considering to reduce the number of refugees arriving at its borders (especially from Somalia), with the government insisting on the closure of Dadaab Refugee Camp (Di Bartolomeo, Jaulin & Perrin, 2012). Nevertheless, contrary to many migrants in the region, South Sudanese migrants tend to stay in the region instead of engaging in irregular migration to Europe (i.e. their former colonial masters).

4   Refugee Problem and Health in Post-Independence East Africa

Most of the civil strife experienced in East Africa was witnessed after colonialism when most of the African states got independence. A number of African states were either under military or authoritarian rule, which fuelled civil strife leading to the rise in the number of refugee cases in the post-independence period. With independence, East African states nationalized the health system, the same way other sectors of the economy were nationalized. Since the end of the Cold War, funding for several rebel organizations and governments allied with one or the other superpower dried up, and many of these conflicts petered out. Although there was a decline in conflict after the end of the Cold War period in East Africa and Africa in general, new post-Cold War conflicts such as in Liberia, Darfur, Somalia, Ethiopia and Sudan have generated significant refugee flows (Salehyan, 2007:127).

Most of the newly independent East African states embarked on the preparation of medium and long-term health development plans of one sort or another. These usually proposed the relatively rapid expansion of virtually all aspects of the health services, essentially in their existing forms. In addition, they sometimes introduced such new elements as "primary health centers" or "community participation" into the health services. Gish (1979:206) argues that if these plans were in their formulation primarily only "more of the same", in application they become at best only that, and at worst allocated health sector resources that are even more sharply geared towards elite and/or urban groups and populations than had been the case before national independence. The leaders of the newly independent countries and, more particularly, the medical leadership did not question the essential character of the health services they had inherited; instead, they aspired to spread these services to the whole of the population. The new services were to be of "high standard" as defined by the medical elite, while at the same time serving the needs of the general population. The comprehensiveness of the plans almost always meant that only a fraction of them could be implemented, thus forcing (or allowing) the implementers to single out only particular projects for development. More often than not it was the prestigious hospital plan that was thus singled out, and not the health centers in rural climes, or preventive programs. The rhetoric of the plans was, and still is, almost always in stark contrast with proposed expenditures. The rhetoric emphasized preventive and rural priorities while, at the same time, expenditures were overwhelmingly curative and urban (Gish, 1979: 206).

The plans reflect not only the social and class views and interests of the medical doctors and their political superiors who develop them, but also the narrow initial clinical training of members of the medical profession. The postindependence period then saw a continuation of the kind of health care systems that had been in operation during the days of colonial rule. Of course, it was an expanded system that was coming to be staffed by nationals at all levels rather than by foreigners as well as being more readily accessible to a somewhat larger proportion of the entire population. Nonetheless, the system could not be characterized as being in any way other than different in size. However, over time states would rely on these public health and rural health centres as forms of western knowledge, in cases of emergencies and outbreaks of disaster. The current refugees in East Africa have also benefitted from these postcolonial medical system structures, symbolizing the fact that postcolonial relationships were not just about resistance but also about collaboration (Mbembe, 2001:104).

As refugees do not live in isolation, but rather in diverse communities, their health status has an impact on the community at large. It is therefore the responsibility of and in the best interest of the host state alongside other international non-governmental agencies to cater for the basic health needs of this group. Refugees are a particularly vulnerable group when it comes to access to health care. Health care needs remain largely unmet due to the persistence of language barriers and the perceived poor quality of care and appropriateness of care. However, women and children remain an even more vulnerable group of refugees compared to men. Some of them have been subjected to unfair treatment or been turned away, e.g. from dentists or walk-in clinics, due to their status and lack of insurance (Newbold et al, 2014:445). Their medical choices at times become limited as a direct consequence of being refugees. Some refugees lack access to settlement agencies that provide access to language and translation services, and to counselors who can help them navigate the health care system. In most cases, illiterate refugees – especially in places like Kakuma Refugee Camp – would only rely on fellow literate refugees, who sometimes live outside the camp, in order to explain their health conditions to doctors. Nevertheless, the UNHCR and IRC and volunteers have tried to provide some medical services to the refugees through their own arrangements. Other refugees have also managed to access health care through a handful of physicians, dentists, and pharmacies willing to accept them as clients. At the same time, the smaller social networks that refugees tend to have mean that they are often more isolated and have limited opportunities. But more importantly, the rise of terrorism has really restricted the movement of refugees in their search for better health care outside refugee camps within the East African region. In most cases, they are (especially Somali refugees) highly suspected to be either Al-Shabaab or sympathizers of the Al-Shabaab terror group. For these reasons, refugees are likely the most vulnerable group as far as accessing health services outside the camp is concerned. To address some of these challenges, Newbold et al. (2014:446) argue that low-cost and professional language and translation services in health care settings must remain a priority, not just for refugees but for other immigrants as well in order to help them express themselves and state the kind of health problems affecting them.

However, not all migrants and mobile populations are equally at risk to adverse health. It is not people moving, per se, that aggravates poor health, but the way in which they move and the context within which movement takes place. For example, income disparities, separation from family, or alcohol abuse are factors that may deteriorate people's wellbeing. Further, cramped habitats in refugee camps make inhabitants prone to tuberculosis transmission, and a lack of effective prevention programs increases the chances of risky sexual behavior, and thus HIV transmission, along transport corridors (IOM, 2011:5). Collier et al. (2003) observe that there is a link between refugees and infectious diseases such as malaria and human immunodeficiency virus/acquired immune deficiency syndrome (HIV/AIDS). Similarly, Refugees fleeing war may also place burdens on health infrastructures and hospitals, which are often not prepared to deal with large population inflows, especially inflows that require special treatment related to the ailments forced migrants might have. These huge migration flows sometimes pose heavy challenges to the host nation whenever there are outbreaks of diseases.

East Africa boasts two major refugee camps, that is, Kakuma and Dadaab, both based in Kenya. The first camp was established in 1991, when refugees fleeing the civil war in Somalia started to cross the border into Kenya. A second large influx occurred in 2011, when some 130,000 refugees arrived, fleeing drought and famine in southern Somalia (Rono, 2017:1). As Somalia descended into civil war, Dadaab was established by the United Nations in 1991, and has since mushroomed, with more refugees streaming in, uprooted by drought and famine as well as on-going insecurity. Many have lived there for years. The camp has schools, hospitals, markets, police stations, graveyards and a bus station (The Standard, 29/3/2019). Other refugee camps are Nyarugusu in Tanzania and Yida in South Sudan. It is worth noting that accessibility to health services sometimes is cumbersome for refugees, especially for irregular refugees who often only seek medical assistance when there is no other alternative option and who tend to miss out on important promotive health measures such as immunizations, pregnancy care, and safe childbirth (IOM, 2009). This is true especially for refugees who do not live inside the refugee camps.

According to UNHCR (2011) data, Kakuma Refugee Camp in Kenya accommodates refugees from 14 nationalities, with most coming from the Republic of South Sudan, Sudan, Rwanda, Congo, Uganda, Burundi and Somalia, with minority representations from Iran, Congo Brazzaville, Cameroon, Tanzania and Zimbabwe. Looking at reproductive health among refugees, it is evident that a number of factors such as gender, religion, as well as medical and legal restrictions, affect accessibility and acceptability of these services especially by women in the refugee camps. Kiura, (2014:153) supports this argument by stating that religious prohibition and opposition by husbands are some of the major barriers to contraceptive use and family planning among Somali urban refugee women in East Africa, and more so in Kenya. Therefore, it can be argued that problems of reproductive health amongst refugees are to greater extent related to gender-based power relations, which systematically marginalizes and discriminates women's access to health care in the refugee camps (see also Larris & Smyth, 2001).

Most refugee camps in East Africa are under the management of the UNHCR and the Department of Refugee Affairs within individual states. They are always assisted by local NGOs such as the International Rescue Committee (IRC), Médecins Sans Frontières (MSF) and the National Council of Churches of Kenya which provide health care services. For food, the refugees mainly rely on the World Food Program (WFP) and. to a smaller extent, on small-scale trading ventures operated within the camp by the refugees themselves (Kiura, 2014:148). As some health issues related to trans-border mobility cannot be solved by individual states alone, international collaboration is required. This is where organizations such as IRC and the NCCK come in. Considering that refugees are foreigners, the health systems should be made more "migrant friendly". The role and effectiveness of NGOs is a particularly sensitive issue within the context of refugee camps. These camps are not only a reflection of regional instability but can also be a source of political, economic, social and health concern for host states (Hannah & Cunliffe, 2011:67). The United Nations High Commissioner for Refugees (UNHCR) holds overall responsibility for providing all aspects of health assistance, including HIV/AIDS management programs and services, to refugees. However, the UNHCR recognizes that it cannot achieve its goals alone and therefore relies upon a number of other organizations, including NGOs, to work alongside them as implementing partners in these camps. As a result, a number of NGOs and other organizations are involved in the provision of aid to, and care of, refugees in both camps (Hannah & Cunliffe 2011: 65).

Based on UNHCR and various NGO recommendations, the IRC have implemented ABC prevention programs[1] in relation to the HIV/AIDS scourge in Kakuma Refugee Camp. They have been implemented as part of each NGO's broader HIV/AIDS awareness programs. This program addresses the abstinence element of HIV prevention. The camp has comprehensive condom awareness and distribution programs, and also provides condoms and educational materials to local communities. Staff in Kakuma's healthcare centre actively distribute condoms and train healthcare workers to do the same in Voluntary Counseling and Testing (VCT) clinics. Condom dispensers have also been installed in frequently visited areas of the camp and surrounding villages (Hannah and Cunliffe, 2011:72).

A number of on-site and off-site clinical facilities are also available to Kakuma's refugees and Turkana's local population. The on-site medical facilities provided by the NGOs are staffed by healthcare professionals with an up-to-date knowledge of modern medicine, Western medical qualifications and accreditation. On-site services, repeatedly reported to have high standards of care, are

---

1   This is a prevention mechanism against contracting HIV/AIDS based on the first three letters of the alphabet, that is ABC, where letter 'A' stands for Abstinence, 'B' stands for Being faithful and 'C' stands for Condom usage. This strategy, if correctly followed, either reduces or completely eliminates HIV/AIDS.

free to both refugees and locals and provide all of the HIV healthcare services recommended by the UNHCR; VCT, preventing mother-to-child transmission (PMTCT), antenatal care (ANC) and post-exposure prophylaxis (PEP) programs (Hannah & Cunliffe, 2011: 75). In Turkana district in Kenya, where some refugees have settled, there are two government-run hospitals and numerous smaller clinics. As a way of managing the HIV/AIDS pandemic in the refugee camps, the UNHCR and UNAIDS strongly advocate the provision of easily accessible, voluntary and confidential voluntary counselling and testing program services with appropriate counselling delivered by trained personnel (Cabassi, 2004). The IRC's PEPFAR-funded VCT program, which meets these standards, is considered by the UNHCR to be a model for other refugee camps in sub-Saharan Africa. Additionally, there are clinics situated in the camp and surrounding communities which are free to both refugees and locals and distribute condoms and provide antiretroviral therapy (ARVT) for people living with AIDS (PLWA). According to Hannah and Cunliffe (2011), the IRC train and use local women as counsellors, thereby improving the long-term sustainability of the programs and providing locals with a new skill set and job opportunities.

Furthermore, as part of the Community-Based Rehabilitation Program[2], the IRC trained community healthcare staff to provide social and medical assistance for all ailments, not just HIV-related illness. They also trained staff and other volunteers to co-ordinate community awareness campaigns, designed to reduce the social stigma associated with HIV/AIDS; and to create a community-based social support network for PLWA and encourage their families to become involved in ensuring community participation and the long-term sustainability of the program (Hannah and Cunliffe, 2011: 75). The success of this program and the enthusiasm amongst its recipients has provided the foundations for facilitating the IRC's new and more comprehensive Home-Based Care (HBC) program. This replacement project ensures that PLWA and their families receive educational material on HIV/AIDS, appropriate psychosocial support, treatment and prophylaxis for opportunistic infections (Hannah and Cunliffe, and Cunliffe, 2011:75).

As part of the IRC's new HIV/AIDS management program, triple combination antiretroviral therapy regimes and specially trained HIV/AIDS staff, available to both refugees and locals, were introduced into Kakuma's main health centre, smaller satellite clinics and VCT clinics. Following the program's introduction in 2005, the number of people on ARVT by 2006 had increased by 30% (UNHCR, 2006). As much as the IRC and other agencies have been dealing

---

2   The Community-Based Rehabilitation Program is a program by the IRC where community healthcare staff is trained to provide social and medical assistance for all ailments to refugees living within the Kakuma Refugee Camp in Kenya and its surroundings.

with health issues at the Kakuma Refugee Camp and amongst refugees who are settled outside the camp is concerned, in Tanzania, Sudan and Ethiopia, similar interventions on the health of refugees have also been carried out.

In the year 2015, Burundians sought refuge in Tanzania at the outset of political violence in that country, leading to the creation of Nyarugusu Refugee Camp. In order to address health matters of refugees at the camp, the National Laboratory in Tanzania, as well the Kenya Medical Research Institute (KEMRI)/Centre for Disease Control and Prevention (CDC) in Nairobi became useful in handling blood samples of refugees in cases of suspected outbreaks of deadly diseases such as cholera. The Health Centre in Nyarugusu's Zone 8 also became operational with a 40-bed capacity for inpatients and is run by partners Tanzania Red Cross Society (TRCS), Spanish Red Cross and International Federation of the Red Cross (IFRC). Similarly, Médecins Sans Frontières (MSF) commenced use of a stabilization centre for severely malnourished cases with complications. Six ambulatory feeding centres were also put in place and are being used for severely malnourished cases without complications. In August 2015, the fifth health post in Nyarugusu became operational. Located in Zone 9, the health facility is run by Tanzania Red Cross Society (TRCS), the Spanish Red Cross and IFRC. Furthermore, three (3) mobile clinics were introduced to supplement health services in the camp. The maternity wing in Zone 8's health centre is also operational. However, more facilities are needed to respond to the growing number of refugees in the camp. According to UNHCR (2015), there has been a decrease in severe malnutrition cases, though malaria and respiratory tract infections continue to be the main causes of morbidity in Nyarugusu (Millimouno, and Munuo, 2018).

IrishAid, a vital donor support is helping UNHCR facilitate access for refugees to primary healthcare and reproductive health, HIV prevention and treatment. Refugees are also given opportunities to attend awareness campaigns on family planning methods and their benefits. UNHCR works with TRCS to provide health services in Nyarugusu and Mtendeli Camps, while Médecins Sans Frontières (MSF) runs health facilities in Nduta Camp. In Nyarugusu, for instance, there are 11 health facilities providing maternity care, as well as inpatient and outpatient services, although the facilities cannot meet the high demand for services (Millimounu & Munuo, 2018). It is, therefore, evident that women giving birth in areas of conflict are at a high risk of developing debilitating, and sometimes life-threatening, medical conditions. 20 years of civil war, chronic famine, and severe poverty have left Somalia, for instance, with some of the highest maternal mortality rates in the world. An estimated 1,200 women die from pregnancy-related causes per 100,000 live births (Millimouno, and Munuo, 2018).

In South Sudan, the German Federal Government has also promoted health services to internally displaced South Sudanese persons as well as to those in refugee camps in the neighboring countries in East Africa. This has been done through Welthungerhilfe, VSF Germany and AMREF by focusing on food security, water supply, the fight against cholera and the provision of basic health services. These are to benefit IDPs in various conflict regions in South Sudan and in the receiving communities, and refugees in camps or refugee settlements outside the country (Millimouno & Munuo, 2018).

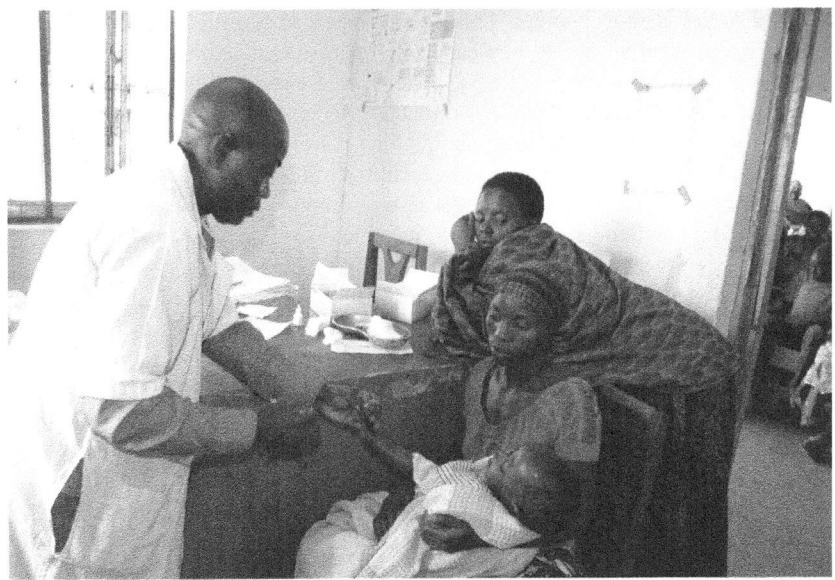

Figure 1: A mother looks on as a health worker caters to her sick child at a clinic in Nyarugusu Camp, Tanzania. © UNHCR/Faya Foko Millimouno

5   Conclusion

The objective of this paper was to give a historical reflection and perspectives on health and migration with a view to the refugees of East Africa. The diversity of health among Africans and African refugees in East Africa is informed by the colonial system, which bequeathed to African countries health system which most postcolonial states in East Africa inherited. Since the colonial regime was concerned more with the benefit for Europeans and colonial administrators, the diversity of the health systems was seen in terms of the racial nature under which the health system operated. There were specific hospitals for whites, blacks and Indians in racially segregated zones. Although colonialism was violent and exploitative, it did not witness external migration of Africans from their colonially defined regions to foreign countries. Rather, these Africans were confined to African reserves or existed as squatters, accessing medical services from specific African district hospitals or health centres.

With independence coming up in the early 1960s, East African states witnessed major civil strife leading to mass flows of refugees giving rise to the establishment of refugee camps such as Kakuma, Nyangarusi and Dadaab, among others. It is within these camps that the accessibility and diversity of health services provided both by national governments, the UNCHR and NGOs have been played out. While the national governments have concentrated on containing the spread of communicable diseases in the refugee camps, the UNCHR and other NGOs such as the IRC have been involved with the provision of all kinds of health services amongst refugees within the camps. However much they have been able to manage health situations within these camps, more resources need to be put in place to supplement the efforts of these NGOs. It has also been observed that gender, religion, language and terrorism also play a major role as far as accessibility of health services amongst refugees is concerned. More so, women and children continue to be more vulnerable to diseases within the camps. From the foregoing above, it would be prudent for East African states, to embrace ideal governance systems in order to avoid civil strife in the region. The paper also recommends a friendly multi-sectoral approach while providing health services to the refugees. There is also a need to have a health service within the refugee camps that is fully integrated into the national health system, with a minimum health service package (including vaccinations) provided to new refugees. This should be accompanied by a good nutrition system, and supplementary feeding programs for malnourished children and those at risk of malnutrition respectively, in order to prevent opportunistic diseases among refugees. However, with poor governance structures in East Africa, the refugee problem might continue to be a long-term issue.

Bibliography

Andrej, K. & Andes, S. (2017). The King is Dead: Political Succession and War in Europe, 1000-1799, University of Gothenburg Working Paper.

Azam, J. P. & Hoeffler, K. (2002).'Violence Against Civilians in Civil Wars: Looting or Terror.' Journal of Peace Research 39:461-85.

Beck, A. (1970). A History of the British Medical Administration of East Africa, 1900-1950, New York: Harvard University Press.

Bhabha, H. (1994). The Location of Culture, London: Routledge.

Cabassi, J. (2004). Renewing Our Voice: Code of Good Practice for NGOs Responding to HIV/AIDS, Oxford: Oxfam.

Collier, P., Elliot, V.I., Haavard H., Anke H., & Marta R., (2003). Breaking the Conflict Trap: Civil War and Development Policy, Washington DC: World Bank/Oxford UP.

Davenport, C.A., Will H. & Steven C. P. (2003). 'Sometimes You Just Have to Leave: Threat and Refugee Movements, 1964-1989.' International Interactions 29:27-55.

Di Bartolomeo, A., Jaulin, T. & Perrin, D. (2012). Sudan CARIM–Migration Profile. European University Institute.

East African Standard (2018). East Africa Host Countries at a Crossroads: Are Refugees Welcome or Not?

Elbadawi, I. & Sambanis, S. (2000). 'Why Are There So Many Civil Wars in Africa? Understanding and Preventing Violent Conflict', Journal of African Economies, Vol. 9, No. 3 pp. 244-269.

Fearon, J.D. (1995). 'Rationalist Explanations for War' International Organization 49(3) pp. 379-414.

Fearon, D. & Laitin, D. (2003). Ethnicity, Insurgency and Civil War, American Political Science Review, Vol. 97, Issue 1.

Fevre, E.M. (2004). 'Reanalyzing the 1900-1920 Sleeping Sickness in Uganda' Emerging Infectious Diseases, Vol. 10, No. 4, pp. 567-573.

Ghervas, S. (2017). 'Balance of Power vs. Perpetual Peace: Paradigms of European Order from Utrecht to Vienna, 1713–1815', The International History Review, 39:3.

Gibney, M. (1988). 'A "Well-Founded Fear" of Persecution', Human Rights Quarterly 10/1 pp. 109–21.

Gish, O. (1979). 'The Political Economy of Primary Care and Health by the People: An Historical Exploration', Social Science and Medicine, Vol. 130, pp. 203-211.

Gleditsch, K. S. (2003b). Transnational Dimensions of Civil War. Manuscript, Department of Political Science, University of California, San Diego.

Gurr, T. R. & Marshall, M. (2003). Peace and Conflict, College Park, MD: Center for International Development and Conflict Management.

Hannah G. & Cunliffe, A., (2011). 'Non-Governmental Organisations and the Management of HIV and AIDS in Refugee Camps: A Comparison of Marratane Camp in Mozambique and Kakuma Camp in Kenya', Journal of Contemporary African Studies, 29:1, 63-81.

Harris, C. & Smyth, I. (2001). The Reproductive Health of Refugees: Lessons Beyond ICPD. Gender and Development, 9(2), 10–21.

Headrick, D.R. (2014). 'Sleeping Sickness Epidemics and Colonial Response in East and Central Africa, 1900-1940', PLOS Neglected Tropical Diseases, 8 (4).

IOM (2011). Migration in Sudan – A Country Profile. Khartoum: International Organization for Migration. Retrieved on May 20 from http://publications.iom.int/system/files/pdf/mpsudan_18nov2013_final.pdf

IOM (2011). An Analysis of Migration Health in Kenya, Nairobi: International Organization for Migration.

Iqbal, Z., & Zorn, C. (2007). 'Civil War and Refugees in Post-Cold War Africa', Journal of Civil War, Vol. 9, pp. 200-213.

Kiura, A. W. (2014). 'Constrained Agency on Contraceptive Use among Somali Refugee Women in the Kakuma Refugee Camp in Kenya', *Gender, Technology and Development, 18:1, 147-161.*

Laurie, M. & Petchesky, R. (2008). 'Gender Health and Human Rights in Sites of Political Exclusion', Global Public Health, Vol. 3, Issue 1.

Leon, G. (1987). Refugees in International Politics, New York: Columbia UP.

Loescher, G. (1993). *Beyond Charity: International Cooperation and the Global Refugee Crisis,* New York: Oxford University Press.

Marchand, K., Roosen, I., Reinold, J. & Siegel, M. (2016). *Irregular Migration from and in the East and Horn of Africa.* A report commissioned by the Deutsche Gesellschaft für Internationale Zusammenarbeit (GIZ) in the framework of the EU-funded Better Migration Management Program.

Marchand, K. & Reinol, J. (2017). *Study of Migration Routes in East and Horn of Africa,* Maastricht: Maastricht University.

Mbembe, A. (2001). *On the Postcolony,* Berkeley: University of California Press.

MGSoG (2017). Sudan Migration Profile: Study of Migration Routes in the East and Horn of Africa, Maastricht: Maastricht University.

Moore, H., & Shellman, S. (2004). 'Fear of Persecution: Forced Migration, 1952–95', *Journal of Conflict Resolution* 48/5, pp.723–45.

Muller, E.N. & Weede, E. (1990). "Cross-National Variation in Political Violence: A Rational Action Approach." *Journal of Conflict Resolution 34:624-51.*

Millimouno, F. & Munuo, H. (2018). Vital Support in Helping Thousands of Refugees Get Primary Health Care in Tanzania, UNHCR unhcr.org/afr/news/stories/2018/6/5b28ed5a4/vital-support-is-helping-thousands-of-refugees-get-primary-health-care.html

Newbold, K., Cho, J. & McKeary, M. (2013). 'Access to Health Care: The Experiences of Refugee and Refugee Claimant Women in Hamilton, Ontario', Journal of Immigrant and Refugee Studies, Vol. 11, Issue 4.

Nindi, B.C. (1987). The Problem of Refugees in Africa: A Case Study, Institute of Muslim Minority Affairs, Vol. 8, Issue 2.

Odinga, A. (1990). A History of Health Services in Nairobi C. 1899-1963, M.A. Thesis, Kenyatta University.

Posen, B. (1996). 'Military Responses to Refugee Disasters', *International Security* 21/1, pp. 72–111.

Rono, B. (2017). World Mental Health Day Marked in Dadaab, Nairobi: UNHCR.

Salehyan, I. (2006). Refugee Flows and the Spread of Civil War, International Organization, *Vol. 60, No. 2, pp. 335-366.*

Salehyan, I. (2007). 'Refugees and the Study of Civil War', *Journal of Civil Wars, Vol. 9, Issue 2.*

Sandler, T. & Murdoch, J. (2004). "Civil War and Economic Growth: Spatial Dispersion." *American Journal of Political Science 48:138-51.*

Standard Newspaper (2019). Kenya Orders Closure of Dadaab Refugee Camp, accessed 29 May 2019 at https://www.standardmedia.co.ke/business/article/2001318717/kenya-orders-closure-of-dadaab-refugee-camp

Tilley H. (2011). *Africa as a Living Laboratory: Empire, Development, and the Problem of Scientific Knowledge, 1870-1950.* Chicago, IL: University of Chicago Press.

Tilley, H. (2016). 'Medicine Empire and Ethics in Colonial Africa', *AMA Journal of Ethics 18 (7) 743-753.*

UNHCR (1991). *Refugees and Displaced Women and Children,* New York: UN Economic and Social Council.

UNHCR (2010). Improving Material Care in Dadaab Refugee Camps, Kenya: Field Brief, Nairobi: UNHCR.

UNHCR (2015). Tanzania Factsheet, UNHCR.

UNHCR (2006). United Nations High Commissioner on Refugees 2006 . UNHCR's HIV and AIDS Policies and Programmes: http://www.unhcr.org/doclist/publ/4028bb914.html (accessed 15 April 2019).

UNHCR (2011). *Kenya Statistical Package Nairobi: UNCHR.*

Walter B. F. (2009). "Bargaining Failure and Civil War." *Annual Review of Political Science* 12: 243–261.

Webb, L.A. (2014). *The Long Struggle Against Malaria in Tropical Africa,* Cambridge: Cambridge University Press.

Wesseling H.L. (1996). *Divide and Rule: The Partition of Africa, 1880-1914.* Westport, CT: Praeger Publishers.

World Bank & UNHCR (2015). Forced Displacement and Mixed Migration in the Horn of Africa, Geneva: WB/UNHCR.

3. Legal Perspectives: Health as a Human Right

Dimensions of Health Care and Social Services Accessibility for Disabled Asylum Seekers in Germany

Cornelius Lätzsch[1]

Keywords: disability; refugees; asylum seekers; displacement; health care and social services

Abstract

This chapter examines the dimensions of health care and social services accessibility for disabled asylum seekers in Germany. The United Nations Convention on the Rights of Persons with Disabilities (UNCRPD), the EU Reception Conditions Directive (Directive 2013/33/EU) and the German Asylum Seekers' Benefits Act (AsylbLG) are framing the lived experiences differently. Where UNCRPD and the Reception Conditions Directive open ways for specific support and the examination of barriers, the Asylum Seekers' Benefits Act limits accessibility. Inaccessible housing, restricted health care access and lack of information characterise the conditions disabled asylum seekers have to cope with. To overcome those challenges, social work, politics and academia need to create spaces that do not foster the marginalisation of disabled asylum seekers.

---

1   Cornelius Lätzsch | University of Hamburg | cornelius.laetzsch@uni-hamburg.de

© Springer Fachmedien Wiesbaden Gmbh, part of Springer Nature 2020
K. Crepaz et al. (eds.), *Health in Diversity – Diversity in Health*,
https://doi.org/10.1007/978-3-658-29177-8_4

Contents

Abstract 51

1   Introduction and Researchers' Own Social Position 53

2   Intersections of Disability and Displacement 55

3   Dimensions of Health Care and Social Support for Refugees with
     Disabilities in Germany 56

3.1 Legal Framework 56

3.2 Research Results 59

3.3 Procedure to Identify Vulnerability among Refugees 65

4   Ways forward 66

5   Conclusion 69

Bibliography 70

1 Introduction and Researcher's Own Social Position

A study conducted in the UK at the beginning of the 21st century (Harris and Roberts 2004) was a turning point for myself to focus on access to health care and social services for disabled asylum seekers in Germany. Despite the growing number of publications on the intersection of forced migration and disability it is a still widely underrepresented topic in academic research (Anderson et al. 2017). Thus, this article seeks to add a German perspective to foster awareness for the specific circumstances that shape disabled asylum seekers' access to health care and social services in Germany.

My own social position as a *white*, male, able-bodied academic shapes my reality and my way of thinking. It also shapes how I can reconstruct the experiences disabled asylum seekers make. It further shapes the questions I ask during my research and it defines the relationship during the research process in terms of power etc.

Harris and Roberts (2003) opted for a participatory approach during their research. Unfortunately, during my own research, I experienced a set of (financial) limitations that did not allow me to design a participatory research project. Thus in 2015, seven interviews were conducted in two German cities with persons working on the nexus of forced migration and disability, and these interviews were analysed using a qualitative content analysis approach (Mayring 2015). While one could argue that these results, due to the quickly changing German asylum law, might not be valid anymore, the German Institute for Human Rights (Deutsches Institut für Menschenrechte 2018, p. 21) states:

> "The structural problem areas have not improved [since the last report, C.L.], despite lower numbers of refugees arriving and they are still dramatic: The needs of refugees with disabilities are not recognised systematically as such in Germany [...]."

Expert interviews cannot reconstruct the lived experiences of disabled refugees and asylum seekers. Nevertheless, I conducted these expert interviews at a time when there was almost no research in this field in Germany. Thus, they offer a first insight into the main problem areas professionals point at when working with disabled refugees and asylum seekers. This chapter intends to add these insights from a German perspective to the growing number of international analyses on different aspects of disabled refugees' living conditions, access to health care and to social services (Bogenschutz 2014; Carta et al. 2016; Soldatic et al. 2015; King et al. 2016).

The definition of health for this purpose goes further than the WHOs definition of health: "Health is a state of complete physical, mental and social well-being and not merely the absence of disease or infirmity." (World Health Organisation 2006, p. 1). I understand health as a complex interplay of different factors that define one's own experience of being healthy. Those factors can be internal factors (such as one's own immune system) or external factors (such as living conditions, legal regulations, etc.) (Hurrelmann and Franzkowiak 2018, p. 4). I will therefore discuss dimensions that seem to be indirectly related to health at first sight. Those dimensions, however, influence very much directly how healthy an individual might, or might not, feel: Inaccessible accommodation might influence one's feeling of isolation; lacking personal and professional support networks might result in a lack of information on health issues and are thus related to health.

Disability, likewise, is constructed through a complex interplay of individual impairments, societal barriers and cultural attitudes[1]: "Persons with disabilities include those who have long-term physical, mental, intellectual or sensory impairments which in interaction with various barriers may hinder their full and effective participation in society on an equal basis with others." (United Nations Convention on the Rights of Persons with Disabilities, Article 1). These barriers might be as clearly visible as in the construction of buildings, but might remain under the surface as well: They can be found in a society's attitude towards disability, in exclusionary laws and in many other settings. Thus, disabling experiences cannot be discussed as an individual "problem", impairments alone do not cause exclusion – but can only be understood if cultural, structural, political and economic exclusionary mechanisms and their intersections are taken into consideration (Plangger and Schönwiese 2013, pp. 58–59).

The problems that come with categorising and labelling people have been outlined in various articles, (Burns 2017, pp. 1467–1468; Otten 2019, pp. 186–187; Müller 2010, p. 60). Pisani et al. (2016) title a paragraph within their article "Label, Categorise, Exclude", which clearly shows the problematic usage of categories: On the one hand, they construct hierarchies, they homogenise, and they simplify (289). On the other hand, such categorisation is used to implement protection mechanisms for disadvantaged persons and might be a way to point out existing barriers.

Under such circumstances, the term "refugee" has to be treated with caution and examined critically. It is shaped by political interests and lacks analytical power (Scalettaris 2007, p. 37). Differentiation is made between those who *are believed* to flee forcibly and those who flee voluntarily. This line draws a wrong distinction: People leave their places of origin for various, often interconnected reasons: war and armed conflicts, environmental crises, oppression, socio-economic problems, lack of perspectives, and all are equally relevant. I,

---

1   For a first overview of models of disability see e.g. Waldschmidt 2017; Degener 2015; Shakespeare 2013.

hereby, support the argumentation Pisani et al. (2016) offer when they call for a renegotiation of forced migration since "human security must necessarily incorporate socio-economic threats and not be limited to violence and persecution." (287)

This chapter focuses on disabled asylum seekers in Germany who, for 18 months after their arrival, have limited access to health care and social services[2]. The analysis outlined later will thus focus on the situation within this time but, as mentioned earlier, remains limited to practitioners' perspectives. Taking into account the problems that come along with labelling and categorisation, it still seems to be necessary to point at the circumstances that shape the lives of disabled asylum seekers in Germany. This article does not aim to give a comprehensive overview of the challenges disabled asylum seekers face but seeks to add one perspective to this neglected issue.

2   Intersections of Disability and Displacement

Disability and displacement may intersect in various ways (Köbsell 2018, pp. 68–69). Armed conflicts and wars are a reason to flee and often go along with maltreatment and torture in the places of origin. Disabled persons hereby are especially exposed to specific risks (Murphy 2002, p. 855; Kanter and Dadey 2000, p. 1118). Insufficient (access to) health care characterises conflicting areas. Inaccessible buildings and structures as a result of armed attacks are typical of conflicting regions and are especially relevant for disabled persons since the ability of the latter to escape may be hindered (Mostafa 2015, p. 554). Nevertheless, those characteristics are not limited to areas of conflict and war but are also likely to be experienced where poverty shapes everyday life. Hence, not war and conflict alone, but extreme poverty with "no access to health care and rehabilitation [...] triggers flight [...]" as well (Pisani et al. 2016, p. 292). Disabling experiences are likely to occur during the flight itself, where physical and structural barriers might weigh even higher for disabled forced migrants: overcoming technically highly equipped borders (as to be found e.g. in Melilla and Ceuta) is problematic when one has difficulties seeing, walking or hearing (Pisani et al. 2016, pp. 290–292). Surviving in refugee camps with limited access to sanitary systems, water and medication poses serious threats to the life and well-being of disabled refugees. Furthermore, disabled persons are more likely to be victims of violence and discrimination, cannot participate in decision-making processes and lack access to disability-related health care (Pearce 2015, pp. 465–471). Disabling reception conditions in the receiving countries

---

2   Formerly, 'limited access' was limited to a maximum of 15 months. This regulation changed in June 2019 in line with the new dispensation of justice. (Pro Asyl e.V. 2019, p. 26.)

might even amplify those experiences (Straimer 2010, p. 4; Bogenschutz 2014, pp. 64–65). This accounts for living conditions (as to be shown later) and for the asylum procedure likewise[3]. Crock et al. (2013) name – and later on demand adjustments of structural barriers as well – some of the difficulties regarding the asylum interview:

> "The range of challenges that persons with disabilities can experience is broad. Examples include: difficulties in understanding questions and instructions (for example, where an asylum seeker has limited cognitive ability); difficulties in communicating (for example, where an asylum seeker has limited speech, is deaf or is severely hard of hearing); and behavioural difficulties, difficulties in delivering a coherent and consistent testimony, and/or difficulties in recalling and recounting events (for example, where an asylum seeker has a psychosocial disability)." (Crock et al. 2013, p. 763).

Valid data on disabled refugees and forced migrants is scarce (Burns 2017, p. 1468) and statistical information about the situation in Germany non-existent (Engin 2018, pp. 106–107; Deutscher Bundestag 2017, p. 2). Handicap International (2017, p. 2) points out that several hundred disabled refugees were identified by (social work) institutions in major German cities. Research conducted in Syria presents 22.4 percent of interviewed people with "some functional limitations to physical mobility, vision, hearing or intellectual ability." (Help Age International und Handicap International 2014, p. 11). Other research highlights the neglect of disabled refugees and non-existent identification structures in refugee camps (Morgan 2017, p. 896). Nevertheless, disabled people flee, regardless of ever-growing border security systems as Pisani et al. (2016, p. 292) point out. This – apart from the challenges disabled refugees must face – primarily shows the great capabilities disabled refugees do have. Facing and overcoming these barriers, they portray their strengths, skills and abilities.

3 Dimensions of Health Care and Social Support for Refugees with Disabilities in Germany

3.1 Legal Framework

The Bundesamt für Migration und Flüchtlinge (BAMF) is the competent decision-making authority for asylum seekers in Germany. During the regular asy-

---

3   While the living conditions of disabled refugees and asylum seekers have recently received more attention in social work and academic communities in Germany, research on the asylum proce dure remains underrepresented. Thus, my PhD project focuses on the asylum interview and the specific experiences disabled asylum seekers have: https://www.ew.uni-hamburg.de/forschung/vtdf/mitglieder/text/laetzsch.html

lum procedure, the BAMF, after an asylum seeker's application and a personal interview, decides on whether or not to grant protection status. During this interview, an interpreter is mandatory but access to legal assistance before the interview is not systematically available to asylum seekers (European Council on Refugees and Exiles 2019). Thus, many asylum seekers only receive necessary legal information after the interview. Germany differentiates between four forms of protection: refugee status, entitlement to asylum, subsidiary protection and a national ban on deportation. The different forms of protection go along with different legal entitlements regarding e.g. access to the labour market and family reunification (BAMF 2019).

To understand the legal situation that shapes the lives of disabled asylum seekers in Germany, this chapter gives a brief introduction to national and international legal documents that affect the access to health care and social services. **The United Nations Convention on the Rights of Persons with Disabilities (UNCRPD)** was ratified by Germany in 2009 and applies to everybody living in Germany, regardless of residential status (Schülle 2018, p. 160). Article 25 specifies that: *"States Parties recognize that persons with disabilities have the right to the enjoyment of the highest attainable standard of health without discrimination on the basis of disability. States Parties shall take all appropriate measures to ensure access for persons with disabilities to health services that are gender-sensitive, including health-related rehabilitation."* Article 26 continues: *"States Parties shall take effective and appropriate measures, including through peer support, to enable persons with disabilities to attain and maintain maximum independence, full physical, mental, social and vocational ability, and full inclusion and participation in all aspects of life."* Article 9 and 28 claim appropriate and accessible accommodation for all persons with disabilities (Leisering 2018, p. 1).

Nevertheless, **the German Asylum Seekers' Benefits Act (AsylbLG)**[4] limits the access to health care for asylum seekers – and consequently does this for disabled asylum seekers likewise. Asylum seekers in Germany are entitled, for the first 18 months after their arrival, only to health services that are related to pregnancy and birth, to acute diseases or problems related to experiences of pain as well as to vaccinations (§ 4 AsylbLG) (Razum et al. 2016, p. 711). Further treatment can be granted in individual cases according to § 6 AsylbLG, if it is *"necessary to safeguard the health"* [translation C.L.]. In practice, those discretionary decisions appear to be interpreted differently (in different regions) by the local social security offices, who are the competent decision making authorities. Many of those applications and discretionary decisions are specifically relevant in the context of disability: physiotherapy, prostheses and even medica-

---

4   Asylbewerberleistungsgesetz (AsylbLG)

tion[5]. Before 1993, asylum seekers were entitled to health care access similarly to people who were regularly covered by the German Health Insurance system (Razum et al. 2016, p. 711; Kleger 2006, p. 32). The implementation of the Asylum Seekers' Benefits Act in 1993 has changed these entitlements and falls together with a series of restrictive legal "adjustments" made during this time (Martin 2014, p. 233; Kannankulam 2014, pp. 108–109) and has ever since received massive criticism from refugees, lobbies, advocacy organisations and from other activists.

Its medical regulations have seen different interpretations by courts, especially when it was contextualised with regard to the aforementioned UNCRPD and other European legislation (Schülle 2018, p. 160). In perspective, the restrictive interpretation of § 6 AsylbLG might not be able to be maintained anymore, after two court decisions[67]. Schülle and Frankenstein (2019) have examined these judgements and conclude that they highlight a change in current case-law towards a less restrictive interpretation.

The EU Asylum Reception Conditions Directive (2013/13/EU) regulates the standards of the reception of Asylum seekers in Europe. In this context, the directive also takes into account the situation of "vulnerable persons". This term applies to *"[...] minors, unaccompanied minors, disabled people, elderly people, pregnant women, single parents with minor children, victims of human trafficking, persons with serious illnesses, persons with mental disorders and persons who have been subjected to torture, rape or other serious forms of psychological, physical or sexual violence, such as victims of female genital mutilation"* (Art. 21). All of them should be *"provide[d] necessary medical or other assistance [...] including appropriate mental health care where needed."* (Art. 19/2).

This means that health care entitlements for disabled asylum seekers should go further than the aforementioned limited entitlements according to § 4 and § 6 of the Asylum Seekers' Benefits Act (Schülle 2018, p. 160). Clara Straimer (2011) analysed this and two other asylum-specific directives. She summarises that "disability is explicitly linked to healthcare, establishing a representation of persons with disabilities as patients. On the other hand [...] the recast [of the directives, C.L.] is [...] a highly valuable step in rendering visible the diverse

---

5   This situation is illustrated by the case of Shabab Al-Aziz: The Iraqi asylum seeker, who suffered from epilepsy and underwent psychiatric treatment, had to apply regularly for his medication with the authorities in Pirna (a town in the Eastern German region of Saxony). In reported cases his application got rejected. (http://www.taz.de/!5422411/, last access 15/04/2019)

6   LSG Hessen – L 4 AY 9/18 B ER

7   LSG Niedersachsen-Bremen – L 8 AY 16/17 B ER

barriers persons with disabilities face in the context of asylum." (Straimer 2011, p. 544). However, these addressed barriers continue to exist in Germany: The directive should have been transformed into national law by 2015 (Engin 2018, p. 105; Europäische Kommission 2016) – but such has never happened: The EU has, therefore, launched an infringement proceeding against Germany[8] (Europäische Kommission 2016). In a minor inquiry by the German party BÜNDIS 90/Die Grünen, the German government was asked about the transposition of the directive into national law. The German government hereby argues that the transposition is the responsibility of Germany's federal states (Deutscher Bundestag 2017). Furthermore, the assertion of the above-mentioned regulations are subject to an individual assessment, that, likewise, has not been implemented in Germany comprehensively (Schülle 2018, p. 160; Thomsen, p. 8) (see also paragraph 3.3 of this chapter).

3.2 Research Results

Having briefly shown the legal basics that disabled asylum seekers do find themselves in, the following chapter aims to outline the main problem areas that social work professionals have pointed out. Those professionals were either working in organisations that provided counselling services for disabled asylum seekers or worked in related fields (such as disability advocacy organisations or migration services) or organisations that tried to bring those two fields together. For further contextualisation, the experiences of K. are illustrated:

K.[9] arrived in Germany at the beginning of 2016. When K. fled his home country, he had experienced severe physical impairments after a mine explosion. K. had lost extremities as well as one eye. Because of severe retina damage, the second eye since then is constantly losing its vision.

After having arrived in Germany, he was at first accommodated in an initial reception centre in a major German city. From there he was moved several times within the city area. There he had to stay in a room that he shared with 14 others. He was assigned the upper part of a bunk bed in which he – due to the extraction hood above – could not find any sleep. Difficulties in communicating due to language barriers during this time were common: The only employed

---

8   In a press release from 10 October 2019 the Representation of the European Commission in Germany informed that the infringement proceedings against Germany regarding directive 2013/33/EU and 2013/32/EU have been terminated. According to the press release the directives have been transferred into national legislation.

9   Name changed; I met K. during the research for my PhD project, where K. kindly allowed me insight into his experiences on arriving in Germany and allowed me to publish his case here.

person who was able to understand him was a security guard who spoke a few words of his mother tongue.

After having been moved again, K. was accommodated in a setting on the outskirts of the city. While several asylum seekers spoke K's mother tongue, interpreters were only available once a week for two hours – which left many of the asylum seekers without a possibility of consultation in their mother tongue. Thus, much relevant information about asylum seekers' access to health care, the asylum interview and other questions were just communicated mouth to mouth within the community.

When K. got in contact with an organisation that assists disabled asylum seekers, even more neglected issues became obvious: Staff at the housing was unaware of the possibility to apply for a disabled persons pass[10]. When K. started the application process, he experienced a set of bureaucratic barriers (application forms only in German, etc.) as well as an application process that lasted several months.

Insufficient interpreting skills have been described by K. and his counsellor as a common problem: Especially in medical settings, interpreters were unable to translate medical terms from one language to another. Exemplary is the following situation: After having described his problems (sleeplessness, headache, nervousness) via an interpreter to the neurologist, the neurologist answered he could not help with such problems. This suggests that the interpreter was unable to translate the medical terms properly. K.'s counsellor has described this problem on several occasions.

This case shows the strength K. has in navigating through such an inaccessible, uninviting surrounding. It shows the great capabilities and problem-solving skills that K. has, but it furthermore points to the shortcomings of the reception conditions disabled asylum seekers experience in Germany. Hence, some of the issues that K. faced after his arrival will be discussed in detail.

Legal Framework and Decision-Making Processes

As stressed above, the legal framework leaves disabled asylum seekers in a precarious situation. All interviewees named the legal situation as the most crucial barrier for disabled asylum seekers' access to health care and social services. In contrast to German citizens, (disabled) asylum seekers experience the

---

10   The German "Schwerbehindertenausweis" (disabled person's pass) is a document issued to
      disabled persons for them to be able to furnish proof of their disablement. It is issued in order
      to access several compensations for disadvantages (such as free access in public transporta-
      tion, etc.)

approval of many forms of medical treatment in accordance with discretional powers of administration.

As pointed out earlier, in reality, that often leads to the rejection of a wide range of medical treatment, technical support and therapeutic assistance. Interviewees stressed unanimously that discretionary powers are handled rather restrictively. Accordingly, reported cases of rejected applications for physiotherapy, speech therapy, ergotherapy, wheelchairs, single-use gloves, incontinence materials support this. When one interviewee argues that "[t]his law is not used for health preservation but only to protect people from dying" it underlines the overall perception of the interviewed professionals.

Interviewees mentioned further that administrators use these discretionary powers unequally in different regions. That means that the support a disabled refugee might receive is not allocated according to the needs she or he might have, and additionally depends on the region they live in – and on the discretion of the communal services that are responsible for them. Long decision-making processes aggravate this all:

> "The normal procedure is: If you hand in an application you won't hear anything for weeks, sometimes months. Then [...] if you are lucky, you might hear that the application has been handed to the next institution and it is been looked at. Then it takes again months until the application has been looked at. Usually, they decide without seeing the clients themselves. Mostly the decision is negative. Then we submit an objection. Usually the decision then still is negative" [translation C.L.].

It is obvious that this is most problematic for medical problems that need urgent treatment. An example of a young child with a deformed pelvis illustrates this: A clinic tried to apply for the financial support needed to perform the procedure, but ended up withdrawing the application: They had had too many experiences where such applications were rejected and had no hope that their patient's case would be different.

Accommodation and Distribution

Asylum seekers in Germany are accommodated in specific houses for asylum seekers. Hence, having the possibility to choose a desired form of accommodation is not what disabled asylum seekers experience after their arrival in Germany. Furthermore, they are distributed to parts of Germany according to a specific distribution formula (known as "Königsteiner Schlüssel" – Königstein Quota System). The accommodation systems also differ between the German federal states (Flüchtlingsrat NRW e.V.). These ways of accommodation and the distribution of asylum seekers are another access barrier to a healthy life in various ways:

"Refugee accommodations are often in an isolated location and hence not adequately integrated into the local support system. In many cases, there are no support facilities for people with disabilities in the vicinity of the accommodation" (Deutsches Institut für Menschenrechte 2017, p. 8). The houses and their interiors are often (at least in part) inaccessible, which puts asylum seekers in a situation in which they cannot make choices according to their wishes. Leaving the house and coming back home independently may be restrained. This is illustrated by the case of a wheelchair-using asylum seeker who had to wait in front of the main door until others came and were willing to carry him up or down the steps.

Inaccessible accommodation leads to further problems: Whereas an asylum seeker cannot leave the place she or he is living at, she or he is likely to experience isolation. Not being able to leave one's own accommodation of one's own free will limits participation widely (Mirza and Heinemann 2012, p. 546). It limits, for instance, the access to refugee and disability advocacy and counselling organisations, and it limits access to shared spaces with others and thus a way of socialising in a new environment or the possibility of political organising. Asylum seekers who may have been imprisoned in the countries they fled from might experience this even more dramatically (Roberts and Harris, pp. 15–16).

The distribution of asylum seekers to certain areas might increase these problems further. The support systems installed at the place where the refugees first arrived might collapse once the refugees are forced to live somewhere else. In some reported cases, well-working support systems (around the migrant community, social work institutions and/or volunteers) were set up and collapsed, as has also been stressed in research from other counties (Ward et al. 2008, p. 55). Rural areas are often less well-equipped to meet the needs of refugees with disabilities: While in metropolitan areas some formal and informal structures do exist, they are not in place in rural regions to the same extent. This is illustrated by the case of a blind refugee who formerly lived in a major German city and was forced to move to a rural region in the surroundings of it. He then had to attend German classes. The rural area he was assigned to live in did offer German classes, but no German classes specifically for blind people, like the ones he could attend in the city. Therefore, to be able to attend classes, he constantly had to travel to the city, the place he was forced to move away from. Each day, he had to be accompanied by his father to go there, two hours each way.

Access to Information

Access to information about social services and health care has been described as "rather random and a question of being lucky or not" by an interviewee. While on the one hand, staff in initial receptions centres often seem to be unaware about the legal basics regarding access to health care for disabled refugees (as clearly pointed out by the case of K. earlier), authorities appear to lack the capacity to provide sufficient language services. Information is rarely provided in asylum seekers' native languages, let alone Braille or easy language[11]. This applies to information on health care and social services, but can equally be argued for information about the asylum system and the asylum interview, which leaves asylum seekers in uncertainty about their rights, their duties and such issues as objection deadlines.

Thus, disabled asylum seekers mostly rely on the information they receive from others who have gone through similar processes. While this again shows capabilities of navigating in a precarious system, it can also be a trap for misinformation and shows how dependency is created in such settings. In reported cases, disabled (and sick) asylum seekers had to rely on their children's translations because of a lack of professional translators. In a context where serious medical problems have to be discussed (between doctors and patients; social workers and clients; etc.), this appears to be an inadequate solution: Firstly, it remains unclear whether all necessary information has been translated in such cases; secondly, children are put in the position of delivering potentially bad news.

Lack of Networking

Social work responses in Germany tend to exist along two "lines": Organisations predominantly focus on either disabled persons (thus lacking knowledge of the asylum system) or on asylum seekers and refugees (thus lacking knowledge on disability-related issues). This can be pointed out especially for rural regions rather than larger cities where organisations try to connect the two fields (e.g. Berlin[12], Cologne[13], Hamburg[14], Munich[15]). Interviewees named the lack of

---

11 Easy language describes a – usually written – specific version of German language. It is directed to the specific needs of people with limited skills in German reading or writing (or in reading or writing in general) and follows a specific set of regulations that makes it applicable nationwide.

12 Fachstelle Migration und Behinderung
The unit offers counselling for institutions that work on the intersection of disability and migration (implementation of programs, networking, collection of material)

linguistic skills and cultural sensitivity as the main gaps in disability-related organisations, as well as a lack of knowledge of the complex legislation for asylum seekers on the one hand. On the other hand, knowledge on social services for disabled people and on concepts of disability were missing in migration-related organisations – which in one case almost led to the death of a young asylum seeker. This lack of knowledge has been pointed out here for social work organisations but can likewise be applied to the administrative level. An interviewee, asked asked about the knowledge organisations working with refugees have on disability and vice versa referred to it as "very, very rudimentary" and "minimal to non-existent". Pisani et al. (2016) stress that "[t]he ramifications are that those working in migration remain unaware of and lack understanding of disability and those working in disability remain uninformed about migration." (Pisani et al. 2016, p. 286).

Again, this is a problem that Germany shares with other countries: The intersections of forced migration and disability remains unclear. This culminates in a "worrying variation in the level of knowledge about the entitlements of disabled refugees and asylum seekers" (Roberts and Harris 2002b, p. 20), that has been criticised for Great Britain (Ward et al. 2008, p. 65) as well as the U.S. (Mirza and Heinemann 2012, pp. 548–549) already years ago but can still be pointed out as a major barrier in Germany.

Informal Support Structures

Since formal support systems seem to have only limited abilities to cater to the needs of disabled asylum seekers, informal support systems step in. Families (Roberts and Harris 2002b, p. 15) and other refugees (Ward et al. 2008, 37) might assist with different daily tasks as one of the interviewees explains:

> "In the room next door lives a women [...] and she [...] cooks for him. In the opposite room is somebody who helps him take a shower. And another one is coming to buy the groceries for him."[transl. C. L.].

---

13   Kompetenzzentrum Flucht, Migration und Behinderung
      The unit offers (peer) counselling for disabled refugees (application process for social services; spare time activities; finding a workplace) as well as networking

14   Flucht UND Behinderung
      The unit offers counselling for disabled refugees and assists individually with questions of access to health care, health insurance, language courses, etc.

15   Crossroads – Flucht.Migration.Behinderung
      This project targets lobbying, capacity building and empowerment to improve the situation of disabled refugees and asylum seekers on local, regional and national levels.

While on the one hand, this shows how solidarity and mutual assistance is organised in an exclusionary setting, it also leaves disabled refugees dependent on the goodwill of others. When – as in reported cases – volunteers collect money to finance medical treatment an ambivalent situation is created: A person receives individual help but thereby the political dimension of this intervention must not be forgotten.

Furthermore, forming bonds of solidarity by connecting with people who have similar life experiences appears to be more difficult for disabled asylum seekers. Firstly and primarily, because inaccessible housing, sometimes away from metropolitan areas, simply does not allow for finding each other. Secondly, disabled persons' organisations, as well as the refugee community, do not focus on "cross-cutting minority identities" (Yeo 2015, pp. 540–541).

Summarising Access to Health Care and Social Services

The illustrated cases clearly outline a precarious situation where access to health care and social services are restricted for disabled asylum seekers. This illustrates the view from a legal, but also from a practical perspective (Schülle 2018, p. 160): Among others do the Asylum Seekers' Benefits Act, lacking linguistic skills, lacking professional knowledge and inaccessible accommodation define if and how disabled asylum seekers can access services in Germany. This perpetuates a hierarchy between those who "belong" and have access – and those who "do not".

All of this is enhanced by the fear that demanding equal access to health care might influence the outcome of the asylum process. Interviewees reported cases where an asylum seeker's suggestion to others "[...] to, by all means, not tell anyone about having a severe disease or impairments since it could influence the asylum decision [...]" discouraged them to apply for medical assistance.

3.3   Procedure to Identify Vulnerability[16] among Refugees

A way for having better access to health services that go further than the limited entitlements of § 4 Asylum Seekers' Benefits Act is to be categorised as "vulnerable" (Köbsell 2018, pp. 68–69) in accordance with the Asylum Reception Conditions Directive (Directive 2013/33/EU). Jenny Baron and Nina Hager (Baron and Hager 2017, p. 17) examine how (for traumatised and mentally ill asylum seekers) this assessment remains a question of chance, luck and persistence. They do this for the context of the asylum interview and the related Asy-

---

16   The term "vulnerability" is hereby used in reference to article 21 and 22 of the Asylum Reception Conditions Directive.

lum Procedures Directive (2013/32/EU). This article focuses on reception conditions and not on traumatised asylum seekers and might thus not be entirely comparable. Nevertheless, some dimensions can be applied from their analysis to the situation disabled refugees experience.

While non-governmental organisations point out the lack of structured assessments, the German government contradictorily argues to have implemented several stages in which vulnerability could be assessed (Baron and Hager 2017, p. 17). Where specific needs are clearly visible the assessment might be done easily: Pregnant women and elderly people are more likely to be identified then victims of human trafficking or persons with cognitive impairments (Baron and Hager 2017, p. 20). This is even amplified because the latter might experience limitations in reconstructing their own biographic experiences. Since no structured system exists that identifies vulnerable asylum seekers as such, it is likely that many fall through the net, leaving their needs hidden. The few organisations that, with all their expertise, try to change this situation are often confronted with limitations (mainly personal and financial resources) that hinder their work. While the EU Asylum Receptions Directive (Directive 2013/33/EU) states in Article 5 that "Member States shall ensure that applicants are provided with information on organisations or groups of persons that provide specific legal assistance and organisations that might be able to help or inform them concerning the available reception conditions, including health care", practitioners point out that "there is no structure [to examine disability or vulnerability] or a leaflet that somebody might be given, because of a, perhaps at best visible, impairment […], so I would not call this a structured way." (translation C.L.).

4   Ways forward

As I have shown, disabled asylum seekers in many cases do not have access to the social services they require. Professionals work primarily focused on either disability or forced migration. The implementation of networks, connecting those two fields (and others) remains an ongoing task for those working in either field. Even though some of the networks have been implemented during the last years (primarily in the metropolitan areas), interviewees still point out that professionals working with disabled people lack knowledge on the topic of forced migration and vice versa. Participation of disabled refugees themselves must not be underestimated hereby: On the one hand, social work has the chance to open spaces for making the voices of disabled refugees heard. On the other hand, social work is a continuous reminder for those who are involved in it that disability and forced migration do intersect with other categories (such as gender, class and others): "Providers, however, should remain aware that individuals will call upon all of the complex interrelations of their identity when interfacing with the health care system and providers." (Bogenschutz 2014, p. 68). Empathy, respect, advocacy and the construction of trustful relations between social workers and disabled refugees are the central qualifications that Ottosdottir and Evans (2014) point out. Especially in a setting characterised by structural exclusion, relationships of solidarity seem to be necessary (62). The problematisation of gaps in the support systems and the articulation of political demands can add to individual support. Clara Straimer stressed already in 2011: "It is time for advocacy organisations within Europe to rise to the legal challenges and effect the conceptual shift necessary to create a disability-sensitive asylum system." (548).

The Asylum Seekers' Benefits Act, however, remains the main reason that prevents disabled asylum seekers in Germany from accessing health care and social services. Therefore, interventions need to be made on a political level as well. Unanimously, interviewees named the Asylum Seekers' Benefits Act as the most crucial barrier. Thus, the abolition of this law would consequently be a way to reduce the barriers faced by disabled asylum seekers. As mentioned above, it has been criticised since its implementation. An implementation of the regulations according to the EU Asylum Receptions Conditions Directive could lead to changes here: A structured assessment of asylum seekers' specific needs of protection are inherent to the directive and are a basis to collect valid data required to implement support structures (Köbsell 2018, pp. 68–69). Insufficient service provision and lacking implementation also shows how, in Germany, the higher standards of law remain ignored (Weiser 2016, p. 25). The aforementioned acknowledgements regarding the implementation process of the UNCRPD illustrate this.

The situation in Germany varies: In many parts, asylum seekers have to ask for a medical voucher[17] from the authorities. This procedure is – among other reasons – criticised because the voucher is not issued by medically qualified personnel but by administrative staff (Schülle 2018, p. 156). Alternatives exist in some other parts of Germany: An electronic health card is issued that allows easier access to the health care system (Razum et al. 2016), minimises the administrative work and reduces barriers. A nationwide solution with the electronic health card would reduce barriers and minimise unequal access in different regions (Schülle 2018, p. 159).

Even though the German scientific community is slowly starting to recognise the various situations disabled refugees experience as a field of research, it remains underrepresented: "Not only are disabled people missing from migration data and debates; migrants are missing from disability data and policy."

---

17   Medical vouchers were used before the implementation of electronic health cards in Germany (Schülle, 2018, p. 156)

(Burns 2017, p. 1468; Westphal and Wansing 2018). In these contexts, questions of participatory research are most relevant. Participatory research offers opportunities to avoid victimisation but opens spaces for cooperation (Otten 2019, p. 184). This offers the opportunity for a different relation between researchers and "the field". Those who were formerly seen as research objects become participating subjects whose opinions, questions and focuses are relevant and enriching (Flieger 2013, p. 163). More often than not, research projects experience limitations regarding financial and/or personal resources, and regarding timeframe (Harris and Roberts 2003). Thus, participatory approaches often remain limited to particular parts of the research (Otten 2019, p. 184). Participatory research can be understood as an aspect of ethically sound research. But furthermore, the perspectives of those who are experts for themselves may broaden the researchers' perspectives and might be a way to minimise the difficulties that arise not only, but also linguistically: "[u]nless one is fluent in a foreign language or culture, much of the complexity inherent in the data is lost to the researcher." (Corbin and Strauss 2015, p. 80).

Furthermore, perspectives are not only shaped by flight and disablement: Race, class, gender, age, sexuality, literacy and other factors form identities and influence lived experiences. The recognition of such intersectional identities and research under an intersectional umbrella helps to "[...] analyse and transform power relation[s] and [is] a unique interdisciplinary space for engaging with various disciplines and in social movement activity" (Stienstra and Nyerere 2016, p. 255). Thus, the recognition of persons' own identities, motives and life plans is crucial to such research projects (Otten 2019, p. 188), as well as a" [...] debate [that] moves forward and beyond labelling and legal categorisation to incorporate broader issues of discourse, construction of subjects, the right to rights and borders (Pisani et al. 2016, p. 290)". Hence, ethical considerations of research must also be a core issue to research in a field that is characterised by exclusion and, in part, life-threatening living conditions. This requires the reflection of researchers' own roles and the relationship between research participants in terms of power relations and the transformation of such (von Unger 2018). Moreover, when Hugman et al. (2011) conclude that to "'[d]o no harm' is a necessary but insufficient principle alone as the ethical basis for such work", it furthermore opens the discussion for reducing harmful situations, but also on the use of the research outcomes for the participants (von Unger 2018). Especially for research at the intersection of forced migration and disability, the preparation of research results in an adequate form can be a contribution here (Clark-Kazak 2017, p. 13). Roberts and Harris (Roberts and Harris 2002a, p. 3), for instance, devoted the last months of their research to dissemination activities and ran workshops to inform refugees and social care practitioners about their research results. Similarly, Unger shows (2018) how research findings can be made accessible by organising an open day. Hereby not only research findings were discussed between research participants; the invited civil society organisations and individuals offered counselling and support for legal as well as medical questions the researchers could not answer. Ways into German universities programs were also discussed.

5   Conclusion

This chapter has shown the variety of barriers for disabled refugees in accessing the German health system. Illustrated by the case of K., the exclusionary legal system has been contextualised within other dimensions that limit disabled asylum seekers' full participation. Apart from having to cope with the regulations of the Asylum Seekers' Benefits Act, asylum seekers' access to health care is a matter of chance. Nothing describes the German situation better than the term 'patchwork': Regional differences in access to health care, individually committed social workers rather than grown structures, lacking linguistic and intercultural skills and the overall invisibility of disabled asylum seekers are patterns, stitched together by uncertainties. Predominantly, those barriers are politically constructed – and thus need to be addressed politically. With the EU Asylum Reception Conditions Directive in place since 2013, with a range of advocacy organisations having raised their voices for improvements and the dismantling of barriers for years (Deutsches Institut für Menschenrechte 2018), with brief inquiries to the German government by other political parties on different aspects of the lives of disabled asylum seekers[18][19][20]during the last years, and with disabled asylum seekers fighting for their rights it is hard to imagine that disabled asylum seekers have remained invisible to decision makers. Much more likely, it seems that their rights and needs have been consequently ignored.

Not only do disabled asylum seekers find themselves on the intersection of two prominent human rights documents: The Convention of Geneva and the UNCRPD (Crock et al. 2013, pp. 736–737). They are also situated in a position where concepts and policies of inclusion (for the area of disability) and restrictive mechanisms of exclusion (for the area of flight and migration), on the other hand, collide (Otten et al. 2017, p. 197; Otten 2018). The interventions derived therefrom for politics, social work and the scientific community are complex and need to navigate between a disclosure of structural barriers whilst not perpetuating victimisation.

---

18   Deutscher Bundestag 2016.

19   Deutscher Bundestag 2017.

20   Deutscher Bundestag 2019.

Reviewed research on the reception conditions for disabled asylum seekers in the Global North shows, at first sight, striking similarities (while a scientific analysis is still to be made (Schülle 2018, p. 160)). This suggests that barriers faced by disabled asylum seekers are not limited to a specific region, but need to be discussed on a transnational dimension. A broadened view that takes into account the less heard voices from the Global South is overdue in this regard (Meekosha 2011).[21]

Bibliography

Anderson, Philip; Langner, Anke; Mecheril, Paul; Schroeder, Joachim; Seukwa, Louis Henri; Thielen, Marc et al. (2017): Vernachlässigte Themen der Flüchtlingsforschung. Kooperatives Graduiertenkolleg in den Bildungs-und Sozialarbeitswissenschaften. Universität Hamburg/HAW Hamburg. Available online at https://www.ew.uni-hamburg.de/forschung/vtdf/files/forschungsprogramm.pdf, checked on 4/18/2019.

BAMF (2019): Forms of protection. Available online at http://www.bamf.de/EN/Fluechtlingsschutz/AblaufAsylv/Schutzformen/schutzformen-node.html, checked on 6/18/2019.

Baron, Jenny; Hager, Nina (2017): Eine Frage von Glück und Zufall. Zu den Verfahrensgarantien für psychisch Kranke oder Traumatisierte im Asylverfahren. In *Beiträge zum Asylmagazin* (7-8).

Bogenschutz, Matthew (2014): "We Find a Way". Challenges and Facilitators for Health Care Access among Immigrants and Refugees with Intellectual and Developmental Disabilities. In *Medical Care* 52 (10), pp. 64–70.

Burns, Nicola (2017): The Human Right to Health: Exploring Disability, Migration and Health. In *Disability & Society* 32 (10), pp. 1463–1484. DOI: 10.1080/09687599.2017.1358604.

Carta, Mauro Giovanni; Moro, Maria Francesca; Preti, Antonio; Lindert, Jutta; Bhugra, Dinesh; Angermeyer, Mattias; Vellante, Marcello (2016): Human Rights of Asylum Seekers with Psychosocial Disabilities in Europe. In *Clinical Practice and Epidemiology in Mental Health : CP & EMH* 12, pp. 64–66. DOI: 10.2174/1745017901612010064.

Clark-Kazak, Christina (2017): Ethical Considerations: Research with People in Situations of Forced Migration. In *Refuge* 33 (2), pp. 11–17. DOI: 10.7202/1043059ar.

Corbin, Juliet; Strauss, Anselm (2015): Basics of Qualitative Research (4th ed.). Techniques and Procedures for Developing Grounded Theory. London: Sage.

Crock, Mary; Ernst, Christine; AO, Ron McCallum. (2013): Where Disability and Asylum Intersect: Asylum Seekers and Refugees with Disabilities. In *International Journal of Refugee Law* 24 (4), pp. 735–764.

---

21 During a conference prior to this chapter, discussion went viral on whether access to health care for disabled asylum seekers in Germany is still better than it is in many countries of origin. I would strongly argue that even this might be the case, the inherent asymmetry in Germany remains between those who have access (and thus belong) and those who do not have access (and thus do not belong): "Race, ethnicity and disability [...] intersect to shape experiences of who is allowed to be a citizen as well as which citizens can access what they need." (Stienstra and Nyerere 2016, p. 260). Discussing whether access to health care in the country of origin is better or not then becomes irrelevant.

Degener, Theresia (2015): Vom medizinischen zum menschenrechtlichen Modell von Behinderung. Konzepte für Behindertenrecht und -politik. In Iman Attia, Swantje Köbsell, Nivedita Prasad (eds.): Dominanzkultur reloaded. Neue Texte zu gesellschaftlichen Machtverhältnissen und ihren Wechselwirkungen. Bielefeld: Transcript-Verl. (Sozialtheorie), pp. 155–168.

Deutscher Bundestag (2016): Antwort der Bundesregierung auf die Kleine Anfrage der Abgeordneten Katrin Werner, Ulla Jelpke, Sigrid Hupach, weiterer Abgeordneter und der Fraktion DIE LINKE. Situation von geflüchteten Menschen mit Behinderungen. Drucksache 18/7831. Edited by Deutscher Bundestag.

Deutscher Bundestag (2017): Antwort der Bundesregierung auf die Kleine Anfrage der Abgeordneten Corinna Rüffer, Luise Amtsberg, Maria Klein-Schmeink, weiterer Abgeordneter und der Fraktion BÜNDNIS 90/DIE GRÜNEN. Zur Lage von geflüchteten Menschen mit Behinderungen. Drucksache 18/11603. Edited by Deutscher Bundestag.

Deutscher Bundestag (2019): Antwort der Bundesregierung auf die Kleine Anfrage der Abgeordneten Ulla Jelpke, Sören Pellmann, Dr. André Hahn, weiterer Abgeordneter und der Fraktion DIE LINKE. Situation von Geflüchteten mit Behinderungen im Asylverfahren. Drucksache 19/9419. Edited by Deutscher Bundestag. Available online at http://dip21.bundestag.de/dip21/btd/19/094/1909419.pdf, checked on 7/2/2019.

Deutsches Institut für Menschenrechte (2017): Development of the Human Rights Situation in Germany July 2016 – June 2017. Report to the German Federal Parliament in Accordance with Sec. 2 Para. 5 of the Act regarding the Legal Status and Mandate of the German Institute for Human Rights. Edited by Deutsches Institut für Menschenrechte. Berlin.

Deutsches Institut für Menschenrechte (2018): National CRPD Monitoring Mechanism. Pre-List of Issues on Germany Submitted by the National CRPD Monitoring Mechanism of Germany to the CRPD Committee on the Rights of Persons with Disabilities on the Occasion of the Preparation of a List of Issues by the Committee. Available online at https://www.institut-fuer-menschenrechte.de/fileadmin/user_upload/PDF-Dateien/Sonstiges/MSt_2018_Pre_LoI_English_bf.pdf, checked on 4/18/2019.

Engin, Kenan (2018): Deutsche Versorgungsstrukturen im Umgang mit geflüchteten Kindern mit Behinderung im Lichte von Grundlagen des internationalen und nationalen Rechts. In Manuela Westphal, Gudrun Wansing (eds.): Migration, Flucht und Behinderung. Herausforderungen für Politik, Bildung und psychosoziale Dienste. Wiesbaden: Springer VS, pp. 103–120.

Europäische Kommission (2016): Umsetzung des Gemeinsamen Europäischen Asylsystems: EU-Kommission geht in neun Fällen zur nächsten Verfahrensstufe über. Available online at europa.eu/rapid/press-release_IP-16-270_de.pdf, checked on 4/15/2019.

Europäische Kommission (2019): Vertragsverletzungsverfahren im Oktober: Entscheidungen zu Deutschland. Available online at https://ec.europa.eu/germany/news/20191010-vertragsverletzungsverfahren-deutschland_de, checked on 11/7/2019.

European Council on Refugees and Exiles (2019): Regular Procedure. Germany. Available online at http://www.asylumineurope.org/reports/country/germany/asylum-procedure/procedures/regular-procedure, checked on 6/18/2019.

Flieger, Petra (2013): Durch Partizipation zu mehr Gerechtigkeit in der Forschung zu Behinderung. In Markus Dederich, Heinrich Greving, Christian Mürner, Peter Rödler (eds.): Behinderung und Gerechtigkeit. Heilpädagogik als Kulturpolitik. Originalausgabe. Giessen: Psychosozial-Verlag (Therapie & Beratung), pp. 153–168.

Flüchtlingsrat NRW e.V.: Unterbringung von Flüchtlingen. Edited by Flüchtlingsrat NRW e.V. Available online at https://www.frnrw.de/themen-a-z/unterbringung-von-fluechtlingen.html, checked on 4/18/2019.

Handicap International (2017): Stellungnahme zum Thema Flüchtlinge mit Behinderung für das Deutsche Institut für Menschenrechte. Available online at https://www.netzwerk-iq.de/fileadmin/Redaktion/Downloads/Fachstelle_Einwanderung/TT8/Fachstelle_Einwanderu ng_8.Thementage_Stellungnahme_DIMR_Handicap_International_2017.pdf.

Harris, Jennifer; Roberts, Keri (2003): Challenging Barriers to Participation in Qualitiative Reserach: Involving Disabled Refugees. In *International Journal of Qualitiativ Methods* 2 (2), pp. 14–22.

Harris, Jennifer; Roberts, Keri (2004): 'Not our Problem': The Provision of Services to Disabled Refugees and Asylum-Seekers. In Debra Hayes, Beth Humphries, Steve Cohen (eds.): Social Work, Immigration and Asylum. Debates, Dilemmas and Ethical Issues for Social Work and Social Care Practice. London, New York: Jessica Kingsley Publishers, pp. 151–161.

Help Age International and Handicap International (2014): Hidden Victims of the Syrian Crisis: Disabled, Injured and Older Refugees. Available online at http://d3n8a8pro7vhmx .cloudfront.net/handicapinternational/pages/454/attachments/original/1397045203/Hidden_Vi ctims_of_the_Syrian_Crisis%E2%80%94disabled__injured_and_older_refugees.pdf?1397045 203, checked on 6/14/2019.

Hugman, R.; Pittaway, E.; Bartolomei, L. (2011): When 'Do No Harm' Is Not Enough: The Ethics of Research with Refugees and Other Vulnerable Groups. In *British Journal of Social Work* 41 (7), pp. 1271–1287. DOI: 10.1093/bjsw/bcr013.

Hurrelmann, Klaus; Franzkowiak, Peter (2018): Gesundheit. Edited by Bundeszentrale für gesundheitliche Aufklärung (BZgA). Available online at https://www.leitbegriffe.bzga.de /alphabetisches-verzeichnis/gesundheit/, checked on 7/20/2019.

Kannankulam, John (2014): Kräfteverhältnisse in der bundesdeutschen Migrationspolitik. Die Asyldebatte als Schlüsselereignis des schwerfälligen Wandels vom Gastarbeitsregime hin zu Managed Migration in der Bundesrepublik Deutschland. In Forschungsgruppe "Staatsprojekt Europa" (ed.): Kämpfe um Migrationspolitik. Theorie, Methode und Analysen kritischer Europaforschung. 1st edition. Bielefeld: transcript (Kultur und soziale Praxis), pp. 93–112.

Kanter, Arlene; Dadey, Kristin (2000): The Right to Asylum for People with Disabilities. In *Temple Law Review* 73 (4), pp. 1117–1158.

King, Julie; Edwards, Niki; Correa-Velez, Ignacio; Darracott, Rosalyn; Fordyce, Maureen (2016): Restrictive Practices on Refugees in Australia with Intellectual Disability and Challenging Behaviours: A Family's Story. In *Adv Mental Hlth Intell Disabil* 10 (4), pp. 222–232. DOI: 10.1108/AMHID-02-2016-0004.

Kleger, Heinz (2006): Toleranz und 'tolerantes Brandenburg'. Münster: LIT (Region - Nation - Europa, No. 34).

Köbsell, Swantje (2018): "'Disabled asylum seekers? … They don't really exist'". Zur Unsichtbarkeit behinderter Flüchtlinge im Hilfesystem und im behindertenpolitischen Diskurs. In Manuela Westphal, Gudrun Wansing (eds.): Migration, Flucht und Behinderung. Herausforderungen für Politik, Bildung und psychosoziale Dienste. Wiesbaden: Springer VS, pp. 63–80.

Leisering, Britta (2018): Geflüchtete Menschen mit Behinderungen. Handlungsnotwendigkeiten für eine bedarfsgerechte Aufnahme in Deutschland. Edited by Deutsches Institut für Menschenrechte. Available online at https://www.institut-fuer-menschenrechte.de/fileadmin /user_upload/Publikationen/POSITION/Position_16_Gefluechtete_mit_Behinderungen.pdf, checked on 5/6/2019.

Martin, Philip (2014): Germany. Managing Migration in the Twenty-First Century. In James Hollifield, Philip Martin, Pia Orrenius (eds.): Controlling Immigration. A Global Perspective. 3rd edition. Stanford: Stanford University Press, pp. 224–250.

Mayring, Philipp (2015): Qualitative Inhaltsanalyse. Grundlagen und Techniken. 12th completely revised and updated edition. Weinheim, Bergstr: Beltz, J (Beltz Pädagogik).

Meekosha, Helen (2011): Decolonising Disability: Thinking and Acting Globally. In *Disability & Society* 26 (6), pp. 667–682. DOI: 10.1080/09687599.2011.602860.

Mirza, Mansha; Heinemann, Allen W. (2012): Service Needs and Service Gaps among Refugees with Disabilities Resettled in the United States. In *Disablity & Rehabilitation* 34 (7), pp. 542–552.

Morgan, Jules (2017): Disability—A Neglected Issue in Greece's Refugee Camps. In *The Lancet* (389), p. 896.

Mostafa, Ayman (2015). Disability and Forced Migration: The Experience of a Syrian Doctor. In *Disability and the Global South* 1 (2), pp. 551–555.

Müller, Doreen (2010): Flucht und Asyl in europäischen Migrationsregimen: Metamorphosen einer umkämpften Kategorie am Beispiel der EU, Deutschlands und Polens: Universitätsverlag Göttingen.

Murphy, Megan (2002): Give Me Your Tired, Your Poor, Your Disabled?: Why the Disabled Should Qualify for Asylum under the Immigration and Nationality Act. In *The George Washington Law Review* 70 (4), pp. 854–865.

Otten, Matthias (2018): Flucht, Behinderung und Inklusion: Wechselwirkungen und Widersprüche der Policy Regime und der professionellen Sozialen Arbeit. In Monika Pfaller-Rott, Esperanza Gómez-Hernández, Hilaria Soundari (eds.): Soziale Vielfalt. Internationale Soziale Arbeit aus interkultureller und dekolonialer Perspektive. Wiesbaden: Springer VS (Springer VS research), pp. 89–114. Available online at https://doi.org/10.1007/978-3-658-21090-8_9.

Otten, Matthias (2019): Partizipative Forschung zur Teilhabe von geflüchteten Menschen mit Behinderung. In Verena Klomann, Norbert Frieters-Reermann, Marianne Genenger-Stricker, Nadine Sylla (eds.): Forschung im Kontext von Bildung und Migration. Kritische Reflexionen zu Methodik, Denklogiken und Machtverhältnissen in Forschungsprozessen. Wiesbaden: SpringerVS, pp. 181–194.

Otten, Matthias; Farrokhzad, Schahrzad; Zuhr, Anna (2017): Flucht und Behinderung als Schnittstellenaufgabe der Sozialen Arbeit. In *Gemeinsam leben* (4).

Ottosdottir, Gudbjorg; Evans, Ruth (2014): Ethics of Care in Supporting Disabled Forced Migrants: Interactions with Professionals and Ethical Dilemmas in Health and Social Care in the South-East of England. In *British Journal of Social Work* 44 (1), pp. 53–69.

Pearce, Emma (2015): 'Ask Us What We Need': Operationalizing Guidance on Disability Inclusion in Refugee and Displaced Persons Programs. In *Disability and the Global South* 1 (1), pp. 460–478.

Pisani, Maria; Grech, Shaun; Mostafa, Ayman (2016): Disability and Forced Migration: Intersections and Critical Debates. In Shaun Grech, Karen Soldatic (eds.): Disability in the Global South. The Critical Handbook. Cham, Switzerland: Springer (International Perspectives on Social Policy, Administration, and Practice), pp. 285–301.

Plangger, Sascha; Schönwiese, Volker (2013): Bildungsgerechtigkeit zwischen Umverteilung, Anerkennung und Inklusion. In Markus Dederich, Heinrich Greving, Christian Mürner, Peter Rödler (eds.): Behinderung und Gerechtigkeit. Heilpädagogik als Kulturpolitik. Originalausgabe. Giessen: Psychosozial-Verlag (Therapie & Beratung), pp. 55–76.

Pro Asyl e.V. (2019): Stellungnahme zum Entwurf eines Zweiten Gesetzes zur besseren Durchsetzung der Ausreisepflicht (Geordnete-Rückkehr-Gesetz). Frankfurt am Main. Available online at https://www.proasyl.de/wp-content/uploads/PRO-ASYL_Stellungnahme-zum-Geordnete-R%C3%BCckkehr-Gesetz.pdf.

Razum, O.; Wenner, J.; Bozorghmehr, K. (2016): Wenn Zufall über den Zugang zur Gesundheitsversorgung bestimmt: Geflüchtete in Deutschland. When Chance Decides About Access to Health Care: The Case of Refugees in Germany. In *Gesundheitswesen* (78), pp. 711–714.

Roberts, Keri; Harris, Jennifer (2002a): Disabled People in Refugee and Asylum-Seeking Communities. Bristol: The Policy Press.

Roberts, Keri; Harris, Jennifer (2002b): Disabled People in Refugee and Asylum Seeking Communities. Bristol: The Policy Press; Policy Press (Social Care, Race and Ethnicity Series).

Scalettaris, Giulia (2007): Refugee Studies and the International Refugee Regime: A Reflection on a Desirable Separation. In *Refugee Survery Quartlery* 26 (3), pp. 36–50.

Schülle, Mirjam (2018): Medizinische Versorgung für Menschen mit Behinderungen, die Leistungen nach dem Asylbewerberleistungsgesetz erhalten. Rechtliche und praktische Barrieren der Barrierefreiheit. In Manuela Westphal, Gudrun Wansing (eds.): Migration, Flucht und Behinderung. Herausforderungen für Politik, Bildung und psychosoziale Dienste. Wiesbaden: Springer VS, pp. 145–165.

Schülle, Mirjam; Frankenstein, Arne (2019): Europa- und verfassungsrechtliche Anforderungen an die Auslegung von § 6 Abs. 1 AsylbLG in Hinblick auf Leistungen für geflüchtete Menschen mit Behinderungen. Anmerkungen zu LSG Hessen, Beschl. vom 11.07.2018 – L 4 AY 9/18 B ER und LSG Niedersachsen-Bremen, Beschl. vom 01.02.2018 – L 8 AY 16/17. In *RP Reha* (1), pp. 20–27.

Shakespeare, Tom (2013): The Social Model of Disability. In Lennard J. Davis (ed.): The Disability Studies Reader. 4th ed. New York, NY: Routledge, pp. 214–221.

Soldatic, Karen; Somers, Kelly; Buckley, Amma; Fleay, Caroline (2015): 'Nowhere to be Found': Disabled Refugees and Asylum Seekers within the Australian Resettlement Landscape. In *Disability and the Global South* 2 (1), pp. 501–522.

Stienstra, Deborath; Nyerere, Leon (2016): Race, Ethnicity and Disability: Charting Comlex and Intersectional Terrains. In Shaun Grech, Karen Soldatic (eds.): Disability in the Global South. The Critical Handbook. Cham, Switzerland: Springer (International Perspectives on Social Policy, Administration, and Practice), pp. 255–268.

Straimer, Clara (2010): Vulnerable or Invisible? Asylum Seekers with Disabilities in Europe. Edited by UNHCR.

Straimer, Clara (2011): Between Protection and Assistance: Is there Refuge for Asylum Seekers with Disabilities in Europe? In *Disability & Society* 26 (5), pp. 537–551.

Thomsen, Jenny: Evaluation zur Früherkennung besonders Schutzbedürftiger im Aufnahmeverfahren. Umsetzung der EU-Aufnahmerichtlinie 2013/33/EU in Niedersachsen. Available online at https://www.ntfn.de/wp-content/uploads/2018/06/NTFN-Evaluationsbericht-zur-Umsetzung-der-EU-Aufnahmerichtlinie-2013-33-EU-in-Niedersachsen.pdf, checked on 6/19/2019.

von Unger, Hella (2018): Ethische Reflexivität in der Fluchtforschung. Erfahrungen aus einem soziologischen Lehrforschungsprojekt. In *Forum: Qualitiative Sozialforschung* 19 (3), no page reference.

Waldschmidt, Anne (2017): Disabiltiy Goes Cultural: The Cultural Model of Disability as an Analytical Tool. In Anne Waldschmidt, Hanjo Berressem, Moritz Ingwersen (eds.): Culture - Theory - Disability. Encounters between Disability Studies and Cultural Studies. Bielefeld: transcript (Disability Studies, Volume 10), pp. 19–27.

Ward, Kim; Amas, Neil; Lagnado, Jacob (2008): Supporting Disabled Refugees and Asylum Seekers: Opportunities for New Approaches.

Weiser, Barbara (2016): Sozialleistungen für Menschen mit einer Behinderung im Kontext von Migration und Flucht. Eine Übersicht zu den rechtlichen Rahmenbedingungen. Edited by passage gGmbH, Universität Hamburg. Hamburg. Available online at https://www.fluchtort-hamburg.de/fileadmin/user_upload/Expertise_Sozialleistungen_2016_web.pdf, checked on 7/20/2019.

Westphal, Manuela; Wansing, Gudrun (2018): Schnittstellen von Behinderung und Migration in Bewegung. In Manuela Westphal, Gudrun Wansing (eds.): Migration, Flucht und Behinderung. Herausforderungen für Politik, Bildung und psychosoziale Dienste. Wiesbaden: Springer VS, pp. 3–24.

World Health Organization (2006): Constitution of the World Health Organization. Available online at https://www.who.int/governance/eb/who_constitution_en.pdf.

Yeo, Rebecca (2015): 'Disabled Asylum Seekers?...They Don't Really Exist': The Marginalisation of Disabled Asylum Seekers in the UK and Why it Matters. In *Disability and the Global South* 2 (1), pp. 523–550.

Protecting the Health Care Rights of Refugees: Some Legal Perspectives from the Republic of South Africa

Letlhokwa George Mpedi[1]

"…access to health is a step towards dignity and social inclusion for those who had been forced to leave their country behind."[2]

Keywords: Bill of Rights, Health Care, Human Rights, Refugees

Abstract

This chapter analyses the protection of health care rights of refugees in the Republic of South Africa from a legal point of view. It does that with a particular focus on the key concepts (i.e. 'health' and 'refugee'); the right to health as contained in the Constitution of South Africa, 1996; international and regional instruments; and pertinent domestic laws such as the National Health Act 61 of 2003, the Refugees Act 130 of 1998, and the National Health Insurance Bill of 21 June 2018. This is followed by a discussion of issues and challenges facing refugees in their quest to access health services in South Africa. These issues and challenges include an imperfect public service and expensive private service; limited ability to enforce the right to health care and related fundamental

---

1   Letlhokwa George Mpedi | Faculty of Law, University of Johannesburg | lgmpedi@uj.ac.za.
    Visiting Professor | Faculty of Law | University of Cape Coast | Cape Coast | Ghana.

2   Jesuit Refugee Service "South Africa: Towards Dignity and Social Inclusion, JRS's
    Healthcare Services" – accessed at http://www.jrssaf.org/news_detail?TN=NEWS-
    20190405092404 (30 April 2019).

rights (e.g. access to courts); language barriers; lack of access to information; and ignorance and xenophobia.

Contents

Abstract 77

1 Introduction 79

2 Key Concepts 79

2.1 Health 79

2.2 Refugee 80

3 Right to Health 82

3.1 Constitution 83

3.2 International and Regional Instruments 85

3.3 Pertinent Domestic Laws 88

4 Issues and Challenges 92

4.1 Imperfect Public Health Services and Expensive Private Health Sector 92

4.2 Limited Ability to Enforce Rights 94

4.3 Language and Cultural Barriers 95

4.4 Lack of Access to Information 97

4.5 Ignorance and Xenophobia 98

5 Conclusion 99

Bibliography 99

1 Introduction

The Republic of South Africa (hereinafter South Africa) transitioned from a refugee-producing to a refugee-hosting country on the African continent. Refugees are human beings of flesh and blood just like everybody else. Therefore, they similarly have basic rights which include the right to health care. This chapter deals with the protection of the health care rights of refugees in South Africa with a particular reference to the Constitution of the Republic of South Africa, 1996 (hereinafter the Constitution), international and regional instruments and relevant domestic laws.

2 Key Concepts

2.1 Health

The World Health Organization (hereinafter WHO) defines health as "a state of complete physical, mental and social well-being and not merely the absence of diseases or infirmity."[1] South Africa, which is a member of the WHO,[2] subscribes to this definition in the sense that it views health as more than simply the absence of disease. The point is that the South African national health system[3] endeavours to encompass promotive, preventative and curative services.[4] This is in line with the African National Congress' National Health Plan for South Africa (May 1994)[5] which argued that:

> "It should also be emphasised that promotion and protection of health constitutes a major component of each and every health activity, as envisaged in this plan, which is committed to healthy living and healthy life style rather than curative care as the

---

[1] The Preamble of the World Health Organization (Adopted by the International Health Conference held in New York from 19 June to 22 July 1946, signed on 22 July 1946 by the representatives of 61 States.

[2] South Africa was one of the founding members of the World Health Organization (hereinafter the WHO). It resumed full membership of the WHO on 3 May 1994 subsequent to its suspension due to its apartheid policy.

[3] Section 1 of the National Health Act 61 of 2003 defines 'national health system' as "the system within the Republic [of South Africa], whether within the public or private sector, in which the individual components are concerned with the financing, provision or delivery of health services."

[4] These concepts can also be found in section 1 of the National Health Insurance Bill of 2018 which defines 'universal health coverage' as "a service that is available to all persons, including promotive, preventative, curative, rehabilitative and palliative health services, regardless of socio-economic or health status of those persons."

[5] Accessed at http://www.africa.upenn.edu/Govern_Political/ANC_Health.html (1 May 2019).

main thrust. To redress the imbalance of the inherited health status from the apart-heid period, curative, palliative and rehabilitative measures will be supported by promotion and prevention measures in the health services."

The importance of healthy living and its interconnectedness with health care rights was highlighted in *Soobramoney v Minister of Health, KwaZulu-Natal* 1998 (SA) 765 (CC).[6] The Constitutional Court asserted in paragraph 54 that:

"Health care rights by their very nature have to be considered not only in a tradi-tional legal context structured around the ideas of human autonomy but in a new analytical framework based on the notion of human interdependence. A healthy life depends upon social interdependence: the quality of air, water, and sanitation which the state maintains for the public good; the quality of one's caring relationships, which are highly correlated to health; as well as the quality of health care and sup-port furnished officially by medical institutions and provided informally by family, friends, and the community."

In light of the preceding pronouncements, it follows naturally that health care rights are not stand-alone rights. Accordingly, when catering for these rights, policy makers need to, *inter alia*, make provision for measures aimed at the realisation of other public services (e.g. access to clean water and sanitation), which are crucial in ensuring that the health care rights are enjoyed in a mean-ingful manner.

2.2 Refugee

In accordance with article 1A (2) of the United Nations (hereinafter the UN) Convention Relating to the Status of Refugees[7] a 'refugee' is:

"...any person who...owing to well-founded fear of being prosecuted for reasons of race, religion, nationality, membership of a particular social group or political opinion, is outside the country of his nationality and is unable or, owing to such

---

6   The case concerned the refusal by a public hospital to provide renal dialysis treatment to a patient suffering from a terminal illness (i.e. chronic renal failure and other diseases). The Constitutional Court found that the patient's situation was not an 'emergency' but and 'ongo-ing state of affairs' (paragraph 21) and it could not "interfere with rational decisions taken in good faith by the political organs and medical authorities whose responsibility it is to deal with such matters" (paragraph 29). The essence of the *Soobramoney v Minister of Health, KwaZulu*-Natal judgement is that the courts will not interfere with policy decisions if they are made in good faith and in a rational manner irrespective of the dire consequences of such pol-icy decisions to those affected. This approach is particularly influenced by the lack of re-sources which entails that not every person requiring access to public services can or will be granted access to such services.

7   Adopted on 28 July 1951 by the United Nations Conference of Plenipotentiaries on the Status of Refugees and Stateless Persons convened under General Assembly resolution 429 (V) of 14 December 1950 and entry into force on 22 April 1954.

fear, is unwilling to avail himself of the protection of that country; or who, not having a nationality and being outside the country of his former habitual residence as a result of such events, is unable or, owing to such fear, is unwilling to return to it."

A key criticism levelled against the UN's definition orbits around the issue of persons (to be) recognised as refugees and, thus, accorded the necessary protection.[8] The UN's definition stands accused, by its detractors, of failing to extend protection to (a) individuals who flee armed conflict, (b) internally displaced persons and (c) individuals in a refugee-like situation.[9] The Organisation of African Unity (now the African Union (hereinafter the AU)) Convention Governing the Specific Aspects of Refugee Problems in Africa (AU Convention)[10] makes provision for a definition which is somewhat expanded when compared to the UN Convention.[11] It states that the concept 'refugee' shall be applicable to:

"...every person who, owing to external aggression, occupation, foreign domination or events seriously disturbing public order in either part or the whole of his country of origin or nationality, is compelled to leave his place of habitual residence in order to seek refuge in another place outside his country of origin or nationality."[12]

South Africa has signed and ratified the UN Convention (12 January 1996) and AU Convention (15 December 1995). The Refugee Act 130 of 1998 has been enacted to, *inter alia*, give effect within South Africa to the relevant internation-

8   See, for an interesting discussion on the debate regarding the question who is a refugee, Gibney MJ "Political Theory, Ethics, and Forced Migration" in Fiddian-Qasmiyeh E et al (eds) *The Oxford Handbook of Refugee and Forced Migration Studies* (Oxford University Press (2014)) 48 at 49 – 50.

9   See Mpedi LG "Africa and the Refugee Crisis: A Socio-Legal Inquiry" in Wacker E et al (eds) *Refugees and Forced Migrants in Africa and the EU: Comparative and Multidisciplinary Perspective on Challenges and Solutions* (Springer (2019)) 69 at 76 – 77. Also, see Newland K *Refugee: The New International Politics of Displacement* (Worldwatch Institute (1981)) 7 – 10.

10   Adopted by the Assembly of Heads of State and Government at its Sixth Ordinary Session, Addis Ababa, 10 September 1969.

11   See, for example, Maunganidze OA "The Forgotten Masses: The Growing Refugee Crisis in Sub-Saharan Africa" (2017) *African Yearbook on International Humanitarian Law* 109 at 114, Odiaka N "The Face of Violence: Rethinking the Concepts of Xenophobia, Immigration Laws and the Rights of Non-Citizens in South Africa" (2017) *IV BRICS Law Journal* 40 at 48 – 49 and 59 – 60, Whittaker DJ *Asylum Seekers and Refugees in the Contemporary World* (Routledge (2006)) 4 – 5 and Newland K *Refugee: The New International Politics of Displacement* (Worldwatch Institute (1981)) 11 – 12.

12   Article 1(2) of the Organisation of African Unity (now the African Union (hereinafter the AU)) Convention Governing the Specific Aspects of Refugee Problems in Africa.

al instruments including the aforementioned. The preamble of the Refugee Act states that:

> "Whereas the Republic of South Africa has acceded to the 1951 Convention Relating to the Status of Refugees, the 1967 Protocol Relating to the Status of Refugees and the 1969 Organization of African Unity Convention Governing the Specific Aspects of Refugee Problems in Africa as well as other human rights instruments, and has in so doing, assumed certain obligations to receive and treat in its territory refugees in accordance with the standards and principles established in international law."

Section 3 of the Refugee Act extends the refugee status in South Africa to a person who

> "(a) owing to a well-founded fear of being persecuted by reason of his or her race, tribe, religion, nationality, political opinion or membership of a particular social group, is outside the country of his or her nationality and is unable or unwilling to avail himself or herself of the protection of that country, or, not having a nationality and being outside the country of his or her former habitual residence is unable or, owing to such fear, unwilling to return to it; or (b) owing to external aggression, occupation, foreign domination or events seriously disturbing or disrupting public order in either a part or the whole of his or her country of origin or nationality, is compelled to leave his or her place of habitual residence in order to seek refuge elsewhere: or (c) is a dependant of a person contemplated in paragraph (a) or (b)."

The above provision of the Refugee Act is progressive in the sense that it combines some elements of both the UN Convention and the AU Convention.

3 Right to Health

The right to health is a fundamental right that should be enjoyed by everyone, inclusive of refugees and their children, in South Africa. This is abundantly clear from the Constitution,[13] international and regional instruments that bind South Africa[14] and relevant domestic laws. However, it should be noted that the right to health care, similarly to any fundamental right, it is not absolute. As explained in 3.1 below, it can be limited.

---

13   The Constitutional Court in *Khosa and Others v Minister of Social Development and Others, Mahlaule and Another v Minister of Social Development* 2004 (6) SA 505 (CC) in paragraph 47 pointed out that "the word 'everyone' in this section cannot be construed as referring only to 'citizens'". It argued further in paragraph 111 that: "The word 'everyone' is a term of general import and unrestricted meaning. It means what it conveys. Once the state puts in place a social welfare system, everyone has a right to have access to that system."

14   Discussed below in paragraph 3.2.

The pertinent provisions contained in the above legal sources of the refugees' right to health care will now be discussed individually.

3.1 Constitution

The Constitution, which is the supreme law of South Africa,[15] contains a Bill of Rights[16] which enshrines the right to health care. The Constitution regards the Bill of Rights as a "cornerstone of democracy in South Africa."[17] It provides everyone with the right to have access to health care services, including reproductive health care.[18] Secondly, it states, "[n]o one may be refused emergency medical treatment."[19] The Constitutional Court explained this right as follows:

> "Section 27(3) itself is couched in negative terms – it is a right not to be refused emergency treatment. The purpose of the right seems to be to ensure that treatment be given in an emergency, and is not frustrated by reason of bureaucratic requirements or other formalities. A person who suffers a sudden catastrophe which calls for immediate medical attention... should not be refused ambulance or other emergency services which are available and should not be turned away from a hospital which is able to provide the necessary treatment. What the section requires is that remedial treatment that is necessary and available be given immediately to avert that harm."[20]

It argued further that:

> "The special attention given by section 27(3) to non-refusal of emergency medical treatment relates to the particular sense of shock to our notions of human solidarity occasioned by the turning away from hospital of people battered and bleeding or of those who fall victim to sudden and unexpected collapse. It provides reassurance to all members of society that accident and emergency departments will be available to deal with the unforeseeable catastrophes which could befall any person, anywhere and at any time."[21]

Furthermore, the Constitution provides everyone with "the right to an environment that is not harmful to their health or well-being."[22] These rights are (to be)

---

15   Section 1(c) and 2 of the Constitution.

16   Chapter 2 of the Constitution.

17   Section 7(1) of the Constitution.

18   Section 27(1)(a) of the Constitution.

19   Section 27(3) of the Constitution.

20   *Soobramoney v Minister of Health, KwaZulu*-Natal in paragraph 20.

21   In paragraph 51.

22   Section 24(a) of the Constitution. Provision regarding environmental health can also be found in article 23 of the Protocol on Health in the Southern African Development Community (SADC) of 1999.

enjoyed by every person in South Africa.[23] Thus, the word 'everyone' includes refugees. It should be noted that the Constitution is explicit where it intends to restrict a right to citizens. For instance, citizens enjoy political rights[24] such as the right to form a political party[25] and the right to vote.[26]

The right to have access to health care is restricted.[27] It is to be realised progressively and it is subject to the availability of resources.[28] This is an internal limitation clause. It entails that the state is not expected to provide more than it can afford or achieve the right instantaneously.[29] However, every child's[30] right to basic health care services[31] is not dependent on the availability of resources.

In addition to the internal limitation, there is the general or external limitation clause. Section 36 of the Constitution provides that:

"(1) The rights in the Bill of Rights may be limited only in terms of law of general application to the extent that the limitation is reasonable and justifiable in an open and democratic society based on human dignity, equality and freedom, taking into account all relevant factors, including – (a) the nature of the right; (b) the importance of the purpose of the limitation; (c) the nature and extent of the limitation; (d) the relation between the limitation and its purpose; and (e) less restrictive means to achieve the purpose. (2) Except as provided in subsection (1) or in any other provision of the Constitution, no law may limit any right entrenched in the Bill of Rights."

In light of the preceding pronouncements, a refugee's right to access to health care can be limited due to the scarcity of resources. The Constitutional Court argued in *Soobramoney v Minister of Health, KwaZulu-Natal* that: "However the right to life may come to be defined in South Africa, there is in reality no meaningful way in which it can constitutionally be extended to encompass the right indefinitely to evade death."[32]

---

23 It should be noted that other rights such as the right to equality (section 9 of the Constitution), the right to dignity (section 10 of the Constitution) and, the right to life (section 11 of the Constitution) support the right to health care.

24 Section 19 of the Constitution.

25 Section 19(1)(a) of the Constitution.

26 Section 19(3)(a) of the Constitution.

27 Section 7(3) of the Constitution.

28 Section 27(2) of the Constitution.

29 *Minister of Health and Others v Treatment Action Campaign and Others* (No 2) 2002 (5) SA 721 in paragraph 32.

30 Section 28(3) of the Constitution defines a child as a "person under the age of 18 years."

31 Section 28(1)(c) of the Constitution.

32 In paragraph 57.

However, in line with section 28(1)(c) of the Constitution alluded to earlier, a child refugee's right to access to health care is not limited by the availability of resources. The point is that a child refugee should be treated the same way as any child who is a citizen of South Africa. This implies that he or she should be granted the same access to health care in the same manner as any child who is a citizen of the country.

The abovementioned rights are definitely worth the paper that they are written on. First, the state has a duty to respect, protect, promote and fulfil the rights contained in the Bill of Rights.[33] In addition, "the Bill of Rights applies to all law, and binds the legislature, the executive, the judiciary and all organs of state."[34] Furthermore, they are enforceable. The Constitution makes provision for the "right to approach a competent court, alleging that a right in the Bill of Rights has been threatened or infringed and the court may grant appropriate relief, including a declaration of rights."[35] The following persons enjoy the right to approach a court of law and enforce the right to health care and associated rights contained in the Bill of Rights:

> "(a) anyone acting in their own interest; (b) anyone acting on behalf of another person who cannot act in their own name; (c) anyone acting as a member of, or in the interest of, a group or class of persons; (d) anyone acting in the public interest; and (e) an association acting in the interest of its members."[36]

This right has a close link with the right to access to courts. Every person in South Africa has a right "to have any dispute that can be resolved by the application of law decided in a fair public hearing before a court or, where appropriate, another independent and impartial tribunal or forum."[37]

3.2   International and Regional Instruments

South Africa is a member of international (e.g. United Nations) and regional bodies (e.g. African Union). Accordingly, it is a party to a number of instruments stemming from these organisations. The binding effect of international agreements on South Africa is provided for in the Constitution.[38] First, customary international law is law in South Africa unless it is inconsistent with the

---

33   Section 7(2) of the Constitution.

34   Section 8(1) of the Constitution.

35   Section 38 of the Constitution.

36   Ibid.

37   Section 34 of the Constitution.

38   Section 231 of the Constitution.

Constitution or an Act of Parliament.[39] Second, courts have a duty to consider international law when they interpret the Bill of Rights.[40] Furthermore, when interpreting the legislation, courts have a constitutional duty to "prefer any reasonable interpretation of the legislation that is consistent with international law over any alternative interpretation that is inconsistent with international law."[41] In light of the foregoing, South Africa has adopted an international-law-friendly approach.

South Africa is a member country of the United Nations Organisation. Therefore, the UN's instruments which constitute soft and hard law are of great relevance to the subject of this chapter. First, article 25(1) of the Universal Declaration of Human Rights (1948) provides that:

> "(1) Everyone has the right to a standard of living adequate for the health and well-being of himself and of his family, including food, clothing, housing and medical care and necessary social services, and the right to security in the event of unemployment, sickness, disability, widowhood, old age or other lack of livelihood in circumstances beyond his control."

This article does not distinguish between persons (e.g. citizens and non-citizens (such as refugees, asylum seekers, documented and non-documented migrants, etc.)). Apart from the aforementioned right, the Universal Declaration of Human Rights bestows upon every person the right to social security.[42]

Second, the provisions of the Convention Relating to the Status of Refugees bind South Africa. These provisions include the right not to be discriminated against because of race, religion, or country of origin[43] and the right to equality of treatment with respect to public relief and assistance[44] as well as social security.[45] The Convention Relating to the Status of Refugees recognises the refugees' right of access to courts[46] as well as any legal assistance provided by the state to nationals.[47]

---

39   Section 232 of the Constitution.
40   Section 39(1)(b) of the Constitution.
41   Section 233 of the Constitution.
42   Article 22 of the Universal Declaration of Human Rights.
43   Article 3 of the Convention Relating to the Status of Refugees.
44   Article 23 of the Convention Relating to the Status of Refugees.
45   Article 24 of the Convention Relating to the Status of Refugees.
46   Article 16(1) of the Convention Relating to the Status of Refugees.
47   Article 16(2) of the Convention Relating to the Status of Refugees.

In addition, South Africa signed (in 1993) and ratified (in 1995) the United Nations Convention on the Rights of the Child.[48] Article 22 of the Convention requires South Africa to:

> "…take appropriate measures to ensure that a child who is seeking refugee status or who is considered a refugee in accordance with applicable international or domestic law and procedures shall, whether unaccompanied or accompanied by his or her parents or by any other person, receive appropriate protection and humanitarian assistance in the enjoyment of applicable rights set forth in the present Convention and in other international human rights or humanitarian instruments…"

The applicable right referred to in the Convention includes the right to health care. Article 24 of the Convention makes provision for "the right of the child to the enjoyment of the highest attainable standard of health and to facilities for the treatment of illness and rehabilitation of health." In addition, it directs state parties such as South Africa to "strive to ensure that no child is deprived of his or her right of access to such health care services."[49] Thus, South Africa has a constitutional and international law obligation to provide access to health care to refugee children. Notwithstanding, refugee children do experience discrimination in their quest to access basic services, which include basic health care services, in South Africa. The Committee on the Rights of the Child has flagged this as a concern.[50] Accordingly, it recommended that South Africa should "[p]lace strong focus on the eradication of structural inequality and discrimination in all legislative, policy and programmatic measures to advance the rights of the child, paying particular attention to …[*inter alia*] asylum-seeking and refugee children…"[51]

Furthermore, South Africa has signed (on 3 October 1994) and ratified (on 12 January 2015) the UN Covenant on Economic, Social and Cultural Rights (hereinafter the Covenant).[52] Article 12 of the Covenant makes provision for "the right of everyone to the enjoyment of the highest attainable standard of physical and mental health." A similar right can be found in the African Charter on Human and Peoples' Rights (hereinafter the Charter).[53] Article 16(2) of the

---

48   Adopted and opened for signature, ratification and accession by General Assembly resolution 44/25 of 20 November 1989 and entered into force on 2 September 1990.

49   Article 24(1) of the United Nations Convention on the Rights of the Child.

50   Committee on the Rights of the Child *Concluding Observations on the Second Periodic Report of South Africa* (United Nations (2016)) 5.

51   Ibid at 6

52   Adopted and opened for signature, ratification and accession by General Assembly resolution 2200A (XXI) of 16 December 1966 and entered into force on 3 January 1976.

53   Adopted in Nairobi on 27 June 1981 and entered into force on 21 October 1986. South Africa signed and ratified the African Charter on Human and Peoples' Rights on 9 June 1996.

Charter provides every individual with "the right to enjoy the best attainable state of physical and mental health." It requires member countries to "take the necessary measures to protect the health of their people and to ensure that they receive medical attention when they are sick."[54]

Moreover, the Convention Governing the Specific Aspects of Refugee Problems in Africa makes provision for the non-discrimination of refugees on grounds of race, religion, nationality, membership of a particular social group or political opinions.[55]

South Africa has enacted several laws in its quest to give effect to its international obligations and the right to health care contained in the abovementioned instruments and the Constitution. These laws include the National Health Act 61 of 2003 and the Refugees Act 130 of 1998. In addition, the Department of Health (South Africa) published the National Health Insurance Bill on 21 June 2018 for broader public comment. All the aforementioned pertinent domestic laws are discussed in paragraph 3.3 below.

3.3 Pertinent Domestic Laws

(a) National Health Act

The health care provisions in South Africa strive to ensure "access to health care services for all people in South Africa through a caring and quality health system."[56] The framework for a structured uniform health system in South Africa is set out in the National Health Act 61 of 2003. The National Health Act provides a legislative framework that endeavours to enable the State to comply with, *inter alia*, the various constitutional obligations.[57] These are the duty to respect, protect, promote and fulfil the health care rights contained in the Bill of Rights[58] and the duty to take reasonable legislative and other measures within its available resources to achieve the progressive realisation of the right to have access to health care services.[59]

The National Health Act makes provision for free health services in public health establishments for certain vulnerable groups.[60] These groups include

---

54   Article 16(2) of the African Charter on Human and Peoples' Rights.

55   Article IV of Convention Governing the Specific Aspects of Refugee Problems in Africa.

56   National Treasury (Republic of South Africa) *Budget Review 2019* (National Treasury (Republic of South Africa) 2019) 57.

57   Preamble of the National Health Act.

58   Section 7(2) of the Constitution.

59   Section 27(2) of the Constitution.

60   Section 4 of the National Health Act.

women, children, older persons and persons with disabilities.[61] State clinics and community centres funded by the State are obliged to provide pregnant and lactating women, and children below the age of six years, who are not members or beneficiaries of medical aid schemes, with free health services.[62] Secondly, all persons, except members of medical aid schemes, and their dependants and persons receiving compensation for compensable occupational diseases, are entitled to free primary health care services.[63]

Furthermore, women are, subject to the Choice on Termination of Pregnancy Act 92 of 1996, eligible for free termination-of-pregnancy services.[64] The entitlement to the abovementioned free services is extended subject to conditions prescribed by the Minister of Health and it, most importantly, covers refugees who belong to the aforementioned groups of vulnerable persons. Apart from the right to free health services, the National Health Services Act makes provision for the right to emergency treatment. It prohibits health care providers, health workers, and health establishments from refusing a person emergency medical treatment.[65] This gives effect to a similar right which is found in section 27(3) of the Constitution. However, as shown in paragraph 4 below, this is easier said than done, since in practice access for refugees to these services is often impeded.

Additionally to the aforementioned provisions, section 6(1) of the National Health Act regulates the right of a user[66] to have full knowledge as follows:

"Every health care provider must inform a user of (a) the user's health status except in circumstances where there is substantial evidence that the disclosure of the user's health status would be contrary to the best interests of the user; (b) the range of diagnostic procedures and treatment options generally available to the user; (c) the benefits, risks, costs and consequences generally associated with each option;

---

61   Section 4(2)(a) of the National Health Act

62   Section 4(3)(a) of the National Health Act.

63   Section 4(3)(b) of the National Health Act.

64   Section 4(30)(c) of the National Health Act.

65   Section 5 of the National Health Act.

66   A 'user' means "the person receiving treatment in a health establishment, including receiving blood or blood products, or using a health service, and if the person receiving treatment or using a health service is (a) below the age contemplated in section 39(4) of the Child Care Act, 1983 (Act 74 of 1983), 'user' includes the person's parent or guardian or another person authorised by law to act on the first mentioned person's behalf; or (b) incapable of taking decisions, 'user' includes the person's spouse or partner or, in the absence of such spouse or partner, the person's parent, grandparent, adult child or brother or sister, or another person authorised by law to act on the first mentioned person's behalf" (section 1 of the National Health Act).

and (d) the user's right to refuse health services and explain the implications, risks, obligations of such refusal."

In his or her quest his to comply with the above duty, a health care provider is required to, where possible, inform the user in a language that the user understands and in a manner which takes into account the user's level of literacy.[67] This provision is crucial particularly in light of the language barriers to access to health care which are articulated in paragraph 4.3 below.

Most importantly, it gives effect to the constitutional right to privacy.[68] Section 86A of the National Health Act directs that:

"Any entry upon or search of any premises or health establishment in terms of this Act must be conducted with strict regard to decency and good order, including (a) the right of a person to dignity; (b) the right of a person to freedom and security; and (c) the right of a person to privacy."

Alongside the right to confidentiality, there is a provision regarding confidentiality that must be complied with. The information concerning a user is to remain confidential.[69] Such information includes information relating to his or her health status, treatment or stay in the health establishment.[70] This information may be disclosed if the user grants his or her consent to that disclosure in writing if a court order or any law requires that disclosure or in a case where the non-disclosure of the information represents a serious threat to public health.[71] The right to privacy and the right to confidentiality extends to refugees. This is

---

67   Section 6(2) of the National Health Act.

68   Section 14 of the Constitution provides that: "Everyone has the right to privacy, which includes the right not to have (a) their person or home searched; (b) their property searched; (c) their possessions seized; or (d) the privacy of their communications infringed."

69   Section 14 of the National Health Act. However, in *Tshabalala-Msimang and Another v Makhanya and Others* 2008 (6) SA 102 (W) the court found that the publication of a public figure's private medical records by a newspaper without the user's consent can be done if such publication is in the public interest. It argued in paragraph 38 that "[t]he public has the right to be informed of current news and events concerning the lives of public persons such as politicians and public officials. This right has been given express recognition in Section 16(1)(a) and (2) of the Constitution which protects the freedom of the press and other media and the freedom to receive and impart information and ideas. The public has the right to be informed not only on matters which have a direct effect on life, such as legislative enactments, and financial policy. This right may in appropriate circumstances extend to information about public figures."

70   Section 14(1) of the National Health Act.

71   Section 14(2) of the National Health Act.

in line with the principle of confidentiality[72] and the right to privacy[73] as contained in international instruments.

(b) Refugees Act

The Refugees Act 130 of 1998 is, as pointed out in paragraph 2.2, the key legislation that "gives effect within South Africa to the relevant international legal instruments, principles and standards relating to refugees."[74] These instruments include the international conventions that South Africa has acceded to such as the 1951 Convention Relating to the Status of Refugees, the 1967 Protocol Relating to the Status of Refugees and the 1969 Organization of African Unity Convention Governing the Specific Aspects of Refugee Problems in Africa as well as other pertinent human rights instruments.[75] Thus, South Africa has to receive and treat, within its geographical boundaries, refugees in accordance with the standards and principles set in international law.[76] In the area of access to health care, the Refugees Act entitles refugees to the same basic health services which the inhabitants of South Africa receive from time to time.[77] Accordingly, refugees are entitled to free basic health care services provided in terms of the National Health Act discussed in paragraph (a) above. However, as discussed below, there is a discrepancy between the refugees' entitlement to health care services as contained in statute books and in practice.

(c) National Health Insurance Bill

The National Health Insurance Bill, published on 21 June 2018 for broader public comment, seeks to, *inter alia*, "achieve the progressive realisation of the right of access to good quality health services by South African citizens and permanent residents"[78] and establish a National Health Insurance Fund in South Africa.[79] It makes provision for the right to health care.[80] Section 7(2) of the National Health Insurance Bill entitles refugees and asylum seekers to the right

---

72   Scripnic V "Principles and guarantees in the protection of refugees" (2016) *11 EIRP Proceedings* – accessed at http://www.proceedings.univ-danubius.ro/index.php/eirp/article/view /1725/1817 (17 May 2019).

73   Article 12 of the Universal Declaration of Human Rights.

74   Preamble of the Refugees Act.

75   *Ibid.*

76   *Ibid.*

77   Section 27(g) of the Refugees Act.

78   Preamble of the National Health Insurance Bill of 2018.

79   Section 3(1) of the National Health Insurance Bill.

80   Part 2 of the National Health Insurance Bill.

to emergency health care services, services for notifiable conditions of public health concern and paediatric and maternal services at primary health care level. This is in line with the Constitution and related national legislation and international instruments. The implementation of the planned National Health Insurance is a policy priority for the health sector in South Africa.[81] Accordingly, the government needs to address staff shortages and other problems in the public health facilities before the full implementation of the policy.[82] This is essential for the success of the envisaged scheme.

4   Issues and Challenges

The legal regulation of the right to health for refugees is impressive on paper. However, in reality, there seems to be a gap between the legal entitlement in law and in practice. The root courses of this situation are diverse and they include the following: imperfect public services and expensive private services, limited ability to enforce the right to health care and related rights, language barriers, lack of access to information, and ignorance as well as xenophobia.

4.1   Imperfect Public Health Services and Expensive Private Health Sector

The South African national health system comprises a (substandard) public health[83] sector and a (world class) private health[84] sector.[85] Some commentators describe this, rightfully so, as a reflection of South Africa's social divide.[86] The public health sector is challenged by the lack of (human and financial) resources,[87] as well as by corruption and fraud. The private health system – while

---

81   National Treasury (Republic of South Africa) *Budget Review 2019* (National Treasury (Republic of South Africa) 2019) 57.

82   *Ibid.*

83   A 'public health establishment' is defined as a "health establishment that is owned or controlled by an organ of state (section 1 of the National Health Act 61 of 2003). Section 239 of the Constitution defines an 'organ of state' as "(a) any department of state or administration in the national, provincial or local sphere of government; or (b) any other functionary or institution – (i) exercising a power or performing a function in terms of the Constitution or a provincial constitution; or (ii) exercising a public power or performing a public function in terms of any legislation, but does not include a court or a judicial officer."

84   A 'private health establishment' is defined as "a health establishment that is not owned or controlled by an organ of state" (section 1 of the National Health Act).

85   Section 2(a)(i) of the National Health Act.

86   Burger R and Christian C "Access to Health Care in Post-Apartheid South Africa: Availability, Affordability, Accessibility" (2018) *Health Economics, Policy and Law* 1 at 2.

87   See, for example, South African Human Rights Commission *Public Inquiry: Access to Health Care Services* (South African Human Rights Commission (2007)) 37 – 40.

ranked amongst the best in the world – is prohibitively expensive. This entails the circumstance that it is accessible to well-off persons and those that are covered by private medical schemes. The majority of users of the private health care services are described as affluent, skilled, educated and belonging to a medical aid scheme.[88] Refugees with adequate resources are able to attend private hospitals.[89] However, the majority seeks health care at public institutions due to their being persons of limited means.[90] It is essential that the gap between public and private health services be bridged. This is one of the reasons for South Africa's drive to introduce a National Health Insurance scheme.[91]

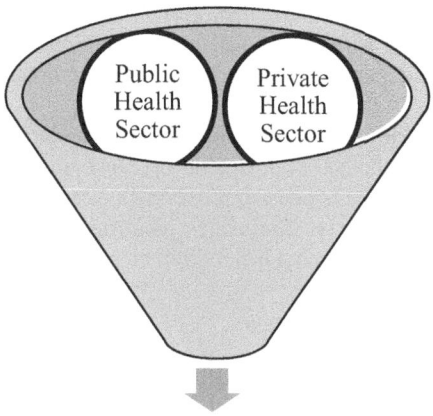

National Health System

Figure 1: Adapted from Mahlathi P and Dlamini J *Minimum Data Sets for Human Resources for Health and the Surgical Workforce in South Africa's Health System: A Rapid Analysis of Stock and Migration* (African Institute for Health and Leadership Development (2015)) 4. Macro-organisation of the South African Health System.

---

88   Burger R and Christian C "Access to Health Care in Post-Apartheid South Africa: Availability, Affordability, Accessibility" (2018) *Health Economics, Policy and Law* 1 at 2.

89   Apalata T et al *Refugees' Perceptions of their Health Status & Quality of Health Care Services in Durban, South Africa: A Community-Based Survey* (Health Systems Trust (2007)) 19.

90   *Ibid.*

91   See paragraph 3.3 (c) above.

The National Health Insurance scheme is based on the following principles: right of access, social solidarity, effectiveness, appropriateness, equity, affordability and efficiency.[92] The envisaged scheme seeks to bridge the public-private divide alluded to earlier by providing sustainable and affordable universal access to health care services. Such access will arise from an approach "whereby funding contributions would be linked to an individual's ability to pay and benefits from health services would be in line with an individual's need for care."[93] Accordingly, the scheme intends to improve cross-subsidization in the entire health system.[94] It should be mentioned that the scheme does not explicitly cater for migration-related measures other than the eligibility of refugees and asylum seekers to health care.[95] Legal permanent residents will be covered alongside the nationals.[96] Individuals with a tenuous link to the country such as short-term residents, foreign students and tourists are expected to obtain compulsory travel insurance.

Although efforts towards the setting-up of a legislative framework for the full implementation of the National Health Insurance are at bill stage, it must be pointed out that the scheme is phased in over a 14-year period. It started in 2012 with ten pilot health districts. Challenges identified through the pilot include human resources constraints and a lack of vehicles.[97]

4.2 Limited Ability to Enforce Rights

As pointed out in paragraph 3.1 above, the rights contained in the Bill of Rights, inclusive of the right to health care and emergency treatment, are enforceable. However, having an enforceable right does not automatically translate to the ability to enforce such a right in practice. The point is that enforcing rights in a court of law invariably requires the assistance and guidance of a lawyer. Refugees and many South Africans are indigent. Thus, they are not in a position to engage the services of a lawyer as and when they require it. Legal services in

---

92 Department of Health (South Africa) *National Health Insurance in South Africa: Policy Paper* – accessed at https://www.gov.za/sites/default/files/nationalhealthinsurance.pdf (14 June 2019).

93 *Ibid.*

94 *Ibid.*

95 Section 7(1)(e) of the National Health Insurance Bill.

96 Department of Health (South Africa) *National Health Insurance in South Africa: Policy Paper* – accessed at https://www.gov.za/sites/default/files/nationalhealthinsurance.pdf (14 June 2019).

97 Department of Health (Republic of South Africa) *Status of NHI Pilot Districts: Progress Report* (Department of Health (Republic of South Africa) (2016)) 32.

South Africa, as it is the case elsewhere, are expensive.[98] This makes it difficult for refugees to approach courts and enforce their fundamental rights. Thus, access to courts and, invariably, justice by those who need it the most is constrained. While legal services are in the main not cheap, the situation in South Africa is exacerbated in some instances by the unethical conduct of some legal practitioners who overreach their clients. The notion of 'overreaching' has been described by the Supreme Court of Appeal in *Melamed & Hurwitz Incorporated v Goldberg*[99] as follows:

> "Where an attorney and his fees are concerned, the word 'overreach' may be taken as conveying the extraction by the attorney from his client, by the taking by the former of undue advantage in any form of the latter, of a fee which is unconscionable, excessive or extortionate, and in so overreaching his client that attorney would be guilty of unprofessional conduct."

Overreaching is dishonest[100] and morally reprehensible. Thus, such cases need to be dealt with harshly by the courts and the legal profession. Notwithstanding the challenge of high legal fees, it must be acknowledged that refugees have been able to enforce their rights in South Africa through the support of, *inter alia*, civil society, non-governmental organisations (NGOs), legal aid clinics and university law clinics. These institutions play an important role by providing the much-needed legal services to the refugees and other indigent persons in South Africa. They approached the court on a number of occasions on behalf of refugees whose various rights were trampled by, among others, the government institutions.[101] Therefore, it is clear that the broad approach adopted by the Bill of Rights with regard to who can approach the courts to enforce rights[102] is instrumental in ensuring that civil society and similar organisations can assist otherwise helpless refugees to enforce their fundamental rights.

4.3 Language and Cultural Barriers

South Africa is a multilingual and multicultural country. It has eleven official languages, namely: Sepedi, Sesotho, Setswana, siSwati, Tshivenda, Xitsonga,

---

98   See, for example, South African Law Reform Commission *Investigation into Legal Fees* (South African Law Reform Commission (2019)).

99   [2009] ZASCA 15 (19 March 2009) in paragraph [3].

100   See, for example, *General Council of the Bar of South Africa v Geach and Others* 2013 (2) SA 52 (SCA) in para. [52].

101   *Somali Association of South Africa v Limpopo Department of Economic Development, Environment and Tourism* 2015 (1) SA 151 (SCA).

102   See section 38 of the Constitution (on enforcement of rights) and paragraph 3.1 above.

Afrikaans, English, isiNdebele, isiXhosa and isiZulu.[103] Furthermore, every person in South Africa has "the right to use the language and the right to participate in the cultural life of their choice, but no one exercising these rights may do so in a manner inconsistent with any provision of the Bill of Rights."[104] In addition, the Constitution provides that:

> "Persons belonging to a cultural, religious or linguistic community may not be denied the right, with other members of that community – (a) to enjoy their culture, practice their religion and use their language; and (b) to form, join and maintain cultural, religious and linguistic associations and other organs of civil society. (2) The rights in subsection (1) may not be exercised in a manner inconsistent with the provision of the Bill of Rights."

Refugees in South Africa come from different linguistic and cultural backgrounds. Some of the languages spoken by refugees are not (widely) spoken in South Africa. This makes medical consultation difficult. Furthermore, language serves as a barrier to suitable treatment and follow-up assessment of refugees admitted in public hospitals.[105] The situation is compounded by the lack of translators for refugees in public hospitals.[106] There are no easy fixes to these challenges. However, they must be addressed. The Constitution provides every accused person with a right to a fair trial, which includes the right to be tried in a language that the accused person understands or, if that is not practicable, to have the proceedings interpreted in that language.[107] This approach can be emulated in the quest to ensure that the right to health care is accessible to all. Therefore, South Africa should make certain that health facilities that serve individuals that may experience language and cultural challenges (e.g. refugees) are well-equipped to deal with such challenges. This may involve the appointment of linguistically and culturally diverse health professionals and translators or interpreters.[108]

It should be recalled that South Africa subscribes to the policy of local integration and not the encampment of refugees. Thus, refugees in South Africa are free to settle anywhere in the country. They are not confined to a camp

---

103   Section 6(1) of the Constitution.

104   Section 30 of the Constitution.

105   Apalata T et al *Refugees' Perceptions of their Health Status & Quality of Health Care Services in Durban, South Africa: A Community-Based Survey* (Health Systems Trust (2007)) 12.

106   *Ibid* 20.

107   Section 35(3)(k) of the Constitution.

108   See, for an illuminating discussion on the need for the appointment of interpreters to deal with the language barriers in the South African health care sector, Benjamin E et al "Language Barrier in Health: Lessons from the Experience of Trained Interpreters Working in Public Sector Hospitals in the Western Cape" (2016) *SAHR* 73.

where their health needs can be attended to through interpreters if necessary. This may raise challenges such as increased overheads for providing health care or the violation of privacy. As regards the costs, the aforementioned proposal need not be realised overnight. In line with the spirit of the Constitution, this may be provided progressively and subject to the availability of resources.[109] As regards privacy, the standard provisions regarding the patient's right to confidentiality[110] need to be respected and enforced.

4.4 Lack of Access to Information

Refugees are generally unaware of their legal entitlements such as the right to be treated in the same way as nationals when it comes to access to health care in South Africa. NGOs are playing an important role in this regard. However, their capacity is invariably hamstrung by the shortage of resources and negative perceptions. For instance, as regards negative views regarding the role of NGOs, Apalata et al[111] argue that there is a perception that:

> "... many NGOs working with refugees do not involve the refugees in their work and, therefore, do not understand the real problems faced by the refugees. In addition, they felt that some exploit refugees and use the money donated to the NGO for their own purposes rather than providing services to refugees."

In light of the foregoing pronouncements, it is important that information regarding the rights and duties within the health sector be made freely accessible to all, inclusive of refugees. This should include "the right to seek, receive and impart information and ideas concerning health issues."[112] It follows naturally that the doctor/patient confidentiality should and must be respected at all times. Accordingly, personal information must, as required by section 14 of the National Health Act, be handled with the confidentiality it deserves. Provision should be made in the National Health Act for the publication of a summary of the rights and duties of individuals within the context of health care in South Africa. Such a summary should be publicly displayed at health facilities throughout the country. Such a step would not be unusual in the South African context. For instance, section 30 of the Basic Conditions of Employment Act 75 of 1997 requires employers to inform their employees about the rights as con-

---

109   See section 27(2) of the Constitution.

110   See paragraph 4.4 below.

111   Apalata T et al *Refugees' Perceptions of their Health Status & Quality of Health Care Services in Durban, South Africa: A Community-Based Survey* (Health Systems Trust (2007)) 19.

112   South African Human Rights Commission *Public Inquiry: Access to Health Care Services* (South African Human Rights Commission (2007)) 25.

tained in that Act by displaying a statement, containing such rights, in the workplace in an official language spoken at that workplace. Secondly, the health sector needs to collaborate more closely with civil society, inclusive of NGOs.

4.5   Ignorance and Xenophobia

Section 2(2)(e) of the Immigration Act 13 of 2002 imposes a duty on the Department of Home Affairs to "educate communities and organs of civil society on the rights of foreigners, illegal foreigners and refugees, and conduct other activities to prevent xenophobia." However, anti-foreigners sentiments remain widespread in South Africa.[113] The issue is that section 44 of the Immigration Act unwittingly promotes xenophobia while purporting to curb it. The section directs any organ of state, which includes public health care providers, to establish the status or citizenship of the person receiving its services and report to the Department of Home Affairs any illegal foreigners or any person whose status or citizenship cannot be determined. This results in what has been termed medical xenophobia.[114]

The provisions of section 44 of the Immigration Act are indeed problematic. As argued by Odiaka:[115]

> "Such provisions are very intrusive and could mean that a foreigner does not enjoy a free and undisturbed sojourn within the country. Consequently, the focus is shifted from border control to control by institutions and members of the community. Such an environment encourages vigilantism and may degenerate into xenophobic witch-hunts. Ultimately, the mistreatment of undocumented migrants results in their alienation and criminalization in the eyes of the community. The result is that all foreigners, even documented migrants are under constant suspicion and become [...] targets for police harassment and xenophobia."

To address the aforementioned problem, the earlier recommendation cited in paragraph 4.4 above is equally relevant here. That is, the main rights and duties contained in the applicable legislation must be prominently displayed in health facilities throughout South Africa. In addition, efforts to sensitise health care service providers about refugees and their rights should be prioritised and offered on a continuous basis.

---

113   Zihindula G et al *"Access to Health Care Services by Refugees in Southern Africa: A Review of Literature"* (2015) 16 Southern African Journal of Demography 7 at 27.

114   *Ibid* at 28 – 29.

115   Odiaka N "The Face of Violence: Rethinking the Concepts of Xenophobia, Immigration Laws and the Rights of Non-Citizens in South Africa" (2017) IV *BRICS Law Journal* 40 at 62.

5   Conclusion

As shown in this contribution, the provision and protection of the refugees' health care rights in South Africa has two sides, i.e. the 'on paper' side and the 'in practice' dimension. It can easily be argued that the protection of the right to health care, as contained in laws and related instruments in South Africa, is amongst the best in the world. The point is that this right and other supporting rights are protected in the Constitution and given effect to in national laws. In addition, South Africa has signed and ratified several germane international and regional instruments requiring it to protect the right to health care of refugees. However, when it comes to the practical implementation of the right to health care of refugees the situation is different. The right is provided on paper but denied in reality due to factors such as language barriers, ignorance and xenophobia. Therefore, the elephant in the room for South Africa is: How can the gap between the right to health care be bridged in law and in reality? Addressing this question is easier said than done. However, it goes without saying that the mere maintaining of the status quo is untenable. Accordingly, South Africa must enhance the ability of refugees to enforce their rights, eradicate language and cultural barriers, render relevant information accessible and address the perennial problem of ignorance and xenophobia if it is to protect the right of refugees to health care in a meaningful manner. It is of vital importance to implement the solutions proposed in this chapter as part of the broader quest to ensure that refugees are not artificially denied their fundamental rights. This should, undoubtedly, include the successful implementation of the envisaged National Health Insurance scheme.

Bibliography

African National Congress "National Health Plan for South Africa" (May 1994) – accessed at http://www.africa.upenn.edu/Govern_Political/ANC_Health.html (1 May 2019).

Apalata T *et al Refugees' Perceptions of their Health Status & Quality of Health Care Services in Durban, South Africa: A Community-Based Survey* (Health Systems Trust (2007)).

Benjamin E *et al* "Language Barrier in Health: Lessons from the Experience of Trained Interpreters Working in Public Sector Hospitals in the Western Cape" (2016) SAHR 73.

Burger R and Christian C "Access to Health Care in Post-Apartheid South Africa: Availability, Affordability, Accessibility" (2018) *Health Economics, Policy and Law* 1

Committee on the Rights of the Child *Concluding Observations on the Second Periodic Report of South Africa* (United Nations (2016)).

Department of Health (Republic of South Africa) *National Health Insurance in South Africa: Policy Paper* – accessed at https://www.gov.za/sites/default/files/nationalhealthinsurance.pdf (14 June 2019).

Department of Health (Republic of South Africa) *Status of NHI Pilot Districts: Progress Report* (Department of Health (Republic of South Africa) (2016)).

Gibney MJ "Political Theory, Ethics, and Forced Migration" in Fiddian-Qasmiyeh E *et al* (eds) *The Oxford Handbook of Refugee and Forced Migration Studies* (Oxford University Press (2014)) 48 – 59.

Jesuit Refugee Service "South Africa: Towards Dignity and Social Inclusion, JRS's Healthcare Services" – accessed at http://www.jrssaf.org/news_detail?TN=NEWS-20190405092404 (30 April 2019).

South African Law Reform Commission *Investigation into Legal Fees* (South African Law Reform Commission (2019)).

Mahlathi P and Dlamini J *Minimum Data Sets for Human Resources for Health and the Surgical Workforce in South Africa's Health System: A Rapid Analysis of Stock and Migration* (African Institute for Health and Leadership Development (2015)).

Maunganidze OA "The Forgotten Masses: The Growing Refugee Crisis in Sub-Saharan Africa" (2017) *African Yearbook on International Humanitarian Law* 109.

Mpedi LG "Africa and the Refugee Crisis: A Socio-Legal Inquiry" in Wacker E *et al* (eds) *Refugees and Forced Migrants in Africa and the EU: Comparative and Multidisciplinary Perspective on Challenges and Solutions* (Springer (2019)) 69 – 94.

National Treasury (Republic of South Africa) *Budget Review 2019* (National Treasury (Republic of South Africa) 2019).

Newland K *Refugee: The New International Politics of Displacement* (Worldwatch Institute (1981)).

Odiaka N "The Face of Violence: Rethinking the Concepts of Xenophobia, Immigration Laws and the Rights of Non-Citizens in South Africa" (2017) IV *BRICS Law Journal* 40.

Scripnic V "Principles and Guarantees in the Protection of Refugees" (2016) 11 *EIRP Proceedings* – accessed at http://www.proceedings.univ-danubius.ro/index.php/eirp/article/view/1725/1817 (17 May 2019).

South African Human Rights Commission *Public Inquiry: Access to Health Care Services* (South African Human Rights Commission (2007)).

Whittaker DJ *Asylum Seekers and Refugees in the Contemporary World* (Routledge (2006)).

Zihindula G *et al* "Access to Health Care Services by Refugees in Southern Africa: A review of Literature" (2015) 16 *Southern African Journal of Demography* 7.

4. Political Perspectives: Health Care Policy, Social Policy, and Diversity

What Happens to the Healthy Immigrant Later in Life? – The Health of (Forced) Migrants Through the Life Course

Andrea Goettler[1]

Keywords: Immigrant Health, Life Course, Forced Migration, Labour Immigrants

Abstract

Studies on immigrant health continuously provide evidence for the "healthy migrant effect" and discuss the associated "healthy migrant paradox". This contribution reviews the relationship of health and migration and considers the role of social determinants of health associated with labour and forced migration over the life course. Studies among older labour immigrants in Germany show the long-term effects of health risks in the receiving country. While older immigrants' health is increasingly addressed through prevention, health promotion and care services, improvements for the recognition of long-term socioeconomic barriers to health are still needed. To conclude, the relationship of health and migration is linked to future health risks of current forced immigrants in Europe.

Contents

Abstract 103

---

1   Andrea Goettler | Technical University Munich, Department for Sport and Health Sciences, Chair of Sociology of Diversity | andrea.goettler@tum.de

© Springer Fachmedien Wiesbaden GmbH, part of Springer Nature 2020
K. Crepaz et al. (eds.), *Health in Diversity – Diversity in Health*,
https://doi.org/10.1007/978-3-658-29177-8_6

1   Introduction 105

2   Healthy Immigrants? 105

2.1   Migration of the Fittest 106

2.2   Salmon Bias Hypothesis: Unhealthy Return Migration 106

2.3   Healthy Forced Migrants? 107

3   The Social Determinants of Migration 107

4   Health of Older (Forced) Immigrants 109

4.1   Exhausted Migrants Later in Life 109

4.2   The Health of Older Forced Migrants 110

5   Older Immigrants in Germany and Health 111

5.1   Health Determinants of Older Labour Immigrants 112

5.2   Health Situation of Older Labour Immigrants in Germany 113

6   Addressing Immigrant Health in Older Age 114

6.1   Prevention and Health Promotion 114

6.2   Care and Health Services 114

7   Discussion and Conclusion 115

Bibliography 116

1 Introduction

The relationship between health and migration has often been viewed from two different perspectives. On one hand, evidence for healthy immigrants especially shortly after arrival is presented; on the other hand, diseases and health problems are highlighted, particularly with reference to forced migrants (Beiser 2005). However, the health of migrants is influenced by socioeconomic and environmental factors before, during, and after migration, and by the specific reasons for migration and associated risk factors. The positive view on immigrant health refers to the "healthy immigrant effect", the phenomenon that immigrants seem to experience lower mortality compared to the native population. This effect has been shown in several international studies (Lariscy et al. 2015). These results are surprising because socioeconomic status tends to be lower in immigrant populations, which is associated with more health risks (Kristiansen et al. 2016; Ronellenfitsch et al. 2006). Hence, the "healthy immigrant effect" has also been termed the "healthy immigrant paradox". However, this positive picture of healthy migrants is not supported in the literature on forced migrants and refugees. Here, infectious diseases and psychological conditions are emphasised at the time of arrival in the host country (Pavli and Maltezou 2017). Overall, the focus often remains on the time shortly after arrival in the immigration country.

This chapter will bring the issue of immigrant health into a life course perspective with an emphasis on health in older age. Immigrant health will be discussed for both voluntary and forced migrant populations. Looking at older labour immigrants in Germany provides an example of how social determinants of health impact healthy life expectancy when growing old in the receiving country.

2 Healthy Immigrants?

The "healthy immigrant effect" or the "healthy immigrant paradox" refers to the results of international studies that show that immigrant populations seem to be in better health than the autochthonous population. Several studies from North America (Lariscy et al. 2015; Markides and Eschbach 2011; Singh and Hiatt 2006) and Europe (Brzoska et al. 2015; Anson 2004; Ronellenfitsch et al. 2006; Uitenbroek and Verhoeff 2002) have shown lower all-cause mortality risks among immigrant populations. This can be seen as a paradox as immigrants often face higher risk factors, which include poverty, lower education, and precarious working conditions (Lu and Zhang 2016; Kristiansen et al. 2016). However, it is important to note that not all migrant populations experience lower mortality rates after migration. To better understand this phenomenon, it is important to consider migration-related factors and processes that influence mortality statistics.

2.1 Migration of the Fittest

One explanation focuses on selection effects of migration that influence health differences in the host country. It is assumed that good health facilitates migration whereas sickness or disability constrain people's mobility. Migrants might thus be in better health than the average population of their origin country. Migration is, therefore, a self-selection of healthy people who find it easier to move internationally. This effect is usually described as the "migration of the fittest" (Lu and Zhang 2016). Furthermore, migration is in most cases associated with the labour market, which favours young and healthy individuals (Lu and Zhang 2016). In the case of labour immigrants in Europe, health selection also took place in the arrival countries to ensure the immigration of healthy workers (Bolzman et al. 2004). In addition to physical health, migrating requires resilience to cope with stress caused by uncertainties and unexpected challenges. Individuals who are psychologically and physically more resilient might thus find it easier to migrate internationally (Acevedo-Garcia et al. 2012; Lu and Zhang 2016).

Health as a prerequisite for migration becomes even more valuable in the context of forced migration. Therefore, selection effects might also take place in forced migrant populations. Yet, given the dangerous journeys forced migrants experience together with the vulnerabilities associated with seeking refuge, the combination of selection and health risk effects during forced migration are complex (Abubakar et al. 2018; Norredam et al. 2012). Health threats such as physical and psychological stress during migration and insecurities at arrival are common and severe (Norredam et al. 2012). While health is an important factor for the decision and opportunity to migrate, the health selection effect only indicates health benefits at the time of migration but does not consider health risks during and after migration.

2.2 Salmon Bias Hypothesis: Unhealthy Return Migration

Later in life return migration provides a further explanation for migrant mortality benefits. This so-called "salmon bias" gets its name from the migration of the salmon fish that returns to its place of birth before spawning and subsequently dying. According to the salmon bias or the "unhealthy return migration" hypothesis, people are likely to return to their home country when faced with health deterioration later in life. This explanation particularly concentrates on statistical errors, which occur when people return to their home country but remain in official statistics. They consequently become "statistically immortal" as their death is only registered in the return country (Abraído-Lanza et al. 1999). Their healthier counterparts, on the other hand, might be more likely to stay than individuals faced with health problems. Yet, the evidence is not clear, it seems, as this hypothesis cannot entirely explain lower mortality rates among migrants. In longitudinal studies, for example, it has been shown that the beneficial mortality effect remains even when the return bias is controlled for (Abraído-Lanza et al. 1999). Thus, uncertainty regarding the healthy migrant paradox remains and selection effects do not seem to suffice as an explanation (Lu and Zhang 2016; Razum 2006a).

2.3   Healthy Forced Migrants?

Does the healthy migrant effect that has been discovered in many international studies also refer to the health of forced migrants? Here the evidence is contradictory. While some research shows that refugees are overall in good health, other studies highlight infectious or mental health risks. Interestingly, there seems to be a higher awareness of the refugee's health status, creating two contradictory pictures: that of the healthy immigrant and that of the sick refugee (Beiser 2005; Abubakar et al. 2018).

While there is a higher prevalence of infectious diseases and mental illness, the overall health status of refugees at arrival is very heterogeneous depending on the receiving country and the health risks experienced during migration (Pavli and Maltezou 2017). In a Danish study, all-cause and cause-specific mortality rates from cancer and cardiovascular disease were lower in refugees compared to native Danes (Norredam et al. 2012). Yet, representative data is not always available on forced migrants (Frank et al., 2017). In Germany, analysing the results of initial examinations on arrival provides some indications but no complete picture of health conditions at arrival. These examinations have shown that refugees show a higher prevalence of tuberculosis, Hepatitis B and other infectious diseases (Frank et al. 2017). Higher prevalence regarding mental health conditions has been reported but results vary based on different studies (Frank et al., 2017). Mental health is more vulnerable because of the specific life contexts that have led to leaving the home country and seeking refuge (Pavli and Maltezou 2017; Abubakar et al. 2018).

3   The Social Determinants of Migration

Studies on immigrant health frequently focus on cultural explanation, specifically the relevance of "acculturation" and neglect commonly accepted frameworks to understand health such as the social determinants of health (Viruell-Fuentes et al. 2012; Acevedo-Garcia et al. 2012). However, environmental, sociocultural, and economic aspects in the sending and the receiving country influence individuals' health over the life course. How these transnational factors affect health depends on the age at migration, socioeconomic status and time of exposure in different living contexts. Acevedo-Garcia and colleagues (2012) suggest a framework which considers determinants of health cross-nationally and across the life course. According to this framework, health is influenced by factors in the sending country before migration, which influence the decision to migrate and health during migration, by factors during migration and by factors in the receiving country after migration. Age at migration plays a significant role within this framework. Migrating during childhood or after the age of 40 have both been shown to be associated with socioeconomic and health risks (Gustafsson et al. 2019; Acevedo-Garcia et al. 2012).

As for the *sending country*, determinants of health include socioeconomic factors, health distribution and epidemics, exposure to infectious diseases and environmental hazards, which in the case of forced migration are highly unfavourable due to conflict, violence, poverty or environmental catastrophes (Acevedo-Garcia et al., 2012). Furthermore, disadvantageous socioeconomic situations before migration can have long-lasting health effects. Exposure to health risks in sending countries can manifest later in the receiving country (Razum 2006b; Razum and Spallek 2012). Later-in-life cancer cases, for example, have been associated with early-in-life infectious diseases (Razum and Spallek 2012). Especially in the case of forced migration, the push factors in the sending countries, such as violence/war, political crisis or lack of public health infrastructure, relate directly to health risks. Nevertheless, health selection effects influence migration intentions and opportunities. Thus, both voluntary and forced migrants may constitute a healthier or more resilient population compared to the average population of the sending country.

Risk factors *during migration* are predominantly relevant for forced migrants who experience high-risk journeys as undocumented migrants. First points of arrival, for example in refugee settlements, pose a considerable risk factor due to highly populated accommodations and associated infectious diseases (Pavli and Maltezou 2017; Abubakar et al. 2018).

Health determinants in the *receiving country* include the same factors as in the sending country: socioeconomic determinants, health distribution, epidemics, exposure to infectious diseases and environmental hazards (Acevedo-Garcia et al. 2012). The immigrant-receiving context is related, primarily, to social status, working and living conditions and the quality of health services. Discrimination or uncertainty and psychological strain in the receiving country act as severe stressors (Acevedo-Garcia et al., 2012; Viruell-Fuentes, Miranda, & Abdulrahim, 2012). Furthermore, economic factors in the receiving countries such as poor housing and working conditions as well as barriers to health care access and social exclusion can lead to worse health outcomes (Warnes et al. 2004). Access to healthcare services can be especially difficult depending on the socio-economic situation, health literacy barriers or legal status (Kristiansen et al. 2016).

When looking at the difference between sending and receiving countries and associated health risk behaviours such as smoking and quality of food, it needs to be recognised that immigrant health behaviours are flexible. Health behaviours can change over time, remain similar to the sending country or as-similate with the culture of the receiving destination. Additionally, social factors play an important role. A better socioeconomic situation and environmental benefits in the receiving country might come with a loss of social support due to a separation from family and social networks in the sending country (Spallek et al. 2016).

4   Health of Older (Forced) Immigrants

Immigrants are predominantly a younger population at the time of migration. However, the diversity of older migrants also includes people who migrate later in life. For example, Warnes and Williams (2004) describe "retirement migra-tion" as an increasing phenomenon of people migrating, for example, to South-ern Europe from other European countries, or to Florida in the case of the Unit-ed States after retirement. While migration takes place at all ages, this chapter focuses on what happens over time in the receiving country and on the health aspects of reaching older age in the host country.

4.1   Exhausted Migrants Later in Life

As discussed by numerous studies, it seems as if a health benefit for immigrants exists with regard to lower mortality. However, this is not the case when looking at the older migrant population. While the majority of research indicates lower mortality among immigrants, the healthy immigrant effect seems to decrease with the length of stay in the receiving country (Anson 2004; Kristiansen et al. 2016; Lanari and Bussini 2012; Solé-Auró and Crimmins 2008). This has been described as the "exhausted migrant effect" (Bolzman et al. 2004). After arriv-ing in good health but working under strenuous conditions, migrants have lost their initial health advantage due to physical and psychological stress through-out the life course. These health stressors start with uncertainties after arrival related to residency and working permission. Physically strenuous working conditions in high-risk sectors follow together with short-term or part-time con-tracts. In addition, psychological burdens such as discrimination can be com-mon. Over time, these health stressors result in worse health outcomes later in life. Studies on older migrants in Europe continuously report worse self-rated health, chronic conditions, problems with activities of daily living, and depression compared to the non-migrant older population (Solé-Auró and Crimmins 2008; Lanari and Bussini 2012; Carnein et al. 2015).

Some studies show that not just younger migrants after arrival experience lower mortality benefits; also, older migrants experience lower all-cause mortality compared to older native populations (Reus-Pons et al. 2017; Carnein et al. 2015; Lariscy et al. 2015). The mortality difference, however, diminishes with age and time spent in the receiving country. Other researchers have looked beyond all-cause mortality to assess morbidity and quality of life among older migrants. Reus-Pons and colleagues (2017) demonstrate that healthy life expectancy is lower among older migrants in the Netherlands, Belgium and England and Wales compared to the older non-migrant population. The reason for lower healthy life expectancy, despite mortality advantages, is lower self-rated health (Reus-Pons et al. 2017). Lower self-rated health has been shown in several studies comparing older migrants to non-migrant populations (Lanari and Bussini 2012; Evandrou et al. 2016; Hoffmann and Romeu Gordo 2016). Additionally, higher rates of depression are reported by older migrants (Lanari and Bussini 2012; Aichberger et al. 2010). Other studies point to limitations in terms of functionality, activities of daily living and disability status among older migrants in Europe (Evandrou et al. 2016; Carnein et al. 2015).

It seems that the potential health benefit or selection effect declines over the life course leading to worse health outcomes over the age of 65 years. This poses the question whether the health disadvantages are related to migration-associated health risks or specific socioeconomic risks of the current older generation in Europe. Many of the older immigrants in European countries arrived as labour migrants and experienced socioeconomic disadvantages in the receiving countries.

4.2   The Health of Older Forced Migrants

Similarly to the term "older migrants", the group of older forced migrants and refugees includes people who are forced to migrate to another country at an older age and those who grew old in exile (Bolzman 2014). The population of migrants being forced to move later in life is statistically small but does make up a small percentage of the forced migrant or refugee population. In Germany, persons older than 60 years filed 1.2 per cent of all first asylum applications in 2017 (BAMF 2018). In 2011, it was estimated that 3 per cent of all refugees were 60 years and older (Bolzman 2014).

Alternatively, "older refugees" also refers to people that grow old in exile. Although forced migrants share social and economic difficulties with other migrant populations, the challenges are intensified due to insecurities related to the migrant status (Becker and Ferrara 2019). Lower socioeconomic status, as well as traumatic migration experiences, among forced migrants can have a negative impact on health over the life course (Bolzman 2014). For example, Bolzman and colleagues (2012) show that forced migrants from former Yugoslavia who lived in precarious legal statuses experienced poorer health indicators than immigrants from Italy or Spain. Even at younger ages, this group of forced immigrants had more physical and mental health problems than the older migrant population from Italy and Spain (Bolzman et al. 2012). Looking at life expectancies, Kohls (2012, p. 218) remarks that undefined precarious or limited rights of residence can lead to higher mortality due to stress and associated unemployment. Overall, the data on forced migration and health is still limited or very recent but it is likely that the health challenges of older migrants also apply to older forced migrants.

5   Older Immigrants in Germany and Health

Migrant populations are loosely defined by a migration event in the life course; this inevitably leads to a very heterogeneous group of people. The same is true for older migrants in Germany who come from a range of countries and have migrated to Germany at different times in their lives and due to different reasons (Baykara-Krumme et al. 2012). However, in this mixed group of people, it is possible to identify shared migration histories. One shared characteristic is that the great majority, 97.5 per cent, of immigrants above 64 years are first-generation immigrants who moved to Germany in their lifetime (Schimany and Baykara-Krumme 2012). About 40% have a foreign nationality; the remaining majority are German citizens. The number of older migrants has been increasing significantly in the last decade and is likely to rise in the future as the percentage of immigrants is higher in younger age groups (Schimany and Baykara-Krumme 2012). One group that can be identified in terms of shared migration histories is that of former guest labour migrants in Germany. Recruitment agreements were in place from 1955-1973 with Italy, Spain, Greece, Turkey, Morocco, Portugal, Tunisia, Yugoslavia and South Korea. Among the people who migrated to Germany themselves, immigrants from countries with recruitment agreements make up a third of all immigrants older than 65 years (Hoffmann and Romeu Gordo 2016). The majority of them moved to Germany before 1973. After 1973, when the labour agreements were suspended, spouses and other family members migrated to Germany to reunite their families. Another group of shared migration histories characterises the group of repatriates. The terms 'late repatriates' or 'late re-settlers' refers to ethnic Germans who resettled to Germany after the fall of the Soviet Union. This group makes up 38 per cent of older people above 65 years with migration experience. Other migrants predominantly come from other EU countries as well as other global regions (Hoffmann and Romeu Gordo 2016).

5.1 Health Determinants of Older Labour Immigrants

The group of older labour immigrants is particularly interesting as people have stayed in the receiving country for several decades and are now reaching older age. The specific socioeconomic situations of labour migration demonstrate the relationship between health and migration over the life course. While some decided to return home, others have found a compromise of moving between countries and some are staying in Germany for their time in retirement (Strumpen 2018). The focus of the labour agreements was on manual labour employment for a restricted period; yet, a large percentage of labour migrants ended up staying in Germany. Integration policies were limited as labour migration was thought to be a short-term occurrence which, however, had long-lasting effects. For instance, due to the lack of focus on language classes, communication barriers remain until today (Ciobanu et al. 2016). Manual and physically intensive work and lower-skilled employment led to lower income and a higher risk of poverty. Moreover, higher unemployment rates, part-time working contracts, and early pension due to sickness pose additional economic risks (Brzoska et al. 2010; Schimany et al. 2012; Bolzman et al. 2004; Ciobanu et al. 2016). For example, work accidents are more frequent among immigrants and especially Turkish immigrants compared to native German workers due to employment in higher-risk occupations in the industrial sector (Brzoska et al. 2010). Brzoska and colleagues (2010) also found a higher risk of early retirement for health reasons among immigrants in the period from 2001 to 2006.

Former labour migrants, their reasons to migrate and the related consequences differ considerably from current forced migration processes (Becker and Ferrara 2019). Yet, there are some similarities, which should raise awareness of future health risks among current forced migrants. Labour migrants were not expected to stay permanently in Germany and integration services were thus limited (Schimany and Baykara-Krumme 2012). Likewise, forced migrants are often stuck in a short-term perspective, which has a negative effect on psychological health. Uncertain residence status and insecurities regarding work permits, housing and residency will have a negative impact on health, not just with a view to the period after arrival but also as regards the long-term health perspective (Kohls 2012).

5.2   Health Situation of Older Labour Immigrants in Germany

These socioeconomic disadvantages have a significant effect on health later in life. Data on older migrants is still limited although this field has been gaining rapid attention in the last decade.

Despite common health risks, Kohls (2012) shows that mortality is lower among labour migrants and late repatriates until the age of 60 years, after which mortality rates increase. Furthermore, immigrants who stayed longer in Germany demonstrated fewer health benefits associated with migration than immigrants with a shorter time after arrival (Kohls 2012, p. 217). As described above, Carnein and colleagues (2015) argue that lower mortality needs to be understood together with morbidity by considering healthy life expectancy. Turkish women and men experienced more years with health limitations despite similar or longer life expectancy than Germans. Health disadvantages were measured using the Global Activity Limitations Indicator, which measures the effect of health conditions or disabilities influencing people's everyday lives (Carnein et al. 2015). Klaus and Baykara-Krumme (2017) present that labour migrants indicate the highest risk for functional limitations among migrant populations or people without a migration background. Studies on psychological health found a higher risk of depressive symptoms, which are only partially explained by differences in socioeconomic status (Klaus and Baykara-Krumme 2017; Lanari and Bussini 2012). Besides, older migrants report more worries regarding their own health and rate their health subjectively lower. Worries regarding own health were stronger among older labour immigrants than late repatriates or older people without a migration background (Hoffmann and Romeu Gordo 2016). Lower subjective health compared to the non-migrant population was shown in a number of studies (Özcan and Seifert 2006; Baykara-Krumme and Hoff 2006; Razum et al. 2008). Subjective health generally corresponds with other "objective" health measures across different populations and cultures (Razum et al. 2008). Lower subjective health thus reflects other health problems relating to functional limitations and mental conditions. Furthermore, detrimental living and working conditions such as work in the industrial sector, lower payment, times of unemployment and part-time working contracts can have a negative effect on functional as well as subjective health. Some studies have shown that worse health outcomes persist even when controlling for socioeconomic status. This is, for example, the case when considering health care access and medical rehabilitation, where negative outcomes of medical rehabilitation remained even when considering lower socioeconomic status (Brzoska et al. 2010). Yet, in other studies, for example, on subjective health, health differences between migrant and non-migrant population were associated with socioeconomic differences (Baykara-Krumme and Hoff 2006). It seems that disadvantages at least partially remain even under consideration of socioeconomic status.

6 Addressing Immigrant Health in Older Age

The health risks of older (forced) migrants and the diversity of the ageing population has led to an increased awareness of immigrants or ethnic minorities in older age. In the last two decades, internationally and in Germany, studies on older migrants, their health and socioeconomic situations have gained attention in research and politics. Thus, quality and accessibility of care and prevention and health promotion are now being increasingly discussed in regard to older migrant populations.

6.1 Prevention and Health Promotion

As health risks and lack of access seem prevalent among older immigrants, the demand for prevention and health promotion has been emphasised for this population group. Researchers ask what barriers exist and how prevention and health promotion attend to the needs of older immigrants. To overcome these barriers, language differences, costs, cultural preferences or lack of knowledge on such services need to be addressed. Furthermore, it is important to recognise both sociocultural factors as well as economic, environmental influences without highlighting cultural or ethnic differences.

Another limitation regarding health promotion of older immigrants was shown in a project on primary prevention and health promotion for older immigrants in Germany (Olbermann et al. 2011). Experts in this field report that older migrants are not a core area in communal work, but are generally seen as a side issue. Therefore, only limited capacities are available. To address these limitations, research in this field has highlighted several points of improvement: providing culturally sensitive services, strengthening existing resources, creating connections between social groups/networks and contact persons and following a settings-based approach. The aim is to situate services in the community to facilitate easy access through decreasing distances and building on existing contacts (Olbermann et al. 2011).

6.2 Care and Health Services

Despite prevention and health promotion initiatives, the ageing of society will result in an increased demand for care. Especially as the literature indicates various health risks in old age, it is important to assess how sickness and disability among older immigrants are currently addressed.

The role of cultural backgrounds and ethnicity on healthcare has been the main focus to understand barriers to health or long-term care access (Arora et al. 2018). For example, social connections, including family members, play an important role in healthcare access and act as facilitators for gaining knowledge about healthcare services. In the literature on long-term care, there is a strong focus on the importance of family for care in immigrant populations. Often references to traditional family structures are emphasised and presented as the main reason why care predominantly takes place in the family (Strumpen 2018; Arora et al. 2018). Care is thus often associated with family resources or other forms of informal support. On the one hand, the family is the preferred option to provide care in a culturally sensitive and private manner. On the other hand, it is acknowledged that the care provided by family members puts stress on the carer and leads to a certain dependence on the family. Furthermore, older migrants rely predominantly on their social capital such as family, friends and social networks to access health services, which are not always available.

While the support from family and informal support systems is crucial to older immigrant populations, it is also essential to recognise economic factors that influence the sociocultural circumstances. Language skills, literacy, education and social responsibilities are greatly influenced by socioeconomic status and need to be taken into account. Especially, as older immigrants endure more socioeconomic risks such as higher poverty rates, it is important to remain critical when the focus is put predominantly on informal solutions to care.

7 Discussion and Conclusion

Despite initial health advantages through selection effects, health in older age is marked by health disadvantages in migrant populations. While younger or newly arrived immigrants display lower mortality rates than native populations, older immigrants experience more health risks in regard to activities of everyday life, mental and subjective health. This is due to long-term socioeconomic stress factors for health that are often experienced in the receiving country. The example of labour immigrants in Germany demonstrates how socioeconomic factors, such as precarious and physically strenuous working conditions, can influence health later in life. It is thus important to look beyond mortality rates at specific points in time and, instead, to consider quality of life and healthy life expectancy over the life course. This perspective should keep in mind the determinants of health before, during and after migration and recognise long-term health stressors in the receiving country.

The presented socioeconomic risks for older labour migrants in Germany should raise awareness of the future health of current (forced) migrants. Short-term perspectives on health and integration have been linked to increased health risks in both labour immigrant populations and forced migration. It is therefore important to acknowledge a long-term perspective that does not neglect the future of (forced) migrants independently of the country of residence. Research and data on the health of forced immigrants in Europe is currently still sparse but will become an important topic in the future. Health determinants need to be identified in order to be able to consider health processes without simply categorising into "healthy", "sick" or "exhausted" migrants.

Lastly, examination of older immigrant health will continue to gain relevance with a view to the increasing percentage of immigrants in the older populations in Germany. Long-term care in older age is one of the main challenges of an ageing society. This includes the provision of access to care for migrant populations, especially as older migrants are an increasing group in many European countries. A critical perspective is needed that recognises sociocultural factors but looks beyond cultural differences to improve prevention, health promotion and long-term care in the future.

Bibliography

Abraído-Lanza, Ana F.; Dohrenwend, Bruce P.; Ng-Mak, Daisy S.; Turner, J. B. (1999): The Latino mortality paradox: a test of the "salmon bias" and healthy migrant hypotheses. In American Journal of Public Health 89 (10), pp. 1543–1548.

Abubakar, Ibrahim; Aldridge, Robert W.; Devakumar, Delan; Orcutt, Miriam; Burns, Rachel; Barreto, Mauricio L. et al. (2018): The UCL–Lancet Commission on Migration and Health: the health of a world on the move. In The Lancet 392 (10164), pp. 2606–2654.

Acevedo-Garcia, Dolores; Sanchez-Vaznaugh, Emma V.; Viruell-Fuentes, Edna A.; Almeida, Joanna (2012): Integrating social epidemiology into immigrant health research: a cross-national framework. In Social science & medicine (1982) 75 (12), pp. 2060–2068.

Aichberger, Marion C.; Schouler-Ocak, Meryam; Mundt, A.; Busch, M. A.; Nickels, E.; Heimann, H. M. et al. (2010): Depression in middle-aged and older first generation migrants in Europe: results from the Survey of Health, Ageing and Retirement in Europe (SHARE). In European Psychiatry 25 (8), pp. 468–475.

Anson, Jon (2004): The Migrant Mortality Advantage: A 70 Month Follow-up of the Brussels Population. In European Journal of Population 20 (3), pp. 191–218.

Arora, Sanjana; Bergland, Astrid; Straiton, Melanie; Rechel, Bernd; Debesay, Jonas (2018): Older migrants' access to healthcare. A thematic synthesis. In International Journal of Migration, Health and Social Care 14 (4), pp. 425–438.

Baykara-Krumme, Helen; Hoff, Andreas (2006): Die Lebenssituation älterer Ausländerinnen und Ausländer in Deutschland. In Clemens Tesch-Römer, Heribert Engstler, Susanne Wurm (Eds.): Altwerden in Deutschland. Sozialer Wandel und individuelle Entwicklung in der zweiten Lebenshälfte. 1. Auflage. Wiesbaden: VS Verlag für Sozialwissenschaften, pp. 447–518.

Baykara-Krumme, Helen; Motel-Klingebiel, Andreas; Schimany, Peter (Eds.) (2012): Viele Welten des Alterns. Ältere Migranten im alternden Deutschland. Wiesbaden: Springer VS (Alter(n) und Gesellschaft, 22).

Becker, Sascha O.; Ferrara, Andreas (2019): Consequences of forced migration: A survey of recent findings. In Labour Economics Article in Press.

Beiser, Morton (2005): The health of immigrants and refugees in Canada. In Canadian Journal of Public Health/Revue Canadienne de Sante'e Publique 96 Suppl 2, S30-44.

Bolzman, Claudio (2014): Older refugees. In Elena Fiddian-Qasmiyeh (Ed.): The Oxford handbook of refugee and forced migration studies. 1. ed. Oxford: Oxford Univ. Press, pp. 409–419.

Bolzman, Claudio; Poncioni-Derigo, Raffaella; Vial, Marie (2012): Elderly immigrants in Switzerland: Exploring their social and health situation. In Analele Ştiintifice 5 (1), pp. 174–190.

Bolzman, Claudio; Poncioni-Derigo, Raffaella; Vial, Marie; Fibbi, Rosita (2004): Older labour migrants' well being in Europe. The case of Switzerland. In Ageing and Society 24 (03), pp. 411–429.

Brzoska, Patrick; Ellert, Ute; Kimil, Ahmet; Razum, Oliver; Sass, Anke-Christine; Salman, Ramazan; Zeeb, Hajo (2015): Reviewing the topic of migration and health as a new national health target for Germany. In Int J Public Health 60 (1), pp. 13–20.

Brzoska, Patrick; Voigtländer, Sven; Reutin, Barbara; Yilmaz-Aslan, Yüce; Barz, Irina; Starikow, Klara et al. (2010): Rehabilitative Versorgung und gesundheitsbedingte Frühberentung von Personen mit Migrationshintergrund in Deutschland: Abschlussbericht. In 0174-4992 FB402, VII, 124.

Bundesamt für Migration und Flüchtlinge (Ed.) (2018): Das Bundesamt in Zahlen 2017. Asyl, Migration und Integration. Nürnberg.

Carnein, Marie; Milewski, Nadja; Doblhammer, Gabriele; Nusselder, Wilma J. (2015): Health Inequalities of Immigrants: Patterns and Determinants of Health Expectancies of Turkish Migrants Living in Germany. In Gabriele Doblhammer (Ed.): Health among the elderly in Germany. New evidence on disease, disability and care need. Opladen u.a: Budrich (Beiträge zur Bevölkerungswissenschaft, 46), pp. 157–190.

Ciobanu, Ruxandra Oana; Fokkema, Tineke; Nedelcu, Mihaela (2016): Ageing as a migrant. Vulnerabilities, agency and policy implications. In Journal of Ethnic and Migration Studies 43 (2), pp. 164–181.

Evandrou, Maria; Falkingham, Jane; Feng, Zhixin; Vlachantoni, Athina (2016): Ethnic inequalities in limiting health and self-reported health in later life revisited. In Journal of epidemiology and community health 70 (7), pp. 653–662.

Frank, Laura; Yesil-Jürgens, Rahsan; Razum, Oliver; Bozorgmehr, Kayvan; Schenk, Liane; Gilsdorf, Andreas et al. (2017): Gesundheit und gesundheitliche Versorgung von Asylsuchenden und Flüchtlingen in Deutschland. In Journal of Health Monitoring 2 (1), pp. 24–47.

Gustafsson, Björn; Mac Innes, Hannah; Österberg, Torun (2019): Older people in Sweden without means: on the importance of age at immigration for being 'twice poor'. In Ageing and Society 39 (6), pp. 1172–1199.

Hoffmann, Elke; Romeu Gordo, Laura (2016): Lebenssituation älterer Menschen mit Migrationshintergrund. In Statistisches Bundesamt/Wissenschaftszentrum Berlin für Sozialforschung (Hrsg.), Datenreport.

Klaus, Daniela; Baykara-Krumme, Helen (2017): Die Lebenssituationen von Personen in der zweiten Lebenshälfte mit und ohne Migrationshintergrund. In Katharina Mahne, Julia Katharina Wolff, Julia Simonson, Clemens Tesch-Römer (Eds.): Altern im Wandel. Wiesbaden: Springer Fachmedien Wiesbaden, pp. 359–379.

Kohls, Martin (2012): Leben ältere Migranten länger? In Helen Baykara-Krumme, Andreas Motel-Klingebiel, Peter Schimany (Eds.): Viele Welten des Alterns. Ältere Migranten im alternden Deutschland. Wiesbaden: Springer VS (Alter(n) und Gesellschaft, 22), pp. 201–222.

Kristiansen, Maria; Razum, Oliver; Tezcan-Güntekin, Hürrem; Krasnik, Allan (2016): Aging and health among migrants in a European perspective. In Public Health Rev 37 (1), p. 46.

Lanari, Donatella; Bussini, Odoardo (2012): International migration and health inequalities in later life. In Ageing and Society 32 (06), pp. 935–962.

Lariscy, Joseph T.; Hummer, Robert A.; Hayward, Mark D. (2015): Hispanic older adult mortality in the United States: new estimates and an assessment of factors shaping the Hispanic paradox. In Demography 52 (1), pp. 1–14.

Lu, Yao; Zhang, Alice Tianbo (2016): The link between migration and health. In Felicity Thomas (Ed.): Handbook of Migration and Health: Edward Elgar Publishing, pp. 19–43.

Markides, Kyriakos S.; Eschbach, Karl (2011): Hispanic Paradox in Adult Mortality in the United States. In Richard G. Rogers, Eileen M. Crimmins (Eds.): International Handbook of Adult Mortality, vol. 2. Dordrecht: Springer Science+Business Media B.V (International Handbooks of Population, 2), pp. 227–240.

Norredam, Marie; Olsbjerg, Maja; Petersen, Jorgen H.; Juel, Knud; Krasnik, Allan (2012): Inequalities in mortality among refugees and immigrants compared to native Danes – a historical prospective cohort study. In BMC Public Health 12 (1), p. 757.

Olbermann, Elke; Drewnik, Arthur; Lak, Claudia; Naegele, Gerhard (2011): Gesundheitsförderung und Primärprevention bei älteren Menschen mit Migrationshintergrund. Schlussbericht zum Forschungsprojekt. Edited by Forschungsgesellschaft für Gerontologie e.V. Institut für Gerontologie an der TU Dortmund. Dortmund. Available online at https://www.gesundheitliche-chancengleichheit.de/docext1.php?idx=276&pfb=44518.pdf.

Özcan, Veysel; Seifert, Wolfgang (2006): Lebenslage älterer Migrantinnen und Migranten in Deutschland. In Lebenssituation und Gesundheit älterer Migranten in Deutschland. Expertisen zum Fünften Altenbericht der Bundesregierung 6, pp. 7–75.

Pavli, Androula; Maltezou, Helena (2017): Health problems of newly arrived migrants and refugees in Europe. In Journal of travel medicine 24 (4).

Razum, Oliver (2006a): Commentary: of salmon and time travellers--musing on the mystery of migrant mortality. In Int. J. Epidemiol. 35 (4), pp. 919–921.

Razum, Oliver (2006b): Migration, Mortalitat und der Healthy-migrant-Effekt. In Matthias Richter, Klaus Hurrelmann (Eds.): Gesundheitliche Ungleichheit. Grundlagen, Probleme, Konzepte, vol. 89. Wiesbaden: VS Verlag für Sozialwissenschaften | GWV Fachverlage GmbH Wiesbaden, pp. 255–270.

Razum, Oliver; Spallek, Jacob (2012): Erklärungsmodelle zum Zusammenhang zwischen Migration und Gesundheit im Alter. In Helen Baykara-Krumme, Andreas Motel-Klingebiel, Peter Schimany (Eds.): Viele Welten des Alterns. Ältere Migranten im alternden Deutschland. Wiesbaden: Springer VS (Alter(n) und Gesellschaft, 22), pp. 161–180.

Razum, Oliver; Zeeb, Hajo; Meesmann, Uta; Schenk, Liane; Bredehorst, Maren; Brzoska, Patrick et al. (2008): Migration und Gesundheit. Schwerpunktbericht der Gesundheitsberichterstattung. With assistance of Hannelore Neuhauser, Ursula Brucks. Edited by Robert Koch-Institut (RKI) (Gesundheitsberichterstattung des Bundes).

Reus-Pons, Matias; Kibele, Eva U. B.; Janssen, Fanny (2017): Differences in healthy life expectancy between older migrants and non-migrants in three European countries over time. In International Journal of Public Health 62 (5), pp. 531–540.

Ronellenfitsch, Ulrich; Kyobutungi, Catherine; Becher, Heiko; Razum, Oliver (2006): All-cause and cardiovascular mortality among ethnic German immigrants from the Former Soviet Union: a cohort study. In BMC Public Health 6, p. 16.

Schimany, Peter; Baykara-Krumme, Helen (2012): Zur Geschichte und demografischen Bedeutung älterer Migrantinnen und Migranten in Deutschland. In Helen Baykara-Krumme, Andreas Motel-Klingebiel, Peter Schimany (Eds.): Viele Welten des Alterns. Ältere Migranten im alternden Deutschland. Wiesbaden: Springer VS (Alter(n) und Gesellschaft, 22), pp. 43–73.

Schimany, Peter; Rühl, Stefan; Kohls, Martin (2012): Ältere Migrantinnen und Migranten. Entwicklungen, Lebenslagen, Perspektiven. Edited by Bundesamt für Migration und Flüchtlinge (BAMF) (Forschungsbericht, 18).

Singh, Gopal K.; Hiatt, Robert A. (2006): Trends and disparities in socioeconomic and behavioural characteristics, life expectancy, and cause-specific mortality of native-born and foreign-born populations in the United States, 1979-2003. In Int. J. Epidemiol. 35 (4), pp. 903–919.

Solé-Auró, Aïda; Crimmins, Eileen M. (2008): Health of Immigrants in European countries. In The International migration review 42 (4), pp. 861–876.

Spallek, Jacob; Reeske, Anna; Zeeb, Hajo; Razum, Oliver (2016): Models of migration and health. In Felicity Thomas (Ed.): Handbook of Migration and Health: Edward Elgar Publishing, pp. 44–58.

Strumpen, Sarina (2018): Ältere Pendelmigranten aus der Türkei. Alters- und Versorgungserwartungen im Kontext von Migration, Kultur und Religion. Bielefeld: transcript (Kultur und soziale Praxis).

Uitenbroek, Daan G.; Verhoeff, Arnoud P. (2002): Life expectancy and mortality differences between migrant groups living in Amsterdam, the Netherlands. In Social science & medicine 54 (9), pp. 1379–1388.

Viruell-Fuentes, Edna A.; Miranda, Patricia Y.; Abdulrahim, Sawsan (2012): More than culture. Structural racism, intersectionality theory, and immigrant health. In Social science & medicine 75 (12), pp. 2099–2106.

Warnes, Anthony M.; Friedrich, Klaus; Kellaher, Leonie; Torres, Sandra (2004): The diversity and welfare of older migrants in Europe. In Ageing and Society 24 (03), pp. 307–326.

Refugee-Environment Nexus: Socio-Cultural Acceptability of Eco-Friendly Options for Household Cooking in Kenyan Refugee Camps

Godffrey Nyongesa Nato[1]

Keywords: Refugee camp, energy options, household cooking

Abstract

Emergency situations require that the migrating communities are provided with basic services. The basic services often revolve around the provision of temporary shelter, food, water, basic sanitation and health. A lot of infrastructural interventions have often focused on shelter, water and sanitation. Investment in sustainable energy infrastructure has not been given much attention. It has probably been looked at as a long-term investment and was thus deemed inappropriate in the context of immediate emergency relief (Lehne et al. 2016). The development of an energy infrastructure has not been well developed in most refugee camps. According to UNHCR only 7% of funds received are allocated to the energy and environment sector in Kakuma Refugee Camp, most of which is channelled towards the procurement and supply of firewood to the over 185,000 refugees. With their limited budgets, the agencies responsible for firewood supply never meet the demands, thus necessitating supplementation by refugees themselves, often from local resources. This has placed pressure on the environment within and outside of refugee camps, with attendant conflicts with host communities. Responsible organizations have thence come up with various initiatives that would address the cooking energy requirements but at the same

---

1   Godffrey Nyongesa Nato | County Government of Mombasa | natogodffrey@gmail.com

© Springer Fachmedien Wiesbaden GmbH, part of Springer Nature 2020
K. Crepaz et al. (eds.), *Health in Diversity – Diversity in Health*,
https://doi.org/10.1007/978-3-658-29177-8_7

time relieve pressure on the sensitive environment within and around refugee camps. This paper takes a critical look at three of such initiatives and their acceptability among the refugees. The paper underscores the need for socio-cultural considerations with regard to target refugee communities when designing eco-friendly energy options.

Contents

Abstract 121

1   Introduction 123

2   Research Problem 123

3   Methodology 124

4   Findings and Discussion 124

4.1 Sustainable Provision of Fuel Wood 124

4.2 Provision of Energy-Efficient Cooking Stoves 128

4.3 Alternative Source of Fuel: Container-Based Toilet with Solid Fuel
    Briquettes 129

5   Conclusion 132

Bibliography 133

1   Introduction

The link between an influx of refugees in a location and environmental degradation has long been established. Increased refugee camp populations are often hypothesized to trigger biodiversity loss, soil erosion, air pollution, water depletion and contamination, as well as energy and transportation problems. To address such consequences, humanitarian agencies, organized under UNHCR, often put in place care and maintenance programmes which focus on providing refugees with food, shelter, and other basic services. The provision of the said services has often been based on the assumption that the refugee situation is temporary, thereby failing to address the long-term needs, situation and prospects of refugees and host communities, considering that displacement situations might drag on for several decades.

Recent developments show a paradigm shift focusing on the integration of refugees in host communities and on the reduction of over-dependence on humanitarian aid. This shift requires aid agencies to develop durable solutions that are ecosystem-friendly.

Located in Turkana County in north-western Kenya, Kakuma Refugee Camp was established 1992 to serve Sudanese refugees. However, it has since expanded to serve refugees from other counties in East Africa and the Horn of Africa. The camp is currently hosting about 188,513 refugees and asylum seekers, about 15% of the total population of Turkana County. The camp hosts 40% of the total refugee population in Kenya. The majority are from South Sudan (109,140), followed by Somalia (33,966), DRC (12,305), Ethiopia (10,547) and Burundi (10,173)[1]. About 21 nationalities are found in the camp. The ongoing care and maintenance programme, which was based on the assumption that the refugee situation is temporary, focuses on providing refugees with basic humanitarian assistance, including free food, non-food items and basic services.

2   Research Problem

Emergency situations require that the migrating communities are provided with basic services that include provision of temporary shelter, food, water, basic sanitation and health. A lot of infrastructural interventions have often focused on shelter, water and sanitation. Investment in sustainable energy infrastructure has not been given much attention, probably because it is regarded as a long-term investment and thus inappropriate in the context of immediate emergency

---

1   Figures obtained from www.unhcr.org/data, retrieved on 5th March 2019

relief. With a limited budget, the agencies responsible for energy provision can never meet the demands, necessitating supplementation by refugees themselves often from local resources. This has placed pressure on the environment within and outside refugee camps, with the attendant conflicts with host communities further compounding the vulnerability of the refugees.

There has been increasing interest in the refugee-environment nexus among aid agencies, particularly for the development of initiatives that would address the cooking energy requirements of refugees while at the same time relieve pressure on the sensitive refugee/host environment. Unsustainable and ineffi-cient cooking technologies or practices can have a direct impact on food prepa-ration, and indirect effects on local biomass resources overexploitation, the health of locals, and social conflicts between hosted and hosting communities (Riva et al. 2017). In the past decade, UNHCR has taken an environmental pro-tection approach towards household energy focusing on: sustainable provision of fuel wood, promotion of efficient energy use, and supply of alternative fuels (Lyytinen, 2009). This paper takes a critical look at the initiatives within the three focal areas and the acceptability thereof among the refugees within the social cultural context of Kakuma Refugee Camp in Kenya.

3   Methodology

The methodology employed to collect data for this study was in-depth inter-views with refugees and staff of the Norwegian Refugee Council and LOKADO[2], who are involved in sanitation and energy services respectively in Kakuma Refugee Camp. Data was collected over a period of two weeks in Feb-ruary 2019, involving four project specialist officers and thirty refugees associ-ated with the provision of firewood, energy saving cooking stoves, and fuel briquettes.

4   Findings and Discussion

4.1   Sustainable Provision of Fuel Wood

Firewood remains the main source of fuel for cooking in refugee camps (Lyyt-inen, 2009) and it is projected to take considerable time and effort for sustaina-ble alternatives. The current demand for firewood in Kakuma Refugee Camp stands at approximately 60-90kgs per person per month against a supply of 5kgs per person per month by the UNHCR implementing partner, LOKADO.

---

2   Lotus Kenya Action for Development Organization, NGO mandated by UNHCR to provide energy and environmental services

UNHCR has contracted this local NGO (LOKADO) to provide firewood to all the 188,000 refugees in Kakuma. The NGO supplies 10kgs of dry firewood per person for every two months.

Figure 1: Firewood distribution centre in Kakuma Refugee Camp (Nato, 2019)

Cognizant of the fact that replacing firewood as a main source of fuel for cooking takes considerable time and effort, the agency given the responsibility to supply firewood to the refugee population has resorted to species selection, targeting the invasive species *Prosopis juliflora*[3], in order to protect the environment. This environmental protection option takes advantage of a government directive on the utilization of this invasive species which has raised serious environmental concerns in Turkana West sub-county, where the camp is located. Although this shrub has a number of disadvantages necessitating its eradication, the invasive species is a prolific seeder, fast-growing, and producing good

---

3   An invasive species. The Kenyan government has given directives for its eradication

quality fuel of high calorific value even when freshly cut (Mwangi and Swallow, 2008), which makes it ideal for household cooking. 70 percent of the current firewood supply comes from *Prosopis juliflora* and 30 percent is harvested from dead wood of indigenous tree species[4].

All the refugees interviewed revealed that the firewood supplied was not sufficient, necessitating other interventions. 47 percent of the 30 respondents indicated that, in order to meet the shortfall in the supply from UNHCR, they sought more firewood from the surrounding forest and bushes, whereas 40 percent purchased charcoal from local communities. This initiative promotes the existing trade between local communities and refugees where more often than not, the trading of butter is practiced, involving food rations from the refugee camp and, in turn, firewood or charcoal from local communities.

It emerged from the interviews that firewood was not the most preferred source of household cooking energy. Charcoal happens to be the most preferred source of fuel because of its perceived health safety, and as it is viewed as a cheaper alternative to gas that can be easily traded with the host community. In fact, 64 percent of the refugees interviewed confirmed a preference for charcoal over firewood, while the rest preferred either gas or bioethanol.

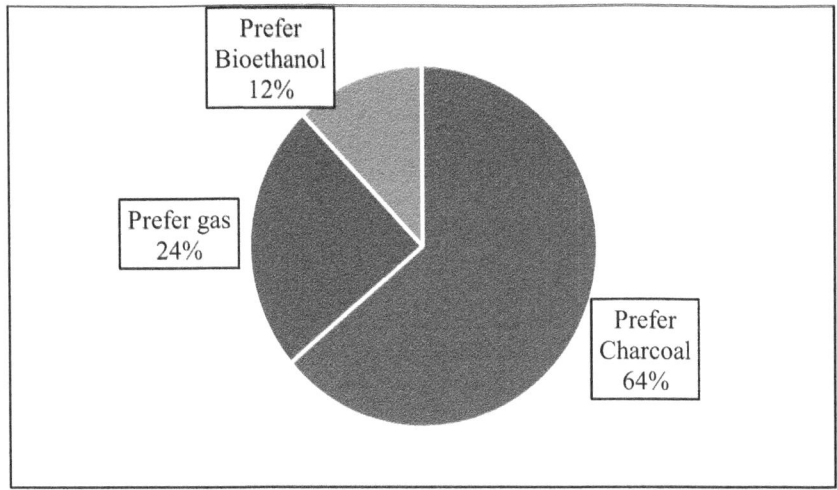

Figure 2: Preference for various energy options over firewood (Nato, 2019)

---

4   Interview with project manager, LOKADO, 21 February 2019

The preference for charcoal over firewood and other sources is evident in the following narratives, where for reasons of easy availability of charcoal from the local host community, the refugees opted to exchange food rations for charcoal. Two narratives by women refugee explained this as follows:

> 'As the firewood given to us is too little, barely enough to last few weeks, we have to look elsewhere. So we use some of the food rations given to us, to exchange them for charcoal from the local host community members'.[5]

> 'The firewood supplied is not sufficient enough to cater for the whole month, and the family has to depend on different sources [of fuel] for cooking. My husband gets charcoal from the neighbourhood [i.e. local host communities outside the camp]. We prefer the charcoal as it is easier to use than the firewood. The firewood produces a lot of smoke and pollutes the entire house area and even the neighbours' [houses]'.[6]

As explained in the above narrative, the preference for charcoal was also due to the health implications caused by firewood smoke. The compactness of households and houses within close proximity in the camp affects the health of the inhabitants due to smoke rising during the cooking process – both inside and outside the house, as is described below:

> 'The smoke from the firewood is unbearable. It hurts the eyes and also spoils the utensils. When you have kids in the house, the kids are affected. The kids cough and their eyes are affected too because of the smoke'.[7]

Apart from health risks, there are other safety concerns, such as the risk for women to be sexually assaulted on their trip outside the camp to fetch firewood:

> 'There are cases where women are sexually abused or raped as they go out of the camp to collect firewood'.[8]

Charcoal is expensive compared to firewood, hence some refugee families buy firewood from other refugee families that use other alternatives.

> 'As the firewood given to each house is not enough, we have to buy firewood from other fellow refugees who sell theirs during distribution. We would prefer charcoal, but we can't afford it. Buying firewood from other refugees [who use other types of

---

5   Interview with a Sudanese refugee woman in Kakuma Camp, zone 1, block 1, 23 February 2019.

6   Interview with a Ugandan refugee woman in Kakuma Camp, zone 2, block 12, 24 February 2019.

7   Interview with a Sudanese refugee woman in Kakuma Camp, zone 1, block 9, 23 February 2019.

8   Interview with a refugee woman in Kakuma Camp, zone 2, block 1, 24 February 2019.

fuel for cooking in the camps] is a cheaper option to our family as charcoal is expensive'.[9]

However, charcoal is cheaper compared to gas as a fuel used for cooking. Some households have the means to buy gas and prefer the option of gas for cooking. Nevertheless, the majority cannot afford the use of gas and the second best option is charcoal:

'There are few among us who use gas for cooking. It's a very good option but very expensive. Most of us cannot afford it. So when our firewood runs out, we have no option but buy charcoal as it's better than firewood'.[10]

4.2   Provision of Energy-Efficient Cooking Stoves

One of the traditional responses by aid agencies to wood fuel shortage has been the promotion of fuel-efficient cooking stoves. Like other fuel-saving systems, it relies on the two principles of enclosing the fire and insulating the cooking stove (Lynch, 2002). The agency responsible for energy established a production unit within the camp to produce and supply efficient cooking stoves to all refugee households. The cooking stoves are assembled from locally sourced materials. The lining material is made from clay soils sourced from Turkana and the neighbouring Baringo County. The linings are prepared in locally configured kilns within the camp, employing local population.

The introduction of the stove aimed at conserving cooking energy, thereby reducing wastage associated with traditional cooking stoves.

'To avoid fuel wastage while cooking, we sought out the alternative of promoting fuel-efficient cooking stoves. This has helped reduce fuel wastage to an extent, helping to conserve up to 30% of energy'.[11]

This strategy ensures that the firewood rations provided last longer and it reduces the need to seek for firewood beyond the boundaries of the refugee camp. However, there are serious doubts regarding whether 30% energy conservation can be achieved, putting into consideration how the cooking stove is used. According to figure 3, the cooking stove can use either charcoal or firewood and is often used outside dwelling units. In the case of firewood, enclosure and control

---

9   Interview with a Congolese Refugee woman in Kakuma Camp, zone 1, block 3, 23 February 2019.

10   Interview with a South Sudanese refugee woman in Kakuma Camp, zone 2, block 7, 24 February 2019.

11   Interview with LOKADO official in Kakuma Refugee Camp, 21 February 2019.

Figure 3: Cooking setup by use of energy-saving cooking stove in Kakuma Refugee Camp (Nato, 2019)

of airflow is difficult to achieve, thereby compromising the efficiency of the stove.

4.3 Alternative Source of Fuel: Container-Based Toilet with Solid Fuel Briquettes

The UNHCR in conjunction with the World Food Programme's SAFE initiative has a multi-faceted approach to meet the energy needs of the refugees through sustainable energy related activities that protect both people and the environment. One of these initiatives is the production of briquettes as an alternative fuel source and the establishment of briquette production units (UNHCR, 2016). Biomass briquettes have advantages with regard to environmental protection and health living. Besides production and sale of the briquettes can form a good income generating activity. The shift to biomass briquettes has the advantage of lowering firewood consumption hence easing the pressure on local forests. Interventions to make people aware of the advantage of briquettes often go hand in hand with programmes to train and employ refugees to make briquettes and sell them (UNHCR, 2017). Briquettes have a high calorific value; however, related social and health implications inhibit acceptability thereof in Kakuma Refugee Camp.

The biomass briquettes produced for use in Kakuma Refugee Camp use human faecal material as the main raw material. As such, a container-based portable toilet has been designed to harvest and store the material before its transportation to the briquette production plant.

Figure 4: Container-based toilet for harvesting faecal material (Nato, 2019)

Despite its functional design, the portable toilet for harvesting material for bio-mass briquettes has been met with scepticism and doubtful acceptance on a social and cultural level. The biggest acceptability challenge is associated with the harvesting of faecal material. It is expected that the faecal content be harvested devoid of urine and water, and this is where the challenge lies. Furthermore, on visiting the toilet the Somali community, being Muslim, practice wash as opposed to wipe after visiting the toilet. The above design, however, is ideal for the wipe hence locking out a significant proportion of refugees, considering that the Somali community is the second largest in the camp. Secondly, the faecal material is retained in the container for a whole day before collection. Persons using the toilet are expected to spread ash on the faecal matter after each use. This arrangement is not compatible with the culture of some South Sudanese communities.

> 'In Kakuma, a number of communities from South Sudan are culturally prohibited from a defecation process that mixes contents of the head of the household, the spouse and that of children'.[12]

This design is therefore not acceptable to such communities. Consequently, the design would also require training and retraining on the proper use to avoid a mix of liquid and solid excrements. The design raises important hygiene concerns as indicated by respondents, who raised the following concerns:

> 'The faeces in the container produce a bad smell which distracts the people living around the household. This happens when we fail to pour ashes or charcoal residue over the faeces'.[13]

> 'The toilet is smelly, attracting flies which move around and may contaminate food. It is also difficult to maintain cleanliness since no water is allowed to leak into the container'.[14]

> 'There is no proper knowledge of the cleaning process of the bucket that holds the faeces. People need to be made aware of how the entire cleaning process works for the project to be accepted by the community. [...] the briquettes also take a lot of time to light up'.[15]

While the end product has very high calorific value for cooking, it is designed for outdoor use only. This is due to the characteristic foul odour while burning. Besides, it is not as simple as charcoal to use, as additions cannot be made during the cooking process. It is therefore associated with inconveniences when preparing several meals. An interview with some of those who use the briquettes raised the following concerns:

---

12   Interview with an official from the Norwegian Refugee Council in Kakuma Refugee Camp, 21 February 2019.

13   Interview with a South Sudanese refugee, Kakuma Refugee Camp, 26 February 2019.

14   Interview with a South Sudanese refugee, Kakuma Refugee Camp, 26 February 2019.

15   Interview with a refugee, Kakuma Refugee Camp, zone 2, block 6, 24 February 2019.

'It produces an abnormal smell when lighting and cooking, leading to victimization by neighbours. The smoke produced when igniting the briquettes is felt in the neighbourhood and is associated with flu.[16]

'Some people refuse to eat food that is cooked with recycled faeces.[17]

It is evident that the design and operational modalities of the portable toilet raised health, cultural and social concerns that limit its adoption. According to Chatham House (2016), any successful and improved cooking programme must also consider the cultural and operational aspects of stove design alongside operating costs, financing options and promotional approaches.

5   Conclusion

Amidst the availability of alternative and environmentally friendly options for household energy requirements, firewood and wood-based products such as charcoal remain the primary sources of energy for the majority of refugees. In Kakuma Refugee Camp, the use of firewood is predominant because it falls within the usual relief supplies, while the preference for charcoal is influenced by its availability within the host community. Charcoal is a commodity of trade between the refugees and host communities and more often than not, it's bartered for food rations.

The adoption of efficient energy cooking stoves has been impressive owing to the fact that local communities have been sufficiently informed; moreover, they are produced within the camp, often with local resources and a local workforce. However, the efficiency of the cooking stoves supplied requires further analysis since efficiency depends on how accurately they have been used (Gunning, 2014). On the other hand, the adoption of briquettes as a source of energy has been hampered by social and cultural concerns related to the design and source of the raw material.

The key to establishing a sustainable fuel solution for refugee camp populations lies in addressing socio-cultural aspects as well as health concerns that would otherwise curtail its adoption. There is a need for designing an appropriate faecal harvesting infrastructure, as well as a special cooking stove for briquettes that not only addresses the burning efficiency but also minimises the characteristic smell. Other alternatives should be explored such as the adoption of community cookers that convert solid waste generated in the camp into energy.

---

16   Interview with a refugee, Kakuma Refugee Camp, 28 February 2019
17   Interview with a refugee, Kakuma Refugee Camp, 27 February 2019

Bibliography

Barbieri, Jacopo (2019) Comprehensive Energy Solutions in Humanitarian Settlements. From the Energy-Food Nexus to a Holistic Approach to Energy Planning. A Thesis.

Chatham House (2016) A Review of Cooking Systems for Humanitarian Settings. The Royal Institute of International Affairs, London.

Gunning, Rebecca (2014) The Current State of Sustainable Energy Provision for Displaced Populations: An Analysis. Chatham House, London.

Lehne, Johana; Blyth, William; Lahn, Glada; Bazilian, Morgan and Grafham, Owen (2016) Energy Services for Refugees and Displaced People. In: *Energy Strategy Reviews*. 13-14 (2016) 134-146.

Lynch, Maureen (2002) Reducing Environmental Damage Caused by the Collection of Cooking Fuel by Refugees. Refuge. Vol. 21 (1).

Lyytinen, Eveliina (2009) Household Energy in Refugee and IDP Camps: Challenges and Solutions for UNHCR. In: *New Issues Refugee Research* 2009:20.

Mwangi, Esther and Swallow, Brent (2008) *Prosopis juliflora* Invasion and Rural Livelihoods in the Lake Baringo Area of Kenya. In: *Conservation and Society*; 6(2):130-140.

Riva, Fabio; Colombo, Emanuela and Barbieri, Jacopo (2017) Cooking in Refugee Camps and Informal Settlements: A Review of Available Technologies and Impacts on the Socio-Economic and Environmental Perspective. In: *Sustainable Energy Technologies and Assessments*.

UNHCR (2016) Kenya Comprehensive Refugee Programme 2016: Programming for Solutions, UNHCR.

UNHCR (2017) Container-Based Toilets with Solid Fuel Briquettes as a Reuse Product – Best Practice Guidelines for Refugee Camps.

Social Integration and Racist Discrimination of Young African Refugees in Germany

Albert Scherr[1]

Keywords: Refugees, Integration, Legal Framework, Social Support

Abstract

The article examines the situation of young African refugees in Germany on the basis of an empirical study. Biographical interviews were a central component of this study. The different burdens that refugees have to cope with after their arrival in Germany are shown. This concerns not least the handling of a hardly transparent constellation of legal and institutional conditions as well as the uncertainty of a future perspective. The high importance of informal and institutional support becomes just as clear as the fact that considerable personal contributions on the part of the refugees are necessary.

Contents

Abstract 135

1   Introduction 137

2   Central Burdens and Risks 138

3   Political and Legal Framework 139

1   Albert Scherr | Pädagogische Hochschule Freiburg | scherr@ph-freiburg.de

© Springer Fachmedien Wiesbaden GmbH, part of Springer Nature 2020
K. Crepaz et al. (eds.), *Health in Diversity – Diversity in Health*,
https://doi.org/10.1007/978-3-658-29177-8_8

4   Racial Discrimination..141

5   Young Refugees, Social Support, and Their Own Contribution to
     Coping with the Situation..142

6   Some General Remarks on the Relationship between Flight, Social
     Policy and Health Issues 145

Bibliography 147

1   Introduction

In this article, I will present some reflections on the challenges and burdens refugees face after their flight to Germany and on the conditions under which their social integration can succeed. I will only go into health issues a little more closely using one case study. However, I will be dealing with topics such as social stress, experiences of failure and quality of social support, which in my view are obviously relevant for a person's health. My considerations are partly based on biographical interviews that we conducted in an ongoing research project with young refugees from West and East Africa (Scherr/Breit 2018 and 2019).[1]

When making statements about the living conditions of refugees in Germany, nevertheless, considerable differences between subgroups have to be taken into account; generalisations are problematic. An important reason for this is that the living conditions and future prospects of refugees in Germany are influenced by complex legal provisions. Therefore, focus shall be put on the situation of young male refugees who have come to Europe and Germany as unaccompanied minors. You might get the impression that the situation is, overall, complicated and almost absurd; but then, in fact, you have understood a central aspect of the considerations mentioned here.

First of all, I would like to share some important data on this topic: At the end of the year 2016 about 65,000 persons were registered as unaccompanied minors by the responsible institutions (Tangermann/Hoffmeyer-Zlotnik 2018: 19). If all refugees under the age of 25 are additionally taken into account, the number amounts to more than 500,000 persons. Over 70% of those who enter Germany as unaccompanied minors have already reached the age of 16 years, and over 90% are male adolescents (ibid.). Experts assume that this is because young male adolescents are willing to take risks, and are considered to be healthier and less vulnerable than other subgroups of the population. Therefore, they are believed to better cope with the risks involved in the process of fleeing their home countries. The most significant countries of origin are Afghanistan, Ethiopia, Eritrea, Gambia, Guinea, Iraq and Syria.

---

1   Essential findings of the relevant research in German are summarised in these publications: BMFSFJ 2017; Lechner/Huber 2017; Müller 2014; Tangermann/Hoffmeyer-Zlotnik 2018.

2   Central Burdens and Risks

It is not hard to determine that young refugees are, in terms of their biographical and present circumstances, affected by social and psychological stress. As numerous studies from international research have shown, this applies firstly to the living conditions and experiences that have led to their flight. In the case of our interviews, this ranges from neglect and lack of perspective in the country of origin to direct confrontation with war and violence. Secondly, the flight itself was and is often a process that is characterised by serious afflictions, such as traumatic experiences of abuse, torture, or the death of friends and travel companions. Thirdly, after entering Europe, young refugees find themselves in a situation in which they have to adapt to living conditions which are fundamentally different from those in their country of origin and the countries they transit during their flight. They are confronted with an assortment of institutions, legal regulations and informal expectations which they have to adapt to, even if they can hardly see through them. Furthermore, unaccompanied minors have to cope with this situation separated from their families of origin, i.e. without emotional support and practical assistance from their families. In some cases, this is combined with the expectation of making money as quickly as possible in order to be able to pay off the costs of the flight and contribute to the livelihood of the family left behind in the country of origin.[2] Under the conditions of the German labour market, this is usually only possible if some knowledge of the German language and vocational qualifications have been acquired, as there is little demand for unskilled work. This results in a pressure to qualify.

From a social science perspective, it is obvious that the situation outlined above involves numerous burdens and risks of failure. As has become evident in our research, it is also relatively easy to explain in social science terms, why some young refugees fail when faced with these challenges, i.e. manifest serious psychological symptoms, are unable to meet school or job requirements or even become delinquent. Empirically, however, it can also be seen that a large part of young refugees is successfully coping with these difficult circumstances (see Mattes 2018). I will go on to explain why this is so and which factors contribute to their successful coping with the refugee situation.

---

2   An instructive typology of the motives and mandates of young refugees is proposed by Étiemble/Zanna 2013.

3 Political and Legal Framework

First, I would like to give some brief background information on a) the political discourses and b) the socio-political and legal contexts that are important for the understanding of the situation of refugees in Germany.

a) As far as the political discourses are concerned, it should first be noted that a broad debate has developed in which uncontrolled migration is seen as a threat. As a result, numerous measures have been implemented to reduce unwanted migration from Africa to Europe. One element of this is the attempt to impose a clear distinction between so-called "real" refugees who are entitled to protection and those who are presumed to be abusing refugee law (Scherr 2018a). In this context, it is openly discussed that these measures have led people to choose more dangerous escape routes to Europe, and it is beyond dispute that a consequence of this is a growing number of refugees dying on their way through the Sahara and across the Mediterranean (Campbell 2019). In this context, a controversy has developed over the social integration of young refugees: On the one hand, they are seen as potential workers who can contribute to meeting the demand for labour in the industrial and skilled manual labour sector, and in the low-skilled sector of the service industry too. This is apparent from the fact that representatives of the business community have repeatedly demanded a right of residence for those refugees who have taken up employment or vocational training even when courts refused to accept them as refugees under existing law. This was also evident in our study: In one of our cases, a company actively prevented the deportation of a refugee by employing a lawyer and giving an employment contract to the person concerned already at an early stage. On the other hand, young refugees from Africa are considered in the public discourse as a particularly problematic group. This is especially true with regard to crime, drug trafficking and sexual offences: incidents in which young refugees were involved in violent and sexual offences have been widely reported in the media and have led to the dissemination of generalised prejudices that portray young refugees as potential offenders (Scherr 2018). As a result, it remains controversial whether young refugees are more likely to be regarded as a group whose social integration through schooling and vocational training represents an important and worthwhile social challenge, or as a threat that must be viewed primarily from a security perspective.

b) This controversy corresponds to a highly contradictory legal framework concerning the treatment of young refugees. Social policy and social law regulations aimed at promoting the social integration of young people overlap with regulations under alien law and refugee law aimed at preventing undesirable immigration (Cremer 2014; Schaumann 2016). The result is a complex legal situation, which is scarcely transparent to those affected.[3] Roughly simplified, the following can be said in this respect:

b1) For young refugees who enter Germany as minors, the provisions of the UN Convention on the Rights of the Child apply and they fall within the legal competence of the German Child and Youth Welfare Act, which is a branch of social legislation in Germany. This has several consequences: Up to the age of 18, unaccompanied minors are effectively protected from deportation, unlike adults and families. Their legal status as minors guarantees them access to the education system and support through state welfare measures and social work. In concrete terms, this means for example, that young refugees up to the age of 18 are obliged and entitled to attend school. If they entered the country without their parents, they will not be forced to live in refugee camps, where adult refugees and families have to stay up to 18 months. Rather, they are accommodated in independent child and youth welfare institutions, where they are taken care of by social workers. They are also entitled to health care, to the treatment of illnesses and, if necessary and achievable, to psychotherapeutic measures. Moreover, measures under the Child and Youth Welfare Act can be extended beyond the age of 18 up to the age of 21. Consequently, in comparison, unaccompanied minors are a relatively privileged subgroup of refugees.

b2) However, all of this takes place in a situation that is superimposed by the provisions of refugee law. For young refugees from Africa, this can lead to consequential uncertainties concerning their future prospects. Depending on the country of origin, the chances of being legally recognised as a refugee and thus achieving a long-term perspective to remain in Germany vary significantly. Refugees from Eritrea and Syria currently have very good chances, but for all other African refugees the prospects are considerably worse. At the beginning of 2018, 99.6% of all refugees who had entered Germany from Syria, 96.7% of refugees from Eritrea and 73.8% of refugees from Somalia had received a permanent or temporary residence permit, compared with 10.2% from Gambia and 7% from Guinea (Bundesregierung 2018). In concrete terms, this means that young refugees often find themselves in a long-term situation during their asylum procedure, in which their future prospects are uncertain and in which they must expect to be deported to their country of origin. But even the rejection of their asylum application does not necessarily and directly lead to a deportation from Germany. In many cases, refugees can remain in Germany even after their rejection for reasons where their return fails due to administrative difficulties or where they are granted a temporary right of residence for other reasons, a so-called "Duldung" (toleration). In addition, under certain conditions, it is possible to obtain a right of residence for several years by successfully enrolling in a

---

3   The relevant legal regulations are summarised by Tangermann/Hoffmeyer-Zlotnik (2018).

school or by commencing vocational training. This requires self-discipline on the part of the refugees in the organisation of their everyday life. But if they fail in school or during their vocational training, for example due to the language requirements, this also jeopardises their right of residence. Therefore, their chances depend considerably on their ability to discipline themselves to study at school and at work.

As our own research has shown, this uncertainty constitutes a considerable burden for young refugees.[4] It confronts young refugees with the paradoxical necessity to invest as much effort as possible into the development of a life perspective in Germany, without however, having any certainty as to whether this effort will prove worthwhile. Experts in the field of social work report that two different ways of dealing with this situation can be distinguished: Some of the young refugees systematically focus their efforts on developing a perspective in Germany through language acquisition, school-based qualification and vocational training. Another part of the young refugees experiences this situation as an excessive demand and is therefore unable to engage in language acquisition and qualification.

4   Racial Discrimination

In order to understand the situation of African refugees in Germany and the burdens they face in their everyday lives, it is essential to address another problem: In many ways, they experience their situation as essentially better than in their country of origin, but they are repeatedly confronted with racial discrimination. Yet, in this context I cannot deal in detail with the question of how widespread racism is in Germany at present.[5] It must therefore suffice here to simplistically summarise that overt racism against persons of African descent is predominantly rejected in the political discourse, in the media, and by the population in Germany. Part of the established self-image of German society is the conviction that any form of racism must be decisively rejected. Nevertheless, racist thinking and attitudes are still to be found in parts of the population and in right-wing political parties. Also, negative attitudes towards refugees have in-

---

4   A survey of skilled workers comes to this conclusion: "Uncertainties in residence law (95%), separation from the family (90%) and fear of the future (88%) are most frequently cited by respondents as impairments relevant to everyday life. Experiences of racism (very) often according to around 30% of the respondents and according to 50% of the respondents sometimes represent an impairment of everyday life for young people." (Nordheim/Karpenstein/Klaus 2017: 50), author*s translation

5   On racism against persons of African descent in Europe see FRA 2018; on the German situation see Decker/Brähler 2018.

creased considerably in the political discourse in recent years. These are not substantiated with genuine racist arguments, but rather with the assertion of preventing further refugee immigration in order to prevent the social institutions from being overburdened (Scherr 2018). But even such supposedly rational arguments lead to a social climate that can enforce racist attitudes. Accordingly, the interviews we conducted show that experiences with open racism are by no means ubiquitous and commonplace, and that young refugees predominantly report positive experiences. Nonetheless, they also experience racism, as they are often controlled by the police, rejected at entrance checks in discos and clubs, and occasionally confronted with racist remarks in the public sphere or on the part of classmates or work colleagues. Our research also demonstrates that such experiences with racism can have a different, stronger impact on young refugees than on Germans citizens of African descent. In combination with uncertainty concerning residence status and unequal treatment by authorities in comparison to German citizens, this can result in specific experiences of mani-fest racism being interpreted as an expression of general rejection by German society. Against this background, it should be noted that the burden that young refugees have to cope with includes recurrent experiences of racism, which are experienced as shameful and can lead to an injured self-esteem.

My thoughts so far can be summarised as follows: Young refugees are faced with the difficult challenge of adapting to the living conditions in the host society after having experienced burdensome living conditions in their country of origin and an often dangerous and traumatising phase of flight. The necessi-ties of adapting include coping with legal and institutional procedures, language acquisition, obtaining school and vocational qualification, and the development of social relations. They receive considerable support through welfare state measures and social work, with the situation of unaccompanied minor refugees differing positively from that of adult refugees and also from that of children and young people who have fled with their families. All of this takes place under conditions of uncertainty about the individual's future prospects during the asylum procedure and, in the event of rejection, also afterwards. In these cases, school-based vocational qualification efforts are of particular importance as they can contribute to achieving residence status even when legal refugee status is not attainable.

5   Young Refugees, Social Support, and Their Own Contri-bution to Coping with the Situation

In our research, we focus on the question of how young refugees can successful-ly cope with this situation. This means above all else: how they succeed in establishing social contacts which enable them to experience a sense of belonging, appreciation, and recognition; how they shape everyday life in such a way that they can experience a sense of agency and self-efficiency; how they succeed in school and vocational training in order to develop an independent life perspective in the host society; and how they deal with experiences of discrimination. In line with international research (Hutchinson/Dorsett 2012; Seukwa 2018), it becomes apparent that it would be analytically wrong and misleading for educational and therapeutic support to regard young refugees merely as powerless victims of difficult circumstances. For in general, it is indispensable for the social sciences to examine the coping with certain situations as a personal achievement of individuals under given conditions, to assess their subjectivity and their agency as essential factors (see Emirbayer/Mische 1998; Scherr 2012). This corresponds with the empirical finding that young refugees often "demonstrate enormous strength and resilience that facilitates their resettlement process" (Hutchinson/Dorsett 2012: 56). This conclusion is also confirmed by our own empirical research: in our case analyses it is astonishingly recurrent that some young refugees are able to maintain their capacity to act and to reorganise their way of life in the host society within a relatively short period of time. From a social science perspective, however, it is of critical importance in this respect to regard their capacity to act and resilience not as personality trait. Resilience and agency are biographically articulated and socially embedded, i.e. abilities whose development, maintenance and realisation depends upon social relationships and social support. Therefore, to look at the coping with the refugee situation as a quasi-heroic achievement of the individual, while neglecting the significance of the structural and institutional contexts would be theoretically and empirically wrong as well as socio-politically misleading.

In the following, I will briefly illustrate the complex interplay of structural conditions, institutional and informal support, and agency by means of a case study: This case concerns a young refugee, we call him Jamal, who fled Uganda at the age of 14. There he had grown up in a rural region and was able to attend an English-speaking school run by a Christian mission for 6 years. The reason for his flight was that he was recruited by a militia as a child soldier in the civil war, had to take part in violent acts and was separated from his family. After migrating across Africa for two years, Jamal reached Germany at the age of 16. There he was classified as a minor and at first placed in a refugee camp, then after a few weeks transferred to a youth welfare institution. He describes this institution as a place where he received comprehensive support and where he made no experiences of racist discrimination. I quote from the interview: "I must honestly say this is one of the best places a desperate person can go. As I said, this was a very positive experience for me. They gave me great support." During his time in this institution he was able to attend school and graduate. At

the age of 19 he commenced vocational training and moved into his own apart-
ment in a larger city. At his new workplace he was confronted with manifest
racism from one of his co-workers. He responded with a complaint to his super-
visor, who offered to discharge the colleague who had expressed himself openly
racist. However, Jamal did not pursue this avenue because he did not want to be
responsible for the dismissal of an older colleague. In his case, this also related
with the impact of his Christian socialisation in his country of origin. Thus, he
reacted to an experience of discrimination with attempts of understanding and
reconciliation. He expressly emphasised that he refuses to develop an attitude of
hatred and hostility towards people who discriminate against him. At first, he
continued his work in this company, while noting that this was only possible
because he was not discriminated against by all of the other colleagues. It was
therefore possible for him to maintain his social contacts at work and to avoid
social isolation at the workplace. The interview also reveals his high intrinsic
motivation for developing a vocational perspective, because he only left the
company in which he experienced recurring racial discrimination after he had
found another training place at a different company. He has since completed his
vocational training there.

In the interview, Jamal then describes an experience of racist discrimination by the police which he considered quite severe: he was physically attacked
by a policeman during an inspection and then failed in his attempt to obtain a
court order against this policeman. Against the backdrop of his biographical
experience, Jamal experienced this as a massive emotional crisis that led to a
fundamental loss of trust in the police and a fear of going out in public. Initially,
he reacted to this by retreating. He then managed to overcome the crisis by making use of therapy. Jamal describes that at first it was in no way conceivable for
him to undergo therapy, since he was convinced that this was only "something
for crazy people". Yet, a person he trusted was able to convince him in conversations that it was not shameful to attend therapy. Looking back, Jamal recalls that
for him the therapy was of decisive positive importance to overcome his insecurity and restore his capacity to lead a normal everyday life. In the meantime,
Jamal has turned 24 years of age, has successfully completed his vocational
training and is recognised as a refugee. He has good social contacts with his
peers. He no longer perceives of experiences of racism, with which he is still
occasionally confronted, as serious burdens and deals with them in a reflective
manner.

Compared with other cases, six key aspects can be identified which enabled
Jamal to handle his situation successfully: Firstly, Jamal's previous schooling in
his country of origin provided him with the prerequisites to facilitate his integration in Germany. In comparison, refugees who were unable to attend school in
their country of origin report significantly greater difficulties to adapt to school

requirements in Germany. Secondly, he has a general confidence in his own abilities, reinforced by his experiences of success at school and work in Germany, but also by the recognition he receives in his leisure time as a dancer. Thirdly, during his time in Germany, he experienced institutional support from child and youth welfare services as well as informal support, which he consistently describes as appropriate and very positive. This distinguishes him from other refugees for whom institutional support was interrupted by relocations and breaks in social relationships. Fourthly, he was confronted with what he saw as a very serious experience of racism, but which he was able to overcome with the help of therapy, to which he had gained access through informal support. Fifthly, his religious orientation also proved to be helpful by establishing a framework of interpretation that enabled him to deal with racism in a way which did not lead to intensified conflicts. Sixth, he managed to be legally accepted as a refugee, that is, to end the insecurity of his residence status and thus gain certainty on his future prospects. In contrast, other refugees we have interviewed are constantly confronted with the threat of deportation. In one of our cases this has led to resignation because the return to the country of origin is regarded as inevitable; the person concerned is therefore trying to earn and save as much money as possible in order to be able to build up a livelihood in the country of origin, if necessary. In another case, the person concerned attempts to avoid the threat of deportation by moving on to another European country, with the precarious hope of achieving legal status there.

6   Some General Remarks on the Relationship between Flight, Social Policy and Health Issues

I will conclude with some general remarks on the relationship between flight and social policy as well as health issues:[6]

a) The legal and institutional structures of the national welfare state are of crucial importance for the situation of refugees in host societies. These are decisive for the level at which basic needs are guaranteed and how access to health care, schooling, vocational training and care through social workers is provided. In Germany, this means that adult refugees and rejected asylum seekers are subject to certain restrictions compared to German citizens, also in the area of health care. However, they have access to a level of social benefits that is com-

---

6   The situation of young refugees from Africa in some respects differs considerably from that of adults and families with children and adolescents. Also, generalisations of any sort are risky because young refugees from Africa are not a homogeneous group with regard to their chances of being recognised as refugees, their educational and vocational background and their health problems, not least due to traumatisation during their flight.

paratively high by international standards. This contributes to the fact that Germany is an attractive host country for refugees compared to some other European countries.

b) In the case of unaccompanied minor refugees, the existing structures of the German welfare state make it possible to considerably promote school and vocational integration – despite all the problems that can nevertheless be identified in this respect.[7] The available studies show that these, in conjunction with the support of civil society, enable a large proportion of young refugees to be able to develop a viable life perspective in Germany. However, this also requires considerable personal effort on the part of the refugees, not all of whom are in a position to accomplish this. Also, experiences with racist discrimination, existing restrictions under immigration law and the often long-term uncertainty concerning future perspectives make this significantly more difficult.

c) The downside of the existing welfare state structures is that flight and forced migration in Germany has recurrently been discussed politically as a burden or overload on the welfare state. This has led to Germany implementing massive defensive measures against further immigration of refugees and forced migrants in the context of the European Union. The consequence of this is that the number of refugees who have arrived in Germany has been substantially reduced since 2015 and that the risks of flight through the Sahara and across the Mediterranean have correspondingly increased considerably. In this respect, it should be noted that refugees encounter the greatest risks to their health and life during the flight and not when living in Germany.

d) Considerable deficits concerning the health care of refugees in Germany result, on the one hand, from the fact that adult refugees have only limited access to treatment for illnesses during the asylum procedure and after rejection; on the other hand, there is a general lack of specialists in the field of psychotherapeutic treatment, especially of specialists who can provide therapeutic treatment in the native languages of the refugees. In addition, translators needed for medical treatment are not financed by the health insurance funds.

e) Also with regard to health aspects, forced repatriation to the countries of origin and deportations must be regarded as an essential problem. In Europe, recognition as a refugee depends on laws based on the Geneva Convention on Refugees. This means that absolute poverty and other socio-economic conditions which lead to a massive reduction in life opportunities are not recognised as a legally legitimate reason for flight and do not constitute a legal ground for asylum. Thus, the prevalent provisions of refugee law only to a limited extent do justice to the actual causes of forced migration (Scherr 2018a). A particular

---

7   Detailed information can be found on the homepage of the 'Bundesfachverband unaccompanied minor refugees' (https://b-umf.de).

problem can be observed in the case of deportations of children and adolescents who completely grew up as refugees in Germany or spent most of their lives here: For them, deportation is equivalent to being forcibly placed in the living conditions of a so-called country of origin which they have never actually known themselves, or which has become foreign to them.

f) In the case of African refugees, attempts at forced repatriation have so far often failed because of the lack of cooperation on the part of the countries of origin, or because wars and civil wars do not allow repatriation. As a consequence, these refugees then remain in Germany and other European countries without being able to return and, at the same time, without being able to develop a secure long-term residence perspective. In the view of many experts, this is an unacceptable situation that should be ended by changing the relevant laws in order to grant a permanent right of residence to all those who have been living in the host country for a certain amount of years.

Bibliography

BAMF (2018:) Das Bundesamt in Zahlen 2017. Nuremberg.

BMFSFJ (2017): Bericht über die Lebenssituation junger Menschen und die Leistungen der Kinder- und Jugendhilfe in Deutschland. 15. Kinder- und Jugendbericht. Berlin.

Bundesregierung (2018): Antwort der Bundesregierung auf die Kleine Anfrage der Abgeordneten Ulla Jelpke, Dr. André Hahn, Gökay Akbulut, weiterer Abgeordneter und der Fraktion DIE LINKE. Drucksache 19/2186 [https://dipbt.bundestag.de/doc/btd/19/031/1903148.pdf].

Campbell, Zach (2019): Europe's deadly migration strategy. [https://www.politico.eu/article/europe-deadly-migration-strategy-leaked-documents/].

Cremer, Hendrik (2014): Uneingeschränkte Rechte für junge Flüchtlinge. Zur öffentlichen Anhörung des Ausschusses für Familie, Kinder und Jugend und des Integrationsausschusses des Landtags NRW. Berlin: Deutsches Institut für Menschenrechte.

Decker, Oliver/Brähler, Elmar (2018): Flucht ins Autoritäre: Rechtsextreme Dynamiken in der Mitte der Gesellschaft. Giessen: Psychosozial Verlag.

Emirbayer, Mustafa/Mische, Ann (1998): What Is Agency? In: American Journal of Sociology, Volume 104, pp. 962-1023.

Espenhorst, Niels (2016): Unbegleitete minderjährige Flüchtlinge in der Kinder- und Jugendhilfe: ein Rückblick auf die letzten 10 Jahre. In: Albert Scherr/Gökcen Yüksel (eds.): Flucht, Sozialstaat und Soziale Arbeit. Neuwied: Verlag Neue Praxis, pp. 145-156.

Étiemble, Angélina/Zanna, Omar (2013): "Des typologies pour faire connaissance avec les mineurs isolés étrangers et mieux les accompagner". In: Topik. Mission de recherche Droit et Justice. Convention de recherche, pp. 12–22.

FRA (2018): Second European Union Minorities and Discrimination Survey. Being Black in the EU. Vienna (https://fra.europa.eu/en/publication/2018/eumidis-ii-being-black).

Hutchinson, Mary/Dorsett, Patt (2012): What does the literature say about resilience in refugee people? Implications for practice. In: Journal of Social Inclusion, 3(2), 2012, pp. 56-76.

Lechner, Claudia/Huber, Anna (2017): Ankommen nach der Flucht. Die Sicht begleiteter und unbegleiteter junger Geflüchteter auf ihre Lebenslagen in Deutschland. Munich: Deutsches Jugendinstitut.

Matthes, Stephanie et al. (2018): Junge Geflüchtete auf dem Weg in Ausbildung. Ergebnisse der BA/BIBB-Migrationsstudie 2016. Bonn: BIBB.

Müller, Andreas (2014): Unbegleitete Minderjährige in Deutschland. Fokusstudie der deutschen nationalen Kontaktstelle für das Europäische Migrationsnetzwerk (EMN). Working Paper 60 des Forschungszentrums des Bundesamtes. Nuremberg: BAMF.

Parusel, Bernd (2015): Unbegleitete Minderjährige auf der Flucht, in: Aus Politik und Zeitgeschichte (25). Online: http://www.bpb.de/apuz/208007/unbegleitete-minderjaehrige-auf-der-flucht?p=all (16.01.2018).

Schammann, Hannes (2016): Im Zentrum des Paradoxons. Auswirkungen grundlegender Spannungsverhältnisse der Migrationspolitik auf den Umgang mit unbegleiteten Minderjährigen, in: Fischer, Jörg/Graßhoff, Günter (eds.): Unbegleitete minderjährige Flüchtlinge. Sozialmagazin, 1. Sonderband 2016, Weinheim and Basel: Beltz Juventa, pp. 116-121.

Scherr, Albert (2012): Soziale Bedingungen von Agency. Soziologische Eingrenzung einer sozialtheoretisch nicht auflösbaren Paradoxie. In: S. Bethmann et.al. (eds.): Agency. Weinheim and Basel 2012, pp. 99-121.

Scherr, Albert (2018): Ablehnung und Solidarität gegenüber Geflüchteten. In: Möller, Kurt/Neuscheler, Florian (eds.): Wer will die hier schon haben? Ablehnungshaltungen und Diskriminierung in Deutschland. Stuttgart: Kohlhammer, pp. 165–183.

Scherr, Albert (2018a): Who Can Claim Protection as a Refugee? A Sociological Critique of the Distinction between Refugees and Migrants. In: H. Kury/S. Redi (eds.): Refugees and Migrants in Law and Policy. Springer International Publishing 2018, pp. 125-136.

Scherr, Albert/Breit, Helen (2018): Risikobiografien und negative Individualisierung. Die Bedeutung von institutioneller Diskriminierung und Diskriminierungserfahrungen für Bildungsprozesse bei jungen Flüchtlingen. In: Thiersch, S./Silkenbeumer, M./Labede, J. (eds.): Individualisierte Übergänge. Aufstiege, Abstiege, Umstiege und Ausstiege im Bildungssystem. Wiesbaden: VS Verlag für Sozialwissenschaften (forthcoming).

Scherr, Albert/Breit, Helen (2019): Diskriminierung, Anerkennung und der Sinn für die eigene soziale Position. Wie Diskriminierungserfahrungen Bildungsprozesse und Lebenschancen beeinflussen. Weinheim and Basel: Beltz Juventa.

Seukwa, L. H. (2018): Handlungsfähigkeit und Heteronomie - eine kompetenztheoretische Perspektive auf fluchtmigrationsbedingte Bildungskontinuitäten. In: Bröse, J./Faas, S./Stauber, B. (eds.): Flucht. Herausforderungen für Soziale Arbeit. Wiesbaden: Springer Fachmedien Wiesbaden GmbH, pp. 73–93.

Tangermann, Julian/Paula Hoffmeyer-Zlotnik (2018): Unaccompanied Minors in Germany – Challenges and Measures after the Clarification of Residence Status. Focussed Study by the German National Contact Point for the European Migration Network (EMN).

von Nordheim, Franziska/Karpenstein, Johanna/Klaus, Tobias (2017): Die Situation unbegleiteter minderjähriger Flüchtlinge in Deutschland. Auswertung der Online-Umfrage 2017. Berlin: B-UMF.

5. Quality of Life, Diversity and Health

Health for All? Disability, Diversity and Global Health

Isabella Bertmann-Merz[1]

Keywords: Global Health, Diversity, Disability, Quality of Life

Abstract

This article deals with the question of access to health (care) for vulnerable groups of people and discusses how diversity aspects are reflected to the extent that health care is available to all people without barriers and/or discrimination. To this end, the text draws on governance issues by using the differentiation between a) "globalization and health governance", b) "global governance and health" as well as c) "governance for global health", suggested by Lee & Kamradt-Scott (2014: 5). The focus of the text is on the two diversity dimensions disability and migration[2].

Contents

Abstract 151

1   Introduction 153

2   Global Health (Governance) 153

---

1   Isabella Bertmann-Merz | Technical University of Munich | isabella.bertmann@tum.de

2   Migration does not appear in the title of the article due to the fact that the whole conference focus was on refugees and forced migration.

© Springer Fachmedien Wiesbaden GmbH, part of Springer Nature 2020
K. Crepaz et al. (eds.), *Health in Diversity – Diversity in Health*,
https://doi.org/10.1007/978-3-658-29177-8_9

2.1   Approaching Global Health..153

2.2   Areas of Global Health Governance...155

3   Diversity and Global Health...157

3.1   Disability as a Topic in Global Health...157

3.2   Migration and Global Health...159

3.3   Diversity Issues as a Topic in GH - Potential and Challenges...................160

4   Outlook: Health for All?..162

4.1   Universal Health Coverage..162

4.2   Quality of Life and Health...164

4.3   Conclusion...165

Bibliography 167

1   Introduction

This article deals with the question of access to health (care) for vulnerable groups[1] of people. To this end, the text starts off with an introduction to the field of global health (GH) and the question if, and how, diversity aspects are reflected to the extent that health care is available to all people, regardless of issues such as gender, disability, migration, etc.

I will approach global health by presenting some definitions and touching upon governance issues. The field of global health is characterized by a high level of diversity on a variety of layers: A diversity regarding institutions, initiatives, health systems and norms exists. This goes hand in hand with challenges regarding ambitious initiatives such as the intent to achieve "health for all". Differences regarding national health systems, foreign-policy interests, cultural backgrounds and environmental characteristics in various countries and populations lead to the need for approaches that are universal while at the same time taking into account the respective particularities.

In addition, policies and approaches in the field of health – similar to other areas such as social policy – need to take into account human diversity. As a starting point, this article focuses on the dimensions of disability and migration, acknowledging the variety of other dimensions as well as the phenomenon of intersectionality and overlapping of – for example – categories such as gender and disability, or disability and migration. The article will continue by discussing ways of dealing with (health) vulnerability by looking at initiatives such as Universal Health Coverage (UHC), but also health-related quality of life and the role that social protection can play in the field of GH. I will then come to conclusions about the questions of how to achieve health for all and how to deal with diversity and inclusion in the area of worldwide – or more specifically global – health.

2   Global Health (Governance)

2.1   Approaching Global Health

Global health is often used synonymously with international health and public health, but differences exist. Whereas public health usually refers to a specific country, the focus of international health can be narrowed down to health issues of other countries, particularly those in the Global South. As Koplan et al.

---

1   In accordance with Barrientos (2010: 581),"vulnerability" means "the strong likelihood that individuals, households, and communities will be in poverty in the future".

(2009: 1993) state, "[for] decades, it was the term used for health work abroad, with a geographic focus on developing countries and often with a content of infectious and tropical diseases, water and sanitation, malnutrition, and maternal and child health". One legal instrument in the field of health on an international level that is binding for 196 countries worldwide exists in the form of the International Health Regulations (WHO 2005, entry into force in 2007). For example, the rules oblige the states to report public health events. Their purpose and scope are

> "to prevent, protect against, control and provide a public health response to the international spread of disease in ways that are commensurate with and restricted to public health risks, and which avoid unnecessary interference with international traffic and trade" (ibid: 10).

As important as this might be, it does not fully encompass all issues that GH is about, and all dimensions that health protection and health coverage can take globally. The same holds true for documents such as the Alma-Ata Declaration (WHO 1978) with a focus on primary health care and the Ottawa Charter for Health Promotion (1986), which had already introduced the goal of "health for all" with the ambitious achievement date of 2000.

By taking into account worldwide health threats and both individual as well as population-based health issues on a global level (see Koplan et al. 2009: 1994), global health issues go far beyond health topics: poverty, human rights, climate change and other issues are important dimensions to be considered. As a result, global health can, for example, be defined as "those health issues that transcend national boundaries and governments and call for actions on the global forces that determine the health of people" (Kickbusch 2006: 561). Another important aspect, especially in fields that have not yet been explored extensively, is that of "collaborative trans-national research and action for promoting health for all" (Beaglehole & Bonita 2010: 1).

Already in 1978, the World Health Organization (WHO) had phrased the following demand or statement regarding health inequalities:

> "The existing gross inequality in the health status of the people particularly between developed and developing countries as well as within countries is politically, socially and economically unacceptable and is, therefore, of common concern to all countries" (WHO 1978: paragraph 2).

Much has been done and achieved since then, but challenges remain that are dealt with by a variety of institutions and initiatives. The most well-known of all are probably the World Health Organization (WHO) and also the United Nations (UN) and their different agencies, programmes and funds, but also specific initiatives such as Gavi, the Vaccine Alliance (founded by the Bill and Melinda

Gates Foundation) or others. However, there is criticism that can be expressed regarding such a variety or diversity of actors.

The problem with the field of global health, as well as with governance on a global level in general, is a certain "anarchy" (Lee & Kamradt-Scott 2014: 2) that can be found due to the absence of a central authority or a governing body. Collaboration is important for this political field and it does take place on a variety of levels, but there is also a lack of coordination between all actors mentioned above (see e. g. Dodd/Hill 2007). A number of different approaches towards health rights and institutional obligations exists, and health policy is often connected with foreign policy and international interests (see Feldbaum et al. 2010). And the different sources of expertise lead to power being relational, there is no consensus among the actors as to what global health governance implies (see Lee & Kamradt-Scott 2014). In addition, the bindingness is highly questionable, and accountability often unclear.

2.2 Areas of Global Health Governance

Let us discuss these aspects in more detail. Frenk and Moon (2013: 937) argue that the "notion of governance goes beyond the formal mechanisms of government and refers to the totality of ways in which a society organizes and collectively manages its affairs", with global governance being "the extension of this notion to the world as a whole". With the absence of a government on the global level, issues such as rule enforcement, the coordination of action or ensuring of accountability are difficult to achieve (see ibid). This does also hold true for the field of global health. If we look at the topic of GH and respective governance questions in more detail, three different areas of research and practice can be distinguished according to Lee & Kamradt-Scott (2014: 5): "globalization and health governance", "governance for global health"[2] and "global governance and health".

The first one is the connection between globalization and health governance, focusing on health-related institutions with a strong emphasis on the tasks and work of the WHO, and the connections that this organization has with other actors. The problem is that a high complexity exists, while at the same time resource constraints may hinder the performance of the institution. In addition, the WHO is said to have problems in completing its intended tasks, which might also be the case due to the fact that it is an important actor, but not THE global health actor per se (see ibid).

---

2   Frenk & Moon (2013: 939) prefer the term "global governance for health" to "global health governance" when referring to the area of health and global governance in general.

The second aspect is global governance and health. Generally, global governance is about the framework of global norms and binding rules, the respective processes for monitoring/enforcement as well as the group of organizations or institutions that are involved in the solution of global problems (see e. g. Domínguez/Velázquez Flores 2018). With respect to health, this means that the focus is on global institutions without original functions or mandates in the field of global health, but which have nonetheless gained influence, among them the World Trade Organization, the World Bank, etc. In this pillar of global health governance, there is criticism of the market orientation of the institutions that might interfere with issues such as health equity and social justice. The World Trade Organization, for example, is involved in intellectual property issues as far as pharmaceuticals are concerned (Frenk & Moon 2013: 937). One thematic element is thus to focus on improving good governance in these institutions. This means that a strong focus on justice is required (see Lee & Kamradt-Scott 2014). The particular attention on health equity is of specific importance when it comes to vulnerable groups, and the third pillar identified by Lee & Kamradt-Scott relatedly highlights a normative view on global health.

In the area of governance for global health, topics include access to medication, health equity, ethical issues and the health issues and needs that are important as far as the so-called developing world[3] is concerned. As a follow-up framework to the Millennium Development Goals (MDGs, 2000-2015), the topics and aims of the much broader Sustainable Development Goals (SDGs, 2015-2030) are one element that might be counted as belonging to that thematic area. The 17 SDGs and the 2030 Agenda for Sustainable Development (UN 2015) are the international community's attempt to agree on a set of goals and indicators to foster development and social cohesion by tackling inequalities, poverty, poor education and many more of the challenges that exist worldwide. Several of the MDGs were already relevant for the field of health, but the SDGs contain a specific goal called "Ensure healthy lives and promote well-being for all at all ages" (SDG 3). The goals show the interconnectedness of health, poverty and development, and they can be said to belong to the ethical foundations of global health governance.

---

3   Acknowledging the shortcomings of this term, it is used in this text as a discussion of its definition and potential alternatives would go beyond the scope of the article.

3   Diversity and Global Health

3.1   Disability as a Topic in Global Health

According to the UN Convention on the Rights of Persons with Disabilities (CRPD), "[p]ersons with disabilities include those who have long-term physical, mental, intellectual or sensory impairments which in interaction with various barriers may hinder their full and effective participation in society on an equal basis with others (UN 2006, article 1). People with disabilities belong to the most vulnerable groups in each society (for details, see e. g. Larkin 2009). The barriers that they face are manifold – these can be social, cultural, environmental, systemic or other.

With respect to the thematic context of the present article, it can be stated that persons with disabilities often face difficulties in accessing health care programmes or facilities, due to a variety of reasons. These range from inaccessible buildings to exclusion and neglection in the field of health policies, alongside with wrong assumptions about the health status and health risks of persons with disabilities (see Swartz & Bantjes 2016). Further reasons are discriminatory practices, unavailable or inaccessible information and higher costs (alongside with the fact that persons with disabilities are often poorer than the rest of society) (see Kuper & Hanefeld 2018). There is a complex relationship between disability, poverty and ill health, and it is important to stress that disability and illness are not equivalent. However, persons with disabilities are at a greater risk of, for example, intentional injuries and violence (see Swartz & Bantjes 2016). In addition, they have a higher risk of premature death and are often thought not to be the right target group for education about topics such as HIV/AIDS (see e. g. Groce et al. 2013), or regarding sexual and reproductive health services. A related field of concern refers to particular vulnerabilities in cases of natural disaster and catastrophes (see e. g. Peek & Stough 2010 regarding the situation of children with disabilities, or Hemingway & Priestley 2014, highlighting that vulnerabilities are based on disadvantages and social exclusion, not on the personal impairments of the victims).

The "vicious circle of poverty and disability" (Yeo/Moore 2003: 572) leads to the fact that especially persons with disabilities in low-resource settings are affected by and vulnerable due to the aforementioned factors (for details, see e. g. WHO & WB 2011; Palmer 2011; Groce et al 2011; Ingstad/Eide 2011). Two challenges regarding the inclusion of disability as a topic in a variety of fields, including health, are: the fact that the prevalence of disability is often underestimated[4]; and, that the consideration of the interests and concerns of persons with disabilities is often seen as a costly and time-consuming endeavor (see Swartz & Bantjes 2016), as the advantages of a mainstream approach are not taken into consideration (or unknown).

For a long time, medical professionals were regarded as the experts on disability-related questions, and the medicalization of disability has only slowly been replaced by a social model view on disability, acknowledging external factors and moving away from seeing disability mainly as a personal and health-related issue (see e. g. Oliver 1996; Shakespeare 2013). In contrast to the medical understanding of disability, the social model views disability as being a result of discriminatory practices and social aspects, or, more precisely, as the interaction between the impairment and diverse external barriers.[5] Civil rights and social change are important components of this disability conceptualization (see e. g. UN 2006; Waldschmidt 2005). What also remains underestimated are the intersectionalities between disability experiences and a person's health status, as well as between these and other dimensions of diversity (gender, class, etc.). The importance of diversity-sensitive approaches towards the provision of health care becomes as obvious as the acknowledgement and further investigation of dimensions and drivers of inequality (see e. g. Swartz & Bantjes 2016; also Thomas 2007).

With respect to global health, a parallel can be drawn to disability in the sense that both rights issues as well as social aspects and determinants receive more and more attention. Thus, Swartz & Bantjes (2016: 25) state that "if the medical model is bad for disability, it is equally bad for global health". From a resource- and capability-oriented point of view, it can be argued that global health is not about "eliminating disease or infirmity, but about the opportunities

---

4   The World Report on Disability (WHO & WB 2011) explains the challenges regarding data collection on disability. A very important factor is the underlying definition or conceptualization of impairments and disabilities, resulting in the fact that for example, "most developing countries report disability prevalence rates below those reported in many developed countries, because they collect data on a narrow set of impairments" (ibid: 25). Also, the availability of data plays a role. The estimations included in the report, namely 1 billion people or 15% of the global population, reflect the statistics available to date.

5   Despite a more adequate reflection of the phenomenon of disability than the medical model, the social model also has its shortcomings. A variety of discussions among Disability Studies scholars have therefore led to the development of further disability models (such as the cultural model suggested by Waldschmidt (2005)), and social norms as well as the construction of "normality" are now an important part of the current discourse on the definition and understanding of disability.

and capacities people have to manage themselves and their health in their specific contexts" (ibid 2016: 28).[6]

3.2 Migration and Global Health

The international Sustainable Development Goals and the 2030 Agenda claim to "leave no one behind". Many of the goals are also and specifically relevant for vulnerable groups, such as persons with disabilities and migrants, and in contrast to the MDGs, the SDGs[7] explicitly address migration issues (see Piper 2017). They can serve as a reference to demonstrate the particular difficulties when it comes to migration and health. With regard to health care provision and health-related challenges, several goals are important. First of all, migrants are particularly affected by health risks (SDG 3 on good health and well-being) and by the question of clean water and sanitation (SDG 6). Climate-related disasters (SDG 13 – "Take urgent action to combat climate change and its impacts") may lead to migration, and "the issue of trafficking is mentioned in several SDGs, for instance, SDG 16 on peaceful societies" (ibid: 232). They often do not have access to health care and/or (health) education (SDG 4 – "Ensure inclusive and equitable quality education and promote lifelong learning opportunities for all"), leading to further risks and vulnerabilities. Decent work (SDG 8 – "Promote sustained, inclusive and sustainable economic growth, full and productive employment and decent work for all") is an important factor when it comes to safe working conditions and social protection, both closely related to health issues. Many migrant laborers may face precarious employment situations. Lastly, gender equality (SDG 5) plays an important role as women and girls, also among migrants, are specifically vulnerable to inequalities, violence and health risks. Against this background, social inequalities in general are to be considered, too (SDG 10 – "Reduce inequality within and among countries"). A similar argumentation can be used for persons with disabilities.

Yet, equal access to health care does often not exist for non-citizens. For Germany, for example, children with a migration background[8] often do not receive the standard vaccination, and maternal mortality is higher in foreign women. In addition, high vulnerability may hinder equal access to adequate health care, and there is a strong interdependence between the socio-economic

---

6 One further interesting aspect that goes beyond the scope of this paper is the connection with the emergence of global mental health as a new field of research, as described by Swartz & Bantjes 2016.

7 The respective platform with information regarding all goals and recent activities can be found here. https://www.un.org/sustainabledevelopment/, last access: 23/04/2019.

8 For a discussion regarding the term "migration background", see e. g. Gummich 2015.

status and health. More concretely, reasons include unemployment, lack of education, financial aspects and others which persons with a migration background experience in their daily life. However, this does not only hold true for migrants, but also for Germans of a similar social status (see Eichler 2008). As regards the specific situation of persons with a migrant background, several aspects need to be considered, among them the definition of migration and differences that might exist regarding internal and international migration. Also, the consequences of flight and displacement need to be taken into consideration, alongside with psychological stress that might have its roots in migration experiences (e. g. language barriers, separation from the family, etc.) (see e. g. Lorenzkowski 2002). In addition, migrants do not constitute a heterogeneous group, and therefore a variety of risk factors, such as few resources to cope with health challenges etc., are prevalent. Issues of language and culture play as important a role as the potential lack of knowledge regarding the health and social system in general, and concrete possibilities of access to health care in particular. Especially in cases where people with a migration background compose a large group in the health care system, these challenges need to be reflected (see Eichler 2008). Furthermore, the full migration cycle with the different phases of migration needs to be considered (see Piper 2017). Corporality is a central component of health care provision, and ideas/images of the body and health/illness are often culturally influenced (see Eichler 2008). Interestingly, this is also a discussion that is to be found in disability studies, e. g. regarding the definition of the terms disability and impairment (and the related medical/social/cultural models of disability, see e. g. Waldschmidt 2005).

In general, as far as the consideration of migrants in the health care systems is concerned, a tendency exists to view this group of people as having certain problems and deficits (see Eichler 2008, also Gummich 2015). What seems to be lacking is an understanding of migrants as "active agents" with strengths and competences. Once again, the same holds true for the group of persons with disabilities – not only in the health care system.

3.3 Diversity Issues as a Topic in GH - Potential and Challenges

The topic of disability has long played a role in the field of global health, namely through programmes such as community-based rehabilitation (CBR, initiated by the World Health Organization already in 1978 following the Declaration of Alma-Ata) or the publication of the World Report on Disability in 2011, showing that actors such as the WHO and the World Bank are committed to dealing with the situation of persons with disabilities worldwide. There is also the WHO Global Disability Action Plan 2014-2021 (WHO 2015), aiming at "better health for all people with disability" and pursuing the following goals:

- "(1) to remove barriers and improve access to health services and pro-grammes;
- (2) to strengthen and extend rehabilitation, habilitation, assistive tech-nology, assistance and support services, and community-based rehabili-tation; and
- (3) to strengthen collection of relevant and internationally comparable data on disability and support research on disability and related ser-vices" (ibid: 3).

The situation of migrants is also increasingly receiving attention by global or-ganizations and initiatives, reflecting the "volume, nature and (gendered) pat-terns of labour migration" as well as the "politico-economic significance of migration" (Piper 2017: 233). This can, for example, also be seen with respect to the WHO's Global Action Plan on 'Promoting the Health of Refugees and Mi-grants' (2019-2023, currently still a draft). It is important to keep in mind that there is no such person as "the migrants" or "the persons with disabilities"; the challenges they are confronted with and the needs they have concerning health care are manifold due to personal characteristics and the barriers that exist as regards access to the system and its components. In addition, intersectional aspects should not be neglected (for details regarding intersectional analyses, see e. g. Winker/Degele 2009). Wickramage et al. (2018: 2) therefore suggested an approach towards research in the area of health and migration which can be counted as valid also for the practical field, including the following dimensions:

- "(1) incorporate the different phases of migration […];
- (2) adopt a life-course approach; and,
- (3) integrate a social determinants of health (SDH) approach".

A challenge that certainly needs to be reflected on is the need for typologies and categorizations depending on the nature of and conditions for service provision. Similar with social protection programmes, eligibility criteria might perpetuate categorizations and discrimination to a certain extent (see Mont 2010: 324). Therefore, approaches on the basis of human diversity – which do not seem to exist in the field of global health – would be beneficial in the sense that a focus on personal characteristics, problems and a related deficit-orientation would make way for a broader approach based on dealing with differences and a re-flection on "normality" in the field of health care.

In the international arena, also other diversity categories receive attention in strategies and programmes, especially gender and women-related issues (such as maternal and child health, for example). Approaches focusing on discrimina-tion and the elimination thereof, such as the "Agenda for Zero Discrimination in

Health Care Settings", focus on recommendations for discrimination-free health care settings, specifically with regard to HIV/AIDS. Recommendations could, however, be transferred to the fields of disability and migration, too.

4   Outlook: Health for All?

4.1   Universal Health Coverage

According to the World Health Organization, universal health coverage deals with the provision of "promotive, preventive, curative, rehabilitative and palliative health services" for "all people and communities" (WHO n. d.). The definition of UHC includes the systematic consideration of social determinants of health and the reflection of economic, environmental and personal aspects in the provision of healthcare (see WHO 2019b). Service provision is aimed at both individuals and communities/the general population. A strong focus is on participatory approaches and self-determination. UHC is specifically enshrined in Target 3.8 of the Sustainable Development Goals, which also highlights the need for high quality, effectiveness and affordability as far as health-care services are concerned. Vega and Frenz (2013: 468) argue that three dimensions of UHC are repeatedly highlighted by the WHO:

> "(a) coverage for the whole population; (b) for a comprehensive set of services, encompassing prevention, promotion, treatment, rehabilitation, and palliative care, of sufficient quality to be effective; and (c) financial protection from direct payment (free or affordable services)".

An important element of UHC is equity, yet policies and programmes aiming to achieve UHC seem to exclude elderly people and others, such as persons with disabilities. Kuper and Hanefeld (2018: 3) therefore state that "people with disabilities face specific and added difficulties across three dimensions of UHC – coverage, access to servicess [sic] needed, and at reasonable cost", and suggest a twin-track approach in order to consider the specific health needs of persons with disabilities: on the one hand, mainstream services need to be made accessible and available – on the other hand, rehabilitation and assistive devices need to be provided as specific services. Disability-awareness, e. g. by health care providers and professionals, needs to be raised, too. A way of dealing with financial vulnerability is the inclusion of "financial protection for healthcare within the widely available social protection programmes for people with disabilities" (ibid: 4). Also other vulnerable groups (such as elderly people or persons with a migration background) will benefit from measures targeted at persons with disabilities, and the differentiation into a more inclusive mainstream approach and specific services in accordance with the twin-track model could also be considered for a variety of diversity dimensions.

A study by Onarheim et al. (2018) compares UHC approaches in Norway, the United States and Thailand. The authors highlight that all "countries differ in ways that affect their path to UHC – in their health needs, demographics, health systems, financing, priorities and other concerns" (ibid: 3), yet through comparative policy analysis, the extent to which the group of undocumented migrants is included in the programmes and progress could be analyzed. The study found out that only Thailand has achieved to allow access to essential healthcare services for undocumented migrants. Gray and van Ginneken (2012) describe the policy challenges that can arise in the context of healthcare and undocumented migration. Their focus is on countries that have universal health insurance systems, with a particular emphasis on Europe. According to their study, most states only provide for emergency services. However, in countries that offer more than that and provide full access (but under specific conditions as outlined by the authors), three strategies can be identified:

> "1) focusing on segments of the population, like children or pregnant women; 2) focusing on types of services, like preventive services or treatment of infectious diseases; or 3) using specific funding policies, like allowing undocumented migrants to purchase insurance".

Apart from the difficulties that the legal status entails, the group of undocumented migrants also has to deal with challenges and barriers as far as language and culture are concerned. Economic aspects play a further role.[9] Access to information as well as communication barriers are an issue that is also relevant for persons with disabilities – however, the other aspects mentioned are less or not relevant for this group of people.

In any case, whereas UHC seems to be a suitable framework to provide health to all people, much remains to be done and more studies are needed (for criticism regarding the narrow focus of UHC and the neglection of social determinants of health, see Vega & Frenz 2013) in order to achieve the goals set out by WHO: "taking steps towards UHC means steps towards equity, development priorities, and social inclusion and cohesion" (WHO 2019b).

---

9   The authors identify some positive and negative arguments for the provision of medical care to undocumented migrants: on the one side, health care is a human right and the provision of e. g. vaccination also to undocumented migrants can benefit a country's population. On the other hand, the fear exists that further migrants will be attracted, alongside with the argument that this group of people uses a system that the country's inhabitants have to finance. Lastly, there is the concern that higher health costs and less access for the country's population can be the results (see Gray & van Ginneken 2012: 2 f.).

4.2   Quality of Life and Health

In the vast field of quality of life research, several approaches exist to capture health-related quality of life (HRQoL). It has to be noted that "the definitions of HRQoL in the literature are problematic because some definitions fail to distinguish between HRQoL and health or between HRQoL and QoL" (Karimi & Brazier 2016: 645). Many instruments that claim to measure health-related quality of life actually deal with the health status perceived by an individual and not his/her (objective) quality of life (see ibid)[10]. A detailed discussion would go beyond the scope of this article, but the short excursion to the topic of quality of life in the field of health shall serve the purpose of introducing a perhaps innovative way of dealing with diversity in the realm of global health.

This article specifically refers to quality of life as understood by the so-called Capability Approach (CA) (see e. g. Sen 1993), an approach from the field of welfare economics that was originally meant to provide a multidimensional framework to assess poverty. The focus on human capabilities, that means the options and opportunities that are available to people, offers the possibility to apply this "framework of thought" (Robeyns 2005: 96) in a variety of other disciplines and thematic contexts, too. In general, the CA allows for the assessment of "people's ability to live a life they value" (Prah Ruger 2004: 1076). The focus, among others, is on the way a variety of "means to achieve", including a person's net income or transfers-in-kind, can be transferred into options and opportunities, i. e. someone's "capabilities" (see Robeyns 2005: 98). Of importance are the social context, environmental factors and others, but also personal characteristics.

Social justice plays a major role in CA-related literature (see e. g. Nussbaum 2002). Relatedly, the CA also allows for measurements and discussions in the field of health. According to Prah Ruger (2004: 1076), one potential understanding of the relation between health and the CA is that "the ability to lead the life one values can improve one's mental health or well-being. Conversely, the ability to make unhealthy choices can degrade one's health status". The questions to be answered are thus, inter alia: Which health domains does one value most? And what kind of health services does someone want to consume (ibid)?

What the CA offers, against this background, is the opportunity to capture social inequalities and determinants of health, and the framework conditions for health promotion. A focus of the approach would be on health needs rather than resources to pay for healthcare. Its application in (global) health does also pro-

---

10   Another well-known term is QALY, meaning the Quality Adjusted Life Years of a person. This measurement combines the length of one's life with the respective quality, meaning that one year with perfect quality is one QALY.

vide the platform for a "democratic process" through "public reasoning" (ibid: 4, see also Sen 2004[11]) in order to discuss "which type of health care (eg, a list or basic benefits package) should be guaranteed and to what level" (Prah Ruger 2004: 1076). Thus, an approach based on central assumptions and elements of the CA would allow for (more) participatory processes in health, especially on the global level. This could support further orientation towards diversity in national health systems and international/global health initiatives, and it could offer concrete opportunities to groups such as persons with disabilities and persons with a migration background.[12]

4.3 Conclusion

To conclude, the contribution argues that a stronger focus on human diversity is required in global health, keeping in mind also intersectional issues. Several approaches are imaginable, among them a quality-of-life perspective as discussed above. The focus on the Capability Approach as a theoretical framework offers the opportunity to base the thematic discussion on questions of justice, agency and the diversity of living situations.

With respect to the group of persons with disabilities, it might be possible to adapt approaches in the form of "lessons learned" from the field of disability studies (see Swartz/Bantjes 2016) and policy as well as inclusive development. This includes the twin-track approach with a combination of mainstream as well as specifically targeted measures to reach and equally include a specific group of people – a transfer might be possible from the field of disability to the field of migration. Reasons for migration and impairment/disability can be closely related (e. g. war, natural disasters). In addition, migration can lead to impairments/disabilities in all different phases of the process (e. g. physical, psychological), and impairments/disabilities can lead to displacement or migration (e. g. cultural aspects, treatment (chronic illnesses)). Lastly, displacement and related risk factors/situations can be more burdensome for persons with disabilities (e. g. infrastructure in refugee camps, (in-)accessibility of services and information) (see e. g. Lorenzkowski 2002). Thus, it seems to be worthwhile drawing parallels between these two (and other diversity) categories.

Individual experiences of discrimination and exclusion need to be considered. Both groups are viewed as "problems", and often, persons with disabilities

---

11   There is an ongoing debate among CA scholars, especially Sen and Nussbaum, whether or not a pre-defined list of capabilities should exist and how to come to conclusions about which capabilities should be selected.

12   In addition to that, it might be worth taking into consideration community-based approaches. However, a more detailed discussion would go beyond the scope of this paper.

and persons with a migration background are physically excluded from main-stream society. This affects several areas of life, such as education, housing and labor – with effects in the field of health care, too (see Gummich 2015). In addition, both these groups are often rather passive recipients than contributing members of society. The "agency-dimension", meaning the view on migrants and persons with disabilities as "agents of development"/change agents (Piper 2017: 234) is required.

From a sociological perspective, the recommendation can be given to understand both disability and migration as dynamic concepts. For both, intra-group differences are the norm – "the typical" migrant/refugee or "the typical" person with disabilities does not exist, therefore measures need to be flexible and adaptable to personal living contexts as well as ideas and values. It is also important to keep in mind that several differences between the groups exist, with persons with disabilities being rather at the edge of society, whereas persons with a migration background are usually considered as "outsiders" (see Gummich 2015). This leads to differences in the provision of healthcare on a national level (citizenship status). Nonetheless, the comparison of the two diversity categories provides an interesting insight into the barriers to healthcare and the importance that a recognition of human diversity plays in regard to the design and implementation of programmes and measures. Accordingly, Crepaz and Dobusch (2017: 15) claim for the recognition of the "Einzigartigkeit gesundheit-licher Voraussetzungen, Bedarfslagen und Handlungsmöglichkeiten", i. e. the uniqueness of health-related preconditions, needs and opportunities for action [own translation].

In addition, elements from the area of social policy and social protection mechanisms are relevant. These include definitions of and perspectives on specific groups of (vulnerable) people as well as an awareness regarding their requirements and potential special needs/living situation. Also, social protection plays a role as far as the financing of health care interventions is concerned.

Generally, more data is needed on disability, migration and (global) health, but also regarding other diversity categories. This includes issues such as participatory research approaches, involving the target group in the planning, implementation and evaluation of scientific projects and data collections. Further sensitization of health care professionals (individual level) and global health players (systemic approach) is another factor that might need enhanced attention. Within international or global health organizations, a focus on diversity management as suggested by Crepaz and Dobusch (2017) could lead for the global health sector to become more responsive and sensitive to the requirements of a diversity focus. Against this background, it is also required to consider diversity as far as health care professionals are concerned. Coming back to the three-fold definition of governance issues, the aforementioned conclusions can be assigned as follows:

In the field of "globalization and health governance", inclusive approaches need to be intensified and current initiatives be re-thought from a diversity perspective, e. g. UHC. As far as "global governance for health" is concerned, awareness raising and intensified sensitization as well as a diversity mainstreaming/management approach are important factors to be considered. Lastly, the field of "governance for global health" offers the platform to discuss questions of diversity and health equity from a broader perspective and to engage in research-related activities to be able to base future initiatives on scientific evidence.

Bibliography

Beaglehole, R.; Bonita, R. (2010): What is Global Health? In: *Global Health Action*, (3), p. 5142 (2 pages).

Crepaz K.; Dobusch L. (2017): Migration als Herausforderung und Chance für das deutsche Gesundheitswesen: Zur Abkehr vom „Norm(al)patienten", In: *ZFPG*, 3 (2), pp. 12-18.

Domínguez, R.;Velázquez Flores, R. (2018): Global Governance. In: *Oxford Research Encyclopedia of International Studies*. Oxford University Press. https://doi.org/10.1093/acrefore/978019084 6626.013.508

Dood, R.; Hill, P. S. (2007): The Aid Effectiveness Agenda: Bringing Discipline to Diversity in Global Health? In: *Global Health Governance*, I (2), pp. 1-11.

Eichler, K. J. (2008): *Migration, transnationale Lebenswelten und Gesundheit. Eine qualitative Studie über das Gesundheitshandeln von Migrantinnen*. Wiesbaden: VS Verlag für Sozialwissenschaften.

Feldbaum, H.; Lee, K.; Michaud, J. (2010): Global health and foreign policy. In: *Epidemiologic reviews*, 32 (1). pp. 82-92.

Frenk, J.; Moon, S. (2013): Governance Challenges in Global Health. In: *The New England Journal of Medicine*, 368 (19), pp. 936-942.

Gray, B. H. & van Ginneken, E. (2012): *Health Care for Undocumented Migrants: European Approaches. Issues in International Health Policy*. Commonwealth Fund pub. 1650, Vol. 33. Link: https://www.commonwealthfund.org/sites/default/files/documents/___media_files_ publications_issue_brief_2012_dec_1650_gray_hlt_care_undocumented_migrants_intl_brief. pdf (last access: 13/06/2019).

Groce, N. (2011): Disability and Poverty: The Need for a More Nuanced Understanding of Implications for Development Policy and Practice. In: *Third World Quarterly*, 32, pp. 1493-1513.

Groce, N. et al. (2013): HIV Issues and People with Disabilities: A Review and Agenda for Research. In: *Social Science & Medicine*, 77, pp. 31-40.

Gummich, J. (2015): Migrationshintergrund und Behinderung – Herausforderungen an einer diskriminierungsrelevanten Schnittstelle. In: Domenig, D. et al. (eds.), *Vielfältig anders sein – Migration und Behinderung* (pp. 127-144). Zürich: Seismo Verlag.

Hemingway, L.; Priestley, M. (2014): Natural Hazards, Human Vulnerability and Disabling Societies: A Disaster for Disabled People? In: *Review of Disability Studies*, 2 (3). pp. 57-67.

Ingstad, B.; Eide, A. H. (2011): Introduction – Disability and Poverty: A Global Challenge. In: Eide, A. H.; Ingstad, B. (eds.), *Disability and Poverty. A Global Challenge* (pp. 1-14). Bristol: The Policy Press.

Karimi, M.; Brazier, J. (2016): Health, Health-Related Quality of Life, and Quality of Life: What is the Difference? In: *PharmacoEconomics*, 34 (7), pp. 645-649.

Kickbusch, I. (2006): The Need for a European Strategy on Global Health. In: *Scandinavian Journal of Public Health*, 34 (6), pp. 561-565.

Koplan, J. P. et al. (2009): Towards a Common Definition of Global Health. In: *The Lancet* 373 (9679), pp. 1993-1995.

Kuper, H.; Hanefeld, J. (2018): Debate: Can We Achieve Universal Health Coverage without a Focus on Disability? In: *BMC Health Services Research*, 18 (1), p. 738 (4 pages).

Larkin, M. (2009): *Vulnerable Groups in Health and Social Care*. Thousand Oaks: SAGE.

Lee, K.; Kamradt-Scott, A. (2014): The Multiple Meanings of Global Health Governance: A Call for Conceptual Clarity. In *Globalization and Health*, 10 (1), p. 28.

Lorenzkowski, Stefan (2002). Zusammenhänge von Flucht und Migration mit Behinderung. In: *Zeitschrift Behinderung und Dritte Welt* 2002 (2), pp. 52-58.

Mont, D. (2010): Social Protection and Disability. In: Barron, T.; Ncube, J. M. (Eds.), *Poverty and Disability* (pp. 317-339). London: Leonard Cheshire Disability.

Nussbaum, M. (2002): Capabilities and Social Justice. In: *International Studies Review*, 4 (2), pp. 123-135.

Oliver, M. (1996): *Understanding Disability. From Theory to Practice*. Houndmills: Macmillan.

Onarheim K.H. et al. (2018): Towards Universal Health Coverage: Including Undocumented Migrants. In: *BMJ Global Health*, 3 (5).

Palmer, M. (2011): Disability and Poverty: A Conceptual Review. In *Journal of Disability Policy Studies*, 21 (4), pp. 210-218.

Peek, L.; Stough, L. M. (2010): Children With Disabilities in the Context of Disaster: A Social Vulnerability Perspective. In: *Child Development*, 81 (4), pp. 1260-1270.

Piper, N. (2017): Migration and the SDGs. In: *Global Social Policy*, 17 (2), pp. 231-238.

Prah Ruger, J. (2004): Health and Social Justice. In: *The Lancet*, 364 (9439), pp. 1075-1080.

Robeyns, I. (2005): The Capability Approach: A Theoretical Survey. In: *Journal of Human Development,* 6 (1), pp. 93-114.

Sen, A. (1993): Capability and Well-Being. In: Nussbaum, M.; Sen, A. (eds.), *The Quality of Life* (pp. 30-53). Oxford: Clarendon Press.

Sen, A. (2004): Capabilities, Lists, and Public Reason: Continuing the Conversation. In: *Feminist Economics* 10 (3), pp. 77-80.

Shakespeare, T. (2013): The Social Model of Disability. In: Davis, L. J. (ed.), *The Disability Studies Reader* (pp. 214-221). New York: Routledge.

Swartz L.; Bantjes J. (2016): Disability and Global Health. In: Grech S.; Soldatic K. (eds.), *Disability in the Global South. International Perspectives on Social Policy, Administration, and Practice* (pp. 21-33). Springer: Cham.

Thomas, C. (2007): *Sociologies of Disability and Illness. Contested Ideas in Disability Studies and Medical Sociology*. Basingstoke: Palgrave Macmillan.

United Nations (UN) (2015): *Transforming Our World: The 2030 Agenda for Sustainable Development*. Link: https://www.un.org/ga/search/view_doc.asp?symbol=A/RES/70/1&Lang=E, last access 18/04/2019.

United Nations (UN) (2006): *Convention on the Rights of Persons with Disabilities*. Link: www.un.org/disabilities/documents/convention/convoptprot-e.pdf, last access 18/04/2019.

Vega J.; Frenz P. (2013): Integrating Social Determinants of Health in the Universal Health Coverage Monitoring Framework. In: *Revista Panamericana de Salud Pública* 34 (6), pp. 468-472.

Waldschmidt, A. (2005): Disability Studies: Individuelles, soziales und/oder kulturelles Modell von Behinderung? In: *Psychologie & Gesellschaftskritik,* 29 (1), pp. 9-30.

Wickramage, K. et al. (2018): Migration and Health: A Global Public Health Research Priority. *BMC Public Health,* 18 (1), p. 987 (9 pages).

Winker, G.; Degele, N. (2009): *Intersektionalität: Zur Analyse sozialer Ungleichheiten*. Bielefeld: transcript.

World Health Organization (WHO) (1978). *Declaration of Alma-Ata.* Link: https://www.who.int/publications/almaata_declaration_en.pdf, last access: 19/04/2019.

World Health Organization (WHO) (1986). *Ottawa Charter for Health Promotion*. Link: https://www.who.int/healthpromotion/conferences/previous/ottawa/en/, last access: 19/04/2019.

World Health Organization (WHO) (2005): *International Health Regulations* (IHR). Link (3rd edition 2016): https://apps.who.int/iris/bitstream/handle/10665/246107/9789241580496-eng.pdf;jsessionid=A93130EE5C32F72E1CDD1D5DE1F7EAF1?sequence=1, last access: 19/04/2019.

World Health Organization (WHO) & World Bank (WB) (2011). *World report on disability*. Link: https://www.who.int/disabilities/world_report/2011/report.pdf, last access: 19/04/2019.

World Health Organization (WHO) (2015). *Global Disability Action Plan 2014-2021. Better Health for All People with Disability*. Link: https://apps.who.int/iris/bitstream/handle/10665/199544/9789241509619_eng.pdf?sequence=1, last access: 19/04/2019.

World Health Organization (WHO) (2019a). *Promoting the Health of Refugees and Migrants. Draft Global Action Plan, 2019–2023*. Link: https://apps.who.int/gb/ebwha/pdf_files/EB144/B144_27-en.pdf, last access: 13/06/2019.

World Health Organization (WHO) (2019b). *Universal Health Coverage (UHC)*. Link: https://www.who.int/news-room/fact-sheets/detail/universal-health-coverage-(uhc), last access: 19/04/2019.

World Health Organization (WHO) (n. d.). *Health Financing. Universal Health Coverage and Health Financing*. Link: https://www.who.int/health_financing/universal_coverage_definit ion/en/, last access: 19/04/2019.

Yeo, R.; Moore, K. (2003): Including Disabled People in Poverty Reduction Work: "Nothing About Us, Without Us". In: *World Development,* 31 (3), pp. 571-590.

Quality of Life: Coping Strategies and Innovations among Forced Migrants in Encampment in the Tana Delta in Kenya

Sellah Lusweti, Obeka Bonventure and Halimu Shauri[1]

Key words: forced migration, encampment, flooding, Tana Delta, quality of life.

Abstract

Forced migration brings together different people from all walks of life, drawing into the equation coping abilities of such individuals. In most cases, forced migration is characterized by few job opportunities and harsh economic and social environments. It is notable that such migrants are compelled to bear life as it is presented to them, thereby innovating mechanisms that can support their new lifestyles. This paper explores the coping strategies and innovations of (and for) forced migrants living in encampment in the Tana Delta, Kenya. A phenomenological research design was employed to study forced migrants in encampment in the Tana Delta. Convenience sampling was employed in selecting the respondents. Data was collected from 39 respondents from three refugee camps using interview schedules with the assistance of two locals research assistants recruited from the local community. The findings of the study reveal that forced migrants of the Tana Delta have shown resilience by sustaining their livelihood. While in encampment, they came up with new solutions and/or new applications

1   Sellah Lusweti | Pwani University Kilifi | s.lusweti@pu.ac.ke

Obeka Bonventure | Pwani University Kilifi | obekabonventure@gmail.com

Halimu Shauri | Pwani University Kilifi | hshauri@yahoo.com

© Springer Fachmedien Wiesbaden GmbH, part of Springer Nature 2020
K. Crepaz et al. (eds.), *Health in Diversity – Diversity in Health*,
https://doi.org/10.1007/978-3-658-29177-8_10

of existing products, technologies, services and organizational models to keep up with the realities of life in encampment.

Contents

Abstract...171

1   Introduction 173

2   Problematization 173

3   Methodology 174

4   Findings of the Study 175

5   Discussion of Key Findings 178

6   Innovation Success Stories of Migrants from across the World 179

7   Coping Strategies and Innovations from the Tana Delta Migrants in
     Encampment...180

8   Fears of Migrants in Encampment in the Tana Delta 181

9   Suggested Methodology to Encourage Innovation among Migrants 182

10   Reasons for Supporting Innovation among Forced Migrants.................182

11   Conclusion 183

Bibliography 183

1   Introduction

Forced migration is a phenomenon widely associated with structural, developmental, economic and political factors (Tognetti & Jackson, 2017). Forced migration has been on a steady rise globally; according to the United Nations High Commissioner for Refugees (UNHCR), 68.5 million people around the world have been forced to leave their homes, among them nearly 25.4 million refugees, over half of whom are under the age of 18 years. It is also estimated that 10 million people are stateless – denied a nationality and access to basic rights such as education, healthcare, employment and freedom of movement. Nearly one person is forcibly displaced every two seconds as a result of conflict or persecution (ibid).

Crepeau (2008) observes that migration is related to a multiplicity of causalities that could either be considered compulsive or voluntary. A displacement of persons can happen at national level as well as between countries, depending on the magnitude of trigger factors that may sometimes compel individuals to go cross borders. Furthermore, Tognetti and Jackson (2017) note that forced migration is a phenomenon widely associated with developing countries and is often a result of structural, developmental, economic and political factors. It is noted that, globally, forced migration is on a steady rise with an estimated 65.6 million forced migrants in 2016, up from a paltry 39.9 million in 1997, a situation protracted by natural disasters and regional conflicts (ibid). Dadush and Niebuhr (2016, p. 1) concur with the fact that there is a global refugee crisis that has had a profound impact on families and nations. They further note that forced migration is characterized by few job opportunities, a strain on public services and infrastructure, job losses or falling wages and other negative externalities for the surrounding regions.

2   Problematization

The Tana Delta is located at the Kenyan Coast where River Tana greatly influences the lives of people living in the riverine environment. The Tana Delta is an ecologically and economically rich area, and is significant as a region due to its constant water availability and land fertility on its banks, while it lies within a larger region that is classified as semi-arid. Despite the resource, the River Tana's unpredictable nature has often resulted in destructive floods that have forced inhabitants of the area to migrate (Kirchner, 2013). In 2018, it was estimated that floods displaced over 211,000 people in various parts of the country including in the Tana Delta (Office for the Cordination of Humanitarian

Affairs, 2018). In the Tana Delta, the displaced communities are mostly the Pokomo (who are agriculturalists) and the Orma/Wardei (who are pastoralists).

Evidently, forced migration congregates individuals with differentiated abilities and levels of resilience, which by a greater margin dictates the coping abilities of such individuals. In their study on life in refugee camps in Kenya, Shauri and Obeka (2019) narrate the difficulties refugees – especially those with disability – undergo to cope with life in encampment. In this regard, depending on what is available to them as they leave their homes, the quality of life of many migrants typically plunges. 'Quality of Life' (QoL) broadly encompasses how an individual measures the 'goodness' of multiple aspects of his or her life. These evaluations include one's emotional reactions to life occurrences, disposition, sense of life fulfilment and satisfaction, and satisfaction with work and personal relationships (Diener, Suh, Lucas & Smith,1999 in Theofilou, 2013, p. 151). In this study, QoL was viewed in terms of life satisfaction, measured by the following factors: material living conditions (income, consumption and material conditions), family size, productive or main activity, health and sanitation, leisure and social interactions, and education. Many times, migrants are compelled to put up with life conditions by finding mechanisms that can support their new lifestyles; these mechanisms may or may not be sustainable but are usually the limited option they are forced to make.

Tognetti and Jackson (2017, p. 6) observe that when forced migrants exhaust coping pathways, there is often the danger of food insecurity that may force them to "employ more extreme and potentially damaging strategies that are less reversible and could put them at further risk. It is within this framework that this paper aims at exploring the coping strategies of forced migrants living in encampment in the Tana Delta in Kenya, as compared to coping and innovation in situations of forced migration across the world.

3   Methodology

The output of this paper is a product of real experiences documented from three camps of forced migrants in the Tana Delta in Kenya. The study was conducted through phenomenological research that aimed to qualitatively describe how forced migrants experience life in encampment. The design allowed the researchers to delve into the lived experiences, perceptions, and perspectives of migrants. Data was collected using interview schedules with the assistance of two (2) research assistants recruited from the local community, who had knowledge of the area and an understanding of the language and culture. The assistants were trained in data collection and ethical consideration in conducting research with vulnerable populations.

4   Findings of the Study

In this study, 39 respondents (44% male and 56% female) were purposively sampled from the studied camps. The migrants interviewed were aged between 20 and 61 years; over half (54%) were aged 31-40 years. Over three fifths (61.5%) of the respondents had not attended school and only less than one tenth (5.1%) had completed their secondary school level education.

When asked about the size of households in the camps within the Tana Delta, it was found out that over two fifths (43.6%) of the respondents were living in a house holding 6 to 8 family members, while over one quarter (28%) of respondents reported living in a house with between 9 and 14 members. The makeshift households in the camp, as shown in Plate 1, are structures made from twigs and branches, covered with a canvas of about 3x3 meters.

Figure 1: Homestead for forced migrants in the Tana Delta

From the study findings, about three quarters (74%) of the respondents categorically stated that the housing they had was insufficient for their families. They have had to construct smaller structures that had no canvas protection so that some members of the household could be 'offloaded' to the smaller constructions, a situation that becomes dire especially considering that these families are in encampment during the rainy seasons. Despite this, most (90%) mentioned that there was no need to restructure their place, probably because they view it as a temporary shelter from which they will soon depart.

Quality of life as an indicator of life satisfaction considers the level of income of respondents. Four fifths (80%) of family members were not engaged in any form of income-generating activity, and less than 10% of respondents had 2 or 3 members working. The main source of income for most families was animal keeping (67%), followed by crop farming (15%), and trade (13%), and only 5% reported to be on paid wages/salary. The finding that most (67%) are livestock keepers is in keeping with the Tana Region's economic activity profile as the majority of the residents are pastoralist farmers who do not subscribe to a sedentary lifestyle.

When asked about their monthly income, over three fifths (65%) of the forced migrants had an income of less than USD$50 per month, over one quarter (26%) made between USD$51 and 80 per month, and less than one tenth (9%) had USD$81 to 150 a month. Being that these families are pastoralists, it was noted that most of the income mentioned was from sale of livestock. Field observation shows that there is a livestock sale market every Saturday in the study site. On probing the forced migrants with regard to their economic rights, it was found that three quarters (75%) of respondents agreed that they had the freedom to practice their economic activities. However, given the environmental conditions in which they found themselves, they often faced challenges since there was hardly any grass or foliage for their animals. For those who were farmers, they had the freedom to practice their trade; however, the land is usually not tillable since the area is arid. This implies that life in encampment is inhibiting for forced migrants with regard to the freedom to practice economic activities in the area, and given the limited livelihood opportunities they could explore.

The study further found that over two fifths (45%) of the respondents indicated that their living standards, whether in the camp or in their homes, had remained the same, with over two fifths (42%) saying that life in encampment was worse than the life at home, while slightly more than one tenth (13%) mentioned that life in the camps was better than life in their original places of residence.

Results reveal that over half (54%) of the forced migrants do not have enough to eat while in encampment. Such a reality is typical of many families in camps as they are given rations that are way below their daily needs. As for the residents of the Tana Delta camps, they supplement their few rations with their own supply of meat and milk from their pastoralist activity, and they also sell their livestock when in dire need for foodstuff. Attempts have been made to engage camp residents in livelihood promotion projects. Indeed, over half (51%) of the forced migrants mentioned that they were part of a livelihood project.

However, the majority (90%) mentioned that the projects they were in were unsuccessful.

On a very positive note, it was found that an overwhelming majority (95%) of the forced migrants indicated that they were able to send their children to school despite living in the camps. Of the sample, it was also found that over four fifths (87%) said they were satisfied with the educational facilities provided to their children, although 34% intimated that they were having difficulties paying school fees for their children. Their difficulty in paying fees was corroborated by a key informant, who happened to be a principal of a secondary school neighbouring one of the camps, when he reiterated that:

> "....migrants have difficulties paying fees for their children....in my school we had to innovated a way to help them by allowing them to pay fee balances of their children, either by exchange with livestock or firewood that we use to cook food for the students".

Study respondents further revealed that over four fifths (87%) had tapped water, while one tenth (10%) depended on tanks and less than one tenth (3%) on dam water. The finding on over four fifths (87%) of the respondents mentioning access to tap water is explained by the close proximity of the camps to tap water sources as observed during the field work. This means that the choice of the camp sites was well made to address water access problems, which has implications for the sanitation and health of the displaced populations.

Results of the study also show that the majority (90%) of respondents said they used solar power, with less than one tenth (8%) using wood fuel and 2% using kerosene. The higher (90%) percentage of the displaced population citing the use of solar energy was a surprise finding in the study. However, it was observed during the survey that many homesteads had small solar panels for lighting and charging mobile phones, among other uses. Interestingly, over three fifths (64%) mentioned that the solar lighting was adequate for their needs.

It follows from the findings that availability of water is a very important resource for pastoralist communities and this, together with the advantage of being able to send their children to school, as well as solar lighting, could very well account for the assertion of over one third (45%) of the forced migrants that the standard of living in the camps was the same as the quality of life they had in their former homes; 13% even mentioned that their life in encampment had turned distinctly to the better.

Further, the survey probed on the adequacy of health facilities available to forced migrants. Findings reveal that of the sample, only over one quarter (28%) were satisfied with the health facilities available to them; while less than a fifth (18%) were satisfied with the toilet facilities they had. Health and sanitation is a matter of utmost importance for people in encampment in the Tana Delta given that these communities are in camps close to areas that are often badly flooded, opening them up to many health-related vulnerabilities. These areas are therefore prone to diseases such as malaria, cholera and bilharzia. Additionally, the Tana River is well-known to be heavily infested with deadly crocodiles and Tsetse flies. As the river breaks its banks, these dangerous animals and insects roam the flood waters and have been the cause of many injuries, diseases and deaths for the already struggling migrants, as reported by some respondents during our interviews in the area.

Finally, it was reported that the main source of lighting in the camps is solar energy. Solar power as an innovation in the Tana Delta camps is of key importance, noting that often the regions around camps are depleted of resources as the migrants search for firewood and food for sustenance. The use of solar power also assures the residents a certain level of security and a decent evening life. Above all, such innovations minimize conflict between the residents in camps and the host communities since there is less competition for the limited energy resources available, especially during flood episodes. This finding was interesting in that while the country and the world seem to still be grappling with the question of how to enhance the adoption of green energy, the majority (90%) of forced immigrants in the Tana River Delta have already adopted it.

5   Discussion of Key Findings

When dealing with encampment, the focus of many people is usually on the chaotic scenes experienced in camps. Little attention is paid to the positive events and happenings such as the coping strategies that make migrants prosper against all odds. The boredom and passivity seen in camps is daunting, especially when it is evident that many in the camps have low levels of education, are unemployed or are not gainfully engaged, and that many of them are young persons. These persons are thus 'waiting in temporary exile' until they can safely return home or until safety nets are provided by mitigation stakeholders. While this waiting and passivity is often the breeding ground for negativity and criminal thoughts, it is also often the genesis of innovations. This is probable because many of the encamped migrants want to move beyond humanitarian assistance and are desperately trying to generate livelihoods for themselves and their families in their quest to adapt to or survive these harsh and dehumanizing conditions..

Innovation among migrant communities has been evidenced throughout history; migrants often seize opportunities that might leave the host communities with a feeling that they have been sidelined or excluded. Historically, migrant communities have often succeeded despite the difficulties they encounter. In Kenya, for example, the Somali community is well-known for their ability to start up innovative businesses and to reach places previously considered inaccessible; often they have had to prove themselves worthy of a place in the community, and have had to show a high level of solidarity and integrity to survive economically and socially.

6   Innovation Success Stories of Migrants from across the World

The motivation and consideration for highlighting success stories for the present study was drawn from some successful innovations reported from forced migrant communities across the world. Precisely, Coburawas Primary School in Uganda, started by Congolese refugees, is presently a prestigious and high-performing school sending many of its students to the national university (Athumani, 2018). Still in Uganda, forced migrants in Nakivale Settlement have built their own local radio station by using locally available materials (University of Oxford, 2014). The station has been providing much-needed information to the migrants over a radius of 5 to 10 kilometers, thereby increasing awareness and safety levels.

There have also been new and innovative phone applications for migrants: InfoAid is an application developed by volunteers to assist refugees in transit along the Balkan route traveling through Southeast Europe, offering advice and updates as migrants sought refuge (Benton & Glennie, 2016). BureauCrazy is another application developed by Syrian refugees to help new arrivals in Germany to better navigate German bureaucracy during their asylum seeking process (Kirchner, 2016).

In Ethiopia, UNHCR's Energy Lab partnered with refugees to develop a prototype stove made from oil cans (Corbett, Frey & Marjanovic, 2019). Oxfam and the University of West of England developed electricity-generating urinals to solve two problems at once: waste disposal and energy conservation (Oxfam International, 2015). Further support for migrant innovation is evidenced through the United Nations Refugee Agency, which partnered with Amman Bank in Jordan to pilot iris scanning technology to help refugees access cash assistance without the requirement of a bank card or a pin code (Dunmore, 2015). A similar initiative was started by the World Refugee Fund (WRF), which overcame the bias against refugee lending (Kiva, 2018): they support refugees around the world (Middle East, Colombia, Burundi, Congo, Rwanda and Syria) to start up their businesses so that they can be self-sufficient.

Taking a different approach, Humanitarian Innovation Jam is an annual festival that brings together humanitarians, academicians and the private sector to discuss and problem-solve around humanitarian innovations (UNHCR, 2016). The 2016 edition had a special focus on convening refugee and host community innovators who wanted to develop the best possible solutions to their community's biggest challenges.

Thus, the overwhelming (90%) adoption of greener energy innovations using solar power among the forced migrants in the Tana Delta is an addition to the growing repository of technology and innovations that is useful in helping human populations in desperate situations. What is more crucial is that lessons and best practices can be learned from these forced migrants to enhance the adoption of solar power as an alternative and clean energy source also for households that are not in distressed conditions.

7 Coping Strategies and Innovations from the Tana Delta Migrants in Encampment

Among the forced migrants in the Tana Delta, there are many business start-ups that include the exchange of goods and services in the new settlements. The migrants have good business sense that helps them to transcend from their homes to camps, and back home while sustaining their businesses all through. It was indicated that even when in the camps, migrants are able to sustain and expand their livelihoods and to positively influence their lives when they return home. While in the camps, they are able to import products from their home areas to the host communities, and they also export goods from the host places back to their homelands. Such an expansion and exchange of goods and ideas is born from the need to seal either a social or an economic gap; it eventually reduces and bridges interpersonal differences between communities.

Being mostly pastoral communities (or influenced by pastoral lifestyles), these migrants easily adapt to new housing conditions, and although the conditions are generally very poor both in their original homes and in the camps, they make do with the little provided to them by adapting their traditional housing style to the limited supply of housing material provided to them through humanitarian aid. These migrants also relocate with most of their possessions, including livestock; they are therefore more adaptable than other groups as they are able to supplement the little rations given to them by providing for themselves and getting the most needed proteins (meat and milk) from their salvaged livestock.

When considering aspects of health, very little is provided to migrants. As mentioned by the respondents, only 28% were satisfied with the health facilities they have. Many mentioned the use of the Neem tree (locally called *Mwarobaini*) as a source of medication. Extracts from the tree are believed to treat up to 40 diseases, including malaria, diarrhea, back pain, toothache and others. Green twigs from the tree are also used as medicated toothbrushes, thus there is no need for toothpaste.

Social support systems in migrant camps are wanting; there are many social groupings formed for security purposes, for receiving rations and also for business start-ups. However, these groupings are informal and are typically reflective of failed social support systems from the government. Notwithstanding, the research team was informed that informal groups are often sustained even after departure from the camps, especially knowing that the next rainy season will bring with it a similar plight.

A very positive innovation in the Tana Delta camps was the report that 90% of the migrants were using solar energy for lighting. The use of such sustainable resources in adverse conditions such as camps is an indication that this technology can be adapted even in established communities. The hours of sunshine on any given day in the Tana Delta would range from 6 to 8, accumulating into very effective solar-powered lighting by the end of day. If such innovative ideas could be extended to sources of energy for cooking and to sanitation, then the quality of life in the camps could be significantly improved.

The schooling system for the migrants has been adapted to allow for the continuation of class attendance and progression, whether the communities are in their homes or in camps. The provision of teachers and the ability to accommodate migrants in schools within the host communities is a forward-looking innovative solution for the migrant communities. More precisely, the researchers were told that:

> "...Garsen High school had to accommodate all students whose schools had been destroyed by the floods in the displacement areas".

More so, as was seen from the study, it is mostly those with very low levels of education that often found themselves in the camps. Consistency in educating the younger generations thus assures future generations a possible escape route out of the vicious circle of illiteracy, poverty and flood-related forced migration.

8   Fears of Migrants in Encampment in the Tana Delta

The following are the fears and problems that most migrants in the camps have to deal with as they try to innovate and cope: Camps develop unpredictably; there is hardly any planned structure for their arrival, stay or departure. Further, many camps run on aid which is short-lived. There is a lot of fear of abuse or being taken advantage of since migrants are people in difficult situations and may not really have a strong voice to defend themselves. There are also inefficient legal and political systems regulating entrepreneurial activity. If a very innovative product is made, the migrants fear that there is poor documentation of innovations and achievements, and thus they may be cheated out of what they produce or invent. They also complained about the inefficient infrastructure connecting entrepreneurs to information, consumers or markets. Finally, it was also noted that many financial institutions see forced migrants as risk borrowers; these institutions require documentation and guarantees which the migrants do not have, limiting their opportunities to escape this predicament.

9 Suggested Methodology to Encourage Innovation among Migrants

Forced migrants were challenged during the study on how best they could be encouraged to become innovative and enhance their quality of life. The following suggestions were received:

- Integration of camp activities (social, economic, political, etc.) into host community activities
- Minimize barriers of engagement (such as confinement) with local communities
- Encourage the use of renewable energies and sustainable solutions
- Outsource tasks/jobs to refugees and migrants by local community and organizations
- Encourage business incubation and acceleration among forced migrants
- Embedded knowledge sharing in migrant programs – with peers, with host communities, with experts in diverse areas that can promote their quality of life

10 Reasons for Supporting Innovation among Forced Migrants

In many cases of political and economic crises, it should be recognized that refugees and forced migrants have a variety of professional backgrounds, abilities and skills to offer. Accordingly, they should not only be seen as a burden by the host communities but as a useful resource that can contribute to the social economics of the area. Indeed, like the local population or communities, they have assets and not just needs. Refugees and migrants also have high rates of return, whether it is on education and awareness, or on loan repayment rates (they are at par with non-refugee borrowers, according to the World Refugee Fund as cited in Kiva 2018).

A paradigm shift is thus necessary to understand that refugees and forced migrants have the ability to significantly contribute to the local economies. We must understand that there are unique and specific opportunities emanating from migrants that can be explored. If participatory approaches are used to bring out these potentialities, community inhabitants and migrants are likely to have more peaceful and beneficial encounters between them.

For most of the forced migrants of the Tana Delta, life in the camps is not very different from life in their former homes; both areas suffer difficult environmental and socioeconomic conditions. Yet, the provision of water, lighting, education opportunities, and the freedom to engage in economic activities has significantly improved the quality of life in the camps. It is possible therefore to use innovation and tap into the resilience of migrants to restructure at least one of these environments (either at home or in the camps) for it to be attractive enough in such a way that migrants do not have to move from one difficult terrain to another difficult terrain every year.

11 Conclusion

Forced migrants of the Tana Delta have shown resilience by sustaining their livelihood while in encampment; their coping strategies have been functional. Coming up with new solutions and/or new applications of existing products, technologies, services and organizational models can have a great impact on the quality of life of people living in forced migration. However, more innovation is needed for employment generation, business and technology incubation, health and sanitation solutions and the resolution of social concerns. Apparently, it cannot be denied that managing innovations is terrifying; this is because one has to manage expectations and resistance, and still meet the needs of the people. Embracing technologies such as sustainable energy and lifestyle products can be good innovation, especially if working with the principle of 'putting the last first'. Refugees and forced migrants could lead the way for communities across the world. With a view to the global framework of green energy, the useful lesson of the widespread use of solar energy among forced migrants in camps in the Tana Delta is a good example for communities, stable or in distress, to emulate a sustainable future.

Bibliography

Athumani, A. (2018): Refugee School Gives Hope, Free Education in Uganda. https://www.voanews.com/a/refugee-school-gives-hope-free-education-west-uganda/ 4319053 .html

Benton, M. & Glennie, A. (2016): Digital Humanitarianism; How Tech Entrepreneurs are Supporting Refugee Integration.

Crepeau, F. (2008): Forced Migration. In P. Cane, J. Conaghan, & M. W. David (Eds.), The New Oxford Companion to Law. Oxford University Press .

Dadush, U., & Niebuhr, M. (2016): The Economic Impact of Forced Migraton. OCP Policy Center.

Dunmore, C. (2015): Iris Scan System Provides Cash Lifeline to Syrian Refugees in Jordan. https://www.unhcr.org/news/latest/2015/3/550fe6ab9/iris-scan-system-provides-cash-lifeline-syrian-refugees-jordan.html

Kirchner, K. (2013): Conflicts and Politics in the Tana Delta, Kenya: An Analysis of the 2012-2013 Clashes and the General and Presidential Elections 2013. Master Thesis, University of Leiden, African Studies.

Kirchner, S. (2016): Syrian Refugees Create App to Help Navigate German Bureaucracy. https://www.washingtonpost.com/news/worldviews/wp/2016/08/09/syrian-refugees-create-app-to-help-navigate-german-bureaucracy/?noredirect=on&utm_term=.ca17e07e36e7

Corbett, J., Frey, C. & Marjanovic, S. (2019): How Innovation Can Assist the Refugee Pathway. https://www.rand.org/blog/2017/06/how-innovation-can-assist-the-refugee-pathway.html

Kiva (2018): World Refugee Fund Impact Report. https://www.kiva.org/cms/world_refugee_fund_impact_report_2018_press_release_6.20.18.pdf

Office for the Cordination of Humanitarian Affairs (2018): Floods in Kenya. United Nations Office for the Coordination of Human Affairs.

Oxfam International (2015): 'Pee-Power' to Light Camps in Disaster Zones. https://www.oxfam.org/en/pressroom/pressreleases/2015-03-05/pee-power-light-camps-disaster-zones

Shauri, H., & Obeka B., (2019): Life in Refugee Camps: The Challenges of Refugees with Disability in Kenya, SPRINGER (2019). ISBN No: 978-3-658-24537-5. ISBN No: 978-3-658-24538-2. https://doi.org/10.1007/978-3658-24538-2. Library of Congress Control No: 2018962630.

Theofilou, P. (2013): Quality of Life: Definition and Measurement. Europe's Journal of Psychology. Vol. 9 (1), 152-164

Tognetti, S., & Jackson, J. (2017): Forced Migration and Protracted Crisis: A Multilayered Approach. Food and Agriculture Organization . Food and Agriculture Organization .

UNHCR (2016): Humanitarian Innovation Jam 2016. http://hij.unhcrinnovation.org/

University of Oxford (2014): Forced Migration Review, Supplement, Sept 2014. https://www.fmreview.org/sites/fmr/files/FMRdownloads/en/innovation.pdf.

6. Diversity in Refugee Camps

Violence Against Women in Camps? Exploring Links between Refugee Camp Conditions and the Prevalence of Violence

Ulrike Krause[1]

Keywords: Gender-based violence, refugee camp, women, Uganda.

Abstract

Although refugee camps are set up to provide protective environments for refugees in host countries, refugees can still be confronted with various risks in such situations of encampment. In this chapter, the forms and scope of gender-based violence against women in camps are explored and their relation to camp conditions are assessed. Based on empirical research, mainly conducted with Congolese refugees in a camp in Uganda, the chapter reveals that sexual violence, domestic violence, and structural discrimination constitute the main forms prevalent in the camp. These occur despite humanitarian projects implemented to protect and assist refugees and especially women and, at times, even precisely because of the particular circumstances that exist in these settings. The limitations imposed by the camp and experienced within it, the hierarchical procedures, and the humanitarian focus placed on women can lead to frustration among refugees and directly or indirectly contribute to violence.

---

1   Ulrike Krause | Institute for Migration Research and Intercultural Studies (IMIS) and Institute for Social Sciences, Osnabrück University | ulrike.krause@uni-osnabrueck.de

© Springer Fachmedien Wiesbaden GmbH, part of Springer Nature 2020
K. Crepaz et al. (eds.), *Health in Diversity – Diversity in Health*,
https://doi.org/10.1007/978-3-658-29177-8_11

Contents

Abstract..187

1   Introduction 189

2   Background and Research Approach 190

3   The Camp as a Humanitarian Site of Protection or Context for
     Violence?..193

3.1 Humanitarian Aid and Structures in Kyaka II...194

3.2 Prevalence of Sexual and Gender-based Violence in Uganda's Kyaka II.196

3.3 Associating Violence with Camp Conditions..198

4   Conclusions 203

Acknowledgements 205

Bibliography 205

1   Introduction

Most of the world's refugees have left their homes due to various types of danger that often result from violent conflicts. Once refugees have reached host countries, many are initially settled in refugee camps. These camp sites can be seen as 'safe havens' because refugees receive shelter as well as access to humanitarian protection and assistance. But for the past several decades, scholars working in the field of forced migration and refugee studies have shed light on the often difficult conditions experienced by refugees in camps (see Harrell-Bond 1986; Agier 2011; McConnachie 2014). Insufficient aid, limited economic livelihoods, restricted opportunities for political participation, and confined social living conditions are just some of these issues. Another prevailing problem is violence. Insecurity can affect all refugees in camps, but certain groups may be exposed to particular forms of violence (for an overview, see Krause 2018). Since the 1980s, feminist scholars have stressed that women are at a high risk of being exposed to gender-specific threats of violence in refugee camps, such as sexual abuse (among others, Callaway 1985; Friedman 1992). These threats are central in this chapter.

The chapter seeks to explore the forms and scope of gender-based violence women in camps are confronted with. Moreover, the question of how this violence is linked to the conditions and humanitarian structures present in refugee camps, which are actually put in place to protect and assist the people, is examined. To this end, the chapter draws on empirical research that was carried out in 2014, mainly with refugees from the Democratic Republic of Congo who lived in the camp Kyaka II in Uganda. Gender-based violence is – in line with the Inter-Agency Standing Committee (IASC) – generally understood as acts of harm, threats of violence and force used against a person due to her or his (ascribed) gender identity (IASC 2015: 5). Although gender-based violence is not limited to women as victims, a focus is placed on women in this chapter.

Based on the empirical findings gathered in Uganda's Kyaka II, it is argued that the overall conditions in the camp are difficult; the camp represents a confined and regulated environment which is shaped by humanitarian structures. The most prevalent forms of gender-based violence to which women are exposed are sexual violence, domestic violence, and structural discrimination of denial of resources and early and forced marriage of girls. Although each case of violence is unique, the findings suggest that certain conditions in the camp can contribute to the prevalence of these risks. The confined nature of camp sites and their limited opportunities as well as certain approaches used in humanitarian projects can affect or even increase the likelihood of violence against women.

These arguments are presented in this chapter as follows: After addressing the literature about the subject and outlining the research approach, the general conditions and humanitarian structures in Kyaka II as well as the forms and scope of gender-based violence are explored. Associations between this violence and the camp conditions are subsequently analysed. The chapter concludes with suggestions of possible changes that can be made to humanitarian aid to decrease such risks.

2 Background and Research Approach

Different types of refugee camps such as 'settlements', 'hotspots', or 'reception centres' (in German, *Erstaufnahmeeinrichtungen*) can be formally distinguished from one another, but their overall setup, operation, and decision-making structures are similar worldwide. These camps generally serve to provide shelter, protection and assistance for refugees until one of the three durable solutions[1] is found. As geographically and temporally confined spaces that are usually established in rural regions in host countries, camps are often physically, socially, and economically widely isolated from the surrounding world (Werker 2007; Jaji 2012). Refugee camps are typically under the administrative power of the host countries' governments and often the United Nations High Commissioner for Refugees (UNHCR), while a number of aid agencies run projects for protection and assistance (Agier 2011; Janmyr 2014; Jansen 2011).

Scholars have extensively criticised these camp and aid projects due to the rigidity of the structures and regulations as well as the living conditions of refugees. In her widely recognised book *Imposing Aid*, Barbara Harrell-Bond (1986) provides a detailed account of the 'imposed' approach of protection and assistance, as well as the existence of restrictive and dangerous conditions, for the people in refugee camps. Liisa Malkki (1995: 498) describes camps as a "standardized, generalizable technology of power [...] in the management of mass displacement", and Rose Jaji (2012: 227) refers to them as "a form of human warehousing". Kirsten McConnachie and Simon Turner support these tendencies, emphasising the contradictory nature of camps; these are marked "by restricted autonomy and by resilient agency" (McConnachie 2016: 407), and refugees are invisible in camps but are also the visible objects of humanitarian aid (Turner 2016: 144). Moreover, Sarah Deardorff Miller (2018) discusses how humanitarian agencies in camps constitute "surrogate states", while Michel Agier (2011: 196) frames these agencies as "humanitarian governments".

---

[1]   The three durable solutions are the voluntary repatriation to the country of origin, resettlement to a third country, and local integration into a country of asylum.

Such critical analyses are part of a growing body of research literature. Empirical findings put into question whether refugee camps constitute 'safe havens' for refugees in the way political and humanitarian actors anticipate but reveal that camps represent difficult sites and at times "violent places" (Jansen 2011: 86). Through case studies conducted in various regions of the world, scholars have also demonstrated the diverse forms and high levels of insecurity faced by refugees during encampment, such as robbery, violent attacks, and sexual assault (see, among others, Lischer 2005; Peteet 2005; McConnachie 2014). Still, the forms, conditions, and effects of this violence are not the same for the whole 'camp population'. As noted above, since the 1980s, feminist studies have illustrated the importance of taking gender-sensitive perspectives in research when examining refugees' situations to shed light on the dangers that especially women face (Indra 1987; Greatbatch 1989; Ferris 1990; de Neef/de Ruiter 1984; Ljungdell 1989). Several recent studies have been carried out to explore the gender-specific characteristics and forms of violence against women[2] in refugee situations (see Buckley-Zistel/Krause 2017; Freedman 2015; Martin/Tirman 2009).

The respective insights gained show that women and girls are at a high risk of experiencing such violence in refugee camps on the basis of their gender and attributed characteristics such as passivity and obedience.[3] This violence can take diverse form, among others sexual assault, discrimination, harmful practices such as female genital mutilation, domestic violence, and social exclusion (Horn 2010; Carlson 2005; Hartmann 2017; Fiddian-Qasmiyeh 2010). Various studies have revealed that the risks of violence against women are not necessarily limited to certain refugee camps but are widespread. For example, as a result of her ethnographic research in Algerian camps, Elena Fiddian-Qasmiyeh (2014: 248 ff; 2010) highlights that violence against women takes places in both the public and private spheres. In her study on Somali refugees, Awa Mohamed Abdi (2006: 238) reveals that rape of women was not only "a key weapon in the Somali civil war" but that "violence against refugee women [continued] in and around the camps" in Kenya. Moreover, taking a spatial perspective, Melanie Hartmann (2017) reflects on gender-based violence against women in camp settings in Germany. These are just some of several studies that have shed light on gender-based violence against women in refugee camps.

---

2   This focus placed on gender-based violence against women in this chapter is not meant to prioritize such risks and this particular group over others. In fact, a slowly growing body of research underlines that men and boys also make negative experiences of gender-based violence (see, e.g., Turner 1999; Jaji 2009; Kabachnik et al. 2013).

3   Although the corpus of research is smaller, several scholars have also addressed gender-specific conditions of and violence against men in exile (among others, Turner 1999; Jaji 2009; Lukunka 2011; Kabachnik et al. 2013; Janmyr 2017).

Gender-based violence may be perpetrated by other refugees but also carried out by actors who are supposed to provide protection and security, i.e., staff of humanitarian organisations, security forces, and administrative institutions. Elizabeth Ferris (2007: 585) criticises cases in which "[h]umanitarian workers traded food and relief items for sexual favors. Teachers in schools in the camps exploited children in exchange for passing grades. Medical care and medicines were given in return for sex." This criticism already leads us to the central question asked in this chapter: how gender-based violence against women is associated with the structures in refugee camps.

For the analysis in this chapter, I draw on empirical research carried out in the context of the project *Gender Relations in Confined Spaces. Conditions, Scope and Forms of Violence against Women in Conflict-related Refugee Camps.* This project was led by Susanne Buckley-Zistel, funded by the German Foundation for Peace Research, and carried out by the author of this chapter. The research included empirical work conducted in the refugee camp Kyaka II in Uganda in 2014, where mainly refugees from the Democratic Republic of Congo (DRC) were placed. Data were gathered by means of a mixed-method approach. In addition to participant observations, refugees were involved in 65 ero-epic dialogues (EED)[4]; seven focus group discussions (FGD) with 35 participants; journal writing[5] with 37 adolescents; and two surveys, one of which is used in this chapter with 351 participants.[6] Aid workers took part in 28 structured and semi-structured expert interviews. The data collection process was supported by research assistants, who had backgrounds in clinical psychology and political science and were highly supportive.

Ethical considerations are always crucial when carrying out research with social actors. Because the focus of this research was on gender-based violence in a refugee camp environment, which was likely to involve traumatised individuals, special attention needed to be paid to ethical reflections and standards. The project team considered aspects of research ethics prior, during, and after the data collection seriously and made special efforts to protect participants from possible harm during the research process. For this reason, the methods listed above were chosen (Krause 2017a; see also Hugman et al. 2011; Mackenzie et al. 2007; Block et al. 2013). The team referred to *The Ethical Guidelines for Good Research Practices* of the University of Oxford's Refugee Studies Centre (2007) as the guiding framework for research. During the data

---

4   According to Girtler (2001), ero-epic dialogues constitute an unstructured interview form that takes place in a surrounding that is comforting for the interviewees.

5   Journal writing was employed as a child-sensitive method with open-ended questions.

6   The survey was conducted by means of anonymised, written, and multiple-choice questionnaires.

collection process, the team emphasised the participants' safety and respect for their rights, the need to protect the confidentiality of information and translations, and ensured the refugees' voluntary participation. Thus, all participants were informed of their rights and the objectives of the project so they could make a decision to participate. Moreover, refugees' involvement was crucial, and the team maintained a focus on leaving sufficient room for them to raise issues they considered important and wanted to address. The people not only informed the research process though their stories but also through their active engagement (Krause 2017a).

3   The Camp as a Humanitarian Site of Protection or Context for Violence?

Since the 1960s, the Republic of Uganda has hosted a relatively large number of refugees, which has grown even more in recent years. Uganda is located in Sub-Saharan Africa in the Great Lakes Region, a region that has experienced a long-lasting series of violent conflicts throughout the second half of the 20th century (e.g. in South Sudan and DRC). These conflicts contribute to the flight of many people. In Uganda, many refugees came from neighbouring countries such as DRC, South Sudan, Burundi, and Rwanda, while others came from Ethiopia, Somalia, and Eritrea (UNHCR 2013: 1-2). Renewed violent conflicts in South Sudan and DRC in recent years has led to a population of more than 1.2 million refugees and asylum seekers in Uganda in 2019 (UNHCR 2019). In addition to newly arriving refugees, many refugees find themselves in protracted situations[7], having to stay in Uganda – sometimes for decades – and facing an uncertain future ahead of them.

Uganda's refugee policy is considered to be progressive. Uganda enforced a new Refugee Act in 2009, granting refugees several rights, such as the rights to movement, work, and possessions (Uganda 2006: art. 30, 29). Moreover, the country proceeds with a development orientation in refugee aid and uses 'local rural refugee settlements' where refugees are encouraged to engage in agricultural activities so they can become self-reliant (Betts et al. 2017: 9-10). One of these 'settlements' is Kyaka II, where the research used in this chapter was carried out. Although the new Refugee Act and the development-oriented approach seem to make improvements, it is necessary to take a critical perspective of the assumed progressiveness. The 2009 Refugee Act also notes in Article 44 that

---

7   UNHCR defines protracted refugee situations as those in which refugees are in exile 'for five or more years […], without immediate prospects for implementation of durable solutions' (UNHCR 2009). The agency also often uses the benchmark of '25,000 or more refugees of the same nationality' (UNHCR 2018: 22) to determine these situations.

refugees must live in designated places – i.e., 'settlements' – and can only leave if they receive permission from the respective governmental authorities. These 'settlements' essentially constitute forms of refugee camps that have analogous administrative, hierarchical, and material structures, despite their larger areas and agricultural opportunities offered, which is why the term 'camps' is used in this chapter. Also the development orientation and self-reliance focus has limitations which are addressed below.

3.1 Humanitarian Aid and Structures in Kyaka II

Kyaka II was established in the early 1980s and encompasses an area of more than 80 km² with an estimated capacity for 17,000 refugees. However, during the period of research conducted in spring 2014, 22,680 refugees lived in this camp (UNHCR 2014b). The population subsequently increased to 91,365 by April 2019 due to the ongoing conflicts that occurred in neighbouring countries (OPM/UNHCR 2019). Most of the refugees in the camp originated from the DRC, while others had fled from Rwanda, Burundi, or South Sudan.

The camp is located in a remote and rural region in the Kyegegwa District of central Uganda. It is under the general supervision of the Office of the Prime Minister (OPM), Government of Uganda, and UNHCR. Mainly non-governmental organisations (NGOs) implement the projects in the different sectors to provide protection and assistance. Kyaka II is divided into nine zones and 26 clusters (UNHCR 2014b) that are set up as villages. In these areas, refugees live side by side with nationals and receive two plots of land for residential and agricultural use so they can become self-reliant and, thus, cease to regularly rely on the provision of aid. The 'base camp' is fairly central within Kyaka II. It contains a police station, a clinic, a local market, offices of aid agencies, and the so-called 'safe houses'.

Because the camp is run by OPM and UNHCR and NGOs are delivering aid, the decision-making structures are relatively clear. Organisational rules and institutional norms and values shape the camp setting, and Inhetveen (2010) calls such power relations within camps 'poly-hierarchical'. These relations are visible in the way humanitarian agencies provide protection and assistance projects. During research, aid agencies have carried out many projects, such as the provision of medical care, primary and secondary education (to a lesser extent), water, sanitation and hygiene measures, livelihoods, and psychosocial counselling, among others, for victims of sexual and gender-based violence. In this setting, the aid agencies, thus, not only delivered 'hand-overs' in terms of material assistance but also supported the refugees' livelihoods.

However, these agencies also found themselves in authoritative positions; in their projects, they decided how aid was provided and targeted specific groups, exercising considerable power over refugees. The presence of these power practices and the inherent 'containment politics' mean that the camp essentially serves as an environment within which control is exerted over refugees. Regarding this biopolitical way of governing refugees, Rose Jaji (2012) similarly stresses that "camps constitute a technology of power and control that compartmentalizes refugees and regulates their movement" (Jaji 2012: 225), encompassing "rules, techniques and physical structures and arrangements underpinning the organization, administration and control of populations in particular settings" (Jaji 2012: 223).

In Kyaka II, this contributed to refugees being subject to restrictions, and they complained about insufficient aid and the overall difficult conditions. As a man living in the camp explained: "Here in Kyaka life is difficult for all refugees [in] that they can never access good food for their diet, medication and counselling. People are sick psychologically and need counsellors who can bring them back to their moods of normal people or bring back hope."[8] In a similar vein, others highlighted the lack of common items such as soap, access to employment opportunities, and chances for political participation. Such accounts elucidate the kind of everyday issues people are confronted with in camps like Kyaka II, despite their access to aid.

Being able to farm and yield harvests has not significantly improved the situation of the 'camp population'. The focus on self-reliance in refugee policies in Uganda instead reveals a critical shift in how the responsibilities are assigned in a neoliberal sense. Refugees are made responsible to contribute to and find solutions but these seem to be defined by humanitarian and political agencies (see also Krause/Schmidt 2019; Easton-Calabria/Omata 2018). However, refugees in Kyaka II regularly stated that they were unable to fulfil these responsibilities for various reasons (e.g. inadequate soil conditions), echoing earlier criticism made by Tania Kaiser (2006). One man pointed out the inadequate size of the allotted land, noting that "[o]ne cannot depend on this one acre for both food and money to buy other basics and school fees. There is also a fear that as time goes on, the other refugees will come and then it will also be cut in half."[9]

Moreover, although all refugees were supposed to receive the same kind and amount of assistance based on the humanitarian regulations and funded measures available in Kyaka II, the findings of the study revealed differences. Those who were assumed to be 'vulnerable' received prioritised access to humanitarian support. Under the umbrella of taking a gender-sensitive approach to aid, women were mainly perceived as 'especially vulnerable'. How these differ-

---

8   Male refugee, EED, 18 March 2014, Base Camp, Kyaka II.

9   Male refugee, EED, 5 March 2014, Kaborogota Zone, Kyaka II.

ences affected the people as well as the level of violence in Kyaka II will be discussed in the following sections.

3.2 Prevalence of Sexual and Gender-based Violence in Uganda's Kyaka II

In addition to the overall difficult conditions in Kyaka II, women and men frequently commented on the wide scope and diverse forms of gender-based violence. The most common forms were said to be sexual violence, domestic violence, and structural discrimination as early and forced marriage of girls and denial of resources. Both women and men explained that such violence was mainly directed against women and girls, placing them at risk.

Sexual violence mainly occurred in the forms of sexual harassment, rape, and attempted rape in diverse locations. Several women said that they experienced or witnessed acts of rape or attempted rape by strangers during daily work in the field, when fetching water, or collecting firewood. In addition, many were also confronted with sexual violence at home, acts that were committed by intimate partners or acquaintances, including neighbours. Among the many accounts of such horrific acts of violence collected during the research, one young Congolese woman explained that she became pregnant after being raped. She was attacked by a stranger when she went to the well to fetch water and suffered from injuries, but she said she did not receive any help.[10] Another woman stated that sometimes when she came home from working on the field, her husband would force her to have sex although she was tired and expressed her discomfort.[11] Moreover, girls and boys shared fears about and described acts of sexual violence they had experienced, such as on their way to school – mainly forced upon them by unknown persons – or while at school, by teachers.[12]

Domestic violence was noted to be particularly widespread in Kyaka II. It took place mainly between intimate partners or spouses and within private domestic spheres. How common such risks were is illustrated by the comparison of 'being beaten like a drum' which a number of women and men referred to. One woman also criticised men, saying that some do not "consider women to be people" but that women "are made to work for nothing by their husbands. Not even the food is enough. They are harassed and seen as helpless people in the society".[13] This quote exemplifies not only the intensity of violence but draws associations between such dangers and the generally problematic conditions in

---

10 Female refugee, EED, 12 April 2014, Bugibuli Zone, Kyaka II.

11 Female refugee, EED, 12 March 2014, Bukere Zone, Kyaka II.

12 Male adolescent, 15 years old, journal writing, 4 April 2014, Bujubuli Primary School, Kyaka II; female adolescent, 16 years old, journal writing, 5 March 2014, Bujubuli Secondary School, Kyaka II.

13 Female refugee, EED, 11 March 2014, Bukere Zone, Kyaka II.

Kyaka II. A 17-year-old adolescent, who had been living in Kyaka II since 2006, furthermore illustrated the extent of dangers children can face at home. She said that "some parents give corporal punishments to their children for example they burn them, beat them heavily [...]."[14]

Although women (and girls) were noted to be the main victims of domestic and sexual violence, people in Kyaka II also mentioned that men were respectively at risk. One woman commented that not only women but "men also are being violated and when they report they are not helped because everyone knows it is mainly women who are always beaten".[15] Male adolescents described sexual harassment by women, including female teachers in schools and women who asked for sexual favours.[16]

Structural violence was discussed especially in the context of early and forced marriage of girls and denial of resources. Adolescents frequently noted that girls run the risk of being forced to marry or marry at an early age. The idea that girls should be married at a certain age appears to be related to traditions held by some ethnic groups of refugees, but economic motives also played a role. The latter is discussed in the following section. Denial of resources encompasses the situation when one intimate or marital partner prevents another person or member of the family from gaining access to certain resources. For example, although primary education is supposed to be free and accessible for girls and boys in camps in Uganda, it was observed during the research that girls at times lacked access to primary or secondary education, either because caretakers were unable to pay the school fees or because some held certain beliefs about traditional gender relations (i.e., girls would not need education since women were responsible for the domestic sphere).

Denial of resources was also explained as a cause of domestic violence in many cases. An aid worker explained in an interview that this denial could include "denying shelter to a person, denial of right to economic benefits, denial of support, school fees to the children etc. The women are always denied these things by their spouse or even their family relatives and in-laws."[17] In focus group discussions, participants said that husbands would often sell the harvest and use the money for alcohol without sharing food or money with the wives. When the women asked for their share, men would use physical force, especial-

---

14   Female adolescent, 17 years old, journal writing, 5 March 2014, Bujubuli Secondary School, Kyaka II.

15   Female refugee, EED, 18 March 2014, Swe Swe Zone, Kyaka II.

16   Male adolescent, 15 years old, journal writing, 4 April 2014, Bujubuli Secondary School, Kyaka II; male adolescent, 15 years old, journal writing, 3 April 2014, Bujubuli Secondary School, Kyaka II.

17   Female employee, interview, 20 May 2014, provided in written form.

ly when they were drunk.[18] This expressed belief was supported by numerous people in Kyaka II.

But how widespread was violence against women in Kyaka II? During the research, women and men as well as humanitarian workers in the camp mentioned that many victims tended to refrain from reporting cases of violence, as they were afraid of increased violence or stigmatisation. At times, they preferred to handle cases within their communities or did not report violent events because they could not pay the reporting fees to the police.[19] Public records of violent attacks may therefore not be complete. To gain information about the scope of sexual and domestic violence, respective questions on these topics were included in the survey. Still, the survey participants were asked how often they believed such violence took place, not how often they were confronted with it. Although the data do not reflect exact accounts of the cases of violence, the participants' responses are assumed to have been influenced by their personal experiences. Survey-based findings reveal that 64.67 per cent of the participants believed that sexual violence took place regularly; 14.81 per cent, daily; 18.50 per cent, rarely; and 1.7 per cent, never. Moreover, all participants noted that domestic violence existed; 55.71 per cent believed that it occurred regularly; 36.86 per cent, daily; and 7.43 per cent, rarely. These findings further support the narratives of women and men regarding the high prevalence of gender-based violence against women in Kyaka II.

However, considering the various protection and assistance measures implemented by humanitarian agencies, two questions arise: Why do the diverse forms and the broad scope of gender-based violence exist in Kyaka II? And how are they associated with the camp structures?

3.3 Associating Violence with Camp Conditions

Gender-based violence against women in refugee camps – as well as beyond encampment – is often construed as a socially constructed power practice to demonstrate male dominance (Buckley-Zistel et al. 2014). But how is this related to the structures in refugee camps? Of course, the specific local conditions in camps can vary, despite their general similarities. Each and every case of gender-based violence is, furthermore, certainly unique, and the particular circumstances of each incident are important to be reflected in order to understand the reasons for the violence as well as the effects it has on the victims. Nonetheless,

---

18   FGD with Refugee Welfare Council Leaders, 19 March 2014, Base Camp, Kyaka II; FGD with female refugee, 12 March 2014, Base Camp, Kyaka II.

19   Female refugee, EED, 17 March 2014, Bugibuli Zone, Kyaka II; FGD with Refugee Religious Leaders, 19 March 2014, Base Camp, Kyaka II; female aid worker, interview, 22 April 2014, provided in written form.

it is possible to reveal connections or correlations between the scope of gender-based violence and the conditions in camps like Kyaka II. In the following discussion, I address contributing factors, including the direct effects of violence that are being perpetrated by humanitarians and the more indirect effects of the local camp landscape, humanitarian (power) practices, changing gender relations, and insufficient law enforcement.

Some cases of gender-based violence against women in Kyaka II were directly associated with humanitarian staff in that the latter perpetrated violent acts or attempted such acts. In addition to previously mentioned examples of school teachers[20] who were involved in the sexual abuse or harassment of children, some women noted that aid workers occasionally asked for sexual favours in return for material and immaterial support. While this information supports the criticism made by Elizabeth Ferris (2007: 585), which appeared at the beginning of this chapter, humanitarians in Kyaka II were reluctant to acknowledge such risks. One female aid worker said that there had been "one case" in the past and "the perpetrator was punished"[21], and another mentioned that it happens but "[t]he most common scenarios and perpetrators were partner staff and government officials (police, guards, etc.)".[22] Only one out of the 28 humanitarians interviewed suggested that it was fairly common; she said that "it is very inevitable to a great extent. Though this is often very hard to know or even prove".[23]

In addition to such direct perpetrations of violence, the conditions in the camp, including the humanitarian aid and regulated camp structures, contributed to the level of gender-based violence against women, even though camps like Kyaka II are established for the protection and assistance of the people. The camp architecture of Kyaka II revealed elements of insecurity; women stated that they were attacked while fetching water or collecting firewood. Such locations were sometimes far away from where people lived, and walking there could be risky. Thus, navigating through the camp landscape was associated with dangers, which these women appeared to have to face and deal with so they could go about their daily work. Moreover, insufficient aid and limited livelihoods complicated the lives of many people in the camp. These limitations could also contribute to structural violence, such as early and forced marriage as well as denial of resources. In the case of early and forced marriage, economic

---

20   School teachers might not always be assumed to be 'humanitarians' in the narrow sense, but when employed in the context of camps, they operate within the humanitarian systems and are, at times, even paid by humanitarian agencies.

21   Female aid worker, interview, 27 March 2014, provided in written form.

22   Female aid worker, interview, 10 April 2014, provided in written form.

23   Female aid worker, interview, 11 May 2014, provided in written form.

motivations play roles, as the child brides' families or caretakers receive dowries upon the marriage. In this regard, an adolescent in Kyaka II explained that "[t]here is forced marriage for girls where parents want to get money to care for the family."[24] Thus, considering the shortcomings in the camp, financial or other forms of dowries can act as incentives for some parents or caretakers, convincing them to agree to or help arrange the girl's wedding.

Changing gender relations correspond with the association noted between gender-based violence and camp characteristics, too. In general, refugees experience substantial changes when they flee their regions of origin. Due to the levels of violence (or other motives for flight) in the regions of origin, the process of forced migration, and the new environments in the host regions with different settings, regulations, and opportunities, refugees can rarely maintain their familiar social and gender structures. As a result, the people have to re-negotiate gender roles and relations in exile (Hans 2008; Turner 1999; Carlson 2005; Krause 2015a). Due to the regulated spheres that exist within refugee camps, such re-negotiations not only take place among the refugees, but are also influenced by humanitarian actors, practices, and camp structures.

In Kyaka II, some of this influence can be seen in the way aid projects are run and in the the description of women as 'vulnerable', which was commonly used by humanitarian agencies. This assumption about the vulnerability of women is not only critical and can contribute to their victimisation; the vulnerability label also had material effects, as women labelled as 'vulnerable' received prioritised access to assistance and specific training programmes, such as those about their rights. Several women described their ability to claim their rights and enhance their social position by means of this support and knowledge, whereas several men critically commented on these measures and changes.[25] In Kyaka II, men were generally not or only in rare cases understood as 'vulnerable' in humanitarian terms, and it remains unclear whether and how they were informed about women's rights. The aid workers' responses to this aspect varied greatly, ranging from stating that men participated "in trainings, sensitisations"[26] to pointing out that men were "not involved".[27] Most men who took part in the research expressed similar sentiments, and several complained about the focus that was placed on women while men were neglected.[28]

---

24   Female adolescent, 17 years, journal writing, 05 March 2014, Bujubuli Secondary School, Kyaka II.

25   FGD with local leaders, 20 March 2014, Base Camp, Kyaka II.

26   Female aid worker, interview, 22 April 2014, provided in written form.

27   Female aid worker, interview, 14 April 2014, provided in written form.

28   Discussion with local leaders, 10 March 2014, Base Camp, Kyaka II.

These statements cannot be generalised to apply to aid structures in refugee camps worldwide, but other studies have also noted that the risks of gender-specific violence against men often remain neglected or are even trivialised (Brun 2000; Jaji 2009; Kabachnik et al. 2013). If we examine UNHCR – the key agency for refugee protection – and its age, gender, and diversity mainstreaming approach, for example, we see that aid is not supposed to be provided only to women but to people who fall into various relevant categories (see, among others, UNHCR 2007: 9). The vulnerability screening tool also takes into account that the 'situations of vulnerability' experienced by forcibly displaced people can change dynamically and affect many groups in particular ways (UNHCR/IDC 2016). Such global policy instruments, however, are localised differently by humanitarians in specific regions, and, in the case of Kyaka II, aid agencies maintained a focus on the vulnerability of women. A female aid worker in Kyaka II even said that gender-based violence "usually occurs because the women are considered weak and vulnerable".[29]

As a result of these tendencies, humanitarian agencies are prone to concentrating on certain groups while neglecting others and the dangers they face. Moreover, by prioritising aid for some, agencies contribute to an unfamiliar imbalance of power and gender relations among the refugees. Other scholars discuss in similar ways how the social status and gender roles of women and men can change in refugee situations. For various reasons, women may take on additional responsibilities and head households, which can turn out to be empowering as well as overwhelming experiences for them (Martin 2004: 15; Freedman 2015: 34-42). On the other hand, the restrictive camp conditions may prevent men from fulfilling the gender roles as decision-makers and providers in families, which they perceive as 'traditional' or typical roles for men. Through their aid projects, humanitarian agencies take over these positions of provisional and hegemonic institutions (Krause 2015a; Friedman 1992). Men who live in camps and under the administration of humanitarian agencies may, therefore, lose social status or feel as though they experience 'emasculation'. By taking a human security approach, Barbra Lukunka (2011) explores the phenomenon of emasculation among Burundian men in a camp in Tanzania and shows how socio-psychological issues are connected to insecurity.

While a number of men I spoke with in Kyaka II criticised violence against women and said that they would not use force against women[30], others noted that the aid focus on women could contribute to issues and arguments over resources and, therefore, also an increase the risk of violence. Expressing an opinion that was echoed by others, one man said "[w]e beat women because some

---

29   Female aid worker, interview, 10 April 2014, provided in written form.
30   Male refugee, dialogue, 05.03.2014, Base Camp, Kyaka II.

women disobey."[31] Another man emphasised that violence exists because "some women are big-headed. They don't understand, they want to talk and can do everything."[32] Yet another man reflected that "a man has no power, has no property and […] some women have taken over" in the camp.[33] These quotes illustrate the possible effects of forced migration, aid, and encampment; more specifically, they illustrate how some men felt frustrated and even helpless, dreaded losing their decision-making roles, tried to defend or regain them, and thus maintain their social positions – sometimes even with force.

In essence, the insights provided by the participants indicate the general relevance and influence of aid and power in camps like Kyaka II. Participants in my research complained about the aspect that humanitarian agencies made wide-ranging decisions through aid measures that affected the 'camp population', as well as about the restrictions and the inadequate treatment. Relying on the aid received, the feelings of being stuck and enclosed in a prison-like situation in the camp and having limited future perspectives frustrated the people in the camp. One man even said that "[t]here is no hope for being a refugee in Uganda now. This is because the people who are supposed to help us are not really doing their work."[34] Such feelings of irritation can contribute to heightened drug and alcohol consumption, and the likelihoods of aggression and violence may increase under influence (Carlson 2005; Krause 2015a; Wachter et al. 2018).

The criticism expressed in the quotes about the lack of property and decision-making opportunities goes beyond material assistance; it correlates with regulations and the way law is practiced in camps like Kyaka II. My research on the continuum of violence during conflict, flight, and encampment revealed that violence against women prevails in the camp, not only because of the unfamiliar imbalance of power structures and changing gender roles, but also because of insufficient law enforcement (Krause 2015b, 2017b). Several study participants in Kyaka II commented that cases of gender-based violence were often not reported, because the police and other institutions requested financial compensation, among others, for their transportation to the crime scene. Victims of violence were sometimes unable to pay these fees and, thus, were left without an investigation and a police report. But this report was important for the victims to receive free medical support.

---

31   FGD with male refugees, 13 March 2014, Base Camp, Kyaka II.
32   FGD with local leaders, 20 March 2014, Base Camp, Kyaka II.
33   FGD with religious leaders, 19 March 2014, Base Camp, Kyaka II.
34   Male refugee, EED, 28 March 2014, Base Camp, Kyaka II.

The limited reporting and treatment of cases of violence and, thus, little law enforcement against such acts, seems to influence the prevalence of violence. Some women and men described stories about legal procedures against perpetrators but also mentioned cases in which perpetrators were let go after they paid a certain amount of money. One man explained that, as a consequence of the ineffective punishment of perpetrators, people would "feel that there is no safety here in Kyaka and there is no justice for us"[35]. Moreover, one woman underlined the lack of law enforcement as she recalled experiences of the past: "You know, there are no strict law enforcement here. [... A] person is arrested, after a few day days, 3 or 4, the person is released without being charged anything. However, it's not only me in this situation but many other single women are also facing similar challenges in terms of violence. You find that women who are married, they fear their husbands."[36] Yet another woman said that some perpetrators do go through the legal system and are imprisoned but often only "for a short while and after being released they beat the women even more."[37]

The information included in this section shows how violence against women is associated with the conditions in the refugee camp in a number of different, yet interrelated ways. While precise, mono-causal relationships do not exist between violence and camp structures, the results of this analysis nonetheless shows correlations. The findings illustrate that the way aid is distributed and camps are regulated can affect the level of frustration among the people in such a way as to create an atmosphere where violence prevails.

4   Conclusions

Despite the critically difficult conditions that many people face in refugee camps like Kyaka II, it must be emphasised again that not all men in Kyaka II – or in fact in other camps – use violence against women. It is not the intention of this chapter to portray women as vulnerably victims and men as aggressive perpetrators; instead, it is to shed light on the risks of gender-based violence and elucidate how these are associated with camp structures. Subsequent questions that arose from this analyse and the different camp features that contributed to violence are: What can be done? How can humanitarian structures be altered so that they do not contribute to violence, or at least to a lower extend?

Although several critical factors of refugee protection and assistance have been addressed in this chapter, it is crucial to note that the respective humanitar-

---

35   Male refugee, EED, 27 March 2014, Base Camp, Kyaka II.

36   Female refugee, EED, 18 March 2014, Base Camp, Kyaka II.

37   Female refugee, EED, 18 March 2014, Base Camp, Kyaka II.

ian projects are generally carried out to reduce the insecurity of refugees. UNHCR even rates "[t]he protection of women and girls of concern […] a core activity and an organizational priority" (UNHCR 2008: 5). Still, it appears as though certain projects and approaches, despite the good intentions, can lead to risks. This can occur, for example, when women are categorised as 'vulnerable' and subsequently provided with prioritised access to aid. Although this process is certainly intended to protect women, the people in Kyaka II criticised the focus that was placed on women, the restrictions and regulations in the camp, as well as the lack of chances for refugees to participate in decision-making. These aspects should, therefore, be addressed for improve the situation.

In general, of course, alternatives to refugee camps should be used to keep refugees from having to stay in these confined spaces – often over the course of several years. While UNHCR has been promoting the move towards alternatives with increasing frequency in recent years (see UNHCR 2014a), national governments rather than humanitarian agencies decide whether refugees have to stay in camps or not. The governments are responsible for refugees in their territories and ultimately decide where they are settled. But even if refugees self-settle or live in other areas such as cities, this does not guarantee an end to gender-based violence.

Since issues regarding power asymmetries brought about by humanitarian and political actors in camps frustrate refugees and potentially contribute to violence, it is crucial to avoid strict top-down hierarchies, strengthen cooperative protection structures, and improve the living conditions in camps. This includes preventing the preferential treatment of certain groups if it would mean neglecting others. Thus, rather than maintaining the top-down decision-making process that is imposed on refugees and prioritising aid for certain groups, the rights and needs of all refugees should be regarded equally. Moreover, opportunities for refugees to make their voices heard and influence aid structures should be provided. However, the general criticism about insufficient aid is not exclusive to humanitarian agencies alone; they face chronic underfunding (Loescher et al. 2012: 96-100) and can only provide protection and assistance insofar as it is funded by external authorities, i.e., often Northern donor states.

The aforementioned cooperative protection structures are important, because refugees naturally do not passively wait to be provided with humanitarian aid; they actively contribute to their living conditions in camps. The people create representation systems (Lecadet 2016; Inhetveen 2010: chapter 10) and cope with issues and violence (Krause/Schmidt 2018; Ensor 2014). Thus, humanitarian agencies should meet refugees as equals, involve them, and integrate the specific local mechanisms they put in place to counteract gender-based violence and address other issues. This is not a new suggestion, and UNHCR has been emphasising the need for participatory approaches in refugee protection for decades (UNHCR 1992). There is certainly no panacea that can completely prevent violence in camps, but it would be helpful if the specific actions used by refugees to combat such violence were thoroughly considered and integrate these actions in humanitarian projects.

Finally, although global norms have been established to protect and assist refugees worldwide, also with regard to gender-specific needs, humanitarian aid for refugees is carried out in various sectors. Aid workers who are involved in projects to improve water availability, sanitation, and hygiene or in infrastructural development may not be trained to identify gender-specific risks. For this reason, it is important to sensitise all staff working in humanitarian and political agencies, as well as other stakeholders such as police or military personnel active in camp settings, to the possible effects of their actions, the rights of refugees, and the need for protective procedures.

Acknowledgements

This chapter is based on findings from the research project *Gender Relations in Confined Spaces. Conditions, Scope and Forms of Violence against Women in Conflict-related Refugee Camps* led by Susanne Buckley-Zistel, carried out by the author, and funded by the German Foundation for Peace Research (DSF). I sincerely thank the DSF for their generous funding, Susanne Buckley-Zistel for her continuous support, the research assistants in Uganda for their invaluable collaboration, and the editors and reviewers for their valuable comments. Moreover, I especially thank all the refugees and aid workers in Kyaka II who took the time and trusted us to share their stories.

Bibliography

Abdi, Awa M. (2006): Refugees, Gender-based Violence and Resistance: A Case Study of Somali Refugee Women in Kenya. In Evangelia Tastsoglou; Alexandra Dobrowolsky (ed.): *Women, Migration and Citizenship.* Hampshire: Ashgate, p. 231-251.

Agier, Michel (2011): *Managing the Undesirables. Refugee Camps and Humanitarian Government.* Cambridge: Polity Press.

Betts, Alexander, et al. (2017): *Refugee Economies: Forced Displacement and Development.* Oxford: Oxford University Press.

Block, Karen; Riggs, Elisha; Haslam, Nick (ed.) (2013): *Values and Vulnerabilities. The Ethics of Research with Refugees and Asylum Seekers.* Toowong: Australian Academic Press.

Brun, Cathrine (2000): Making Young Displaced Men Visible. In: *Forced Migration Review* 9, p. 10-12.

Buckley-Zistel, Susanne; Krause, Ulrike; Loeper, Lisa (2014): Sexuelle und geschlechterbasierte Gewalt an Frauen in kriegsbedingten Flüchtlingslagern. Ein Literaturüberblick. In: *Peripherie: Zeitschrift für Politik und Ökonomie in der Dritten Welt* 34(133), p. 45-63.

Buckley-Zistel, Susanne; Krause, Ulrike (ed.) (2017): *Gender, Violence, Refugees.* New York, Oxford: Berghahn.

Callaway, Helen (1985): *Women Refugees in Developing Countries: Their Specific Needs and Untapped Resources.* Oxford: Refugee Studies Programme.

Carlson, Sharon (2005): Contesting and Reinforcing Patriarchy: Domestic Violence in Dzaleka Refugee Camp. In: *RSC Working Paper Series* 23.

de Neef, C.E.J; de Ruiter, S.J (1984), 'Sexual Violence against Women Refugees: Report on the Nature and Consequences of Sexual Violence Suffered Elsewhere', (Amsterdam).

Deardorff Miller, Sarah (2018): *UNHCR as a Surrogate State: Protracted Refugee Situations.* London; New York: Routledge.

Easton-Calabria, Evan E.; Omata, Naohiko (2018): Panacea for the Refugee Crisis? Rethinking the Promotion of 'Self-Reliance' for Refugees. In: *Third World Quarterly*, p. 1-17.

Ensor, Marisa O. (2014): Displaced Girlhood: Gendered Dimensions of Coping and Social Change among Conflict-Affected South Sudanese Youth. In: *Refuge* 30(1), p. 15-24.

Ferris, Elizabeth G. (1990), 'Refugee Women and Violence', *World Council of Churches* (Geneva).

Ferris, Elizabeth G. (2007): Women in Refugee Camps. Abuse of Power: Sexual Exploitation of Refugee Women and Girls. In: *Signs: Journal of Women in Culture and Society* 32(3), p. 584-591.

Fiddian-Qasmiyeh, Elena (2010): Concealing Violence Against Women in the Sahrawi Refugee Camps: The Politicization of Victimhood. In Hannah Bradby; Gillian L. Hundt (ed.): *Global Perspectives on War, Gender and Health: The Sociology and Anthropology of Suffering.* Farnham: Ashgate, p. 99-110.

Fiddian-Qasmiyeh, Elena (2014): *The Ideal Refugees: Gender, Islam, and the Sahrawi Politics of Survival.* New York: Syracuse University Press.

Freedman, Jane (2015): *Gendering the International Asylum and Refugee Debate.* Basingstoke, Hampshire: Palgrave Macmillan.

Friedman, Amy R. (1992): Rape and Domestic Violence. In: *Women & Therapy* 13(1-2), p. 65-78.

Girtler, Roland (2001): *Methoden der Feldforschung.* Wien, Köln, Weimar: UTB.

Greatbatch, Jacqueline (1989): The Gender Difference: Feminist Critiques of Refugee Discourse. In: *International Journal of Refugee Law* 1(4), p. 518-527.

Hans, Asha (2008): Gender, Camps and International Norms. In: *Refugee Watch* (32), p. 64-73.

Harrell-Bond, Barbara E. (1986): *Imposing Aid. Emergency Assistance to Refugees.* Oxford, New York, Nairobi: Oxford University Press.

Hartmann, Melanie (2017): Spatializing Inequalities: The Situation of Women in Refugee Centres in Germany. In Susanne Buckley-Zistel; Ulrike Krause (ed.): *Gender, Violence, Refugees.* New York, Oxford: Berghahn, p. 102-126.

Horn, Rebecca (2010): Exploring the Impact of Displacement and Encampment on Domestic Violence in Kakuma Refugee Camp. In: *Journal of Refugee Studies* 23(3), p. 356-376.

Hugman, Richard; Pittaway, Eileen; Bartolomei, Linda (2011): When 'Do No Harm' Is Not Enough: The Ethics of Research with Refugees and Other Vulnerable Groups. In: *British Journal of Social Work* 41(7), p. 1271-1287.

IASC (2015): *Guidelines for Integrating Gender-Based Violence Interventions in Humanitarian Action: Reducing risk, promoting resilience and aiding recovery.* Geneva: IASC.

Indra, Doreen Marie (1987): Gender: A Key Dimension of the Refugee Experience. In: *Refuge* 6(3), p. 3-4.

Inhetveen, Katharina (2010): *Die Politische Ordnung des Flüchtlingslagers. Akteure - Macht - Organisation. Eine Ethnographie im Südlichen Afrika.* Bielefeld: transcript Verlag.

Jaji, Rose (2009): Masculinity on Unstable Ground: Young Refugee Men in Nairobi, Kenya. In: *Journal of Refugee Studies* 22(2), p. 177-194.

Jaji, Rose (2012): Social Technology and Refugee Encampment in Kenya. In: *Journal of Refugee Studies* 25(2), p. 221-238.

Janmyr, Maja (2014): *Protecting Civilians in Refugee Camps. Unable and Unwilling States, UNHCR and International Responsibility.* Leiden: Brill.

Janmyr, Maja (2017): Military Recruitment of Sudanese Refugee Men in Uganda: A Tale of National Patronage and International Failure. In Susanne Buckley-Zistel; Ulrike Krause (ed.): *Gender, Violence, Refugees.* New York, Oxford: Berghahn, p. 219-238.

Jansen, Bram (2011): The Accidental City: Violence, Economy and Humanitarianism in Kakuma Refugee Camp Kenya. University of Wageningen.

Kabachnik, Peter, et al. (2013): Traumatic Masculinities: The Gendered Geographies of Georgian IDPs from Abkhazia. In: *Gender, Place & Culture* 20(6), p. 773-793.

Kaiser, Tania (2006): Between a Camp and a Hard Place: Rights, Livelihood and Experiences of the Local Settlement System for long-term Refugees in Uganda. In: *The Journal of Modern African Studies* 44(4), p. 597-621.

Krause, Ulrike (2015a): Zwischen Schutz und Scham? Flüchtlingslager, Gewalt und Geschlechterverhältnisse. In: *Peripherie: Zeitschrift für Politik und Ökonomie in der Dritten Welt* 35(138/139), p. 235-259.

Krause, Ulrike (2015b): A Continuum of Violence? Linking Sexual and Gender-based Violence during Conflict, Flight, and Encampment. In: *Refugee Survey Quarterly* 34(4), p. 1-19.

Krause, Ulrike (2017a), 'Researching Forced Migration. Critical Reflections on Research Ethics during Fieldwork', *RSC Working Paper Series* (No. 123; Oxford: RSC).

Krause, Ulrike (2017b): Escaping Conflicts and Being Safe? Post-conflict Refugee Camps and the Continuum of Violence. In Susanne Buckley-Zistel; Ulrike Krause (ed.): *Gender, Violence, Refugees.* New York, Oxford: Berghahn, p. 173-196.

Krause, Ulrike (2018), 'Gewalterfahrungen von Geflüchteten', *State-of-Research Papier 03, Verbundprojekt ,Flucht: Forschung und Transfer'* (Osnabrück: Institut für Migrationsforschung und InterkulturelleStudien (IMIS) der Universität Osnabrück / Bonn: Internationales Konversionszentrum Bonn (BICC)).

Krause, Ulrike; Schmidt, Hannah (2018): »Being beaten like a drum« Gefahren, Humanitarismus und Resilienz von Frauen in Flüchtlingssituationen. In: *GENDER. Zeitschrift für Geschlecht, Kultur und Gesellschaft* 2018(2), p. 47-62.

Krause, Ulrike; Schmidt, Hannah (2019): Refugees as Actors? Critical Reflections on Global Refugee Policies on Self-Reliance and Resilience In: *Journal of Refugee Studies*, p. *forthcoming*.

Lecadet, Clara (2016): Refugee Politics: Self-Organized 'Government' and Protests in the Agamé Refugee Camp (2005–13). In: *Journal of Refugee Studies* 29(2), p. 187-207.

Lischer, Sarah K. (2005): *Dangerous Sanctuaries: Refugee Camps, Civil War, and the Dilemmas of Humanitarian Aid.* Ithaca: Cornell University Press.

Ljungdell, Stina (1989): *Refugees? Female Asylum Seekers and Refugee Status: Guidelines for Assistance.* Geneva: UNHCR.

Loescher, Gil; Betts, Alexander; Milner, James (2012): *UNHCR: The Politics and Practice of Refugee Protection*. London; New York: Routledge Global Institutions.

Lukunka, Barbra (2011): New Big Men: Refugee Emasculation as a Human Security Issue. In: *International Migration* 50(5), p. 130-141.

Mackenzie, Catriona; McDowell, Christopher; Pittaway, Eileen (2007): Beyond 'Do No Harm': The Challenge of Constructing Ethical Relationships in Refugee Research. In: *Journal of Refugee Studies* 20(2), p. 299-319.

Malkki, Liisa H. (1995): Refugees and Exile: From "Refugee Studies" to the National Order of Things. In: *Annual Review of Anthropology* 24, p. 495-523.

Martin, Susan F. (2004): *Refugee Women*. Lantham: Lexington Books.

Martin, Susan F.; Tirman, John (2009): *Women, Migration, and Conflict. Breaking a Deadly Cycle*. Heidelberg, London, New York: Springer.

McConnachie, Kirsten (2014): *Governing Refugees: Justice, Order and Legal Pluralism*. Abingdon: Routledge.

McConnachie, Kirsten (2016): Camps of Containment: A Genealogy of the Refugee Camp. In: *Humanity: An International Journal of Human Rights, Humanitarianism, and Development* 7(3), p. 397-412.

OPM; UNHCR (2019), 'Uganda - Refugee Statistics April 2019 - Kyaka II', (Kampala: UNHCR).

Peteet, Julie M. (2005): *Landscape of Hope and Despair: Palestinian Refugee Camps*. Philadelphia, PA.: University of Pennsylvania Press.

Refugee Studies Centre (2007): Ethical Guidelines for Good Research Practice. In: *Refugee Survey Quarterly* 26(3), p. 162-172.

Turner, Simon (1999): Angry Young Men in Camps: Gender, Age and Class Relations Among Burundian Refugees in Tanzania. In: *New Issues in Refugee Research* 9.

Turner, Simon (2016): What Is a Refugee Camp? Explorations of the Limits and Effects of the Camp. In: *Journal of Refugee Studies* 29(2), p. 139-148.

Uganda (2006), 'The Refugees Act 2006', (8, Uganda Gazette No.47 Volume XCVIX dated 4 August 2006; Kampala: Government of Uganda).

UNHCR (1992): *A Framework for People-oriented Planning in Refugee Situations Taking Account of Women, Men and Children*. Geneva: UNHCR.

UNHCR (2007): *Handbook for Emergencies*. Geneva: UNHCR.

UNHCR (2008): *UNHCR Handbook for the Protection of Women and Girls*. Geneva: UNHCR.

UNHCR (2009), 'Conclusion on Protracted Refugee Situations', *Executive Committee of the High Commissioner's Programme No. 109 (LXI)* (Geneva: UNHCR).

UNHCR (2013), 'UNHCR Global Report 2012, Uganda', (Geneva: UNHCR).

UNHCR (2014a): *UNHCR Policy on Alternatives to Camps*. Geneva: UNHCR.

UNHCR (2014b), 'Kyaka II. Fact Sheet 2014', (Kampala: UNHCR).

UNHCR (2018): *Global Trends. Forced Displacement in 2017*. Geneva: UNHCR.

UNHCR (2019), 'UNHCR Uganda Operational Update - April 2019', (Kampala: UNHCR).

UNHCR; IDC (2016): *Vulnerability Screening Tool*. Geneva: UNHCR.

Wachter, Karin, et al. (2018): Drivers of Intimate Partner Violence Against Women in Three Refugee Camps. In: *Violence Against Women* 24(3), p. 286-306.

Werker, Eric (2007): Refugee Camp Economies. In: *Journal of Refugee Studies* 20(3), p. 461-480.

Resolving Trauma Associated with Sexual and Gender-Based Violence in Transcultural Refugee Contexts in Kenya

Fathima Azmiya Badurdeen[1]

Keywords: *trauma, sexual and gender-based violence, transcultural contexts, refugees, diversity, mental health care*

Abstract

Refugees and asylum seekers come from various parts of the neighbouring countries of Kenya and belong to different communities. They exhibit a myriad of mental health issues, such as trauma, as a result of sexual and gender-based violence (SGBV) in relation to pre-war contexts, the conflict itself, experiences of flight and refugee camp settings. These complexities connected to the myriad of issues of SGBV make it necessary to address mental health care needs of refugees, who often come from unfamiliar terrains, and thus often challenge health care professionals as trauma issues in differing transcultural contexts need to be addressed. Based on a qualitative research study of two datasets of in-depth interviews with women and girl refugees in Dadaab and Kakuma refugee camps, the paper presents the context of trauma faced by women and refugees of SGBV, and the ways in which they resolve trauma and health issues using social networks and professional health care services. The findings of the

---

1   Fathima Azmiya Badurdeen | Department of Social Sciences, Technical University of Mombasa | fazmiya@tum.ac.ke

© Springer Fachmedien Wiesbaden GmbH, part of Springer Nature 2020
K. Crepaz et al. (eds.), *Health in Diversity – Diversity in Health*,
https://doi.org/10.1007/978-3-658-29177-8_12

study show that there are many ways in which refugee women and girls resolve trauma. Most often, women and girls try to resolve it through the use of social networks in the form of cultural and indigenous methods in order to find healing for mental trauma. Health and social work professionals are more focused on culturally relevant trauma informed systems and the utilization of informal networks to resolve trauma. The study emphasizes the need for an exploration of cultural interpretations of trauma and the need for flexible and adaptive approaches by professionals for interpreting and treating mental trauma and health care.

Contents

Abstract 209

1   Introduction 211

2   Locating the Study in Research 212

3   Methodology 214

4   Trauma and Sexual and Gender-Based Violence against Women and
     Girls in Refugee Settings 216

5   Resolving Sexual and Gender-Based Violence-Related Trauma in
     Refugee Settings 218

6   Practices Used and Challenges Faced by Social and Health Care
     Professionals in Addressing SGBV-Related Trauma 222

7   Conclusion 226

Bibliography 227

1   Introduction

Women and girls are the major victims and survivors of sexual and gender-based violence (SGBV) in refugee camp settings.[1] SGBV in refugee camp settings includes acts such as sexual misconduct, rape, intimate partner violence (IPV), marital violence, early or forced marriages and sexual exploitation. These forms of violence are shaped by the values and circumstances of particular cultures and, in some cases, justified in the name of culture (Wendt and Zannetino, 2015:105). The trauma resulting from SGBV is associated with short-term and long-term psychological consequences such as fear, anxiety, shock, confusion and withdrawal. Long-term effects include Post Traumatic Stress Disorder (PSTD), depression, insomnia, sexual dysfunction, alcohol and illicit drug use, suicidal threats and obsession with one's physical appearance (Yuan, Koss and Stone, 2006:3-4). Often, these related traumas are complex, wherein cultural manifestations of trauma play a significant role. For, culture shapes the subjective meaning of trauma and pain which influences symptom expressions (Frey, 2001:107). Perceptions and individual responses such as psychiatric symptoms are guided by the existing rituals, norms and values within the prevailing culture of the victim (Schubert and Raija-Leena, 2011:175). Success in countering traumas associated with SGBV requires trauma-informed systems and care measures that integrate cultural viewpoints in the building of transculturally relevant frameworks for trauma intervention.

Most often, health and social work professionals find it challenging to provide assistance to refugee women and girls with SGBV-related mental disorders or psychosocial problems due to distinct cultural and religious conceptualizations of mental health and psychosocial wellbeing. This is compounded by lack of understanding of the specific socio-cultural organization of refugee societies in their countries of origin and the complicated migration history of the population.

It is in this context that the article seeks answers for the three interrelated questions: How does women's and girls' positioning in culture influence the interpretion of SGBV-related traumas in refugee camps? How does such positioning in culture explain women's and girls' ability to reach out to health and social services for mental health care in the aftermath of SGBV? And, how do healthcare and social work professionals respond to treat SGBV-related trauma within diverse cultures in refugee settings? These three questions are interlinked with the common problem of local cultures caught between global discourses on

---

1   The author acknowledges men and boys, too, as vulnerable to sexual violence and abuse in refugee camp settings.

human rights of the victim versus collective cultural practices on SGBV and the transcultural understanding of SGBV and trauma manifestations of different communities in refugee settings.

This article uses two data sets from two refugee camps – Dadaab and Kakuma – to understand SGBV-related trauma, and uses a cultural lens and victims' responses to health and social services for mental health care. The article begins by exploring the research approach on locating relevant literature in the research design, framing the research question and the methodology used. This is preceded through an analysis on SGBV and trauma among refugee women and girls in Dadaab and Kakuma refugee camps respectively, examining the various forms of SGBV-related trauma implications and the ways in which refugee women and girls respond to such trauma in terms of mental health care. Finally, the article argues that support systems for SGBV survivors can be enriched through culturally relevant trauma-informed systems and community interventions.

2   Locating the Study in Research

This article is situated in the context of an emerging scholarship of SGBV and trauma in refugee settings. Studies in different refugee contexts have shown that women and girls experience multiple incidents of trauma occurring over an extended period of time due to their exposure to war, flight, displacement, encampment, resettlement and integration (Eileen and Rees, 2006:21-23; Zannetino, 2012:807; Leatherman, 2011:32). Rape, sexual abuse and assault can have long-term negative effects on women's and girl's psychological and physical health (Campbell and Wasco, 2005:127; Wasco, 2003:309). There is a need to focus on the extensive histories of sexual violence and abuse women and girls go through as a result of war and displacement, and how these experiences contribute to the ways in which women and girls face SGBV-related trauma in their present environments in refugee camp settings, during resettlement in another country or even when they return back to their countries of origin (Pittaway (2004:2-4; Rees, 2004:4). Physical and psychological violence are the most prevalent forms of violence attributed to SGBV among refugees and asylum seekers (Keygnaert, et. al., 2008:4). In this context, women and girls from poor countries with low socio-economic backgrounds, living in detention, camps or shelters were the most vulnerable for SGBV (Bonewit and Shreeves, 2016:22).

Trauma may effect physical, psychological, social and spiritual changes in a persons in the long or short term and can impact the survivor's ability to cope with life in places of integration, resettlement or after their return home. Health impacts of trauma can be classified in terms of physical, psychological, reproductive and behavioural impacts. The physical consequences of SGBV include injuries, infections and disability, weight loss, gastrointestinal problems, and other physical complaints. Some victims die of the immediate consequences of violence, others resort to committing suicide, and some may be infected with sexually transmitted diseases, unwanted pregnancies, miscarriages or abortions (Keygnaet, Vittenburg, and Temmerman, 2012:10). Trauma may lead to psychological problems such as depression, anxiety, insomnia and PTSD. Some survivors indulge in risky or unhealthy behaviours as a result of trauma. This includes alcohol and other substance abuse, smoking, and risky sexual behaviours. Some may speak about their SGBV encounters if they accept narration as a healing process, while others keep their stories to themselves for the fear of social stigma and pain (Herman, (2015:2).

Culture plays a vital role in understanding SGBV and trauma. The ways in which individuals discuss trauma is attributed to the culture of the country of origin in which they grew up before displacement, or where they were socialized, such as the new host community or the refugee setting. In some cultures, it is considered a taboo to discuss sexual violence or related issues, and marital rape is deemed normal within the marriage. Therefore, cultural identity has taken a dominant aspect that needs to be explored in SGBV-related trauma. Attention has been drawn to making health professionals and social workers understand cultural identity in the context of addressing mental health problems among migrants. For, cultural identity has the potential to include 'cultural explanations of the individual's illness, cultural factors related to the psychosocial environment and levels of functioning, cultural elements in the patient-clinician relationship and an overall cultural assessment' (Groen, Richters, Laban and Deville, 2018:70).

Cultural identity focuses on norms and values that shape the image of an individual, her view of herself and behaviours considered as right and wrong based on her social or cultural group. Therefore, a refugee woman's or girl's cultural identity includes a range of ethnic and social factors specific to each individual's situation and her perception of this situation. These characteristics are often underexposed in SGBV-related trauma care. In the case of refugee women and girls, cultural identity could be regarded as complex, multiple, ever-changing through potentially traumatic events (PTEs) such as war, flight, displacement, resettlement and integration and, as a consequence, acculturation into a new society (Rohlof, Knipscheer and Kleber, 2009:489). Acculturation explains the ways in which refugees identify themselves with the host culture and/or with the culture of origin. Positive identification with both cultures results in lower risk for mental distress, while negative identification with both cultures leads to higher risks (Kamperman, Komproe and de Jong, 2007:101). Most often, refugees were forced to leave their country of origin and the majority experience PTEs resulting in a higher risk for mental health problems (Porter and Haslam, 2005:602).

Traumatic stress related to SGBV has a strong impact on cultural identity as the experiences associated with one or more PTEs do have distressing effects on identity formation and development. Memories linked to PTEs tend to 'form a cognitive reference point for the organization of other memories leading to an enhanced integration of these PTEs in a person's understanding of him- or herself and the world' (Berntsen and Rubin, 2007:427). Traumatic memory is central for a person's identity as it is shaped by culture. Hence, knowledge and understanding of the individual's cultural identity is necessary for trauma treatment. An insight into the respective cultural identity is needed for better understanding of the SGBV-related trauma. Therefore, cultural competency in health care and of social work professionals may help to understand trauma in specific social cultural contexts on an individual basis (Kirmayer, 2012:254). For, the treatment of psychiatric symptoms in an individual case may still involve misunderstandings between the patient and a health care professional who lacks the cultural understanding of the case.

3   Methodology

Narrative analysis of case stories has been used in this study. This approach has been used as it enabled the capturing and recounting of stories which were emotional and traumatic, bringing to the forefront lives lived in an everyday setting. Amidst varied approaches in narrative analysis, Bruner (1986) emphasizes the narrative's importance as a mode of understanding, where storytelling has a potential to provide ways to minorities or underrepresented communities to author their version of their own story. In this study, stories of refugee women and girls have taken prominence as the main objective is to build on knowledge of trauma as a consequence of sexually gender-based violence in conflict and displaced contexts such as lived through by the narrator. The case-centred life stories collected through in-depth conversational interviews facilitated a narrative inquiry where stories on women's SGBV experiences were gathered and examined to understand women's lived experiences of trauma, tolerance of violence and interventions. Hence, this method of using stories to capture often difficult encounters is fundamentally qualitative and usually ethnographically oriented.

The fieldwork resulted in an individual-level-study on the trauma of women and girls exposed to SGBV. This article does not intend to represent the views of individuals or try to capture the entire communities' perceptions of sexual and gender-based violence. Rather, it captures the narratives of few women who had willingly expressed their concern to share their stories. The aim was not to generalize findings, but to look at contextualized experiences. The article has also been complemented by focused group discussions and key informant interviews conducted during the study period.

The article is based on two data-sets, conducted by the author from November 2013 to February 2014 in Dadaab Refugee Camp, and from January to February 2019 in Kakuma Refugee Camp. The two data sets revealed many similarities in refugee women's and girls' experiences of war, flight and their lives in the refugee camps linked to events related to SGBV. In the two data sets, the narrative form of the interview began with an open question on the women's or the girls' lives as at present in the refugee camp, inviting the interviewee to freely recount her story. The interviewees were asked to narrate their lives, then to narrate their stories in relation to the focus of the study on SGBV. In the first part of the interview, a series of open-ended questions shaped the interview process. The second part comprised a series of follow-up questions emanating from the initial interviewee narrative. The interviewees were purposively selected due to their encounters with SGBV. The selection process was aided by gatekeepers whom the women and girls trusted. The gatekeeper in the first case was a Somali woman who was a community mobilizer working on SGBV issues in Dadaab. In the second case during the research process, the gatekeeper was a Ugandan refugee woman working as a community mobilizer in the Kakuma Refugee Camp. In most of the cases, the researcher conducted the interviews together with the gatekeepers who also assisted as interpreters. Two cases in Kakuma Refugee Camp required a one-to-one interview between the respective respondent and the gatekeeper (due to the familiarity of the latter with the women and girls). While consent was given, some respondents found it difficult to open up to the researcher due to the lack of familiarity between them. Altogether, the study is based on a selection of twenty-one cases, twelve of which are from Dadaab Refugee Camp and nine from Kakuma Refugee Camp.

All responses were thematically analysed based on the context and trauma as a consequence of SGBV, and the ways in which respondents resolved issues related to trauma in refugee camp settings. The analysis was based on combining the two methods of Rosenthal's narrative analysis (Rosenthal, 1993:5-15) and Flick's thematic analysis (Flick, 2009:305). The initial step was to identify certain recurring or important themes. The second step consisted of an analysis of the narratives, where all the data devoid of any subjective interpretation of the interviewee were listed. This step helped to generate answers to the three sections of the analysis on the causes and context, consequences and resolving of SGBV among women and girl refugees. The analysis made it possible to establish specific connections between the various data points. The themes were grouped and named with titles and subtitles in order to understand the structure of the story in relation to the SGBV experience. The third analysis was an in-depth analysis of the story. Each section was coded chronologically according to the themes that emerged. This process was thus a continual alternation between the coding and the establishing of themes. All the names of people were changed to pseudonyms and the specific names of places (camps) were left out so that participants remained anonymous.

4   Trauma and Sexual and Gender-Based Violence against Women and Girls in Refugee Settings

Over the last two decades many discussions and writings have centred on SGBV in the context of war and displacement, bringing out themes of trauma experienced by women and girls. SGBV is the most prevalent form of violence against women and girls in the context of war and displacement, as often it has been known to be a strategy in military campaigns (Burnet, 2012:98) and is used as a reward for troops in terms of access to sex (Heineman, 2008:7). Victimization of women and girls is often linked to their cultural identity of gender, and they are targeted as they are bearers of the future generation and protectors of the community's culture; in this regard, it is a tool to demoralize the enemy, whose community members place high value on women's purity and whose manhood is affected by the inability to protect their women (Heineman, 2008:8-10). Women and girls may go through multiple instances of victimization throughout the various phases of conflict, displacement, camp life, as well as and during and after conflict settlement (Leatherman, 2007:53). This is well encapsulated in the narratives of Seira (Somali) and Susan (South Sudanese), who were subjected to sexual abuse at different phases of the war:

> '...the first time I encountered the terrible incident (rape), I was sixteen. It was four armed men who raided our home in Kismayu...my mother was killed while she defended me from getting raped. The following day, I fled the place with some of my neighbours to Kenya. The journey was difficult as we had to walk through thorny bushes...we were mainly women in the group...on our way we were stopped by armed men...they did not talk nor ask anything...but pulled us (the women) to the jungle...we (three young women) were raped. I don't remember anything of that time...I just hate to remember...we walked and walked in pain.[2]

> '...it was on a morning when I had gone to fetch firewood. I was raped by two men. It took me a while to even understand what had happened.[3]

---

2   Interview with refugee woman, Dadaab Refugee Camp, 27 November 2013.
3   Interview with refugee woman, Kakuma Refugee Camp, 3 January 2019.

The effects of these SGBV acts were physical, emotional and psychological. The immediate physical trauma revealed by the respondents included: injuries from being beaten, bruises, confusion, being shocked, having sleepless nights and being hyper-vigilant.[4] However, the incident becomes a part of the lives of the women affected in that memories tend to linger on in the aftermath of war as they continue to carry out their day-to-day activities amidst the physical and emotional trauma of their injuries (Khanna, 2008:142). They continue to care for children which includes those born of rape (Haleigh, 2008:64) and may be ignored or chased away by their husbands and families (Leatherman, 2007:54). Susan narrated her experiences as follows:

> 'I kept the stress to myself. After all, whom do I share with? [I lost my parents during the war]... I was pregnant [after the rape] and realized after three months. I had no money for abortion and feared on what would happen to myself if I did it [abortion]. I gave birth to a girl. I named her after my lost mum. People see and call her as a child of a bastard, even blaming her for misfortune. But I love her. She is innocent. Today, she gives me hope to live...'[5]

Further, refugee women and girls are more vulnerable to domestic violence due to the traumatic experiences that they have endured prior to their arrival in the host country (Zannettino, 2012:808). This can be attributed to specific cultural norms being threatened where men's traditional roles and identities are threatened by experiences of trauma from persecutions, flight, and time spent at refugee settlements, resulting in increased violence exacerbated by symptoms of post-traumatic stress disorder and other psychological problems (Pittaway and Rees, 2006:18). Another major factor has been the increase in early marriages in refugee camps as a way of "protecting" the girl, and this in turn may attribute to an increase of cases of intimate partner violence (IPV) among refugee women.[6]

> 'I was forced to marry at the age of fifteen. My father forced me to marry as he said women are always a problem and need to be married soon for protection. Usually fathers like to marry off their daughters at an early age. Parents fear that they will not find a potential match while in these dire conditions [poverty resulting from being a refugee and from living in camps]. It is a cultural thing. I was married off to a man who was in his fifties...who already has two other wives. Since he had livestock [goats and camels] my parents felt that it was a good match. My husband is mostly out as he has to graze animals. Even if he does come home, he stays with the second wife...he does not allow me to go out as he feels that I will have relationships with other men in the camp. He rarely comes to me and if he does come he forces himself upon me to have

---

4   Interview with social worker, Dadaab Refugee Camp, 2 December 2013.

5   Interview with refugee woman, Kakuma Refugee Camp, 3 January 2019.

6   Interview with refugee woman, Dadaab, 2 December 2013.

sex...he beats and shouts at me saying I am unwilling...look at these marks [in her arm]...this has become normal to me...I have lost all hopes for a happy marital life with kids...[7]).

Within the framework of refugee settings, forced and early marriages take place for varied reasons such as poverty within refugee families, the need for protection of girls, girls seen as commodities that are exchanged by the family for goods and money, or to be handed over by the family to another to settle disputes within families or to preserve the honour of the family where the girl will have to marry the rapist.

IPV as direct violence against women tends to remain a private affair restricted to the family level in many cultures such as the Somali culture.[8] Physical abuse experienced by women within family homes is not considered a violation of rights.[9] These narratives reveal the need for different interventions regarding psychosocial support for SGBV-related trauma victims in the two contexts – in the public and the private sphere.

The aftermath of sexual violence can bring about a host of other problems associated with virginity and female genital mutilation (FGMs). Usually after rape, the woman is stitched up. This is done by elderly women in the community using traditional methods detrimental to the victim's health. It is a form of re-victimization for the victim. The loss of virginity means she cannot marry a good partner and therefore she loses all hope of getting married[10].

Refugee women who have been sexually violated often keep their trauma hidden in their everyday lives as they fear being viewed as commercial sex workers. A participant revealed that women and girls who had previous experiences of being sexually abused were among the most vulnerable as they were considered to be available for sex in the refugee camps.[11] The shame and psychosocial stigma that survivors of rape suffer in disclosing their plight is another form of re-victimization (Letherman, 2007:53).

5   Resolving Sexual and Gender-Based Violence-Related Trauma in Refugee Settings

James (2010:281) describes that refugee women and girls resolve trauma related to SGBV in different ways, and culture plays a vital role in the ways in which

---

7   Interview with refugee woman, Dadaab, 9 December 2013.

8   Interview with refugee woman, Dadaab Refugee Camp, 6 December 2013.

9   Interview with refugee woman, Kakuma Refugee Camp, 4 January 2019.

10   Interview with social worker Dadaab, 11 December 2013

11   Interview with social worker, Dadaab, 11 December 2013.

they resort to such traumatic experiences. Literature highlights that sexual violence in refugee settings emerges at the intersection of culture, gender and trauma (Pease and Susan, 2008:39), where a theory of intersectionality should shed light on these traumatic experiences for better understanding and to inform policies and health, social and welfare practice concerning refugee communities affected by SGBV. Intersectionality as articulated by the legal scholar Kimberle Crenshaw (1991:1242) focuses on gender inequalities based on race, age, religion, ethnicity, class, sexuality, or marital status. Hence, interventions aimed at SGBV prevention need to contextualize culturally specific factors in particular communities to understand the SGBV experiences and the related trauma experienced by refugee women and girls (Yacob-Haliso, 2016:53).

Refugee women and girls resort to different ways in which they resolve their SGBV experience and the related traumas. Most participants highlighted the aspect of normalizing and tolerating violence as a result of stigma, being labelled or facing shame. Shame was a stronger factor for remaining quiet about their SGBV experience (Josse, 2010:180). The religious and cultural influences of the communities where refugees hail from affect the way the refugee women or girls (as victims) normalize or tolerate the incident of SGBV. Six participants stated that the fear of being stigmatized, shamed and labelled as being raped or abused by the husband (in case of marital rape) or an outsider (stranger) were reasons why they never revealed the incident. While some kept the incident to themselves, other participants such as Basra revealed the incident to her family, 'I told my mother. She said I am a disgrace to the family...'

The usual response when the issue is revealed to family members, is the view of the daughter, or wife, or sister, bringing disgrace to the family. Community stigmatization is such that the family then hides the girl or, in extreme cases, it can result in the girl running away from the family and the community, or committing suicide[12]. In the case of normalizing and tolerating violence, self-blame was often cited as the outcome of the SGBV activity. The criteria of being a faithful woman, the honour of the family, self-sacrificing, a subordinate wife and mother surfaced as key cultural influences that depicted women in their society. As women are the honour of the families and communities, they remain in this abusive cycle of violence – be it early marriages or IPV. Rape victims are looked at as if they were a curse, outlawed, and not fit to be married again. A woman's tarnished image within the community can result in double trauma for her – that of having been raped and that of how the community has viewed her since. According to Basra, communities tend to put the blame of rape on the victim as it "is her fault": '...usually in these contexts [rape] they [the community] shower the blame on us [women]...it's our fault of provoking men'.

---

12   Interview with refugee woman, 13 December 2013.

The shame assigned to women and girls is part of the collective consciousness of many communities grappling with the inability to cope with horrendous ordeals or rape. Being rejected by family members and the community due to shame and blame often makes women and girls keep their plight to themselves, hence they cry in silence or are often unable to cope with the horror of the event(s). Therefore, social and health workers must understand the power of shame or labelling and how this is used to silence women, as well as to destabilize families and communities. Usually, these experiences of what women went through during conflict or flight is not known as it is never revealed by the victim, and this complicates the level of traumatic experiences in their new refugee camp settings. Hence, social and health professionals are often not well-informed about the real incidents, experiences and trauma and may thus not be able to offer the appropriate services (Eckert, Pittaway and Bartolomei, 2010:479).

Being stigmatized or being labelled tends to prevent women from seeking help or reporting the incident to the authorities. While some hide the issue, others settle within the families or within their communities. These women are haunted by the fear that they will not be believed or that they are responsible for the attack. The result is the silence that surrounds such sexual violence, which in turn generates a hidden (but prevailing) culture of violence. In many ways, the rape victims are proven responsible for her condition. The raped or sexually assaulted victim may agonize over herself 'being a woman', or about her behaviour that seemingly led to the attack. This forces us to ask ourselves: had these women acted any differently, would it actually have avoided them being targeted?

The refugee women's and girls' narratives revealed how resilience was a process that operated in the social spaces that linked them to their environment, where they embraced their own personal resources such as their inner will to survive and opportunities available outside such as NGO activities that supported them after the violence. There is much value in applying knowledge on resilience to understand the experiences of refugee women and girls as it offers an opportunity for those involved to move away from their victim status and to be able to contribute as a survivor, which can be of immense help in understanding the SGBV experiences of refugee women and girls in refugee settings. Resilience is conceptualized as an interplay of circumstances involving risks and the fact that some individuals have the ability to well adjust after severe stressors in their lives due to protective factors inherent in their individual personality or their environment. Resilience related to their individual personality is based on factors such as high self-esteem, intelligence and independence, and as regards their environment, on factors like emotional support by the family and the community (Gopal and Nunlall, 2017:64). Resilience in this study was discussed with regard to four aspects: resilience concerning the ordinary daily lives of women, personal characteristics of the survivor, resilience promoted through informal and formal sources, and the social complexities of resilience and stress.

Resilience with regard to the survivors' ordinary daily lives entailed two strategies for their survival on a day to day basis. Either they hid the act of sexual violence or revealed it to their families or the communities. Hiding the issue and going on with their daily lives was the most commonly used strategy among women where their family reputation was at stake, or where they feared losing the love of their husband or the possibility to find a suitor (if unmarried). Losing the love of the husband due to the violent act can be painful, and many women could not envision how their husbands would react to the incident. Rehma stated that '…there was nothing to gain by exposing, but more losses. It's painful memories but still safe to hide it for your family…'[13]

Basra had the courage to open up to her mother and sister. The issue came to light within the community and she became accustomed to the looks and community gossip after some time. Deep inside, she knew she was not the one who had done something wrong. She went about her daily chores of cleaning, cooking and participating in community activities. Sometimes she cursed the perpetrator that he should be punished in hell as her faith would not let her down. Hage (2006:90) describes that finding solace in religious symbolism was a strategy undertaken by many of the victims of social violence. Similarly, interviews with Rehma and Ilhaan included statements like 'my faith kept me alive' or 'Allah will give me a new life'. Faith gave them a new life, or gave hope or expectations for a new life. There was a strong sense of faith, through which women found their strength to endure. This included prayers where they 'became closer to God'[14]. A further aspect of resilience is the personal character of the survivor. Among the narratives two catch words stood out under this aspect: 'courage or will to survive' and 'determination'. Four participants used these words with a view to their children and family life. They tried to forget the incident and move on with their lives for a better tomorrow[15].

The narratives of these refugee women survivors of sexual violence revealed that resilience was both supported through individual will and promoted through informal and formal support networks and organizations. Resilience is both conditional on the assistance of the community and constructed through the support of the community, family, friends and agencies (Chung, Hung and Bruce, 2013:66). The participants revealed the importance of family support

---

13   Interview with refugee woman, Dadaab, 19 December 2013.

14   Field Notes, February 2014.

15   Interview with refugee woman, Dadaab, 19 December 2013; interview with refugee woman, Kakuma Refugee Camp, 3 January 2019.

during their crisis. In cases where family support was high, women found ways to cope and the ability to learn to accept themselves and to go on with their lives. Various counselling sessions carried out in organizations have helped the women in overcoming their plight and assisted them in the process of healing, reporting these crimes and seeking medical advice. Women who had some means of livelihood and had independence had the ability to cope with the situation and move on with their lives[16]. A participant explained that awareness has helped women and girls to freely discuss rape and sexual abuse in the refugee camp setting. Most commented that service providers had created awareness forums and platforms to discuss experiences of sexual violence in the refugee camps.[17] Formal social support mechanisms, such as the forming of women's groups – maintained and financed by NGO activities – provided women with a platform to discuss their issues with likeminded individuals. The exploration of an individual's resilience (the ability of the survivor to connect interpersonally with others) would allow for acknowledgement of "the complex, multi-layered interpersonal and cultural dynamics that affect one's ability to be resilient" (Hartling, 2005:339). The survivors used their interpersonal skills to form supportive relationships outside the family, and within these safe relationships they were able to face their plight and the associated shame of sexual abuse and place the blame on the perpetrator.

6   Practices Used and Challenges Faced by Social and Health Care Professionals in Addressing SGBV-Related Trauma

Effective response to SGBV-related trauma can only be given once refugee women's and girls' experiences are fully understood, and this includes knowledge of their experiences of SGBV during the various stages of the conflict (pre-conflict stage to conflict escalation stage) and the flight experiences. Only then can treatment of the individual begin within the refugee camp setting. For, individual cases are not only dealt with considering present, but also past experiences. The horrendous realities of sexual abuse as a systemic process, or the multiple traumas connected to it, are little understood and integrated into the consciousness and practice of social and health care service providers working with refugee women and girls. It is never easy to interpret cases if the cultural aspect is neglected, e.g. the fact that women and girls are targeted for rape in specific cultures as a means of humiliating and disgracing men of particular

---

16   Interview with refugee woman, Dadaab, 19 December 2013; interview with refugee woman, Kakuma Refugee Camp, 3 January 2019.

17   Interview with NGO personnel, Kakuma Refugee Camp, 5 January 2019.

communities and thus of dehumanizing their entire community. Knowledge of the cultural realities of specific cases can be a basis for the provision of meaningful services for the traumatized individual, as well as for the service provider in that the latter gets a better understanding of SGBV-related trauma cases. Further, refugee women and girls rarely experience traumatic incidents in isolation and have experienced multiple traumatic incidents during war, flight or displacement, revealing that multiple abuse with recurrent memories can make women more susceptible for future violence, as it impacts women's resilience and wellbeing (Bartolomei, Pittaway and Pittaway, 2003:88). Therefore, health care professionals and social workers dealing with trauma healing need to earn credibility by learning about the client's culture, critical issues in the country of origin, and the traumatic experiences these vulnerable groups have encountered throughout their lives as refugees. This includes the need to factor in manifestations of post-traumatic stress disorder and other mental health impacts arising from past and current experiences of trauma (Rees, 2004:117).

An interviewee explained the need for raising awareness and discussing the topic of SGBV with the entire family and the community – above all the husband of the female victim, if she is married. For example, IPV in refugee settings cannot be resolved by the woman alone, hence discussions with both men and women are important[18]. Women usually do not disclose their encounters with violence so as to remain loyal to their husbands and their communities, and the fear of a family breakdown. An NGO worker highlighted that, 'most often, women and girls hide the case of SGBV, with statements such as "it doesn't happen here in our culture," or, often normalize issues such as IPV saying "its normal in our culture" or, "'it's not our culture to admit."[19] Hence there is a need for challenging SGBV happening in the private and public sphere but hidden in the name of culture, specifically in refugee contexts acknowledging intersections of culture, trauma and displacement (James, 2010:276).

Health care professionals and social workers have to be culturally sensitive and culturally aware, and they should know that the silencing of women and girls results from a cultural context and is caused by cultural 'defences.' SGBV in families, such as IPV, is considered normal by some communities and even some refugee women themselves. This makes it difficult for the health care professional to intervene, as refugees involved accept such fate themselves. However, the main causes of sexual violence in IPV in refugee communities is rooted in patriarchal power relations that transcend culture, nationality and religion, and the use of rape is justified as a tool for controlling women in the

---

18   Interview with health care professional, Kakuma Refugee Camp, 2 January 2019.
19   Interview with NGO worker, Dadaab Refugee Camp, 3 December 2013.

household or as a war strategy (Pittaway and Rees, 2006:19). Many refugees in the Dadaab and Kakuma refugee settings have fled from protracted refugee situations with layers of cultural experiences, e.g. their own culture of the country of origin, as well as that of the refugee culture in refugee camps (through accustomization). Most often, the traditional cultures are preserved in these refugee settings, so as to put the lives of women and girls more in line with the traditional norms of their places of origin.

Most often, refugee women and girls find it easier to report their SGBV incident within their community networks rather than seek professional help. Hence, the affected women and girls in these cases even looked forward to trauma healing within their known networks. Some went for professional assistance from health workers as a last resort but preferred to deal with their trauma within their families and the community. This was the case with Basra, who was initially able to tell her mother and sister. Later, slowly, her story was told to the community leaders.[20] However, not all women or girls may have the opportunity to tell family or community members, and those will have to rely on professional help. In the case of Juliet, she has no one to rely on as she had no family and had to rely on professional help from the NGOs.[21]

A social worker in the Kakuma Refugee Camp explained that attitudes towards professional help is changing, and women and girls seize the opportunity to resort to professional help:

> 'Slowly, attitudes towards professional help is changing, affected women go and seek for professional help. The key is secrecy. Many NGOs and INGOs have been successful in gaining trust and empowering women to speak up and treat their traumatic experiences and also give hope via education and employment opportunities.[22]

A health professional highlighted that they rely on community networks when treating cases where women and girls do not want to come out and discuss their problem with health workers: 'We use community networks by creating awareness, responding to emergencies (SMS emergencies) and even treat affected women and girls with the aid of relatives and community members comfortable and close to the victim.'[23] Similarly, another health care professional explained the importance of community networks in the reporting and the treatment of SGBV cases:

---

20   Interview with refugee woman, Dadaab Refugee Camp, 11 November 2013.

21   Interview with refugee woman, Kakuma Refugee Camp, 6 January 2019.

22   Interview with social worker, Kakuma Refugee Camp, 3 January 2019.

23   Interview with NGO worker, Kakuma Refugee Camp, 2 January 2019.

'Most often victims are comfortable with their families, if they fail via family and relatives, they go to the community elders. They also access block leaders, community security personnel of the block or chairladies responsible in each block in the Kakuma Camp. Community health workers and other professional help is sought via these personnel.'[24]

Cultural and other belief systems such as religion play an important role in the trauma healing process. Health care professionals and social workers need to understand these belief systems if they are to help in the trauma healing process. Twelve interviewees highlighted the role of religion and spiritual guidance as the most important factor in their healing process.[25] However, navigating within these belief systems require knowledge on how to use belief systems in the healing process, even on how to use the assistance of religious institutions and leaders.[26] This requires health workers to work together with the client to explore ways in which belief systems can be utilized in the trauma healing process.

Probing into experiences of SGBV can be very traumatic and some health care professionals deem it better not to disturb memories that are painful to the client (Eckert, Pittaway, Bartolomei, 2010:480). However, some have expressed the importance of retelling the stories of their traumatic experiences as vital in the traumatic healing process. This again depends on a case-to-case basis, where professionalism plays a vital role in helping refugee women and girls to reveal their stories in safe spaces where they feel comfortable in the narrating process.[27] Most refugee women and girls have gone through multiple traumas and may need days to talk about different experiences in their narrations. Providing space and time for the affected women and girls is important to heal their emotional wounds. However, this can be a toll on the health care or social worker, too, who constantly gets to hear of traumatic experiences and who may suffer as a result of vicarious traumatization. Hence, professional treatment of such trauma needs to be well thought through, with self-care strategies for a better professional response towards traumatized refugee women and girls.[28]

Refugee women and girls who had undergone various awareness and educative programmes explained that these programmes, which empowered them to take control of their own lives, and equipped them with knowledge and skills on

---

24   Interview, health care professional, Kakuma Refugee Camp, 2 January 2019.

25   Interview with refugee women, Kakuma Refugee Camp, 6 January 2019.

26   Interview with social worker, Kakuma Refugee Camp, 3 January 2019.

27   Interview with NGO worker, Kakuma Refugee Camp, 2 January 2019.

28   Interview with social worker, Kakuma Refugee Camp, 6 January 2019.

advocacy, rights, legal aid, or even employment skills, gave them courage to live amidst their plight[29].

Addressing SGBV involves working with men and boys, too. Sensitization, awareness and educative programmes have included men and boys so that they become part of preventing SGBV against women and girls, and so they can assist women and girls in the SGBV healing process. In fact, an interviewee stated that these programmes are geared towards a cultural change where both male and female members of the community look into these issues together with regard to SGBV prevention. For it is important to stress the need to present SGBV as an issue regarding both men and women.[30] Further, there is also a need to work with the perpetrators of violence in the refugee camp settings. Sometimes, the perpetrators are found within the refugee camps and most often in cases of IPV, they are the victim's abusive partner. Hence, prevention entails working with these individuals for a better future.[31]

7   Conclusion

Culture shapes the ways in which individuals frame and resolve their traumas. This implies how women and girls in specific cultures understand and interpret SGBV, which shapes the ways in which they name and frame SGBV and the ways in which they reveal and resolve their traumas. The study viewed the merging themes on SGBV and trauma in the refugee settings of Dadaab and Kakuma in Kenya. SGBV and trauma has been viewed through a cultural lens considering the intersections between nationality, tribe, religion, power and gender. While cultural explanations of SGBV are a contested terrain, cultural contexts are critical to the analysis of SGBV, as they are always applicable to anyone who has (had) a culture – whether this was during peace times (pre-war) or in displaced contexts (refugee camps). Cultural explanations are contested because they are either used to excuse individual actions or to facilitate stereotyping. Hence, culture is often responsible for how we view the problem of SGBV and related trauma and how we address it (believing that women and girls from a particular culture are passive, normalize and tolerate violence, fear seeking help, refrain from speaking out about abuse as it would shame the family and affect her resilience in the aftermath of the violence). Culture cannot be viewed isolated from religion, for there is an inextricable link between religion and culture in some communities such as the Somali community. Similarly,

---

29   Interview with refugee woman, Kakuma Refugee Camp, 9 January 2019.
30   Interview with NGO worker, Kakuma Refugee Camp, 9 January 2019.
31   Interview with social worker, Kakuma Refugee Camp, 6 January 2019.

culture and ethnicity is closely tied, shaping how refugee women and girls view and respond to trauma, as is the case in the Sudanese and Somali refugee communities.

Transcultural interpretation of SGBV and trauma healing includes the way in which the violent act is viewed, tolerated, normalized, reported and punished and needs to be depicted through culture, religion and a patriarchal interpretation. These patriarchal interpretations are of those of individuals in position of power or means of maintaining power, who define the dominant culture and interpretation of religion (Shaheed, 2008:243). It is important to view these themes through the power relations of the refugee communities to shed light to the context of SGBV in refugee settings. For instance, marital rapes or early marriages in camps and reporting such acts to the authorities are dependent on the women's positioning in their families and communities. Hence, reaching out for assistance and treatment of SGBV trauma is dependent on the cultural positioning of women and girls in their respective refugee communities.

Bibliography

Bailey-Smith, Yvonne (2001). A Systemic Approach to Working with Black Families. In: McMahon, Linnet; Ward, Adrian (eds.), Helping Families in Family Centres. London: Jessica Kingsley Publishers.

Bartolomei, Linda; Pittaway, Eileen; Pittaway, Emma (2003): Who am I? Identity and Citizenship in Kakuma Refugee Camp in Northern Kenya. In: *Development*, 46(3): 87-93.

Berntsen, Dorthe; Rubin, David (2007): When a Trauma Becomes a Key to Identity: Enhanced Integration of Trauma Memories Predicts Posttraumatic Stress Disorder Symptoms. In: Applied Cognitive Psychology, 21(4), pp. 417-431.

Bonewit, Anne; Shreeves, Rosamund (2016): Reception of Female Refugees and Asylum Seekers in the EU. In: Case Study Germany, European Parliament, February, available at: http://www.europarl.europa.eu/RegData/etudes/STUD/2016/536497/IPOL_STU   (2016)5 36497_EN.pdf.

Burnet, Jennie (2012): Situating Sexual Violence in Rwanda (1990–2001): Sexual Agency, Sexual Consent, and the Political Economy of War. In: African Studies Review, 55(2), pp. 97–118.

Campbell, Rebecca; Wasco, Sharon (2005): Understanding Rape and Sexual Assault: 20 Years of Progress and Future Directions. In: Journal of Interpersonal Violence, 20(1), pp. 127-131.

Chung, Karren; Hong, Ellie; Bruce, Newbold (2013): Resilience among Single Adult Female Refugees in Hamilton. Ontario. In: *Refuge,* 29 (1): p. 66.

Crenshaw, Kimberle (1991): Mapping the Margins: Intersectionality, Identity Politics, and Violence against Women of Color. In: *Stanford Law Review*, 43(6), pp. 1241-1299.

Doney, Gil; Eckert, Rebecca; Pittaway, Eileen. (2009). African Women Talking: We Want the Best Thing for our Family, Research Report, Commissioned by ACCES Services Inc., Queensland, Centre for Refugee Research. Sydney: University of New South Wales.

Eckert, Rebecca; Pittaway, Eileen; Bartolomei, Linda (2010): Resettled but Still at Risk: Women at Risk and Resettlement. In: ARRA Submission to UNHCR Geneva, Centre for Refugee Research, University of New South Wales, Sydney, pp. 459-481.

Flick, Uwe (2009): An Introduction to Qualitative Research. London: SAGE Publications, pp. 305-358.

Frey, Cid (2001): Post-Traumatic Stress Disorder and Culture. In: Yilmaz, Tariq; Weiss, Mitchell; Riecher-Rossler Anita; (eds.). Cultural Psychiatry: Euro-International Perspectives. Karger, Basel, pp. 103-116.

Gopal, Nirmala; Nunlall, Reema (2017): Interrogating the Resilience of Women Affected by Violence. In: *Empowering Women for Gender Equity*, 31(2), pp. 63-73.

Groen, Simon; Richters, Annemiek; Laban, Cornelis; Deville, Walter (2018): Cultural Identity among Afghan and Iraqi Traumatized Refugees: Towards a Conceptual Framework for Mental Health Care Professionals. In: Cultural Medical Psychiatry, 42(1), p. 70.

Hage, Sally (2006): Profiles of Women Survivors: The Development of Agency in Abusive Relationships. In: Journal of Counseling & Development, 84(1), pp. 83-94.

Hanlon, Haleigh (2008): Implications for Health Care Practice and Improved Policies for Victims of Sexual Violence in the Democratic Republic of Congo. In: Journal of International Women's Studies, 10(2), pp. 64-72.

Hartling, Linda (2005): Fostering Resilience Throughout our Lives: New Relational Possibilities. In: Dana Camstock (ed.), Diversity and Development: Critical Contexts that Shape our Lives and Relationships. CA: Thomson, Belmont.

Heineman, Elizabeth (2008): The History of Sexual Violence in Conflict Zones: Conference Report. In: *Radical History Review*, 101(1), pp. 5-21.

Herman, Judith Lewis (2015): Trauma and Recovery: The Aftermath of Violence – From Domestic Abuse to Political Terror. New York: Basic Books.

James, Kerrie (2010): Domestic Violence within Refugee Families: Intersecting Patriarchal Culture and the Refugee Experience. In: *The Australian and New Zealand Journal of Family Therapy*, 31(3), pp. 275-284.

Kamperman, Astrid; Komproe, Ivan; de Jong, Jocelyn (2007). Migrant Mental Health: A Model for Indicators of Mental Health and Health Care Consumption. In: *Health Psychology*, 26 (1), pp. 96-104.

Keygnaert, Ines; Wilson, Ruth; Dedoncker, K; Bakker, H; Van Petegem, Marijke; Wassie, Najla; Temmerman, Marleen (2008): Hidden Violence is Silent Rape. Prevention of Sexual & Gender-Based Violence against Refugees & Asylum Seekers in Europe: A Participatory Approach Report. Available at: http://icrhb.org/sites/default/files/Hidden%20Violence%20is%20a%20 Silent%20Rape %20Final%20Report.pdf.

Keygnaert, Ines; Vettenburg, Nicole; Temmerman, Marleen (2012): Hidden Violence is Silent Rape: Sexual and Gender-Based Violence in Refugees, Asylum Seekers and Undocumented Migrants in Belgium and the Netherlands. In: Culture, Health & Sexuality, 14 (5), pp. 505-520.

Khanna, Renu (2008): Communal Violence in Gujarat, India: Impact of Sexual Violence and Responsibilities of the Health Care System. In: Reproductive Health Matters, 16(31), pp. 142-152.

Kirmayer, Laurence (2012): Cultural Competence and Evidence-Based Practice in Mental Health: Epistemic Communities and the Politics of Pluralism. In: *Social Science and Medicine*, 75 (1), pp. 249-256.

Leatherman, Janie (2007): Sexual Violence and Armed Conflict: Complex Dynamics of Re-Victimization. In: *International Journal of Peace Studies,* 12(1), pp. 53-71.

Leatherman, Janie (2011): Sexual Violence and Armed Conflict. Polity Press, Malden, MA.

Pease, Bob; Rees, Susan (2008): Theorising Men's Violence towards Women in Refugee Families: Towards an Intersectional Feminist Framework. In: Just Policy, 47(1): pp. 39-45.

Pittaway, Eileen (2004): From Horror to Hope: Addressing Domestic Violence in Refugee Families Resettled in Australia. Sydney, Australia: Centre for Refugee Research, UNSW and Office for Women, NSW Premiers Department.

Pittaway, Eileen; Rees, Susan (2006): Multiple Jeopardy: Domestic Violence and the Notion of Cumulative Risk for Women in Refugee Camps. In: Women Against Violence: An Australian Feminist Journal, 18, pp. 18-25.

Porter, Matthew; Haslam, Nick (2005): Pre-Displacement and Post-Displacement Factors Associated with Mental Health of Refugees and Internally Displaced Persons: A Meta-Analysis. In: JAMA 294(5), pp. 602-612.

Rees, Susan (2004): Human Rights and the Significance of Psychosocial and Cultural Issues in Domestic Violence Policy and Intervention for Refugee Women. In: *Australian Journal of Human Rights*, 10(1), pp. 97-118.

Rohlof, Hans; Knipscheer, Jeroen; Kleber, Rolf (2009): Use of the Cultural Formulation with Refugees. In: Transcultural Psychiatry, 46(3), pp. 487-505.

Rosenthal, Gabriele (1993): Reconstruction of Life Stories: Principles of Selection in Generating Stories for Biographical Narrative Interviews. In: *Narrative Study of Lives,* 1(1), *pp.* 59-91.

Schubert, Carla; Raija-Leena, Punamaki (2011): Mental Health among Torture Survivors: Cultural Background, Refugee Status and Gender. In: *Nordic Journal of Psychiatry*, 65(3): 175-182.

Shaheed, Farida. (2008). Violence against Women Legitimized by Arguments of 'Culture': Thoughts from a Pakistani Perspective. In: Due Diligence and its Application to Protect Women from Violence. Leiden: Koninklijke Brill. pp. 241-248.

Wasco, Sharon (2003): Conceptualizing the Harm Done by Rape: Applications of Trauma Theory to Experiences of Sexual Assault. In: Trauma, Violence and Abuse, 4(4), pp. 309-322.

Wendt, Sarah; Zannettino, Lana (2015): Refugee Women. In: *Domestic Violence in Diverse Contexts: A Re-Examination of Gender*. Abingdon, Oxon: Routledge, pp. 105-125.

Yacob-Haliso, Olajumoke (2016): Intersectionality and Durable Solutions for Refugee Women in Africa In: *Journal of Peacebuilding and Development,* 11(3), pp. 53-67.

Yuan, Nicole P.; Koss, Mary. P.; Stone, Mirto (2006): The Psychological Consequences of Sexual Trauma. Minnesota: Applied Research Institution, pp. 1-11.

Zannettino, Lana. (2012): "There is No War Here; It is Only the Relationship that Makes us Scared": Factors Having an Impact on Domestic Violence in Liberian Refugee Communities in South Australia. In: Violence Against Women, 18(7), pp. 807-828.

7. Economic Perspectives on Diversity and Health

The e-ICI Framework: How to Support the Development of Digital Services for Forced Migrants Dealing with Health Issues

Annalies Beck, Ayca Nina Zuch[1]

Keywords: *forced migrants, e-services, technology-based innovation, e-Health, mental health, e-inclusion, user-centered design, play theory, mobile applications, social media, blockchain, artificial intelligence*

Abstract

The present article presents a novel approach, the e-Inclusion- and Cohesion-based Innovation (e-ICI) model, as a tool for analysing how digital technologies can help forced migrants suffering from health restrictions. Starting from the example of forced migrants with special needs in Germany, the authors take a closer look at the current situation through statistical indicators, before providing the results of their qualitative analysis of already existing digital services for forced migrants in Germany. Their findings are complemented by deductions from the theoretical concepts of innovation, culture and inclusion. In addition, selected new digital technologies are assessed regarding their applicability and possible risks. The authors argue that the e-ICI model offers a valuable new approach for researchers and practitioners that takes the individual needs of forced migrants dealing with health issues into account.

---

1   Annalies Beck | Friedrich-Schiller-Universität Jena | annalies.beck@uni-jena.de

Ayca Nina Zuch | Hochschule für Wirtschaft und Recht Berlin | e_zuch@doz.hwr-berlin.de

© Springer Fachmedien Wiesbaden GmbH, part of Springer Nature 2020
K. Crepaz et al. (eds.), *Health in Diversity – Diversity in Health*,
https://doi.org/10.1007/978-3-658-29177-8_13

Contents

Abstract..233

1   Introduction..235

2   Analysis of the Current Situation in Research and Practice....................235

2.1 Migration and Health in Germany – Facts and Numbers 236

2.2 Existing e-Services for Forced Migrants in Germany 239

2.2.1 Selected e-(Health)-Services 239

2.2.2 Analyzed Features of the Selected e-(Health-)Services........................240

3   Theoretical Principles of Technology-Based Innovation in the Context
     of Migration and Health..243

3.1 Derivations from the Theoretical Concepts of Innovation, Culture and
     Inclusion 244

3.2 Assessment of Potentials and Risks of Selected Technologies...............248

3.2.1 Gamified Mobile Applications 248

3.2.2 Social Media..249

3.2.3 Blockchain..251

3.2.4 Artificial Intelligence (AI)..253

4   The e-ICI Approach as a new Conceptual Framework...........................257

5   Conclusion and Final Remarks 259

Bibliography 261

Appendix..270

1   Introduction

This contribution aims to explore the impact of technology[1] against the background of the current situation of recently arrived forced migrants in Germany who are dealing with health issues. The topic is considered from the authors' perspectives of intercultural business communication and innovation management. Thereby, the conducted study is based on a literature review and a qualitative analysis of already existing digital services, respectively e-services[2], that follow the intention to support forced migrants with special needs. The key findings result in the conception and presentation of a novel approach, the *e-Inclusion- and Cohesion-based Innovation (e-ICI)* model, which meets the needs of forced migrants with health restrictions in a sustainable way, is supposed to be applied to all creators of digital services in the future and allows follow-up research.

This article is divided into five parts: In the following chapter we focus on the identified present problems that occur when forced migrants in Germany are in need of health support. Besides, the research gap is outlined by highlighting key findings from a literature review and a qualitative analysis of digital services for forced migrants that are already offered in Germany. Chapter three contains the theoretical fundamentals as a base for the development of the theoretical e-ICI model in chapter four. Final remarks are formulated in chapter five.

2   Analysis of the Current Situation in Research and Practice

This chapter aims to explain the present research status with a view to forced migrants, their health issues and the role of digital technology. This implicates a closer look on e-services that are already in use in Germany. First, we present an overview regarding relevant data about forced migrants who arrived in Germany and who are dealing with health issues (2.1). The second half of the chapter concentrates on our research results and the analysis of currently available e-services for forced migrants in Germany by also focusing on the specific functions of these services (2.2).

---

1   In this article, the addition "digital" is omitted for improved readability. Whenever the term "technology/-ies" is used, digital technologies are meant.

2   Following Ronchi (2019) the abbreviation "e-" is used if a product, service or organization is provided via the Internet using information and communication technology (ICT).

2.1   Migration and Health in Germany – Facts and Numbers

In January 2019, the monthly applications for asylum in Germany reached 14,534 (BAMF 2019a). Earlier, in 2017, more than 67% of all migrants in Germany were able to work (OECD 2019). According to the German Asylum Procedures Act, recognized refugees and asylum seekers can work in Germany without any restriction. By contrast, asylum seekers who are still in the asylum procedure are allowed to work in Germany at the earliest after a three months' stay. The same applies to persons who are tolerated[3] in Germany. The Integration Act implies, however, that in the first 15 months access to the labor market is still limited in some regions with high unemployment rates[4] (BAMF 2019b).

Being able to work and to be employed in Germany requires – next to complying with asylum procedure laws – stable health conditions. This chapter focuses on possible health issues of forced migrants that have already arrived in Germany[5]. Complementing the "social determinants of health" that were first mentioned in a report by WHO[6] (CDSH 2008; IOM's GMDAC 2017), further research of the authors cited in tab. 1 demonstrates further challenges that forced migrants face in Germany and that have an impact on their health. When looking at the different extended social determinants of health, one has to keep in mind that the health status of forced migrants varies significantly across the European region (Humphris and Bradby 2017).

It is a fact that people with a migration background differ in terms of health-related aspects from people without a migration background (Brzoska and Razum 2016). Following Frank et al. (2017) and distinguishing communicable and non-communicable diseases, for example, certain chronic diseases are more common among people with a migrant background (ibid.). Even though forced migrants are basically endangered by the same infectious diseases as the population living in Germany, they are particularly vulnerable to infectious diseases due to their living conditions during the flight and possible incomplete vaccination protection (Frank et al. 2017). The Migration Data Portal (2019)

---

3   This applies to persons who are not or who are no longer in the asylum procedure or who have received a negative notification regarding their applications for asylum; if their deportation is suspended, they receive a "certificate for the suspension of a deportation" from the immigration office which is called "toleration" (BAMF 2019b).

4   An exception to the labor market access applies to asylum seekers from "safe countries of origin": they are not allowed to work for the entire time of the asylum procedure (BAMF 2019b).

5   Besides this destination and integration phase, according to the Migration Data Portal (2019) the process of migration consists of three other phases, including pre-departure, travel and transit, and return.

6   WHO (Word Health Organization), see https://www.who.int

adds: "the increasing pattern of 'circulatory migration' moving between immune and non-immune populations also adds a further challenges [sic!] with respect to the prevention and control of emerging infectious diseases."

Extended social determinants of health	Authors
access to information, working and education conditions *(e.g. lack of knowledge about existence of jobs)*	Bagfa-Integration[7] 2019; IOM's GMDAC 2017; Frank et al. 2017; Maier and Straub 2011; Fassaert et al. 2009
social and community factors *(e.g. social isolation)*	IOM's GMDAC 2017; Almohamed 2016; Andrade and Doolin 2016; Almohamed and Vyas 2016; Caidi et al. 2010
culture-related and lifestyle factors *(e.g. limited proficiency in the local language)*	Humphris and Bradby 2017; IOM's GMDAC 2017; Brown and Grinter 2016; Razum and Saß 2015; Bischoff et al. 2003
individual factors *(e.g. old age)*	IOM's GMDAC 2017; Humphris and Bradby 2017
political and socioeconomic factors *(e.g. limited access to health care)*	Humphris and Bradby 2017; Talhouk et al. 2016a/b
living conditions *(e.g. poor diet and housing)*	Bagfa-Integration 2019; Humphris and Bradby 2017; IOM's GMDAC 2017

Tab. 1:   Extended social determinants of forced migrants' health according to literature review

Among the non-communicable diseases mental illness plays a crucial role. Several studies show that forced migrants are at considerable risk of developing symptoms of mental disorders (de Jong et al. 2003; Fazel et al. 2005; Hassan et al. 2016; Steel et al. 2009). Frank et al. (2017) consider this a "priority supply requirement". The main reasons why forced migrants suffer from mental diseas-

---

7   Bagfa (Bundesarbeitsgemeinschaft der Freiwilligenagenturen e.V.), see https://bagfa. de/aktuelles.html.

es such as post-traumatic stress disorder, depression or anxiety disorders are traumatic experiences in the countries of origin or during the flight (Böttche et al. 2016; Bühring 2015). At the current time, generally valid statements cannot be made. In Germany there is no central data collection about the health status of forced migrants, even though numerous initiatives aim to improve the data situation (Frank et al. 2017). One problem is that the initial examinations in the federal states of Germany are not standardized. These initial admission examination results, which asylum seekers according to § 62 "AsylG" (asylum law) (Bundesamt für Justiz 2019a) and § 36 "IfSG" (Infection Protection Act) (Bundesamt für Justiz 2019b) must submit to a shared accommodation before or immediately after admission, represent an important data source. Another challenge lies in the collection of health data from undocumented migrants who cannot identify themselves. Studies to date have shown either a low case number or regional limitations. Thus, binding statements can only be made for individual areas (Frank et al. 2017; Mediendienst Integration 2019). In 2015, it was estimated that of 379,848 forced migrants in need of mental health care only about 5% received treatment (BAfF 2016). The WHO (2012) has indicated that depression will be the leading global disease by 2030 and that "refugees, asylum seekers and irregular migrants are at heightened risk for certain mental health disorders, including post-traumatic stress, depression and psychosis" (WHO 2017). This leads to the question of how Germany is currently handling the situation of forced migrants who just arrived in the country and who are suffering from mental health issues.

The existing findings suggest that action is needed while there is inadequate access to public health care services. Several federal states in Germany have begun handing over an electronic health card (EHC) to asylum seekers with the intention to improve access to the medical system and reduce administrative costs. According to the Asylum Seekers Benefits Act, with this card doctor visits do not have to be requested in advance from the social welfare authorities and the treatment needs are decided directly by the medical staff (MFG 2019, Bundesamt für Justiz 2019a). But even with the EHC, challenges on the way to help and healing remain: Several studies show that people with a migrant background are less likely to use health services, such as early disease detection (Laban et al. 2007; Lamkaddem et al. 2014). The reasons for the lack of use of health services in Germany by migrants coincide and are directly related to the extended social determinants of health (see tab. 1, p. 3). In this context, two aspects come to the fore: Migrants can feel a sense of shame when they seek psychiatric help (Hassan et al. 2015). In addition, it is problematic in the already difficult situation that there seems to be a lack of linguistically and culturally validated screening tools or that, if they exist, they are not yet used to their full potential (Metzner et al. 2016).

If migrants are willing to get treatment, there are waiting lists and according to Baron and Schriefers (2015) only 5% of psychosocial center clients can be passed on each year to resident therapists.

In summary, it can be stated against the background of the current situation and in response to the needs of forced migrants suffering from mental health issues that there is a need of

- special skilled and culturally sensitive workers in psychotherapeutic practice

- functioning and stable treatment structures

- language mediation services[8]

- clear communication of reimbursement of services

- an innovative way of communication to address and actually reach people.

In the next section we will present the findings of our analysis of technology-based services which are already offered, and which are aimed directly at forced migrants in Germany.

2.2   Existing e-Services for Forced Migrants in Germany

2.2.1   Selected e-(Health)-Services

Regarding the current research status, Mehrotra and Tripathi (2018: 379) have shown evidence of the acceptability, feasibility and efficacy of mobile-based mental health interventions for facilitating recovery. Nevertheless, they point out that "more research is needed on implementation and integration of these interventions in diverse real-world clinical and community contexts" (ibid.). Sijbrandij et al. (2017: 5) share the following opinion: "e-mental health interventions may reach clients that would otherwise not have access to mental health treatment due to internal (e.g. fear of stigmatization) or external (e.g. infrastructure) barriers. Additional advantages are the relative brevity of e-mental health interventions and the possibility to automatize parts of the treatment".

Screening the market of mobile applications[9] (hereafter abbreviated as "mobile apps") online which claim to support forced migrants, and also researching relating scientific papers, one paper was especially outstanding:

---

8   Sijbrandij et al. 2017 suggest that that it may be a disadvantage to use a person close to the patient as an interpreter, since then no confidential conversations are possible.

9   Understood as an application software for mobile devices or mobile operating systems (see i. a. Nayebi et al. 2012) .

Bustamante Durante et. al. (2018) have investigated 36 digital (health) solutions[10], and all solutions are available online via open access; see http://appsforrefugees.com/. This list helped us digging deeper into digital services for psychological support addressing forced migrants in Germany.

Tab. 2 "e-support solutions for forced migrants in Germany" (see Appendix) lists 10 examples of digital services provided for forced migrants in Germany. No. 2 and No. 6 are the ones with the most users: 50,000 and 100,000, respectively. Both mobile apps deliver most helpful information for daily life and administration issues. Outstanding here is that No. 2 has been established by a forced Syrian migrant for forced migrants (Arabic speaking) while No. 6 is an app created by the government of North Rhine-Westphalia. Nos. 1, 2, 4, 5, 8, 9 have their own Facebook[11] (FB) channel. No. 2 has the most FB likes and a vibrant FB community (almost 120,000 likes). No. 10 is outstanding because it addresses female forced migrants and offers support (e.g. direct contact to women's houses) and gives information on women's rights in Germany. No. 1 and No. 8 have the second highest amount of users. Both give information on daily life matters. Nos. 1, 6, 8 work offline. All these three services deal with daily life matters. No. 9 is a project by the designer Gosia Warrink, making communication easier, also for refugees by communication via icons.

Nos. 4 and 5 are e-Health solutions, both give psychological support, both claim to have secure online channels.

2.2.2   Analyzed Features of the Selected e-(Health-)Services

The results of our analysis suggest that the common features are (except in one, namely game No. 7) free of charge, digital and at least available in English.
Based on findings that "research shows that online MH [Mental Health] interventions are as effective as traditional face-to-face therapy for disorders such as depression and anxiety" (Yellowlees et al. 2016: p. 233), we analyzed mobile health care solutions addressing forced migrants in Germany as principal users.

Focusing on the e-Health solutions presented in Appendix, tab. 2: "e-support solutions for forced migrants in Germany", we found the following: Solution No. 4, "Ipso-Care" (fig. 1), is a quite hidden[12] but promising support

---

10   Also to be understood as "e-(Health-)solutions" (see i. a. https://www.bundesgesundheitsmini
       sterium.de/service/begriffe-von-a-z/e/e-health.html)

11   As a virtual social network, Facebook is one of the world's most widely used social media
       applications (Hootsuite 2018).

12   E.g. a glimpse into the meta texts of *https://ipso-care.com* showed that the target group cannot
       really find it: "<meta name="description" content="*In einer ausgewogenen und harmonischen
       Weise auf der Grundlage Ihrer eigenen Werte leben, Ihre Ressourcen nutzen und Ihre Visionen*

platform, available in 13 languages, accompanied by a FB channel with about 900 likes. We find it promising because of the 13 languages offered and the so-called "safe room" to enter and start a dialogue with a psychologically trained person (fig. 2).

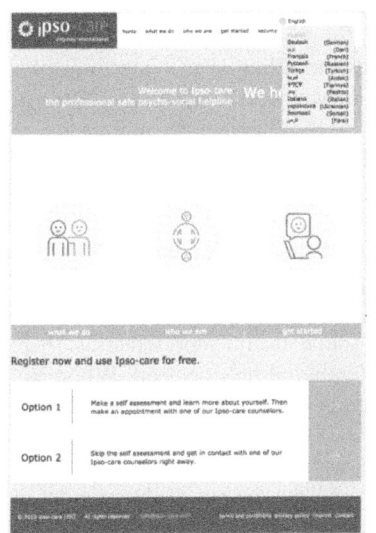

Fig. 1:   "Ipso-Care" landing page (https://ipso-care.com/home.html)

Fig. 2:   First steps at "Ipso-Care" (https://ipso-care.com/get-started.html)

---

und Ideen, die für Sie Sinn erzeugen, umsetzen zu können: Dabei unterstützt Sie der psychosoziale Ipso e-care Berater."> (<meta name="keywords" content="">".

No. 5 is composed of two mobile apps and an online platform, "Ilaj Nafsy", all are part of a current study by Zentrum Überleben e.V. Berlin, available only in three languages maximum. On this platform, one gets information on analyzed papers that show that a web-based therapeutic consultation works. On this website, patients can register for a course to treat post-traumatic stress disorder and/or a course of therapy for depression, and get consultations via written communication over a secure internet portal for free. Their participation in a course or use of the mobile apps also involves the filling in of "questionnaires both before and after (directly after and again two weeks later) the course of therapy in order to assess the effectiveness of the therapeutic approaches in question. Additionally, the patients are asked how they felt about having their treatment carried out over the internet or using their smartphones respectively"[13].

The platform "Ilaj Nafsy" has its own FB channel with almost 6,500 likes and a vivid community. On FB, both mobile apps get supported.

Analyzing the accessibility of the listed services, it seems that there is a strong link between having or not having a social media representation (here shown via an existing own FB channel) and the digital service itself. While No. 2, the one which got created by a single person being himself a forced migrant, has less downloads (50,000+) than No. 6 (100,000+), No. 2 has the most FB likes: almost 120,000 likes (while No. 6 does not even have its own FB channel). This may be linked to given trust to the publisher/owner of the services as he may be seen as "one of them" and the user can identify with the publisher/owner of the service (Liu et al. 2015: 41).

Also No. 1 can register FB likes of 10% measured against the amount of downloads. Access to the usage of No. 4 or 5 by download numbers cannot be gained as download numbers are not visible. Only the FB likes can be mentioned: while No. 4 lists about 900 likes, No. 5 can record about 6,500 likes on FB.

Furthermore, we think it is important to mention the problem of (il)literacy and the variety of languages that services support (Reem et al. 2016, Bustamante Durante et al. 2018). Although most listed services are multilingual, some start in Arabic (Nos. 2, 5), while No. 4 seems to start device-dependent, as the language used on the device is shown on the start page of the website. We advise more focus on user-oriented development. Nos. 1, 6, 8 are accessible offline. Nevertheless, we see a strong need for more offline services as internet connection and services are not always given (also not in camps or in various locations in Germany) (Bustamante Durante et al. 2018).

---

13   See https://ilajnafsy.bzfo.de/portal/en/science/

Tab. 2 (see Appendix) shows that a variety of digital services supporting also health-related issues are available. A strong connection between the service and the representation in social media and the owner/publisher can be shown. This raises the questions of how to build trust in information, how to address the target groups and how to make services as user-friendly as possible so that a service can not only help but is also attractive to people.

Although we were able to identify four promising services (Tab. 2: Nos. 4 and 5) addressing psychological support, we think – especially due to the fact that the three services of No. 5 are part of a study and reach out to offer help, but that being part of a research program might cause users to feel like they serve as human guinea pigs – that further investigation is needed into:

(1) how to address/advertise a psychological support service that meets with the need of trust in information (e.g. evaluate blockchain technology as an approach),

(2) how to get access to the communities visited by potential patients/users/people seeking for help, or access to those who do not even know that there is helping support at all (e.g. strengthen social media presence),

(3) finding alternatives in communicating within therapeutic courses (e.g. interactive or self-helping ways without the need of a psychologist on the other side of the line, as is the case in Nos. 4 and 5), e.g. by using aspects of gamification.

Thus, the building of trust in digital information, the communication of the available support (e-services) by addressing the target groups within their social e-habitats (e.g. groups) with culturally sensitively designed solutions and the creation of user-centered (gamified) mobile apps are key challenges we identified.

To address these findings, we will present a new conceptual framework. Before, we will provide the theoretical principles for the development of our approach by elucidating the references to existing theoretical innovation and culture concepts. Furthermore, we evaluate key technologies that have the potential to meet these identified challenges – despite the risks which are associated with their use at the same time.

3 Theoretical Principles of Technology-Based Innovation in the Context of Migration and Health

The definition of technology-based innovation in the context of the target group of forced migrants who are dealing with health issues first requires a referencing of the theoretical concepts of innovation, culture and inclusion (3.1). Furthermore, it has to be explained which technologies can be distinguished and defined. In this connection, it is also important to identify the opportunities and risks associated with the respective use of technology (3.2).

3.1 Derivations from the Theoretical Concepts of Innovation, Culture and Inclusion

In the following, the question is answered through which theoretical approach the described problem of forced migrants facing health issues can be addressed. With the actual technological progress and a changing of user needs in mind, the underlying intention can be summarized by the creation and offering of something new like e.g. a novel service for forced migrants dealing with mental health problems. According to Schumpeter (1982), the successful introduction of something new can be understood as innovation. The use of the concept of innovation first requires a definition.

> "Innovation is the first economic application of a new technical, economic, organizational or social problem solution [...] It affects the new fulfillment of corporate goals." (Burmester and Vahs 2005)

Basically, innovation aims to add value or bring about improvement (Hilbrecht and Kempkens 2013). According to Tidelski (2002) there are two types of innovation to distinguish: Incremental innovations refer to small changes to an existing product or service to protect the current market position. Radical innovations solve problems in a completely new way. More than 90% of all innovations are incremental, whereas radical innovations are rarer and more elaborate (Gassmann et al. 2017). According to Fueglistaller et al. (2012), there are four different types of innovation:

- Process and method innovation,
- product or service innovation,
- business model innovation and
- social innovation.

The fourth type, social innovation, is defined as the following:

> "New interactions (usually communication or cooperation) between people; or, in the normative sense, "good for society and its members, with the aim of developing new solutions to social problems and challenges." (Fueglistaller et al. 2012)[14]

---

14   See also Brown and Wyatt (2010).

Accordingly, considering the creation of a novel service for forced migrants dealing with health issues, one could define that as both a service and social innovation.

Brown (2016) focuses on the user of an innovation as he explains that innovation starts with humans. In this sense, he presents a theoretical approach whereby innovation arises in the interaction of three components: human (desirability), economy (marketability) and technology (feasibility) (see fig. 3).

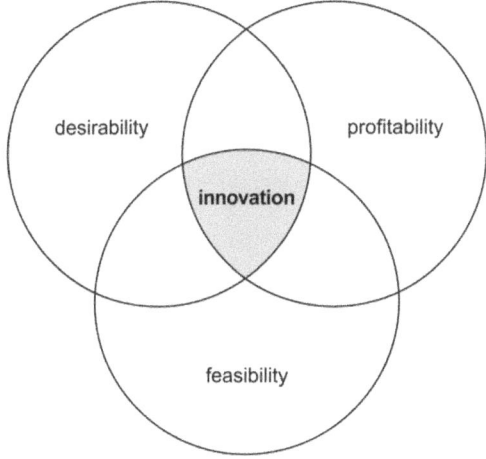

Fig. 3.   Three components of innovation (after Brown 2016)

This user-centering marks the central thought which is shared by the Design Thinking (DT) community. DT is a user-centric innovation technique and the special feature of this method is that solutions for product or service improvements can be generated from the user's perspective (Plattner et al. 2011). The DT approach was first officially introduced in 1991 at the "Research in Design Thinking" symposium at Delft University of Technology. Among the symposium participants was a representative of the consulting firm IDEO[15]. IDEO, located in Palo Alto, California, and above all chairman and CEO Tim Brown started to clearly focus on the customer, respectively user, and his needs and problems (Brown 2016).

---

15   See https://www.ideo.com/eu.

The underlying technique, however, goes back to the time of the invention of the light bulb in 1879[16], when previously 300 prototypes were built and tested. Fig. 2 shows how the typical iterative process of DT works in six phases (see fig. 4):

1) The user's needs and problems are understood,

2) the user is observed

3) the perspective is defined,

4) ideas are generated,

5) prototypes are developed and tested,

6) prototypes are implemented (Grots and Pratschke 2009; Wölbling et al. 2012).

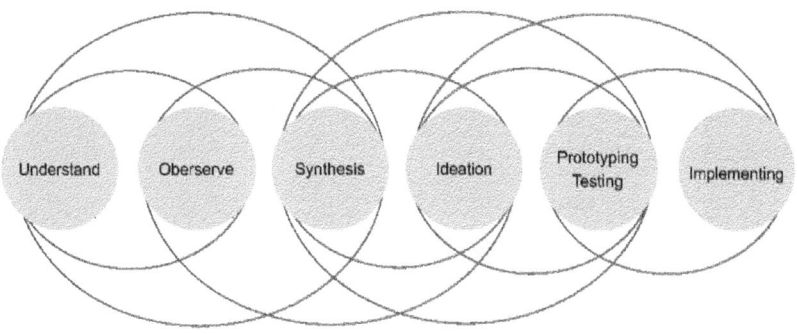

Fig. 4: The iterative DT process (after Wölbling et al. 2012: 121ff)

With this method, it is aimed to meet the user's requirements effectively. In the specific case of forced migrants and against the background of the central research question ("how can technology help forced migrants with health restrictions?") in the present case, an approach that is purely based on innovation theory does not seem to be sufficient. If it is intended to address forced migrants' needs through technology, first of all, the diverse individual conditions (see also chapter 2.1) have to be considered carefully. Starting from the assumption that the focused-on forced migrants come from different countries and have

16   See Rode 2007.

different cultural backgrounds, these individual requirements are culturally shaped. Thus, it seems to be necessary to focus on a suitable concept of culture first. It appears to be an impossible task to classify the term "culture" clearly, as recent discussions on cultural concepts show (see Busche et al. 2018; Schmidt-Lux et al. 2016; Bolten 2015). In terms of the origin of the term and the literal translation, it should be noted that "culture" comes from the Latin word „colere/cultum" and means "cultivate" (Brockhaus Enzyklopädie 2019), whereby both land and relationships can be cultivated (Bolten 2009). When looking at relationships and interactions between different actors, this also means "interculturality" (Bolten 2010). But also, with regard to the concept of interculturality, the attributions of definition have changed over time (see i. a. Jammal 2014).

> "If one transfers this idea of culture to the case of interculturality, then it can be deduced that, if culturality is not characterized by homogeneity, but above all by the awareness of differences, interculturality, on the other hand, is due to unknownness or strangeness distinguished by differences." (Rathje 2006: 22)[17]

In order to transform unknown differences into known ones, it requires intercultural competence[18], as Rathje (ibid.) points out. Consequently, intercultural competence can be defined as the "ability to transform the foreign transient interculture into culture by creating cohesion[19] through normality" (Rathje 2006: 28). Thus, by disseminating differences and diversity, cohesion is achieved. This idea of culture represents a useful concept when carefully taking into account the individual conditions of forced migrants. The theoretical concept of cohesion, respectively the consideration of the individual requirements of forced migrants, put the potential user of technology-based services in focus. Thus, the cohesion-based approach goes hand in hand with the user-centered design and implementation of a new e-service.

If forced migrants with health restrictions are understood as a separate group of society, in addition to the cohesion-based user centering idea, the theoretical concept of inclusion also appears noteworthy. So far, there is no generally accepted, concrete definition of *inclusion* (Grosche 2015) and especially "the concept of *social inclusion*[20] remains unclear, largely due to multiple and con-

---

17   Translated by the authors from the original quote in German.

18   The concept of intercultural competence is discussed controversially. Accordingly, different definitions exist. This article follows a definition that appears relevant in the given context.

19   Originally from physics, the term "cohesion" has become established in recent years as an important component of social science and intercultural theories (Hansen 2000; Rathje 2004; Bolten 2008; Stegbauer 2016). In the context of migration and diversity, often the term "social cohesion" is used (see i. a. Demireva 2017).

20   Hayes et al. (2008) point out that the concepts of social inclusion and exclusion are closely related and that discussions on the subject are inextricably linked.

flicting definitions in research and policy" (Simplican et al. 2015). Following Walker et al. (2011, p. 15) in the thematic context of this article, (social) inclusion shall be understood as societal acceptance of forced migrants with health restrictions and/or disabilities within the community settings. So when it comes to providing integration support with e-services for forced migrants, the concept of inclusion must also be considered.

In order to answer the central research question, i. e. how technology can help forced migrants with health restrictions, an approach seems to be required that considers both the inclusion-oriented user centering from a (social) inclusion perspective and innovation theories as well as a cohesion-based concept of culture.

Discussing technology-based innovation presupposes a common understanding and a valuation of currently available technologies. In the next section we focus on selected technologies and the associated potentials and risks from our point of view.

3.2   Assessment of Potentials and Risks of Selected Technologies

The fact that approx. 80% of Syrian and Iraqi forced migrants had access to a smartphone during their flight (Emmer and Richter 2016: 6) marks the relevance of internet-based information and technology-based services for forced migrants. No exact data shows how big the percentage of smartphone usage of forced migrants in Germany is. Nevertheless, we assume that the percentage of people who had access to a smartphone during their flight is similar to people who still have access to a smartphone during their stay in Germany.

The development of a new conceptual framework for the adequate use of technology within innovative service solutions that support forced migrants who are dealing with health issues requires, first, an assessment of currently available technologies. Due to the limited scope of this article only a selection can be presented. The following sections contain definitions and associated chances and risks of each presented technology.

3.2.1   Gamified Mobile Applications

Our analysis of selected e-(Health-)services (see tab. 2, Appendix) shows that the use of game elements can have a positive effect on the user numbers of a mobile application. Applying the term "gamified mobile applications" requires a definition of the term "gamification" which can be described as "integration of game mechanics into a non-game environment in order to give it a game-like feel" (Deterding et al. 2011: 9).

The following example shows the possible impact of games in the context of (mental) health: Tetris, the 1980s famous Nintendo game, has been proved as a game that helps in therapeutic ways to handle trauma (Holmes et al. 2009; James et al. 2015; Andersson et al. 2018; Iyadurai et al. 2018). Holmes et al. 2009 (p. 1) used the following methodology:

> "All participants viewed a traumatic film consisting of scenes of real injury and death followed by a 30-min structured break. Participants were then randomly allocated to either a no-task or visuospatial ("Tetris") condition which they undertook for 10-min. Flashbacks were monitored for 1-week. Results indicated that compared to the no-task condition, the "Tetris" condition produced a significant reduction in flashback frequency over 1-week."

Holmes et al. 2017 (p. 99) have successfully implemented Tetris into their methodology and concluded that "young people particularly can be reluctant to access psychiatric/psychological services, thus computer-gaming in daily life opens new possibilities to provide support in non-/less-stigmatizing ways".

(Experimental) game theory and the usage of digital games in therapy open doors and windows to access non-game environments and areas which may be abstract or psychologically difficult to get to (Deterding et al. 2011). According to Wilkinson at al. (2008: 370), video games shall be taken into account: "The mental health community can benefit from more collaborative efforts between therapists and engineers, making such innovations a reality."

Nevertheless, there is a lack of serious games specially designed for treating mental disorders (Fernández-Aranda et al. 2012). A new model/tool to analyze therapeutic games and to improve the communication between health experts and game designers, and to evaluate the game design coherency of therapeutic games has been created by Mader et al. 2012. Further research results may enhance the use of serious games in the future, so that the potential can be fully exploited in the context of health and migration as well. At this point, we also want to stress the research taking place on digital games development concerning its game cultures by Wimmer and Elmezeny (2018), who propose a structure to comparatively analyze game cultures.

In the next section, our focus is on social media usage and the associated chances and risks for forced migrants.

3.2.2   Social Media

In 2018, the number of internet users worldwide has crossed four billion, and the fact that 3.2 billion of all internet users worldwide are using social media applications (Hootsuite 2018) makes the thematic relevance in the present context clear. Social Media can be defined as internet-based networks, often profit-based, that enable communication and participation via the used media channel (Gabler Wirtschaftslexikon 2019). Social media platforms and channels such as

FB and WhatsApp are strong marketing tools that can identify target groups, e.g. forced migrants.

Social media seems to be one technological approach to communicate with forced migrants: The results by Alcenar (2018) indicate that social media networking sites were particularly relevant for refugee participants to acquire language and cultural competences, as well as to build both bonding and bridging social capital. Another important finding by Alcenar (ibid.) concerns the role of government, host society and the agency of refugee actors in determining the way refugees experience social media.

Many forced migrants are minors and are stuck in camps. Social media offers platforms to get access to people and offer services and support – e.g. when they are dealing with health issues. New forms of social interaction can be accessed (Trebbe and Paasch-Colberg 2016).

A German report (together with the German Children's Fund) on minor migrants in Germany and their media consumption habits shows that social media has a central role also in exchanging coping strategies during the flight but also while staying in the hosting country (Kutscher and Kreß 2015). As the study of Kutscher and Kreß (ibid.) shows, minors are online and act in various groups on FB, WhatsApp[21] and video content platform YouTube[22] and thus are accessible via analyzing their consumption habits. Minors, help and games promise to be a good cognitive association and causal connection in this context.

The usage of cost-efficient tools like Google Analytics or FB Ads maybe helpful here. Holmes et al. (2017: 98) examine the cost efficiency on behalf of therapeutic costs and propose "that certain behavioral interventions could be delivered at minimal cost, directly (without a therapist/interpreter), by smartphone, in refugees' daily life".

Risks can be evaluated by connecting to communities that distribute fake information via social media platforms: As the chapter before shows, it is really easy to access social media groups and platforms, but in this context also fake information can be distributed.

Furthermore, as mental disorders and attending mental health services are associated with stigma in Syrian cultures (Hassan et al. 2015), we identify a high risk of not accessing the people who are actually looking for/needing help. Social media channels can help to access these groups of people. Also the UNHCR (2016) mentions social media as a helpful tool and network to navigate life.

---

21   WhatsApp was acquired by Facebook Inc. in 2014 and offers users i. a. the ability to exchange text messages, images, videos and sound files (see https://www.whatsapp.com).

22   See https://www.youtube.com.

Another paper has researched on refugees and technology, focusing on Syrian pregnant women who reside as refugees in Lebanon. Their key findings that need to be taken into consideration when working with e-Health solutions for (Syrian) forced migrant women are:

> "The range of literacy levels (technological and language); the hierarchal [*sic!*] nature of social and familial structure; the roles of husbands and the sheikha; the women's medicalized attitudes to healthcare; and the dual formal and informal health advice systems. Furthermore, the particular importance and need to overcome the negative perceptions that the women have of the attitude of healthcare providers towards them is highlighted." (Talhouk et al. 2016b: 340)

Information spread within social media channels and relevant peer groups and communities can help e-services find their users.

We think that is very important to take all these findings and cultural diversities in approaching mental e-Health solutions into account before starting to conceptualize and develop a new service that might, if handled the wrong way, fail to access its target group. Before our conceptual framework is presented, there is one more technological innovation, i. e. blockchain, to discuss.

3.2.3   Blockchain

Blockchain technology requires the proof of independent components towards a piece of information. Only if proved by all of them, in terms of a consensus mechanism, the information gets authorized to pass (Gabler Wirtschaftslexikon 2019b). Consensus is achieved by an algorithm-based method of matching (Nguyen and Kim 2018).

Blockchain as a technological approach in humanitarian contexts has already successfully been implemented. The Munich-based company Datarella GmbH has developed a service called "Building Blocks" for the World Food Programme. The solution is based on blockchain to provide cash transfers "reducing costs by eliminating up to 98% of fees issued by third-party institutions"[23].

Back to blockchain as a technology for forced migrants: First of all, creating a FB account seems to be a pre-condition to one's flight and/or settling in: ">[Social media] is useful for connecting people and allowing them to settle in just by making them aware of what information and services are available, and also giving people an opportunity to draw on these more diffused, looser or weaker ties to find work and other important integration services,< Ahad said" (Kaplan 2018).

---

23   https://innovation.wfp.org/project/building-blocks and https://datarella.com/building-blocks-how-the-world-food-programme-harnesses-blockchain-technology-ro-deliver-aid/

Second, it needs to be mentioned that a SIM card is one of the first things people acquire when arriving in a new country (*"Without Facebook I wouldn't have made it"*, Mohammad Khalefeh, cited in Henrichs 2016), which we also recognized among the services of No. 2, where German providers of SIM cards get mentioned right at the outset.

Returning to fact one: To be part of WhatsApp or FB groups allows forced migrants to get information by people who have already gone through the obstacles a flight brings along, or by people who are at the same stage as the user him-/herself. It seems that the more information on a searched item is congruent with one another, and thus proved by others, the more it can be trusted (Liu et al. 2015: 41). In a non-scientific world and for an immediate response for decision-making, platforms such as FB or WhatsApp groups are needed where people can communicate about a piece of information searched for, so that this information can be proved by others (Dekker et al. 2018).

Talhouk et al. 2016b (p. 340) "also point to a (...) better communication with healthcare providers (possibly through peer networks) and digital media for health advocacy. With these factors and opportunities in mind, we conclude that there is real potential for sensitively designed digital platforms (...)."

Translated into given technology, we see parallels to blockchain technology. Blockchain technology can help to build trust in authorship: The paper "Trust Bit: Reward-based intelligent vehicle communication using blockchain" by Singh and Kim (2018) gives first examples of how blockchain technology can be used to generate trust regarding broadcasted data, in their case on intelligent vehicles.

Huckle and White (2017) have created a prototype that is capable of indicating the authenticity of digital media. They also say that as it "has the potential to be able to verify the originality of media resources, we believe that technology is only capable of providing a partial solution to fake news. That is because it is incapable of proving the authenticity of a news story as a whole. We believe that takes human skills." (Huckle and White 2017: 356)

With them (ibid.) saying that technology is incapable of proving authenticity, the major risk of blockchain technology is that by definition independent components give authorization on the correctness of a piece of information. That means that there can be a community, whose members pretend to be independent, that gives permission to a piece of information that aims to mislead communication: an actual fake information just needs enough members in the blockchain who are willing to confirm this fake information and mark it as approved - although it is fake.

As further articles mention, trust is crucial to forced migrants when retrieving and following information, and we think that more research needs to be done concerning blockchain technologies for trust-building in information gathering. Especially when we think of the already existing trust in information spread within peer groups and communities forced migrants feel associated with, we think that blockchain might help information introduced by externals into these communities to be accepted.

As blockchain works with algorithms, we think that it is important to introduce also the further usage of algorithms in the context of forced migrants.

3.2.4 Artificial Intelligence (AI)

By using or owning a smartphone, almost everybody has come in contact with the AI-based service offered by Google LLC called "Google Translate"[24]. A solution like this seems to be very helpful for people like forced migrants who are looking for support in an area where they are not familiar with the spoken language.

The technologies forming artificial intelligence are based on data-driven processes, such as algorithms. We might know them from keywords such as deep learning, machine learning and others. AI methods are used to enable a computer to solve problems which, if solved by humans, require intelligence; such are e.g. methods for representing knowledge and for the conclusion and deduction for using represented knowledge (Gabler Wirtschaftslexikon 2019c).

AI seems to be a constructive enabler for handling not only language barriers but also for assigning the high number of forced migrants, e.g. concerning the question of integration of forced migrants.

Switzerland has launched an algorithm called "Placement Algorithm"[25], still in its beta version, which has been created by ETH Zurich, Switzerland and Stanford University, USA. This "machine learning–based algorithm for assigning refugees can improve their employment prospects over current approaches (...) [by using] a combination of supervised machine learning and optimal matching to discover and leverage synergies between refugee characteristics and resettlement sites." (Bansak et al. 2018: 325).

A similar approach has been created by an interdisciplinary team from the UK, Sweden and the USA (Trapp et al. 2018): an algorithm helps to classify

---

24   https://translate.google.com

25   "The historical data used to develop the algorithm for Switzerland included information on where refugees were sent, whether they found work, and their age, country of origin, gender, and time of arrival. The algorithm uses this complex history to calculate refugees' probability of employment at each possible resettlement location, and then allocates them in a way that gives each person the best possible match. In Switzerland, only 15 percent of refugee arrivals from 2013 found a job within three years. Using the algorithm could have increased that to 26 percent, according to initial tests on the historical data." https://phys.org/news/2018-05-switzerland-ai-refugee.html

people (such as forced migrants, asylum-seeking persons, etc.) to find a new place to stay and/or a job. The automated decision-making software "Annie Moore", named after the first person received and processed on Ellis Island in 1982[26], aims to match forced migrants to a given location according to their needs, skills and the local number of resources and opportunities available. "Initial back-testing indicates that "Annie" can improve short-run employment outcomes by 22%–37%" (Trapp et al. 2018: 2).

The USA is already testing and working with the software "Annie".[27] According to a report by the University of Toronto, Canada, Canada is experimenting with this solution, too (Molnar and Gill 2018). Critics have accused Canada for discretionary and opaque decision-making and that the experimentation has profound implications for people's fundamental human rights (Molnar 2018).

Also the solution "Rafiqi.net" (fig. 5), founded by Ghida Ibrahim, who works as a Quantitative Engineer in the Edge Infrastructure team at Facebook London[28], tries to support forced migrants through an algorithm-based connection of forced migrants with helpers/inhabitants: "[we] built an algorithm that uses your basic data to match you in real-time to the one(s) that you need most".[29]

AI in combination with natural language processing and deep learning can form chatbots. The "DoNotPay" app (fig. 6) is free of charge and available on iOS and Android. It claims to be:

> "the home of the world's first robot lawyer. Fight corporations, beat bureaucracy and sue anyone at the press of a button. This app is completely free and you keep 100% of what you save"[30]

and is connected by an application-programming-interface (API)[31] to Facebook Messenger and

> "asks users a series of questions (...) and gives them the customized legal help they need, such as helping them through the asylum application process"[32].

---

26   https://www.refugees.ai/

27   https://www.theatlantic.com/international/archive/2019/04/how-technology-could-revolutionize-refugee-resettlement/587383/

28   https://uk.linkedin.com/in/ghida-ibrahim-ph-d-823b4042

29   https://www.rafiqi.net/

30   https://apps.apple.com/app/id1427999657

31   https://wirtschaftslexikon.gabler.de/definition/schnittstelle-44838/version-268142

32   https://www.delltechnologies.com/en-us/perspectives/four-ai-powered-technologies-aimed-at-helping-refugees/

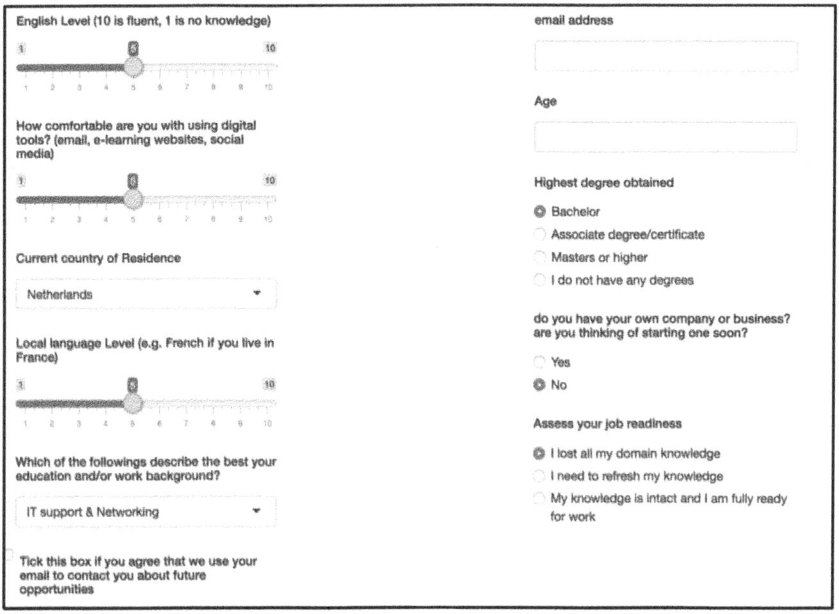

English Level (10 is fluent, 1 is no knowledge)

1 — 6 — 10

1 2 3 4 5 6 7 8 9 10

How comfortable are you with using digital tools? (email, e-learning websites, social media)

1 — 6 — 10

1 2 3 4 5 6 7 8 9 10

Current country of Residence

Netherlands ▾

Local language Level (e.g. French if you live in France)

1 — 6 — 10

1 2 3 4 5 6 7 8 9 10

Which of the followings describe the best your education and/or work background?

IT support & Networking ▾

Tick this box if you agree that we use your email to contact you about future opportunities

email address

Age

Highest degree obtained

◉ Bachelor
○ Associate degree/certificate
○ Masters or higher
○ I do not have any degrees

do you have your own company or business? are you thinking of starting one soon?

○ Yes
◉ No

Assess your job readiness

◉ I lost all my domain knowledge
○ I need to refresh my knowledge
○ My knowledge is intact and I am fully ready for work

Fig. 5: "Rafiqi.net" Matching Tool (https://gibrahim.shinyapps.io/Rafiqi_matching_tool/)

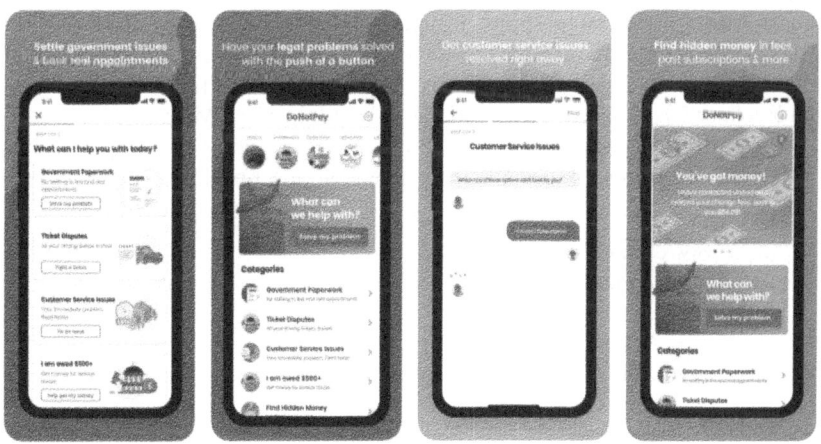

Fig. 6: DoNotPay – Legal help (https://apps.apple.com/app/id1427999657)

AI in the form of a chatbot has also been used in the solution "Tess" and "Karim", developed by US-based company X2AI[33]. Both chatbots simulate a conversation with a psychologically trained person - nevertheless, after testing them, both solutions claim to act rather as a friend than a therapist and hand over to a real person if certain words drop, e.g. "suicide"[34]. While "Tess" is a "mental health chatbot who delivers emotional wellness-coping strategies"[35] available to anyone in the USA, "Karim" has been tested in a Syrian refugee camp[36] together with the non-governmental organization Field Innovation Team, which delivers tech-enabled disaster relief[37].

The advantages are at your feet: Chatbots can be consulted 24/7, are unemotional, take away feelings like shame about seeking out psychologists, they collect data and so also their market is promising: "Healthcare is betting big on AI in areas like fraud detection, image diagnosis, connected machines, robot-assisted surgeries, and so on. By 2021, the AI health market is expected to hit the $6.6 billion mark. And chatbots are emerging as game-changers in unconventional areas in healthcare like counseling."[38, 39]

The up-and-coming economic forecasts relating to AI solutions and the power of algorithms or, rather, their creators – if their suggested solutions/matches/etc. are followed – lead us to stress that further usage of algorithms and artificial intelligence needs to be accompanied by further research. Several research results show that those who create AI systems/programs gain power as they know about the configurations and constitutions of AI systems/programs and thus may become political or economic targets to influence systems and their terminations; plus: the risk of discrimination through the usage of AI-originated suggestions, matches, findings, etc. can be enhanced and might consequently involve the cheating on some but favoring of others, which would mean a disregard of the existing human rights (Martini 2019, Tinnefeld and Buchner 2019, Schaar 2018, Molnar 2018, Molnar and Muscati 2018).

According to Bendig et al. (2019) research on chatbots in therapy requires "corrective measures. Issues like effectiveness, sustainability, and especially

---

33   https://www.x2ai.com/

34   https://www.theguardian.com/technology/2016/mar/22/karim-the-ai-delivers-psychological-support-to-syrian-refugees

35   https://www.x2ai.com/

36   https://www.sueddeutsche.de/digital/kuenstliche-intelligenz-eine-maschine-gegen-die-depression-1.3431873

37   http://fieldinnovationteam.org/

38   https://dzone.com/articles/the-role-of-chatbots-in-mental-healthcare

39   https://www.accenture.com/_acnmedia/PDF-49/Accenture-Health-Artificial-Intelligence.pdf#zoom=50

safety and subsequent tests of technology are elements that should be instituted as a corrective for future funding programs of chatbots in clinical psychology and psychotherapy."

We conclude that technologies like mobile apps, social media, blockchain or AI can help to build trust, address the target groups within their digital social habitats and reach out to minors and actually provide help to get over traumatic experiences and to settle into a new community. At this point, it should be noted that against the background of the limited scope of this article only a selection of technological developments could be considered. Further research in the context of migration and health should definitely also highlight the potentials and risks of other new technologies, e.g. big data.

Following the clarification of relevant theoretical principles of technology-based innovation in the context of migration and health by outlining our deductions from the theoretical concepts of innovation, culture and inclusion, and then sharing our assessment of potentials and risks of selected technologies, in the following chapter a new conceptual framework is presented which will meet the earlier identified challenges and close the identified research gap.

4   The e-ICI Approach as a New Conceptual Framework

The present situation of forced migrants with health restrictions in Germany allows for the following conclusions in the light of current technological developments: On the one hand, there is a need for the careful consideration of the forced migrations' individual conditions. In chapter two we showed that previous practical approaches neglect a user-centered perspective which also combines inclusion and cohesion at the same time. Individual conditions include, i. a., the required access to information, taking into account trust in information, and the comprehensive consideration of cultural characteristics such as communication in a language familiar to forced migrants. On the other hand, there are currently available technologies like mobile apps, social media, blockchain and AI, which can add great value if used wisely (see chapter 3.2). These are the central criteria that need to be considered when developing a new conceptual framework for sustainable and meaningful technological innovation that intends to address the health issues of forced migrants.

The conceptual framework of *e-Inclusion- and Cohesion-based Innovation (e-ICI)* fills the recognized research gap and offers a new approach for addressing the health issues of forced migrants through technology (see fig. 7). By using the term "e-inclusion" we refer to the theoretical concepts of Heidkamp and Kergel (2018), Raya Diez (2018), Yu et al. (2018) and White and Forrester-Jones (2019), and understand e-inclusion as equal access for all users of technology regardless of their technological literacy, background, health or other circumstances.

We recommend the application of this approach to those responsible for the creation of new technology-based services for forced migrants with health restrictions. The e-ICI model aims to change the situation of currently offered e-services that are, in our opinion, not yet adequate for the use by forced migrants. Our analysis in chapter 2.2 showed that within the examined e-services for forced migrants, our approach has not yet been considered.

The practical implementation is about the careful taking into account of three central components of the e-ICI-model:

1. To understand culture and interculturality from a cohesive perspective, and handling the diverse and various conditions of forced migrants dealing with health issues in a culture-sensitive way while referring to the concept of inclusion and aiming for a user-centered approach.

2. Accordingly, to choose sustainable and meaningful technology like mobile apps, social media, blockchain or AI (while keeping in mind the possible risks associated with its use).

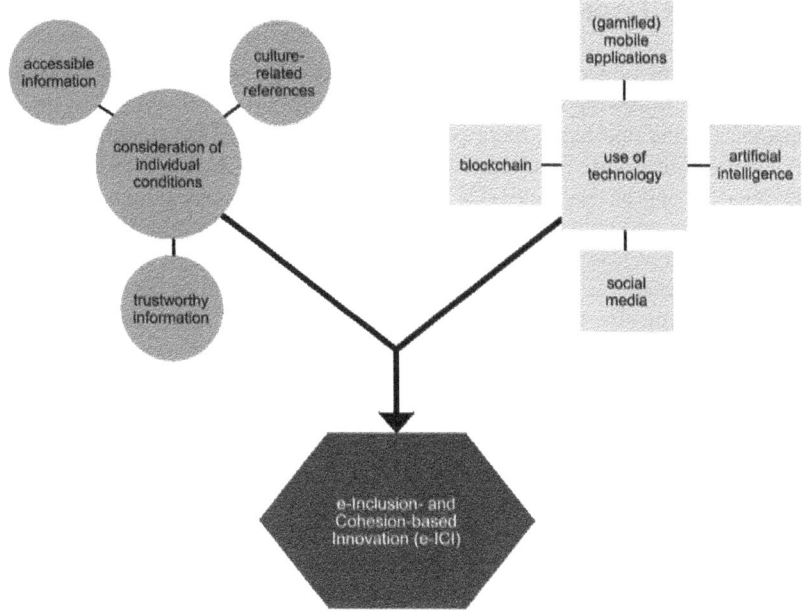

Fig. 7: The e-Inclusion- and Cohesion-based Innovation (e-ICI) approach

From our point of view, this requires not only a collaboration of doctors, scientists, developers, designers and experts in information technologies, but also input from the target group itself, the user – meaning an integration of the perspective of the potential user from the very beginning, starting with an observation and an understanding of the user as suggested within the DT approach (see chapter 3.1). In practice, this means that before developers start with the coding of a new technology-based service, first extensive user data has to be collected e.g. by following a qualitative research design and conducting personal interviews with forced migrants who are dealing with health issues. Personal interviews with the potential user of a new technology-based service will bring about an understanding of the varying individual requirements and can provide sufficient information about the personal user requirements. These in turn provide valuable information for the culture-sensitive design of a new technology-based service.

Such a procedure ensures that the e-service being developed represents a technology-based innovation with a user-centering that is inclusion-oriented and cohesion-based.

5   Conclusion and Final Remarks

This article focuses on forced migrants who arrived in Germany and who are dealing with health issues, and on the question of how technology can help in this case by inducing e-inclusion based on a cohesion-oriented concept of culture, understood as a highly user-centered approach.

It is a fact that forced migrants with health restrictions in Germany are not treated self evidently to the extent necessary. This becomes particularly clear when the focus is on the example of mental health, as used in this study.

In the context of the identified – and in this article extended – social determinants of health, apart from the official regulations connected with the German Asylum Procedures Act, personal reservations related to the individual respective cultural background are responsible for this. With a view to the current pension gap on the one hand, and the limited use of health services by migrants in Germany on the other, our central research question examined in this article was how technology could help forced migrants dealing with health issues, particularly against the background of the new technological possibilities, of which we mentioned a few. When the use of technology in supporting forced migrants was examined in previous research, the key findings resulted in "limited proficiency in the local language, limited Internet access, information complexity, information reliability and timeliness, limited experience of forced migrants with geospatial services, difficulties due to limited functional literacy" (Bustamante Duarte et al. 2018). Our conducted exemplary analysis of 10 mobile applications that were created in Germany with the intention to help forced migrants during the integration process lead to further insights: It has been shown that many e-services support daily life questions but only two of them are actually used by more than 5000 users, and that only a few e-services – which also do not show outstanding usage – address psychological support. This marks the need for optimized services in practice and at the same time points to the research gap. The aim of this article was to present a problem-solving approach that has far-reaching value in both practice and science.

In our study, we investigated how technologies like mobile applications, social media, blockchain and AI can help forced migrants with health restrictions in Germany. The use of technologies holds a great potential if, at the same time, the risks associated with the use of technologies are sufficiently taken into account. Thereby a theoretical framework has been presented that is based on a user-centered approach originating from the innovation theory of design thinking. By looking at interculturality from a cohesion- and inclusion-based perspective, the e-ICI model looks at the individual conditions of forced migrants in a new way. This approach enables doctors, developers and designers to create culture-sensitive, health-related interventions and health services. We believe that based on this approach, sustainable and meaningful services for forced migrants with health restrictions can be developed. It is an added value that the e-ICI model can be transferred and applied to both forced migrants in other countries and also to other target groups with special needs.

Further research will be required in line with the testing of new services created following the e-ICI approach. A qualitative research experiment in combination with the technology acceptance model (TAM) (Davis et al. 1998[40]) would then lead to profound and more detailed insights into user behavior. The findings of this study show that there is a need for

- health data collection among forced migrants
- collaboration between users, doctors, scientists, developers, designers and experts in information technologies
- using the full potential of new technologies like blockchain or AI
- applying gamified digital services, especially to forced migrants dealing with mental health issues
- further research that takes up the findings of this study and will hopefully also have an impact on changes of Germany's legislation and policies affecting forced migrants' health.

---

40   The first version of the TAM was developed by Davis in his dissertation submitted to the Massachusetts Institute of Technology in 1985.

Bibliography

Alencar, Amanda (2018): Refugee Integration and Social Media: A Local and Experiential Perspective. In: *Information, Communication and Society*, 21 (11), pp. 1588–1603. DOI: 10.1080/1369118X.2017.1340500

Almohamed, Asam (2016): 'Designing for the Marginalized: A Step Towards Understanding the Lives of Refugees and Asylum Seekers'. In: *DIS -Proceedings of the 2016 ACM Conference Companion Publication on Designing Interactive Systems*. pp. 165–168.

Almohamed, Asam and Vyas, Dhaval (2016): Vulnerability of Displacement: Challenges for Integrating Refugees and Asylum Seekers in Host Communities. In: *OzCHI 2016 - Proceedings of the 28th Australian Conference on Computer-Human Interaction*, pp. 125–134.

Andersson, Erik; Holmes, Emily A. and Kavanagh, David (2018): Innovations in Digital Interventions for Psychological Trauma: Harnessing Advances in Cognitive Science (last accessed 19 May 2019). In: *mHealth* [Online], 4. DOI: 10.21037/mhealth.2018.09.11

Andrade, A. D. and B. Doolin (2016): Information and Communication Technology and the Social Inclusion of Refugees. In: *MIS Quarterly*, 40 (2), pp. 405–416.

BAfF (2016): Versorgungsbericht zur psychosozialen Versorgung von Flüchtlingen und Folteropfern in Deutschland. 3rd revised edition. Berlin, Germany: Bundesweite Arbeitsgemeinschaft der Psychosozialen Zentren für Flüchtlinge (last accessed 3 Feb 2019). http://www.baff-zentren.org/wp-content/uploads/2017/02/Versorgungsbericht_3-Auflage_BAfF.pdf

Bagfa-Integration 2019: 7. Geflüchtete Menschen informieren und erreichen (last accessed 14 July 2019). URL: https://bagfa-integration.de/Wiki/7-gefluechtete-menschen-informieren-und-erreichen/

BAMF (2019a): Aktuelle Zahlen zu Asyl (Ausgabe April 2019) (last accessed 19/May/2019). URL: http://www.bamf.de/SharedDocs/Anlagen/DE/Downloads/Infothek/Statistik/Asyl/aktuelle-zahlen-zu-asyl-april-2019.pdf?__blob=publicationFile

BAMF (2019b): Infothek – FAQ: Zugang zum Arbeitsmarkt für geflüchtete Menschen. (last accessed 19/May/2019) URL: http://www.bamf.de/DE/Infothek/FragenAntworten/ZugangArbeit Fluechtlinge/zugang-arbeit-fluechtlinge-node.html

Bansak, Kirk.; Ferwerda, Jeremy; Hainmueller, Jens; Dillon, Andrea; Hangartner, Dominik; Lawrence, Duncan; Weinstein, Jeremy (2018): Improving Refugee Integration through Data-Driven Algorithmic Assignment. In: *Science*. 359 (6373) pp. 325–329 (last accessed 7 July 2019). DOI: 10.1126/science.aao4408

Baron, Jenny; Schriefers Silvia (2015): Versorgungsbericht zur psychosozialen Versorgung von Flüchtlingen und Folteropfern in Deutschland. Bundesweite Arbeitsgemeinschaft der Psychosozialen Zentren für Flüchtlinge und Folteropfer. (BAfF e.V.) (last accessed 19 May 2019). http://www.baff-zentren.org/wp-content/uploads/2015/09/Ver-sorgungsbericht_mit-Umschlag_2015.compressed.pdf

Bendig, Eileen; Erb, Benjamin; Schulze-Thuesing, Lea; Baumeister, Harald (2019): Die nächste Generation: Chatbots in der klinischen Psychologie und Psychotherapie zur Förderung mentaler Gesundheit – Ein Scoping-Review. In: *Verhaltenstherapie 2019*, (29) (last accessed 7 July 2019). https://doi.org/10.1159/000499492

Bischoff, Alexander; Bovier, Patrick, A.; Isah, Rustemi; Françoise, Gariazzo; Ariel, Eytan; Louis, Loutan (2003): Language Barriers between Nurses and Asylum Seekers: Their Impact on Symptom Reporting and Referral. In: *Social Science and Medicine*, 57 (3), pp. 503–512 (last accessed 3 Feb 2019). DOI:10.1016/S0277-9536(02)00376-3

Bolten, Jürgen (2008): Reziprozität, Vertrauen, Interkultur. Kohäsionsorientierte Teamentwicklung in virtualisierten multikulturellen Arbeitsumgebungen. In: Jammal, Elias (ed.): Vertrauen im interkulturellen Kontext. Perspectives of the Other (Studies on Intercultural Communication). VS Verlag für Sozialwissenschaften, Wiesbaden, pp. 69–93.

Bolten, Jürgen (2009): Kultur, Reziprozität und Religion. Anregungen zu einem interdisziplinären kulturwissenschaftlichen Diskurs. In: Jürgen Court/ Michael Klöcker (eds.), *Wege und Welten der Religionen. Forschungen und Vermittlungen*. Stuttgart, pp. 39 –45.

Bolten, Jürgen (2010): Interkulturelle Kompetenzvermittlung via Internet. In: Wordelmann, P. (ed.): Internationale Kompetenzen in der Berufsbildung. Bonn, pp. 101–114.

Bolten, Jürgen (2015): Einführung in die Interkulturelle Wirtschaftskommunikation. 2nd revised edition, Göttingen: UTB

Böttche, Maria; Heeke, Carina; Knaevelsrud, Christine (2016): Sequenzielle Traumatisierungen, Traumafolgestörungen und psychotherapeutische Behandlungsansätze bei kriegstraumatisierten erwachsenen Flüchtlingen in Deutschland. In: *Bundesgesundheitsblatt - Gesundheitsforschung - Gesundheitsschutz*, 59 (5), pp. 621–626.

Brockhaus Enzyklopädie (2019): Kultur. (last accessed 19/May/2019) URL: https://brockhaus.de/ecs/enzy/article/kultur

Brzoska, Patrick and Razum, Oliver (2016): Die Gesundheit von Menschen mit Migrationshintergrund aus sozialepidemiologischer Sicht. In: Kriwy, P. and Jungbauer-Gans, M. (eds.): *Handbuch Gesundheitssoziologie*. Springer, pp. 1–17.

Brown, Deana and Grinter, Rebecca E. (2016): Designing for Transient Use: A Human-in-the-loop Translation Platform for Refugees. In: *CH 2016 Proceedings of the 2016 CHI Conference on Human Factors in Computing Systems*. pp. 321–330.

Brown, Tim (2016): Change by Design – Wie Design Thinking Organisationen verändert und zu mehr Innovationen führt. Vahlen.

Brown, Tim and Wyatt, Jocelyn (2010): Design Thinking for Social Innovation. In: *Stanford Social Innovation Review* 8 (1), pp. 30–35.

Bühring, Petra (2015): Traumatisierte Flüchtlinge: Krieg, Verlust und Gewalt. In: *Deutsches Ärzteblatt International,* 112 (40) (last accessed 19 May 2019). https://www.aerzteblatt.de/pdf.asp?id=172403

Bundesamt für Justiz (2019a): Asylgesetz (AsylG) (last accessed 19 May 2019). URL: http://www.gesetze-im-internet.de/asylvfg_1992/index.html

Bundesamt für Justiz (2019b): Asylbewerberleistungsgesetz (AsylbLG) (last accessed 19 May 2019). URL: http://www.gesetze-im-internet.de/asylblg/index.html

Burmester, Ralf and Vahs, Dietmar (2005): Innovationsmanagement – Von der Produktidee zur erfolgreichen Vermarktung. 3rd. ed.

Busche, Hubertus; Heinze, Thomas; Hillebrandt, Frank and Schäfer, Franka (2018): Kultur – Interdisziplinäre Zugänge. VS Verlag für Sozialwissenschaften.

Bustamante Duarte, Ana; Degbelo, Auriol; Kray, Christian (2018): Exploring Forced Migrants (Re)settlement and the Role of Digital Services. In: *Reports of the European Society for Socially Embedded Technologies*, 2 (1) (last accessed 19 May 2919). DOI: 10.18420/ecscw2018_7.

Caidi, Nadja; Allard, Danielle; Quirke, Lisa (2010): Information Practices of Immigrants. In: *Annual Review of Information Science and Technology* 44 (1), pp. 491–531.

CDSH (Commission on Social Determinants of Health) (2008): Closing the Gap in a Generation – Health Equity through Action on the Social Determinants of Health. Final Report of the Commission on Social Determinants of Health. Geneva, World Health Organization (last accessed 19 May 2019). https://apps.who.int/ iris/bitstream/handle/10665/43943/ 9789241563703_eng.pdf;jsessionid=5F95A4ACB46E886271CB04CFD2DC4CE0?sequence= 1

Davis, Fred D; Bagozzi, Richard, P; Warshaw, Paul R. (1989): User Acceptance of Computer Technology – A Comparison of Two Theoretical Models. In: *Management Science,* 35 (8), pp. 982–1003.

Dekker, Rianne; Engbersen, Godfried; Klaver, Jeanine and Vonk, Hanna (2018): Smart Refugees: How Syrian Asylum Migrants Use Social Media Information in Migration Decision-Making. In: *Social Media + Society,* 4 (1) (last accessed 19 May 2019). https://doi.org/10.1177/2056305118764439

Demireva, Neli (2017) Briefing. Immigration, Diversity and Social Cohesion. 4th Revision. The Migration Observatory at the University of Oxford (last accessed 19 May 2019). URL: http://migrationobservatory.ox.ac.uk/wp-content/uploads/2016/04/Briefing-Immigration-Diversity-and-Social-Cohesion.pdf.

Deterding, Sebastian; Dixon, Dan; Khaled, Rilla; Nacke, Lennart (2011): From Game Design Elements to Gamefulness: Defining Gamification. In: *MindTrek '11 Proceedings of the 15th International Academic MindTrek Conference: Envisioning Future Media Environments,* pp. 9– 15.

Emmer, Martin; Richter, Carola; Kunst, Marlene (2016): Flucht 2.0: Digitale Mediennutzung durch Flüchtlinge. Freie Universtität Berlin, Institut für Publizistik und Kommunikationswissenschaft (last accessed 7 July 2019). https://www.polsoz.fu-berlin.de/kommwiss /arbeitsstellen/ internationale_kommunikation/Media/Flucht-2_0.pdf

Fassaert, Thijs; De Wit, Matty A. S.; Tuinebreijer, Wilco C.; Verhoeff, Arnoud. P.; Beekman, Aartjan T. F.; Dekker, Jack (2009): Perceived Need for Mental Health Care among Non-Western Labour Migrants. In: *Social Psychiatry and Psychiatric Epidemiology,* 44 (3), pp. 208–216. DOI:10.1007/s00127-008-0418-x

Fazel, Mina; Wheeler, Jeremy; Danesh John (2005): Prevalence of Serious Mental Disorder in 7000 Refugees Resettled in Western Countries: A Systematic Review. In. *The Lancet,* 365 (9467), pp. 1309–1314. DOI:10.1016/S0140-6736(05)61027-6

Fernández-Aranda, Fernando; Jiménez-Murcia, Susana; Santamaría, Juan J.; Gunnard, Katarina; Soto, Antonio; Kalapanidas, Elias; Bults, Richard G. A., Davarakis, Costas; Ganchev, Todor; Granero, Roser; Konstantas, Dimitri; Kostoulas, Theodoros P.; Lam, Tony; Lucas,Mikkel; Masuet-Aumatell, Cristina; Moussa, Maher H.; Nielsen, Jeppe and Penelo, Eva (2012): Video Games as a Complementary Therapy Tool in Mental Disorders: PlayMancer, a European Multicentre Study, In: *Journal of Mental Health,* 21(4), pp. 364–374. DOI: 10.3109/09638237.2012.664302

Frank, Laura; Yesil-Jürgens, Rahsan; Razum, Oliver; Bozorgmehr, Kayvan; Schenk, Liane; Gilsdorf, Andreas; Rommel, Alexander; Lampert, Thomas (2017): Gesundheit und gesundheitliche Versorgung von Asylsuchenden und Flüchtlingen in Deutschland. In: *Journal of Health Monitoring,* 2 (1). DOI: 10.17886/RKI-GBE-2017-005

Fueglistaller, Urs; Müller, Christoph; Müller, Susan; Volery, Thierry (2012): Innovation und Entrepreneurship. In: Fueglistaller, U., Müller, C., Müller, S. and Volery, T. (eds.): *Entrepreneurship – Modelle - Umsetzung - Perspektiven – Mit Fallbeispielen aus Deutschland, Österreich und der Schweiz.* Springer, pp. 131–171.

Gabler Wirtschaftslexikon (2019b): Blockchain (last accessed 19 May 2019). https://wirtschafts lexikon.gabler.de/definition/blockchain-54161

Gabler Wirtschaftslexikon (2019a): Soziale Medien (last accessed 19 May 2019). https://wirtschaftslexikon.gabler.de/definition/soziale-medien-52673

Gabler Wirtschaftslexikon (2019c): Künstliche Intelligenz (last accessed 07 July 2019). https://wirtschaftslexikon.gabler.de/definition/kuenstliche-intelligenz-ki-40285/version-263673

Gassmann, Oliver; Frankenberger, Karolin; Csik, Michaela (2017): Geschäftsmodelle entwickeln – 55 innovative Konzepte mit dem St. Galler Business Model Navigator. 2nd ed. Carl Hanser Verlag GmbH & Co KG.

Grots, Alexander and Pratschke, Margerete (2009): Design Thinking – Kreativität als Methode. In: *Marketing Review St. Gallen,* 26 (2), pp. 18–23.

Hansen, Klaus P. (2000): Kultur und Kulturwissenschaft. Paderborn: UTB.

Hansen, Klaus P. (2009): Kultur und Kollektiv. Eine Einführung. Passau: Stutz

Hassan, Gghayda; Kirmayer, Laurence J.; Mekki-Berrada, Abdelwahed; Quosh, Constance; el Chammay, Rabih: Deville-Stoetzel, Jean Benoit; Youssef, Ahmed; Jefee-Bahloul, Hussam; Barkeel-Oteo, Andres; Coutts, Adam; Song, Suzan (2015): Culture, Context and the Mental Health and Psychosocial Wellbeing of Syrians: A Review for Mental Health and Psychosocial Support Staff Working with Syrians Affected by Armed Conflict. Geneva, Switzerland: United Nations High Commissioner for Refugees (UNHCR) (last accessed 19 May 2019). https://www.unhcr.org/55f6b90f9.pdf

Hassan, Gghayda; Ventevogel, Peter; Jefee-Bahloul, Hussam; Barkil-Oteo, Andres; Kirmayer Laurence J. (2016): Mental Health and Psychosocial Wellbeing of Syrians Affected by Armed Conflict. In: E*pidemiology and Psychiatric Sciences,* 25 (2), pp. 129–141. DOI:10.1017/S2045796016000044

Hayes, Alan; Gray, Matthew; Edwards, Ben (2008): Social Inclusion: Origins, Concepts and Key Themes. Canberra, Australian Capital Territory: Social Inclusion Unit, 2008 (last accessed 19 May 2019). URL: http://pandora.nla.gov.au/pan/142909/20130920-1300/www.socialinclusion.gov.au/sites/default/files/publications/pdf/si-origins-concepts-themes.pdf

Heidkamp, Birte and Kergel, David (2018): E-Inclusion – Diversitätssensibler Einsatz digitaler Medien. Überlegungen zu einer bildungstheoretisch fundierten Medienpädagogik. Bielefeld. DOI: 10.3278/6004624w

Henrichs, B. (2016): Ohne Facebook wäre ich nicht angekommen. In: *Die Welt (23rd Feb 2016)* (last accessed 19 May 2019). https://www.welt.de/regionales/hamburg/article152540522/Ohne-Facebook-waere-ich-nicht-angekommen.html

Hilbrecht Hester and Kempkens, Oliver (2013): Design Thinking im Unternehmen – Herausforderung mit Mehrwert. In: Keuper F., Hamidian K., Verwaayen E., Kalinowski T. and Kraijo C. (eds.): *Digitalisierung und Innovation.* pp. 347–364.

Holmes, Emily A.; James, Ella L.; Coode-Bate, Thomas; Deeprose, Catherine (2009): Can Playing the Computer Game "Tetris" Reduce the Build-Up of Flashbacks for Trauma? A Proposal from Cognitive Science. In: *PLoS ONE,* 4 (1): e4153. DOI: 10.1371/journal.pone.0004153

Holmes, Emily A.; Ghaderi, Ata; Eriksson, Ellinor; Olofsdotter Lauri, Klara; Kukacka, Olivia M.; Mamish, Maya; James, Ella L. and Visser, Renée M. (2017): 'I Can't Concentrate': A Feasibility Study with Young Refugees in Sweden on Developing Science-Driven Interventions for Intrusive Memories Related to Trauma. In: *Behavioural and Cognitive Psychotherapy,* 45, pp. 97–109. DOI: 10.1017/S135246581600062X

Hootsuite (2018): Social Media Barometer – Global Report (last accessed 19 May 2019). https://hootsuite.com/resources/barometer-2018-global,

Huckle, Steve and White, Martin (2017): Fake News: A Technological Approach to Proving the Origins of Content, Using Blockchains. In: *Big Data*. 5 (4), pp. 356-371. DOI: 10.1089/big.2017.0071

Humphris, Rachel and Bradby, Hannah (2017): Health Status of Refugees and Asylum Seekers in Europe. In: *Oxford Research Encyclopedia of Global Public Health* (last accessed 19 May 2019). DOI:10.1093/acrefore/9780190632366.013.8

IOM's GMDAC (2017): Migration and the Social Determinants of Health (last accessed 19 May 2019). https://migrationdataportal.org/themes/migration-and-health

Iyadurai, Lalitha; Blackwell, Simon E.; Meiser-Stedman, Richard; Watson, Peter C.; Bonsall, Michael B.; Geddes, John R.; Nobre, Anna C. and Holmes, Emily A. (2018): Preventing Intrusive Memories After Trauma Via a Brief Intervention Involving Tetris Computer Game Play in the Emergency Department: A Proof-of-Concept Randomized Controlled Trial. In: *Molecular Psychiatry*, 23, pp. 674–682 (last accessed 19 May 2019). https://doi.org/10.1038/mp.2017.23

James, Ella L.; Bonsall, Michael B.; Hoppitt, Laura; Tunbridge, Elizabeth M.; Geddes, John R., Milton, Amy L. and Holmes, Emily A. (2015): Computer Game Play Reduces Intrusive Memories of Experimental Trauma via Reconsolidation-Update Mechanisms. In: *Psychological Science*, 26 (8), pp. 1201–1215 (last accessed 19 May 2019). https://doi.org/10.1177/0956797615583071

Jammal, Elias (2014): Kultur und Interkulturalität. Interdisziplinäre Zugänge. Wiesbaden: Springer VS

Jong, Joop TVM de; Komproe, Ivan H.; Ommeren, Mark van (2003): Common Mental Disorders in Postconflict Settings. In: *The Lancet*, 361 (9375), pp. 2128–2130. (last accessed 19 May 2019). DOI:10.1016/S0140-6736(03)13692-6

Kaplan, Ivy (2018): How Smartphones and Social Media have Revolutionized Refugee Migration In: *The Globe Post, 19 Oct 2018* (last accessed 19 May 2019). https://theglobepost.com/2018/10/19/refugees-social-media/

Kutscher, Nadia; Kreß, Lisa-Marie (2015): "Internet ist gleich mit Essen". Empirische Studie zur Nutzung digitaler Medien durch unbegleitete minderjährige Flüchtlinge. Vechta 2015 (last accessed 3 May 2019). URL: https://images.dkhw.de/fileadmin/Redaktion/1.1_Startseite/3_Nachrichten/Studie_Fluechtlingskinder-digitale_Medien/Studie_Fluechtlingskinder_und_digitale_Medien_Zusammenfassung.pdf

Laban, Cornelis J.; Gernaat, Hajo B.; Komproe, Ivan H.; Jong, Joop TVM de (2007): Prevalence and Predictors of Health Service Use Among Iraqi Asylum Seekers in the Netherlands. In: *Social Psychiatry and Psychiatric Epidemiology*, 42 (10), pp. 837–844. https://doi.org/10.1007/s00127-007-0240-x

Lamkaddem, Majda; Stronks, Karien; Devillé, Walter D; Olff, Miranda; Gerritsen, Annette A; Essink-Bot, Marie-Louise (2014): Course of Post-Traumatic Stress Disorder and Health Care Utilisation Among Resettled Refugees in the Netherlands. In: *BMC Psychiatry,* 14 (90). https://doi.org/10.1186/1471-244X-14-90

Liu, Xin, Datta, Anwitaman, Lim, Ee-Peng (2014): Computational Trust Models and Machine Learning. New York. https://doi.org/10.1201/b17778

Mader, Stéphanie; Natkin Stéphane; Levieux Guillaume (2012): How to Analyse Therapeutic Games: The Player / Game / Therapy Model. In: Herrlich M., Malaka R., Masuch M. (eds.) *Entertainment Computing - ICEC 2012*. ICEC 2012. Lecture Notes in Computer Science, vol. 7522. Springer, Berlin, Heidelberg. DOI: https://doi.org/10.1007/978-3-642-33542-6_17

Maier, Thomas, and Straub, Miriam (2011): "My Head is Like a Bag Full of Rubbish": Concepts of Illness and Treatment Expectations in Traumatized Migrants. In: *Qualitative Health Research*, 21 (2), pp. 233–248. https://doi.org/10.1177/1049732310383867

Martini Mario (2019): Blackbox Algorithmus – Grundfragen einer Regulierung Künstlicher Intelligenz. Springer, Berlin, Heidelberg (last accessed 7 July 2019). https://doi.org/10.1007/978-3-662-59010-2_5

Mediendienst Integration 2019: Gesundheit und Migration (last accessed 19 May 2019). URL: https://mediendienst-integration.de/integration/gesundheit.html

MFG (Medizinische Flüchtlingshilfe Göttingen e.V.) (2019): Gesundheitskarte (last accessed 19 May 2019). URL: http://gesundheit-gefluechtete.info/gesundheitskarte/

Mehrotra, Seema; Tripathi, Ravikesh (2018): Recent Developments in the Use of Smartphone Interventions for Mental Health. In: *Current Opinion in Psychiatry*, 31 (5), pp. 379–388. DOI: 10.1097/YCO.0000000000000439

Metzner, Franka; Reher, Cornelia; Kindler, Heinz; Pawils, Silke (2016): Psychotherapeutische Versorgung von begleiteten und unbegleiteten minderjährigen Flüchtlingen und Asylbewerbern mit Traumafolgestörungen in Deutschland. In: *Bundesgesundheitsblatt - Gesundheitsforschung - Gesundheitsschutz*, 59 (5), pp. 642–651.

Migration Data Portal (2019): Migration and Health (last accessed 19 May 2019). URL: https://migrationdataportal.org/themes/migration-and-health

Molnar, Petra and Gill, Lex (2018). "Bots at the Gate: A Human Rights Analysis of Automated Decision-Making in Canada's Immigration and Refugee System". International Human Rights Program (Faculty of Law, University of Toronto) and the Citizen Lab (Munk School of Global Affairs and Public Policy, University of Toronto) (last accessed 7 July 2019). https://ihrp.law.utoronto.ca/sites/default/files/media/IHRP-Automated-Systems-Report-Web.pdf

Molnar, Petra and Muscati, Samer (2018): Algorithms are Deciding the Fate of Many Immigrants — and Neglecting Their Rights. In: *Apolitical Group Limited* (GB) (last accessed 7 July 2019). https://apolitical.co/solution_article/algorithms-immigrants-neglecting-rights/

Molnar, Petra (2018): Governments' Use of AI in Immigration and Refugee System Needs Oversight. Institute for Research on Public Policy. Montreal, Canada (last accessed 7 July 2019). https://policyoptions.irpp.org/magazines/october-2018/governments-use-of-ai-in-immigration-and-refugee-system-needs-oversight/

Nayebi, F; Desharnais, Jean-Marc; Abran, Alain (2012): The State of the Art of Mobile Application Usability Evaluation. 25th IEEE Canadian Conference on Electrical and Computer Engineering (IEEE CD: 978-1-4673-6/12), Montreal.

Nguyen, Giang-Truong and Kim, Kyungbaek (2018): A Survey about Consensus Algorithms Used in Blockchain. J Inf Process Syst, 14(1), pp. 101–128, https://doi.org/10.3745/JIPS.01.0024

OECD (2019): Settling In 2018: Indicators of Immigrant Integration (last accessed 19 May 2019). URL: http://www.oecd.org/berlin/publikationen/settling-in-2018-indicators-of-immigrant-integration.htm

Plattner, Hasso; Meinel, Christoph; Leifer, Larry (eds.) (2011): Design Thinking – Understand – Improve – Apply. Springer.

Razum, Oliver and Saß, Anke-Christine (2015): Migration und Gesundheit: Interkulturelle Öffnung bleibt eine Herausforderung. In: *Bundesgesundheitsblatt - Gesundheitsforschung - Gesundheitsschutz*, 58 (6), pp. 513–514.

Rathje, Stefanie (2004): Corporate Cohesion – Handlungsansatz zur Gestaltung interkultureller Unternehmenskultur. In: Bolten, Jürgen (ed.): Interkulturelles Handeln in der Wirtschaft. Sternenfels, pp. 112–124.

Rathje, S. (2006). Interkulturelle Kompetenz – Zustand und Zukunft eines umstrittenen Konzepts [Intercultural Competence – Status and Future of a Controversial Concept]. Zeitschrift für Interkulturellen Fremdsprachenunterricht [Journal of Intercultural Foreign Language Teaching], 11(3), pp. 15–36.

Raya Diez, Esther (2018): e-Inclusion and e-Social work: New Technologies at the Service of Social Intervention, European Journal of Social Work, 21 (6), pp. 916–929. DOI: 10.1080/13691457.2018.1469472

Rode, Hans-Christian (2007): Die Göbel-Legende – Der Kampf um die Erfindung der Glühlampe. Verlag zu Klampen.

Ronchi, Alfredo M. (2019): e–Services – Toward a New Model of (Inter)active Community. Springer International Publishing.

Schaar, Peter (2017): Überwachung, Algorithmen und Selbstbestimmung. In : Gapski, H., Oberle, M., Staufer,W. (eds.). Medienkompetenz - Herausforderung für Politik, politische Bildung und Medienbildung. Bundeszentrale für politische Bildung. pp. 73–81 (last accessed 7 July 2019). https://www.slpb.de/fileadmin/media/Publikationen/Ebooks/Medienkompetenz_PDF.pdf#page =107

Schmidt-Lux, Thomas; Wohlrab-Sahr, Monika; Leistner, Alexander (2016): Kultursoziologie - eine problemorientierte Einführung. Beltz Juventa.

Schumpeter, Joseph A. (1982): Theorie der wirtschaftlichen Entwicklung. Berlin.

Sijbrandij, Marit; Acarturk, Ceren; Bird, Martha; Bryant, Richard A; Burchert, Sebastian; Carswell, Kenneth; de Jong, Joop; Dinesen,Cecilie; Dawson, Katie S.; El Chammay, Rabih; van Ittersum, Linde; Jordans, Mark; Knaevelsrud, Christine; McDaid, David; Miller, Kenneth; Morina, Naser; Park, A-La; Roberts,Bayard; van Son, Yvette; Sondorp, Egbert; Pfaltz, Monique C.; Ruttenberg, Leontien; Schick, Matthis; Schnyder, Ulrich; van Ommeren, Mark; Ventevogel, Peter; Weissbecker, Ilka; Weitz, Erica; Wiedemann, Nana; Whitney, Claire, Cuijpers Pim (2017): Strengthening Mental Health Care Systems for Syrian Refugees in Europe and the Middle East: Integrating Scalable Psychological Interventions in Eight Countries. In: European Journal of Psychotraumatology, 2017, 8 (2): 1388102. DOI: 10.1080/20008198. 2017.1388102.

Simplican, Stacy Clifford; Leader, Geraldine; Kosciulek, John; Leahy, Michael (2015): Defining Social Inclusion of People with Intellectual and Developmental Disabilities: An Ecological Model of Social Networks and Community Participation. Research in Developmental Disabilities, 38 (3), pp. 18–29.

Singh, Madhusudan and Kim, Shiho. (2018). Trust Bit: Reward-Based Intelligent Vehicle Communication Using Blockchain In: 2018 IEEE 4th World Forum on Internet of Things (WF-IoT) 62-67. DOI: 10.1109/WF-IoT.2018.8355227.

Steel, Zachary; Chey, Tien; Silove, Derrick; Marnane, Claire; Bryant, Richard A; van Ommeren, Mark. (2009): Association of Torture and Other Potentially Traumatic Events with Mental Health Outcomes among Populations Exposed to Mass Conflict and Displacement: A Systematic Review and Meta-Analysis. In: JAMA, 302 (5), pp. 537–549. DOI:10.1001/jama.2009.1132

Stegbauer, Christian (2016): Situation und Kultur. In: Stegbauer, Christian (ed.). Grundlagen der Netzwerkforschung. Springer, pp. 37–73.

Talhouk, Reem; Ahmend, Syed Ishtiaque; Wulf, Volker; Crivallero, Clara; Vlachokyriakos, Vasilis; Olivier, Patrick (2016a): Refugees and HCI SIG: The Role of HCI in Responding to the Refugee Crisis. In: *CHI Extended Abstracts on Human Factors in Computing Systems*, pp. 1073–1076.

Talhouk, Reem; Mesmar, Sandra; Thieme, Anja; Balaam, Madeline; Olivier, Patrick; Akik, Chaza; and Ghattas, Hala (2016b): Syrian Refugees and Digital Health in Lebanon: Opportunities for Improving Antenatal Health. In: *Proceedings of the 2016 CHI Conference on Human Factors in Computing Systems (CHI '16)*, pp. 331–342. https://doi.org/10.1145/2858036.2858331; https://eprint.ncl.ac.uk/file_store/production/219015/E81E76FA-7BDB-4699-B460-AA9DDB 11C9B6.pdf, retrieved 7 May 2019

Tidelski, Olaf (2002): Ökonomische Theorien der Innovation. Wirtschaftswissenschaftliches Studium (WIST), 31 (11), 659–663. https://doi.org/10.15358/0340-1650-2002-11-659

Tinnefeld, Marie-Theres and Buchner, Benedikt (2019). Recht und Ethik im digitalen Zeitalter. In: *Datenschutz und Datensicherheit*. 43 (6), p. 321. https://doi.org/10.1007/s11623-019-1114-6

Trapp, Andrew. C; Teytelboym, Alexander; Martinello, Alessandro: Andersson, Tommy; Ahani, Narges (2018): Placement Optimization for Refugee Resettlement, Working Paper 2018:23. University of Lund. Dept, of Economics (last accessed 7 July 2019). https://project.nek.lu.se/publications/workpap/papers/wp18_23.pdf

Trebbe, Joachim and Paasch-Colberg, Sünje (2016): Migration, Integration und Medien. In: *Bundeszentrale für politische Bildung, 09/Dec/2016* (last accessed 19 May 2019). http://www.bpb.de/gesellschaft/medien-und-sport/medienpolitik/172752/migration-integration -und-medien

UNHCR (2016): The UN Refugee Agency, Facebook Group Helps Syrian Refugees Navigate Life in Lebanon, 13 July 2016 (last accessed 19 May 2019). https://www.unhcr.org/en-lk/news/latest/2016/7/577e16064/facebook-group-helps-syrian-refugees-navigate-life-lebanon .html

WHO (2012): Depression – A Global Crisis. World Federation for Mental Health (last accessed 19 May 2019). URL: https://www.who.int/mental_health/management/depression/wfmh _paper_depression_wmhd_2012.pdf

WHO (2017): Migrant Populations, Including Children, at Higher Risk of Mental Health Disorders (last accessed 7 July 2019). URL: http://www.euro.who.int/en/health-topics/health-determinants/migration-and-health/news/news/2017/04/migrant-populations,-including-children,-at-higher-risk-of-mental-health-disorders

White, Pippa and Forrester-Jones, Rachel (2019): Valuing e-Inclusion: Social Media and the Social Networks of Adolescents with Intellectual Disability, Journal of Intellectual Disabilities. https://doi.org/10.1177/1744629518821240

Wilkinson, Nathan; Ang, Rebecca P.; Goh, Deon H. (2008): Online Video Game Therapy for Mental Health Concerns: A Review. In: *International Journal of Social Psychiatry*, 54 (4), pp. 370–382. https://doi.org/10.1177/0020764008091659

Wimmer, Jeffrey and Elmezeny, Ahmed (2018): Games Without Frontiers: A Framework for Analyzing Digital Game Cultures Comparatively. In: Kneer, Julia and Jacobs, Ruud. *Games Matter. Current Theories and Studies on Digital Games. Media and Communication.* 6 (2), pp. 80–89. DOI: http://dx.doi.org/10.17645/mac.v6i2.1330

Wölbling, Anja; Krämer, Kira; Buss, Clemens N; Dribbisch, Katrin; LoBue, Peter M.; Taherivand, Abraham (2012): Design Thinking: An Innovative Concept for Developing User-Centered Software. In: Maedche A., Botzenhardt A., Neer L. (eds.). *Software for People. Management for Professionals*. Springer, Berlin, Heidelberg, pp. 121–136.

Yellowlees, Patrick M; Hilty, Donald M.; Mucic, Devor (2016): Global/Worldwide e-Mental Health: International and Futuristic Perspectives of Telepsychiatry and the Future. In: Mucic D., Hilty D. (eds.): *e-Mental Health*. Springer, Cham, pp. 233–259.

Yu, Biyang; Ndumu, Ana; Mon, Lorri M.; Fan, Zhenjia (2018): E-inclusion or Digital Divide: An Integrated Model of Digital Inequality, Journal of Documentation, 74 (3), pp. 552-574, Emerald Publishing Limited. https://doi.org/10.1108/JD-10-2017-0148.

Appendix

No.	name of service	publisher/owner	technical format	services	unique features	target group	languages	keywords, category in app stores (if available)	number of downloads (if available), Facebook likes (if available)
1	Integreat	TU München (Tuer an Tuer - Digital Factory gGmbH)	(web) app (iOS, Android); FB channel	tips and tricks for daily life, support and contact details of local administrations, initiatives, etc., finding educational programs and internships	local news, jobs, administration contacts; offline	immigrants, local communities, economy (jobs)	EN; GER; FR	social networks	10,000+ https://play.google.com/store/apps/details?id=tuerantuer.app.integreat 7 May 2019; 1,094 likes on FB (8 May 2019)

No.	name of service	publisher/ owner	technical format	services	unique features	target group	languages	keywords, category in app stores (if available)	number of downloads (if available), Facebook likes (if available)
2	الدليل في الجنين المنيا and http://kappelninfo.blogspot.com/	Alfahel Marwan	app (Android); Website; FB channel	daily life advice: from how to behave in a supermarket to how to get a flat	by a forced Syrian migrant for Arabic-speaking forced migrants	by a forced Syrian migrant for Arabic-speaking forced migrants	ARABIC	social networks	50,000+ https://play.google.com/store/apps/details?id=com.deutsclandinfo.mar (May, 7th, 2019); 119.002 likes on FB (8 May 2019)

No.	name of service	publisher/ owner	technical format	services	unique features	target group	languages	keywords, category in app stores (if available)	number of downloads (if available), Facebook likes (if available)
3	Informationen für Flüchtlinge	Herder Verlag GMBH, Freiburg	app (Android, iOS)	daily information to a better understanding of Germany	educative (style an manner (esp. ethical and democratic)	Arabic-speaking refugees and English, Dutch or Scandinavian immigrants to Germany and German helpers	GER; ARABIC; DANISH; ENG; DUTCH; NOR (Bokmål);SWEDISH	Lifestyle, Bildung [lifestyle, education]	5.000+ https://play.google.com/store/apps/details?id=de.herder.deutschland (7 May 2019)

No.	name of service	publisher/ owner	technical format	services	unique features	target group	languages	keywords, category in app stores (if available)	number of downloads (if available), Facebook likes (if available)
4	https://ipso-care.com	Ipso gemeinnützige Gesellschaft mbH, Berlin	portal (Website), FB channel	e-Health: Confidential online counseling services in several languages /certified training for psychosocial counsellors with a focus on migration in Berlin	trains forced migrants in psycho-social counseling in Berlin, Hamburg and Erfurt; gives immediate help via an online "safe room"	forced migrants who want to help others; service is not accessible on FB channel	ENG; GER; FR; ARABIC; FARSI; RUSSIAN; TURKISH; TIGRINYA; PASHTO; IT; BURMESE; UKRAINIAN; SOMALI	-	836 likes on FB (8 May 2019)

No.	name of service	publisher/ owner	technical format	services	unique features	target group	languages	keywords, category in app stores (if available)	number of downloads (if available), Facebook likes (if available)
5	SMILERS - helping with depression in Arabic; ALMHAR - Mental health aid for refugees; https://ilajnafsy.bzfo.de/portal/de	Zentrum Überleben gGmbH (previously: Behandlungszentrum für Folteropfer e.V.)	Smilers: app (iOS only); portal incl. a FB channel; ALMHAR: app (Android)	e-Health: Smilers: Self-help program for Arabic-speaking persons with depression; Website: Online consultations; ALMHAR: self-help app handling stress after the fight/escape	part of a study; also available online at https://ilajnafsy.bzfo.de/portal/de/; content of app is supervised by Free University Berlin and the Berlin Center ÜBERLEBEN gGmbH	Smilers App, portal: traumatized and/or depressed Arabic-speaking refugees; ALMHAR: self-help app :The app explains the most common emotional problems; offers background information on 12 common problem areas; gives practical and easy-to-do tips	Smilers App: Arabic; platform: ENG; ARABIC; GERMAN; ALMHAR App: ENG, FARSI, ARABIC	health, fitness, medicine	Portal: 6,423 likes on FB (8 May 2019); ALMHAR: 500+ installations (https://play.google.com/store/apps/details?id=org.ueberleben.ueberleben 8 May 2019)

No.	name of service	publisher/ owner	technical format	services	unique features	target group	languages	keywords, category in app stores (if available)	number of downloads (if available), Facebook likes (if available)
6	Ankommen	Bundesamt für Migration, Bayerischer Rundfunk	app (Android)	help with application for asylum German language learning; daily life	offline; co-production of Federal Office for Migration and Refugees, the Goethe Institute, the Bundesagentur für Arbeit; Bayerischer Rundfunk (Bavarian Broadcasting)	immigrants and helpers	ENG; FR; GER; ARABIC; PERSIAN	learn	100,000+ https://play.google.com/store/apps/details?id=de.br.ankommen (7 May 2019)

No.	name of service	publisher/ owner	technical format	services	unique features	target group	languages	keywords, category in app stores (if available)	number of downloads (if available), Facebook likes (if available)
7	Cloud Chasers	Blindflug Studios AG, Zurich CH	app (iOS, Android, Amazon); PC game	game; subject to a charge	"A father and daughter on a desperate journey in hope for a future beyond the deserts." http://cloudchasersgame.com/	people interested in flight	ENG	role play	1,000+ https://play.google.com/store/apps/details?id=com.blindflugstudios.rogallo&hl=de (8 May 2019)

No.	name of service	publisher/owner	technical format	services	unique features	target group	languages	keywords, category in app stores (if available)	number of downloads (if available), Facebook likes (if available)
8	Welcome	IT hilft gGmbH, Dresden	web app (iOS, Android, Windows); FB channel	general information on daily life in Germany; contact details of administrations, associations, and aid agencies; local information on cities and counties.	local; available offline	immigrants, refugees, asylum seekers; cities, volunteers	GER,ENG; FR; ARABIC; FARSI; GREEK;TURKISH; SPANISH, SWEDISH; RUSSIAN; POLISH; DUTCH; ROMANIAN; CZECH; BULGARIAN	reference (category in iOS, Windows)	10,000+ https://play.google.com/store/apps/details?id=de.welcome_app_concept.welcome2germany&hl=de 7 May 2019; 869 likes on FB (8 May 2019)

No.	name of service	publisher/ owner	technical format	services	unique features	target group	languages	keywords, category in app stores (if available)	number of downloads (if available), Facebook likes (if available)
9	ICOON for refugees	AMBERPRESS Chausseestr. 116, D-10115 Berlin, Germany	app (Android); FB channel	dictionary of symbols	more than 1,200 symbols in 12 categories	refugees, forced migrants, asylum seekers	GER; ARABIC; CHINESE; ENG; FR; IT; JAP; DUTCH; POLISH; PORTUGUESE. RUS; SPANISH	communication, travel	https://play.google.com/store/apps/details?id=eu.amberpress.icoon.refugees 7 May 2019; 1,087 likes on FB (May 8th 2019) 5,000+

No.	name of service	publisher/ owner	technical format	services	unique features	target group	languages	keywords, category in app stores (if available)	number of downloads (if available), Facebook likes (if available)
10	RefuShe	Ministerium für Heimat, Kommunales, Bau und Gleichstellung des Landes Nordrhein-Westfalen	app (Android)	information on legal protection and contact details of law offices offering advice for female forced migrants	addressing women's' rights, help and supporting contacts (women's houses) for migrant women and girls in Germany; direct contact via phone to aid agencies such as women's' houses	For women and girls	GER; ENG; ARABIC; KURDISH; PASHTO	-	1,000+ https://play.google.com/store/apps/details?id=de.upsource.appff&hl=de 7 May 2019

Tab. 2: e-support solutions for forced migrants in Germany

Costs and Benefits of Forced Migration in Kenya: The Case of Kakuma Refugee Camp

Samuel Mwakubo[1]

Keywords: Forced Migration, Cost Benefit Analysis, Integration

Abstract

Refugees can put enormous pressure on public resources in a country besides security threats that may be linked or associated with them. Besides, most of the refugees are often hosted in ecologically fragile areas and their continued stay without adequate planning could lead to environmental degradation. Kenya is likely to continue hosting refugees for the foreseeable future given the political situation in Somalia and Sudan, and the unfolding instability in Burundi. Given this state of affairs, it is thus critical to understand the costs and benefits of forced migration. This study seeks to assess the costs and benefits to Kenya for having refugees in Kakuma Refugee Camp. The study heavily relies on desk research and uses a Cost-Benefit Analysis (CBA) framework. The results show that household consumption was substantially estimated in 2016 at US $ 56.2 million annually with consumption in the refugee camp amounting to about 30%. Estimates indicate that goods worth about US $ (350,000-400,000) monthly are purchased for purposes related to the refugee camp. Supplies for various goods and services demanded by refugees were sourced from Kakuma, Lodwar, Kitale and Nairobi, thus forming supply chains, which is a positive spin-off. The results strongly suggest that indeed the benefits are substantial for Turkana County although negligible /marginal for the overall country. Simulated Gross Regional Product has been growing by 3.4%, employment by 2.9% and income

1   Samuel Mwakubo | School of Business and Economics, Pwani University Kilifi | samuelmwakubo@gmail.com

© Springer Fachmedien Wiesbaden GmbH, part of Springer Nature 2020
K. Crepaz et al. (eds.), *Health in Diversity – Diversity in Health*,
https://doi.org/10.1007/978-3-658-29177-8_14

per person by 0.5%. Benefits come in the form of health facilities, nutritional status, and overall economy while costs are related to environmental degradation and, in some instances, security issues. A simulation of integration within a host scenario has yielded good results. It suggests that such refugees should be integrated, especially those with Kenyan spouses and/or established livelihoods. Finally, the environmental costs are real especially with a view to ecologically fragile areas. Governments, the UNHCR and NGOs ought to consider viable measures to mitigate negative impacts.

Contents

Abstract...281

1   Introduction..283

2   Conceptual Framework 285

3   Costs of Forced Migration – Evidence..286

4   Benefits of Forced Migration – Evidence 286

5   Conclusions and Policy Implications 295

Bibliography 296

1   Introduction

The number of people in forced migration in the world today is about 68.5 million, with 40 million being internally displaced, 25.4 million classified as refugees, and 3.1 million classified as asylum seekers (UNHCR, 2019). About 86% of these people are in developing countries. A majority of them (57%) are from South Sudan (2.4 million), Syria (6.3 million) and Afghanistan (2.6 million).

The number of people hosted by Kenya was about 475,412 as of January 2019, with 209,979 in Dabaab and 188,513 in Kakuma (UNHCR, 2019). The latter is in Turkana County, which borders South Sudan. The remaining 76920 refugees live in urban areas (UNHCR ibid.).

As Figure 1 below shows, the number of refugees in the country has been fluctuating, with a steep increase in 2010 and a gradual decrease from 2011 onward. The dip in 2015 can be explained by the efforts to repatriate refugees back in their home countries.

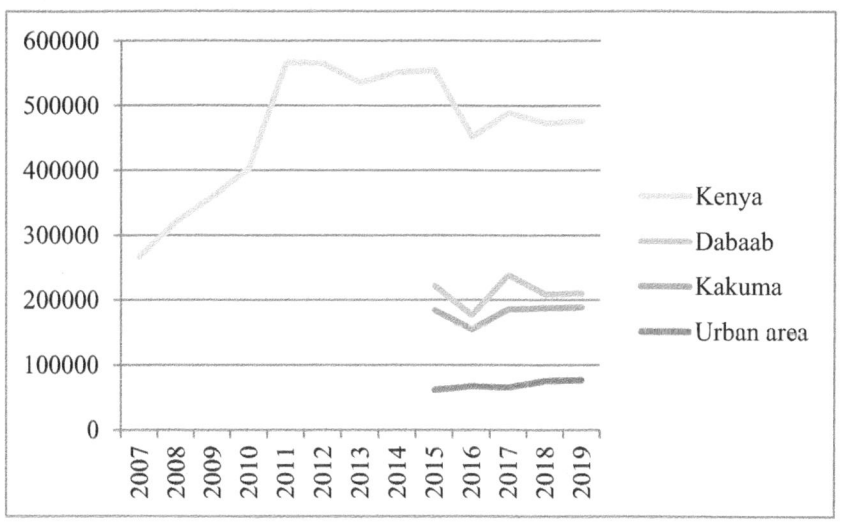

Figure 1: Total number of refugees in recent years in Kenya (after UNHRC, 2019)

Refugees and asylum seekers from Somalia as of December 2018 are the majority (54.5%), followed by those from South Sudan (24.4%), Congo (8.8%); and

Ethiopia (5.9%). Almost half of the refugees in Kenya (44%) reside in Dadaab, 40% in Kakuma and 16% in urban areas (mainly Nairobi), and there are a further 18,500 stateless persons who reside in many parts of the county such as Kwale, Kilifi and Nairobi (UNHCR, 2019).

With regard to Kakuma Refugee Camp, 54.3% of refugees were from South Sudan, and 22.4% from Somalia, with the rest coming from Sudan, Ethiopia, Burundi and the Democratic Republic of Congo (UNHCR, 2018a). Another new refugee camp (Kalobeyei) has been set up to ease the increasing pressure on Kakuma Refugee Camp. Kalobeyei Camp, which is about 40 km from Kakuma and hosts 40,000 people, is of a different arrangement in that there is integration with the local people (UNEP, 2018).

Kenya is likely to continue hosting refugees for the foreseeable future given the political situation in Somalia and Sudan, and the unfolding instability in Burundi. Although there have been efforts under the voluntary scheme program to repatriate refugees, only a paltry 82,925 have returned (UNHCR, 2019).

Given the above state of affairs, it is thus critical to understand the benefits and costs of forced migration. Refugees can put enormous pressure on public resources in a country besides security threats that may be linked or associated with them. Most refugees are often hosted in ecologically fragile areas and their continued stay without adequate planning could lead to environmental degradation (Vemuru, 2016). But on the other hand, hosting refugees also has its benefits. They provide abundant low cost labour, have skills that are unique and, in some instances, capital and financial assets (World Bank and UNHCR, 2016). Aid agencies also invest in necessary infrastructure such as health and water facilities for refugees that the local people can also access (World Bank and UNHCR, 2016; Vemuru et al., 2016; Aokot, 2003; Zetter, 2012).

The quantitative impact of refugee camps on the local people and the economy at large with regard to benefits and costs are not known. Past research on refugees has mainly looked at the qualitative aspect (Aukot 2003 and Oka 2011).

This paper seeks to understand the unique challenges that Kenya is facing in relation to hosting refugees and also assess whether there are any benefits accrued. The objective of the paper is therefore to assess the costs and benefits to Kenya for having refugees in Kakuma Refugee Camp. The camp was established in 1992 and was initially meant to cater for refugees from the Sudan conflict, but it now hosts people from Uganda, Rwanda, Somalia, Ethiopia and Burundi. The camp is about 850 km from Nairobi and 150 km from the South Sudanese border. The study heavily relies on desk research to reach its objective. We use the Cost-Benefit Analysis (CBA) framework in this study. CBA helps to predict whether the benefits of a policy or a project, etc. outweigh its costs, and by how much, relative to other alternatives (Atkinson et al., 2018; Benton and Diegert, 2018).

2 Conceptual Framework

The study relies on the Cost-Benefit Analysis framework (Atkinson et al., 2018; Benton and Diegert, 2018), which helps in the evaluation of alternatives according to their costs and benefits when each is measured in monetary terms. We also examine pathways through which positive and negative impacts of refugees might occur. Since refugee camps have one major characteristic, namely that of hosting a vast number of people, we assess if the presence of many refugees results in labour market competition, or a huge market for locally produced goods.

As Figure 2 shows, there are both market and non-market impacts, with the market impacts affecting the supply and demand side via the eventual increase of prices of non-tradable goods and loss of income for tradable goods.

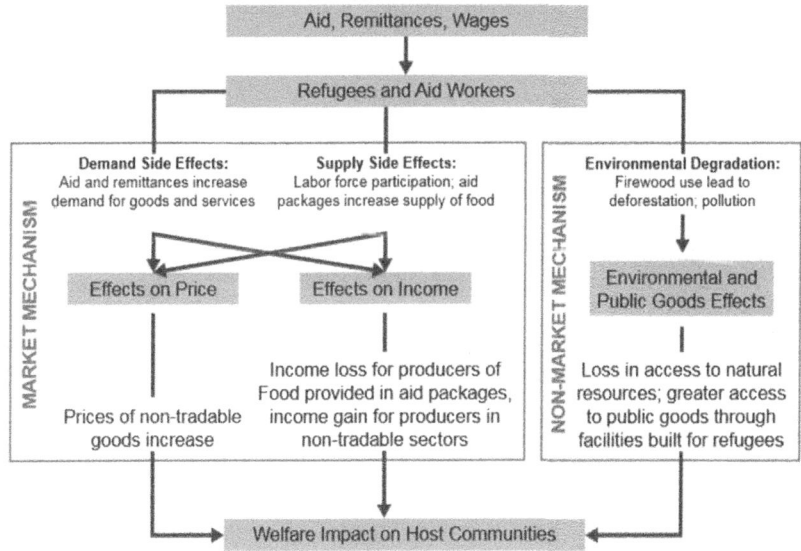

Figure 2: Conceptual framework of refugee impact (World Bank and UNHCR, 2016: 16)

On the non-market side, we have environmental degradation, but also facilities/infrastructure built to cater for refugee needs. All these factors form the sum of the total welfare impact of refugees on a host country.

3   Costs of Forced Migration – Evidence

A number of studies point out the costs/burdens that refugees place on host countries (Zetter 2012, Vemuru 2017). Some of the burdens consist of extra costs on government budgets to cater for refugees, to some extent straining/dragging the growth of the economy, distorting markets, or accelerating the degradation of the environment; and in some cases, causing stress politically in conflict and fragile countries (Zetter, 2012). The host country has to provide services such as water, education, health and security, and build roads, and all these strain the budget (Zetter ibid.). Some of the negative impacts of forced migration include incidences of violence or indignity (Aokot, 2003; Vemuru, 2017). Moreover, the areas where refugee camps are located are less developed and environmentally fragile (Vemuru, 2016). As UNEP (2018) argues, Kakuma experiences environmental degradation arising from an increased demand for wood fuel, inadequate sanitation facilities and inadequate water supplies for people and livestock. Harvesting of firewood and the high demand for water has put a lot of pressure on the local environment not least due to climate change and the growing host and refugee population (Aokot, 2003; UNHCR, 2015). In 2014, about 84% of energy needs of refugees were sourced from firewood obtained from the nearby forests and bushes (UNHCR, 2015). This suggests a certain extent of environmental degradation with regard to the depletion of firewood, water shortages, etc. in the immediate vicinity of the camp (Aokot, 2003; O'Callaghan and Sturge, 2018).

However, we have not been able to get evidence of the magnitude of these costs from past studies.

4   Benefits of Forced Migration – Evidence

Hosting refugees who have been displaced through forced migration comes with benefits for the host country. These include abundant labour that may have new/unique skills and, above all, a market for food and other commodities such as building materials, which stimulates the growth of the host economy. Infrastructure and social services which are provided to cater for refugee needs by UNHCR and other agencies also benefit the local community (Aokot, 2003; Zetter, 2012). Roads built can expand market access and improve the distribution of commodities. New businesses might be started to cater to the increased demand for goods and services arising from the needs of refugees, thereby improving economic activity. Alix-Garcia et al. (2018) used night-time lights data and other data to find long-term-increased economic activity around Kakuma Refugee Camp in Kenya. The telecommunication infrastructure has been upgraded to cater for international calls and remittances (De Montclos and Kagwanja, 2000). This suggests that although some argue that refugees are a burden, they bring economic benefits (Aokot, 2003; O'Callaghan and Sturge, 2018).

Vemuru (2017) argues that some of the beneficial effects of having refugees are improved social interactions and civil networks; improved market access; and better health and physical wellbeing for the local population. The author also argues that the local Turkana women benefit more than men of this circumstance as they provide housework services, collect firewood/water, and deliver goods such as charcoal and firewood. Turkana women have also established social bonds and support networks with the refugees. World Bank (2018) argues that in Kakuma Refugee Camp and the environs, there are significant unmet demands for goods and services. A recent study (Alix-Garcia et al., 2018) estimates that a 10% increase in the refugee population raises consumption by approximately 5.5% within the proximity of the camp.

There is an increase of low-skilled jobs and wage labour, especially for households having secondary education, as proximity to the refugee camp increases (Alix-Garcia et al., 2018). Any negative impact of labour market competition from having refugees is mitigated by increased employment opportunities in the camp and the high demand for goods and services needed by refugees. A recent study finds that in Rwanda, the locals living nearer a refugee camp (within 10 km) are significantly more likely on average to be engaged in wage employment in comparison to farming or livestock production (Loschmann et al., 2019).

There are also differential effects even among refugees and the host population. Bett et al., (2018) finds that refugees from Somalia and Congo are better off than the host population with respect to number of meals, access to electricity and having assets. However, refugees from South Sudan were worse off in comparison (Bett el al., ibid.).

With respect to agricultural commodities, distortions in the market may arise as food given to the refugees is sourced externally. This may lead to lower prices as the overall supply in Kakuma increases (Alix-Garcia et al., 2018). However, prices may in instances increase across a variety of specific products due to the increase in the number of people purchasing these goods, and due to the sale of aid packages for income (Alix-Garcia et al., ibid.). It has been observed that agricultural activities intensify in the vicinity of the refugee camp indicating a positive relation. Livestock prices are noted to be higher closer to the refugee camp suggesting that livestock farmers benefit from refugee presence. Refugee presence seems to have an overall positive effect through a better employment situation, as well as changes in the price of agricultural commodities and livestock which encourage more production (Alix-Garcia et al., ibid.). Most of the firewood, charcoal, and wooden building materials that refugees use are from the host community who sell for money or trade materials for food and other desired goods; and 100% of the meat comes from Turkana livestock (World Bank and UNHCR, 2016). Some studies have also identified high-potential value chains in Kakuma, which include tomatoes, hides & skins, and aloe vera (Hall, 2015).

There are also health benefits related to the hosting of refugees. Gengo et al. (2018) find that local residents have better nutritional status compared to other relevant locations such as Lorengo or Lokichoggio as a result of the existence of Kakuma Refugee Camp. The argument advanced is that there is better access to cereals through the refugee networks and that there are also employment opportunities in the camp. Vemuru (2017) argues that the presence of refugees is highly correlated with greater physical well-being of the host community. Despite the improvement of nutrition levels in Kakuma and Kalebeyei camps, malnutrition is still prevalent (WFP, 2018). With regard to the number of health facilities, Kakuma Refugee Camp has 8 while Kalobeyei has 2 (WFP, 2018). Local people also make use of the opportunity to access medical services within the Camp (Aokot, 2003; Vemuru et al., 2016).

The multi-sectoral simulation model results are presented below showing that impact on the overall economy, on income per local person, and on domestic employment. The Gross Regional Product has been growing by 3.4%, employment by 2.9% and income per person by 0.5%. Non-tradable sectors benefit from the hosting of refugees as measured by the impact on prices, wages and employment (+7.45%) while the tradable sector shrinks (-7.2%) [World Bank and UNHCR, 2016]. However, the impact on the overall Kenyan economy is negligible, as Table 1 shows. This may be due to the size of the economy of Turkana in relation to the overall Kenyan economy.

	BEFORE ARRIVAL	ARRIVAL YEAR	+5 YEARS	+10 YEARS	+15 YEARS	+20 YEARS	+30 YEARS	+50 YEARS
		(Percentage change from initial equilibrium						
TURKANA								
Gross Regional Product (GRP)	0.0	2.6	3.4	3.4	3.4	3.4	3.4	3.4
Tradable	0.0	-5.7	-7.1	-7.1	-7.2	-7.2	-7.2	-7.2
Non-tradable	0.0	5.7	7.3	7.4	7.4	7.4	7.4	7.4
Employment (locals only)	0.0	1.2	2.8	2.9	2.9	2.9	2.9	2.9
Tradable	0.0	-2.7	-6.0	-6.3	-6.3	-6.3	-6.3	-6.4
Non-tradable	0.0	2.7	6.2	6.5	6.5	6.5	6.5	6.5
Gross Regional Income (GRI)	0.0	2.6	3.4	3.4	3.4	3.4	3.4	3.4
GRI per local person	0.0	1.4	0.6	0.5	0.5	0.5	0.5	0.5
Non-tradable prices	0.0	12.0	7.3	7.0	6.9	6.9	6.9	6.9
REST OF KENYA								
Gross Regional Product (GRP)	0.0	0.0	0.0	0.0	0.0	0.0	0.0	0.0
Tradable	0.0	0.0	0.0	0.0	0.0	0.0	-0.1	-0.1
Non-tradable	0.0	0.0	0.0	0.0	0.0	0.0	0.0	0.0
Employment (locals only)	0.0	0.0	-0.1	-0.1	-0.1	-0.1	-0.1	-0.1
Tradable	0.0	0.0	0.0	0.0	-0.1	-0.1	-0.1	-0.1
Non-tradable	0.0	-0.1	-0.1	-0.1	-0.1	-0.1	-0.1	-0.1
Gross Regional Income (GRI)	0.0	0.0	0.0	0.0	0.0	0.0	0.0	0.0
GRI per local person	0.0	0.0	0.0	0.0	0.0	0.0	0.0	0.0
Non-tradable prices	0.0	0.0	0.0	0.0	0.0	0.0	0.0	0.0

Tab. 1: Macroeconomic effects of refugee arrivals (encampment simulation results) suggest the refugee presence has a beneficial effect on Turkana's economy, (after World Bank and UNHCR, 2016: 26)

There have been concerns on whether refugees should be confined to the camps or be integrated into the host community. Tables 2 and 3 below present the "what-if" scenarios of the modelling of the impact of Kakuma Refugee Camp: little economic integration; full economic integration; decampment (camp closure and removal of refugees to other countries). The results show that full economic integration is the best solution (World Bank and UNHCR, 2016), as is shown in Table 2.

The limited integration option yields the following figures: Gross Regional Product (4.7%), employment of locals (-0.8%), Gross Regional Income (0.8%), Gross Regional Income per person (1.6%), and non-tradable prices (2.3%). The figures for the full integration option are: Gross Regional Product (15.1%), employment of locals (-3.6%), Gross Regional Income (2.3%), Gross Regional Income per person (6.1%), and non-tradable prices (7.1%). The decampment option, by contrast, yields the following figures: Gross Regional Product (-2.6%), employment of locals (-1.2%), Gross Regional Income (-2.6%), Gross Regional Income per person (-1.4%), and non-tradable prices (-10.3%).

It is encouraging to note that the new fully integrated scheme (Kalobeyei) that began in 2016 is a move in the right direction. The scheme allows the refugees and the host population to interact and live without restrictions on movement (UNHCR, 2018b). It was meant to decongest Kakuma Camp and attract the more entrepreneurially-minded refugees who could make use of the tiny plots of land on offer and trade with the local community, thereby promoting self-reliance. This suggests that integration reduces market distortions and also encourages interaction in many spheres including economic, social and even cultural interaction. As Werker (2007) argues, refugee camp economies are influenced by restrictions on movement and work, as well as by physical and economic isolation of the site. Moreover, a restriction forcing refugees to remain inside the camp is likely to enhance competition of resources and degradation of the environment (Zetter, 2017). As discussed earlier, the impact for the rest of Kenya (Table 3) is negligible for all the parameters.

The presence of refugees also increases consumption, self-reported incomes and asset ownership among the Turkana people while agriculture benefits (but marginally) from refugee presence (World Bank and UNHCR, 2016). It has also been found that assets and ownership of assets decrease with distance from the camp (World Bank and UNHCR, ibid.). The results are similar to those related to refugee camps in other countries. For instance in Rwanda, locals who live in the vicinity of a refugee camp have more household assets (Loschmann, 2019).

	INTEGRATION/ DECAMPMENT YEAR	+5 YEARS	+10 YEARS	+15 YEARS	+20 YEARS	+30 YEARS	+50 YEARS
	Turkana: Gross Regional Product (GRP)						
	(Percentage change from initial equilibrium)						
Limited integration	4.7	0.1	-0.3	-0.4	-0.4	-0.4	-0.4
Full integration	15.1	0.3	-2.1	-2.7	-2.8	-2.9	-2.9
Decampment	-2.6	-3.3	-3.3	-3.3	-3.3	-3.3	-3.3
	Turkana: Employment (locals only)						
	(Percentage change from initial equilibrium)						
Limited integration	-0.8	-1.2	-0.8	-0.6	-0.5	-0.4	-0.4
Full integration	-3.6	-7.0	-5.2	-3.9	-3.3	-2.9	-2.8
Decampment	-1.2	-2.7	-2.8	-2.8	-2.8	-2.8	-2.8
	Turkana: Gross Regional Income (GRI)						
	(Percentage change from initial equilibrium)						
Limited integration	0.8	-1.6	-1.1	-0.7	-0.6	-0.5	-0.5
Full integration	2.3	-5.3	-4.7	-3.9	-3.6	-3.3	-3.3
Decampment	-2.6	-3.3	-3.3	-3.3	-3.3	-3.3	-3.3
	GRI per local person (GRIplp)						
Limited integration	1.6	-0.5	-0.3	-0.2	-0.1	-0.1	-0.1
Full integration	6.1	1.9	0.5	0.0	0.3	-0.4	-0.5
Decampment	-1.4	-0.6	-0.5	-0.5	-0.5	-0.5	-0.5
	Non-tradable prices						
Limited integration	2.3	-0.6	-0.8	-0.9	-0.9	-1.0	-1.0
Full integration	7.1	-3.5	-5.3	-5.9	-6.1	-6.3	-6.3
Decampment	-10.3	-6.8	-6.5	-6.5	-6.5	-6.5	-6.5

Tab. 2: What-If Scenarios for Turkana County Economy (World Bank and UNHCR, 2016: 47)

	INTEGRATION/ DECAMPMENT YEAR	+5 YEARS	+10 YEARS	+15 YEARS	+20 YEARS	+30 YEARS	+50 YEARS
	Rest of Kenya: Gross Regional Product (GRP)						
	(Percentage change from initial equilibrium)						
Limited integration	0.0	0.1	0.1	0.1	0.1	0.1	0.1
Full integration	0.0	0.4	0.4	0.4	0.4	0.4	0.4
Decampment	0.0	0.0	0.0	0.0	0.0	0.0	0.0
	Rest of Kenya: Employment (locals only)						
	(Percentage change from initial equilibrium)						
Limited integration	0.0	0.0	0.0	0.0	0.0	0.0	0.0
Full integration	0.1	0.2	0.1	0.1	0.1	0.1	0.1
Decampment	0.0	0.1	0.1	0.1	0.1	0.1	0.1
	Rest of Kenya: Gross Regional Income (GRI)						
	(Percentage change from initial equilibrium)						
Limited integration	0.0	0.1	0.0	0.0	0.0	0.0	0.0
Full integration	0.0	0.2	0.1	0.1	0.1	0.1	0.1
Decampment	0.0	0.0	0.0	0.0	0.0	0.0	0.0
	GRI per local person (GRIplp)						
Limited integration	0.0	0.0	0.0	0.0	0.0	0.0	0.0
Full integration	-0.1	0.0	0.0	0.0	0.0	0.0	0.0
Decampment	0.0	0.0	0.0	0.0	0.0	0.0	0.0
	Non-tradable prices						
Limited integration	0.0	0.0	0.0	0.0	0.0	0.0	0.0
Full integration	0.0	0.2	0.2	0.2	0.2	0.2	0.2
Decampment	0.0	0.0	0.0	0.0	0.0	0.0	0.0

Tab. 3: What-If Scenarios for the Kenyan Economy (World Bank and UNHCR, 2016: 48)

Refugee camps generate demand for goods and services. Businesses are thus established to cater for the needs of refugees and town residents in Kakuma. A study by IFC (2016) shows that the estimated total household consumption in Kakuma in 2016 was US $ 56.2 million annually, with US $16.5 million for the camp and US $ 39.7 million for the town. This shows that consumption in the refugee camp is substantial in that it amounts to about 30% of the town total household consumption. Another study (Oka, 2014) shows that remittances to refugees amount to US$ 200,000 monthly, employment in the commercial sector equals US $66,000 and the selling of relief packages amounts to US $ 89,000, generating a total income of US $ 355,000 per month that is available for expenditure. Refugees use this cash to buy goods and services. The remittances come from family and friends in the diaspora, and this is common among the Somalis and Ethiopian refugees (Hall, 2015). Estimates from M-PESA agents show that refugees receive between US$ 100,000- 150,000 monthly (Oka, 2011). Wholesalers estimate that the refugee camp purchases goods worth about US $ 350,000-400,000 monthly (Oka, 2014).

Figure 3 below shows the types of retail business in Kakuma and indicates that the dominant ones includes dukas [retail shops for general merchandise] (19.7%), followed by clothing/shoes (15.7%), vegetables (6.7%) and hotels/restaurants (6.4%). The number of businesses totals at about 2100, and they are run by the private sector. These serve both the town people and residents in the camp. As argued earlier, the overall consumption of goods and services is substantial.

Retail businesses by type in Kakuma camp

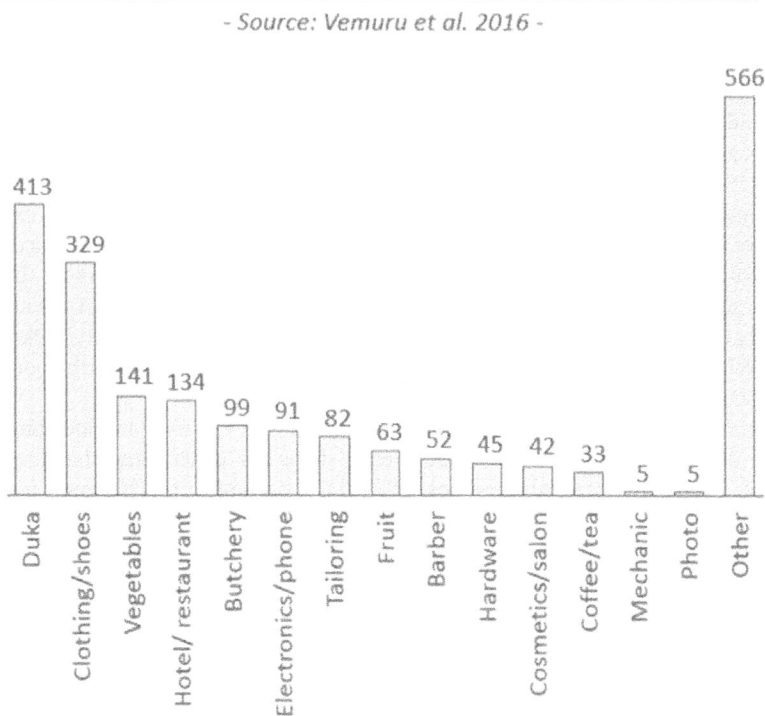

- Source: Vemuru et al. 2016 -

Figure 3: Types of Businesses by Type in Kakuma (IFC, 2018)

As Oka (2014) argues, refugees buy goods and services which bring about social benefits that may exceed the costs or, at the very least, mitigate the costs.
Most of the goods consumed in Kakuma are sourced from wholesalers in Kitale
and other places. The camp is served by a market value chain that follows the
transport corridor that links Nairobi with Lokichoggio and South Sudan (WFP,
2014).

Commercial activities in Lodwar town also benefit heavily from refugee
activities in Kakuma (see Figure 4 below). As the figure shows, some of the
relief food/supplies are secretly sold to Kakuma town and find their way to
Lodwar, Kitale, Eldoret and Nairobi.

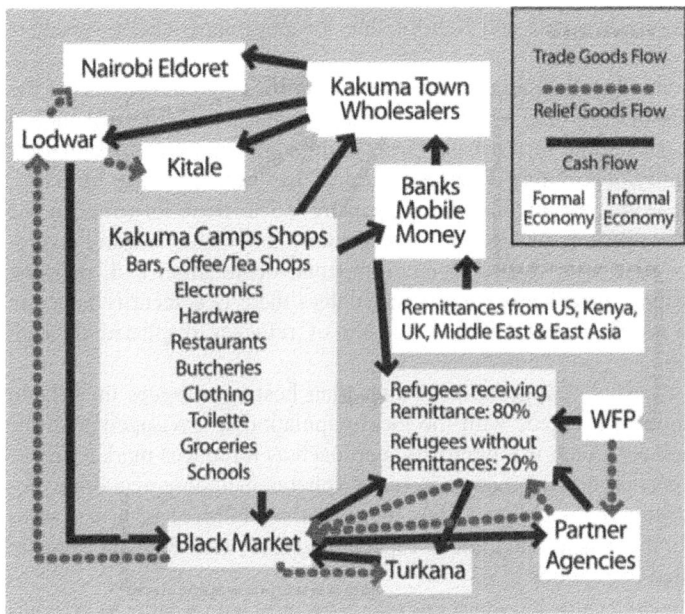

Figure 4: Flow of Goods and Services at Kakuma (Oka, 2014: 28)

The locally produced goods in large quantities in Turkana are livestock, milk and fish. The rest of the food commodities are sourced from outside the county (WFP, 2014).

5 Conclusions and Policy Implications

Kenya is likely to continue hosting refugees in the foreseeable future due to the prevailing political conditions in Somalia and Sudan and the growing instability in Burundi. Given the concerns about budgetary burdens and security, it is thus critical to assess the costs and benefits of hosting refugees in the country.

The study relied on desk research and used a cost-benefit analysis framework. Household consumption is substantial and estimated in 2016 at US $ 56.2 million annually with consumption in the camp making up about 30% of the overall consumption. Estimates indicate that refugee camp purchases relate to goods worth about US $ (350,000-400,000) monthly, which is really significant. Supplies for various goods and services demanded by refugees were sourced from Kakuma, Lodwar, Kitale and Nairobi, thus forming supply chains, which is a positive spin-off.

Although data is still limited particularly in terms of the magnitude of the various elements of costs and benefits, the study strongly suggests that indeed the benefits are substantial for Turkana County, although negligible/marginal for the overall country. The Gross Regional Product has been growing by 3.4%, employment by 2.9% and income per person by 0.5%. Benefits come in the form of health facilities, improved nutritional status, and a better overall economy while costs arise with regard to environmental degradation and, in some instances, security issues. This suggests that unless there is a security concern, countries have no reason to fear the hosting of refugees displaced through forced migration.

Secondly, the study suggests that rather than hosting refugees in isolated camps, integration of refugees with the local population as envisaged with the Kalobeyei Integrated Camp is a pragmatic approach as it reduces market distortions and also encourages interaction in many spheres including economic, social and even cultural interaction. This suggests that refugees in urban areas should be naturalized and integrated, especially those with Kenyan spouses and/or established livelihoods.

Finally, the environmental costs are real especially with a view to ecologically fragile areas. Governments, UNHCR and NGOs ought to consider viable measures to reduce negative impacts.

Bibliography

Atkinson, Giles; Groom, Ben; Hanley, Nicholas; Mourato, Susana (2018). Environmental Valuation and Benefit-Cost Analysis in U.K. Policy. In: *Journal of Benefit-Cost Analysis*, 9(1), p. 97-119. https://doi.org/10.1017/bca.2018.6

Aukot, Ekuru (2003). "It is better to be a refugee than a Turkana in Kakuma": Revisiting the relationship between hosts and refugees in Kenya. In: *Refuge*, 21 (3), p. 73-82.

Benton, Meghan; Diegert, Paul (2018). A needed evidence revolution: Using cost-benefit analysis to improve integration programming. Brussels and Gütersloh. Migration Policy Institute Europe and Bertelsmann Stiftung.

De Montclos, Marc-Antoine P.; Kagwanja, Peter M. (2000). "Refugee camps or cities? The socio-economic dynamics of the Dadaab and Kakuma camps in Northern Kenya". In: *Journal of Refugee Studies*, 13(2), p. 205–222.

Alix-Garcia, Jennifer ; Walker, Sarah; Bartlett, Anne (2017). How Refugee camps benefit host Communities. https://voxdev.org/topic/labour-markets-migration/how-refugee-camps-benefit-host-communities.

Alix-Garcia, Jennifer; Walker, Sarah; Bartlett, Anne (2018). Assessing the direct and spillover effects of shocks to refugee remittances. https://ageconsearch.umn.edu/record/ 274255/files/ Abstracts_18_05_23 _12_35_ 10_50__128_193_152_0_0.pdf.

Alix-Garcia Jennifer; Walker, Sarah; Bartlett, Anne; Onder, Harun; Sanghi, Apurva (2018). Do refugee camps help or hurt hosts? The case of Kakuma, Kenya. In: *Journal of Development Economics*, 130, p. 66–83.

Betts, Alexander; Omata, Naohika.; Sterk, Olivier. (2018). Refugee Economies in Kenya. Oxford: Refugees Studies Centre.

Gengo, Rieti G.; Oka, Rahul; C; Vemuru, Varalakshmi; Golitko, Mark; Gettler, Lee T. (2017). Positive effects of refugee presence on host community nutritional status in Turkana County, Kenya. In: American Journal of Human Biology, 30(1), p.

Hall, Samuel (2015). Rapid Market Assessment and Value Chain Analysis: Kakuma Refugee Program, Turkana, Kenya. http://samuelhall.org/wp-content/uploads/2016/07/Rapid-Market-Assessment-Value-Chain-Analyses-in-Kakuma-May-2016-FINAL.pdf.

International Finance Corporation (IFC) (2018). Kakuma as a Market Place: A consumer and a market study of a refugee camp in northwestern Kenya.

Loschmann, Craig; Bilgili, Özge; Siegel, Melissa (2019). Considering the benefits of hosting refugees: evidence of refugee camps influencing local labour market activity and economic welfare in Rwanda. In: *IZA Journal of Migration and Development*, 9(1), p. 1-23.

O'Callaghan, Sorcha; Sturge, Georgina (2018). Against the Odds: Refugee Integration in Kenya. HPG Working Paper. https://www.odi.org/sites/odi.org.uk/files/resource-documents/12542.pdf.

Ohta, Itaru (2005). Multiple Socio-Economic Relationships Improvised between the Turkana and Refugees in Kakuma Area, Northwestern Kenya. http://www.africa.kyoto-u.ac.jp/eng/enmember/thesis/ Ohta2005_1.pdf.

Oka, Rahul C. (2014). Coping with the Refugee Wait: The Role of Consumption, Normalcy, and Dignity in Refugee Lives at Kakuma Refugee Camp, Kenya. In: *American Anthropologist*, 116(1), p. 23-37.

Oka, Rahul C. (2011). Unlikely Cities in the Desert: The Informal Economy as Causal Agent for Permanent 'Urban' Sustainability in Kakuma Refugee Camp, Kenya. In: *Urban Anthropology and Studies of Cultural Systems and World Economic Development* , 40(3–4) p. 223–62.

Vemuru, Varalakshmi (2017). Understanding the nuanced social impact of Kakuma refugees on their Turkana hosts. http://blogs.worldbank.org/dev4peace/understanding-nuanced-social-impact-kakuma-refugees-their-turkana-hosts.

Vemuru, Varalakshmi; Raina, Ashutosh (2016). Perspectives from the Horn of Africa: Improving livelihoods for communities hosting refugees. http://blogs.worldbank.org/_dev4peace/taxonomy/term/14528.

Vemuru, Varalakshmi; Oka, R; Gengo, Rieti; Gettler, Lee (2016). Refugee impacts on Turkana hosts: a social impact analysis for Kakuma Town and refugee camp, Turkana County, Kenya. World Bank/UNHCR.

UNEP (2018). Managing Environmental Stress in Kenya's Kakuma Refugee Camp. https://reliefweb.int/report/kenya/managing-environmental-stress-kenya-s-kakuma-refugee-camp.

UNHCR (2019). Figures at a glance. https://www.unhcr.org/figures-at-a-glance.html.

UNHCR (2018a). https://data2.unhcr.org/fr/documents/details/64664.

UNHCR (2018b). Kalobeyei Integrated Socio-Economic Development Plan in Turkana West. UNHCR. https://www.unhcr.org/ke/wpcontent/uploads/sites/2/2018/12/KISEDP_ Kalobeyei-Integrated-Socio-Econ-Dev-Programme.pdf

UNHCR (2017a). UNHCR Population Statistics Database. United Nations High Committee on Refugees.

UNHCR (2015). Kenya Comprehensive Refugee Program. https://www.unhcr.org/ke/wp-content/uploads/ sites/2/2016/08/KCRP-2015.pdf.

Werker, Eric (2007). Refugee Camp Economies. In: *Journal of Refugee Studies*, 20(3), p. 461–480. https://doi.org/10.1093/jrs/fem001

World Food Program (WFP) (2018). Nutrition for Refugees in Kakuma Camp and Kalobeyei Settlement. INFOBRIEF No 27. November 2018. https://docs.wfp.org/api/documents/_WFP-0000102588/download/?ga=2.245207046.2074167988.1554894009-942450713.1554894009.

World Food Program (WFP) (2014). Dadaab and Kakuma Refugee Camps Market Assessment. The World Food Program.

World Bank (2018). In Kenya, Refugees are Opening up Frontiers: The Pull of Investing in Underserved Areas. https://www.worldbank.org/en/news/feature/2018/09/27/in-kenya-refugees-are-opening-up-frontiers-the-pull-of-investing-in-underserved-area.

World Bank; UNHCR (2016). In My Backyard? The Economics of Refugees and Their Social Dynamics in Kakuma, Kenya. http://documents.worldbank.org/curated/en/308011482417763778/pdf/111303-WP-Kakuma-Report-Yes-in-my-backyard-December-2016-PUBLIC.pdf.

Zetter, Roger (2017). Impacts and Costs of Forced Displacement Phase II: A Critical Evaluation of Methodological and Analytical Progress on Designing Development-led Strategies and Interventions in Forced Displacement. Refugees Study Centre, Oxford, UK. https://www.rsc.ox.ac.uk/publications/impacts-and-costs-of-forced-displacement-phase-ii-a-critical-evaluation-of-methodological-and-analytical-progress-on-designing-development-led-strategies-and-interventions-in-forced-displacement.

Zetter, Roger (2012). Are refugees an economic burden or benefit? In: *Forced Migration Review*, 41, p. 50-52.

Index of Authors

Fathima Azmiya Badurdeen is presently a Lecturer at the Department of Social Sciences, Technical University of Mombasa. Fathima has worked as a researcher and trainer in the field of countering violent extremism, gender and forced migration in Kenya. She has also worked as a researcher, trainer, and evaluator for conflict transformation and peacebuilding projects in Sri Lanka.

Annalies Beck is a digital strategy consultant based in Munich and holds a M.A. in business communication management and a B.A. in communication in social and economic contexts. As an external Ph.D. candidate at the intercultural business communication department of Friedrich Schiller University in Jena she is currently completing her doctorate on the implementation of sustainably effective collaboration in international development cooperation. Her main research and teaching interests are digital participation, inclusive transformation and user-centered as well as technology-based innovation.

Isabella Bertmann-Merz joined the Chair of Sociology of Diversity at the Technical University of Munich in July 2016 as research associate. In the context of the "Inclusion and Disability" research group at the Max Planck Institute for Social Law and Social Policy, her PhD research focused on the quality of life experienced by persons with disabilities in South Africa. In her current research and teaching at TUM, she concentrates on international development and social policy topics (i. a. social protection and global health) with a focus on persons with disabilities, diversity issues as well as social inclusion.

Obeka Bonventure is a Sociology Tutorial Fellow in the Department of Social Sciences at Pwani University. He is also a PhD candidate at Pwani University (School of humanities and social sciences). Mr. Obeka has over five years teaching and research experience at University level and over the years has amassed a wealth of knowledge in various research areas that greatly focus on; Radicalization, conflict and violent extremism and its consequent prevention, human rights, environmental health and community development. Furthermore, Mr Obeka has a keen interest in maters development especially in the design of social policies. His training coupled with his research background in the area of prevention of conflict and violent extremism (P/CVE) amongst different vulner-

© Springer Fachmedien Wiesbaden GmbH, part of Springer Nature 2020
K. Crepaz et al. (eds.), *Health in Diversity – Diversity in Health*,
https://doi.org/10.1007/978-3-658-29177-8

able populations is deemed to be key in ensuring that the existing framework is critically reviewed and effectively customized to respond to the needs of students to attain a higher level of cohesion in the society.

Katharina Crepaz is a post-doctoral research associate at the Max Planck Institute for Social Law and Social Policy (Fellow-Group: "Dis[cover]ability and Indicators for Inclusion 2015–2020") and at the Chair of Sociology of Diversity, Technical University of Munich. She holds a Ph.D. in Political Science from the University of Innsbruck, as well as Mag. Phil. (M.A.) and B.A. degrees in English and American and Scandinavian Studies from the Universities of Innsbruck and Vienna. Her main research interests are political participation in diversity contexts (e.g. national minorities, migrants, persons with disabilities), Europeanization, transnational civil society, regionalism and federalism, and the European social and human rights policy.

Andrea Göttler works as a Research Assistant and Diversity Officer at the Department of Sports and Health Science at the Technical University of Munich. As a PhD student at the Chair of Sociology of Diversity, she investigates the discourses on older migrants in Germany in regard to health and care. She holds a B.Sc. degree in Anthropology from the University of Kent and a M.Sc. degree in Global Health from Maastricht University. Her research interests focus on older age and ageing, migrant health, as well as culture and ethnicity in (health)care.

Ulrike Kluge, Dipl. Psych., Professor for Psychological and Medical Integration and Migration Research at the Charité, University Medicine Berlin. Head of the Center of Cross-Cultural Psychiatry and Psychotherapy (ZIPP) and senior researcher at the Berlin Institute for Integration and Migration Research (BIM) at the Humboldt University Berlin. Group analyst (Seminar für Gruppenanalyse Zürich- SGAZ) and in psychoanalytical training at the Arbeitsgemeinschaft für Psychoanalyse und Psychotherapie Berlin e.V. (APB). Main research areas are migration, flight and (mental) health, transculturality, social cohesion, ethnopsychoanalysis and psychotherapy with language and cultural interpreters.

Ulrike Krause is Junior Professor for Forced Migration and Refugee Studies at the Institute for Migration Research and Intercultural Studies (IMIS) and the Institute for Social Science, Osnabrück University as well as affiliated Research Associate at the Refugee Studies Centre, University of Oxford. Her research interests are in the areas of humanitarian refugee protection, the nexus of displacement with conflict and peace, resilience, gender and gender-based violence. Her regional focus is on global developments as well as Africa, in particular East Africa. She is a co-founder and co-editor of the German Journal for

Forced Migration and Refugee Studies, and board member of the German Network Forced Migration Research (Netzwerk Fluchtforschung).

Cornelius Lätzsch is a PhD candidate at the University of Hamburg's and University of Applied Sciences Hamburg's joint graduate school "Neglected Topics in Refugee Studies". Furthermore, he is a lecturer at the University of Applied Sciences in Dusseldorf and holds a scholarship by the German Hans-Böckler Foundation. His research interest focuses on the intersection of disability and displacement. As a social worker, he has been working in disability-related institutions in Europa, Asia and Africa and was able to gain knowledge on forced migration through his longstanding voluntary and activist engagement in related contexts.

Sellah Lusweti holds a PhD in Educational Psychology (Measurement and Evaluation), she is a lecturer in the Department of Educational Psychology and Special Needs at Pwani University, and has 9 years' experience in teaching, research and consultancy. She is a seasoned researcher and consultant on quality of education (with a focus in monitoring and evaluation), peace education, and ethics and integrity. She has special interest in the area of educational resilience and champions for the overcoming of impact of adversity on learning; the appreciation of the positive educational experiences of refugees and forced migrants is one such focus area.

Letlhokwa George Mpedi completed his B Juris degree (1996) and LLB degree (1998) at Vista University. In 2001 the LLM degree in Labour Law was conferred upon him by the Rand Afrikaans University. The LLD degree was conferred upon him by the University of Johannesburg (UJ) in 2006. Prior to his appointment as Executive Dean, Prof Mpedi served as Head of Department: Practical Business Law (2011–2012) and Vice-Dean (2013–2015) at the UJ's Faculty of Law. He has published extensively in the fields of social security and labor law in South Africa, Southern Africa and some Anglophone African countries.

Samuel Mwakubo is an Associate Professor of Agricultural and Resource Economics and Dean of the School of Business and Economics, Pwani University, Kenya. He holds a PhD in Environmental Economics from Moi University, Kenya; and an MSc and BSc in Agricultural Economics from Egerton University, Kenya. Mwakubo has been a Research Manager at the African Economic Research Consortium (AERC), and a Policy Analyst with the Kenya Institute for Public Policy Research & Analysis (KIPPRA). He has also lectured at Egerton and Moi Universities, and conducted research on food production, horticultural marketing, farming systems, fertilizer marketing, soil conservation, social capital and wetlands.

Godffrey Nyongesa Nato holds a bachelor's degree in natural resources management and a Master's degree in Human ecology from Egerton University in Kenya. He graduated with a PhD in Sociology from Pwani University in 2017. He has seven years work experience in community development programmes and a six years' service in University teaching and administration in Technical University of Mombasa. He is currently the County Minister of Environment, Waste Management and Energy in the County Government of Mombasa, Kenya. His research interest and publications are in the field of appropriate technology adoption for rural development.

Gordon Onyango Omenya obtained his PhD in History from Université de Pau in France in the year 2016. He is currently a lecturer in the Department of History, Archaeology and Political Studies at Kenyatta University (Nairobi, Kenya). His areas of interest include race relations, gender history, global history, migration and diaspora studies, popular culture and heritage issues as well as history of international relations. Dr. Omenya is also a member of the French Institute of Research in Africa (IFRA), the British Institute of Research in East Africa (BIEA), AEGIS (Africa-Europe Group for Interdisciplinary Studies) and the Council for the Development of Social Science Research in Africa (CODESRIA).

Albert Scherr, sociologist, born 1958, Prof. Dr. is Director of the Institute for Sociology at the Freiburg University of Education. His work focuses on discrimination and racism, sociology of migration, refugee research, sociological theory, theories of social work and qualitative social research. Recent publications deal with the connection between discrimination and educational processes, the interpretation and coping with experiences of discrimination as well as the sociology of forced migration.

Halimu Shauri is an Associate Professor of Sociology, with more than 15 years' experience in research, teaching and community service. He is the current Dean, School of Humanities and Social Sciences, Pwani University, Kenya. He has extensive research experience in refugee studies, conflict resolution, radicalization, Preventing and Transforming Violent Extremism (P/TCVE). His major accomplishments include research in land conflicts, refugees with disability and the internally displaced, returnees, women victims and Social Network Analysis of recruitment into VE in Kenya and Tanzania. His current research is in family and community influencers of recruitment into VE in the Boni Enclave, Kenya.

Elisabeth Wacker holds the Chair of Sociology of Diversity at the Technical University of Munich and is Max Planck Fellow (Fellow-Group: "Dis[cover]ability and Indicators for Inclusion 2015–2020") at the Max Planck Institute for Social Law and Social Policy. Her research focuses on coping with social inequality, diversity and difference when faced with impairment and disability in society (ICF, WHO, cross-cultural comparison). Other topics include the transformation of care systems (prevention, rehabilitation) and social policy (inclusion, participation and disability mainstreaming). She also examines the interdependency of social and context factors (linked to conditions and quality of life) within the human lifespan and with regard to adequate indicators.

Ayca Nina Zuch Creativity and innovation with artistic and scientific practices merge my work scenarios. Born 1981, living in Berlin since 2001, I hold an M.A. in publication sciences and a Meisterschüler degree in Fine Arts. For two years, I have been teaching digitalization methods at the Hochschule für Wirtschaft und Recht in Berlin. Social, economical and political changes challenge the running system. Digital innovation needs creative ideas and workarounds. I pitched one of my ideas at the Falling Walls Lab in Zurich and won a stipend at the Konrad-Zuse Institute Berlin. At the moment I am thinking about founding a publishing agency focusing on artistic knowledge distribution.

The manufacturer's authorised representative in the EU is Springer
Nature Customer Service Centre GmbH, Europaplatz 3, 69115 Heidelberg,
Germany. If you have any concerns regarding our products, please
contact ProductSafety@springernature.com

Printed and bound by CPI Group (UK) Ltd, Croydon, CR0 4YY
24/04/2026
02096335-0006